HOW TO WRITE BRILLIANT PSYCHOLOGY ESSAYS

Sara Miller McCune founded SAGE Publishing in 1965 to support the dissemination of usable knowledge and educate a global community. SAGE publishes more than 1000 journals and over 800 new books each year, spanning a wide range of subject areas. Our growing selection of library products includes archives, data, case studies and video. SAGE remains majority owned by our founder and after her lifetime will become owned by a charitable trust that secures the company's continued independence.

Los Angeles | London | New Delhi | Singapore | Washington DC | Melbourne

HOW TO WRITE BRILLIANT PSYCHOLOGY ESSAYS

PAUL DICKERSON

Los Angeles | London | New Delhi
Singapore | Washington DC | Melbourne

Los Angeles | London | New Delhi
Singapore | Washington DC | Melbourne

SAGE Publications Ltd
1 Oliver's Yard
55 City Road
London EC1Y 1SP

SAGE Publications Inc.
2455 Teller Road
Thousand Oaks, California 91320

SAGE Publications India Pvt Ltd
B 1/I 1 Mohan Cooperative Industrial Area
Mathura Road
New Delhi 110 044

SAGE Publications Asia-Pacific Pte Ltd
3 Church Street
#10-04 Samsung Hub
Singapore 049483

Editor: Donna Goddard
Editorial assistant: Marc Barnard
Production editor: Imogen Roome
Copyeditor: Sarah Bury
Proofreader: Brian McDowell
Indexer: Adam Pozner
Marketing manager: Camille Richmond
Cover design: Wendy Scott
Typeset by: C&M Digitals (P) Ltd, Chennai, India
Printed in the UK

© Paul Dickerson 2021

First published 2021

Apart from any fair dealing for the purposes of research or private study, or criticism or review, as permitted under the Copyright, Designs and Patents Act, 1988, this publication may be reproduced, stored or transmitted in any form, or by any means, only with the prior permission in writing of the publishers, or in the case of reprographic reproduction, in accordance with the terms of licences issued by the Copyright Licensing Agency. Enquiries concerning reproduction outside those terms should be sent to the publishers.

Library of Congress Control Number: 2020934665

British Library Cataloguing in Publication data

A catalogue record for this book is available from the British Library

ISBN 978-1-5264-9731-4
ISBN 978-1-5264-9730-7 (pbk)

At SAGE we take sustainability seriously. Most of our products are printed in the UK using responsibly sourced papers and boards. When we print overseas we ensure sustainable papers are used as measured by the PREPS grading system. We undertake an annual audit to monitor our sustainability.

CONTENTS

ABOUT THE AUTHOR

Paul Dickerson is Principal Teaching Fellow at the University of Roehampton where he has taught for more than 25 years. His research has predominantly adopted a qualitative approach and has largely focused on issues of talk, interaction and autism. He has written a social psychology textbook which sought to empower students to engage critically with the material presented (the second edition is currently in preparation with Sage). Paul has written this book so that you can feel empowered to express your thoughts and ideas in writing, achieve your full potential and rediscover the joy of learning.

ACKNOWLEDGEMENTS

Even when there is just a single author indicated on a book's cover, there are many people involved in making it a reality. My conversations with students, across nearly three decades of teaching, have made me keen to unlock the potential that they – and other students – have, so that they can each write in a way that really shows their mind at work. I am grateful to all of my friends and colleagues at Roehampton, including Jen Mayer, Jean O'Callaghan, John Rae, Gina Pauli and Marta Jackowska, who have been a constant source of inspiration and encouragement regarding writing this text and I am truly grateful to each of them.

I have been really fortunate to have had the benefit of working with a very talented team at Sage. I would like to thank three commissioning editors: Becky Taylor, who got the (metaphorical) ball rolling, then Rob Patterson, who kept the ball rolling, and finally Donna Goddard, whose wise oversight across so much of the project helped (to stay with the metaphor) see the ball safely into the hole/back of the net/ball sanctuary. I have also benefited enormously from the regular contact, encouragement and advice from editorial assistants Katie Rabot and, subsequently, Marc Barnard. I am very grateful to all of the production team at Sage, in particular production editor Imogen Roome and copyeditor Sarah Bury – they have had an incredibly positive influence on the book's development and completion. I am indebted to Wendy Scott for the funky cover design and Camille Richmond and her team for their positive and proactive approach to raising awareness of the book.

Last, but never least, my children, Joshua and Miriam, and my wife, Suba, have been so positive and patient, particularly as writing this text strayed into most weekends over the last year. Without them this book would have been just an unrealised good intention – I can't thank them enough.

DISCOVER YOUR TEXTBOOK'S ONLINE RESOURCES!

The following online resources in support of *How to Write Brilliant Psychology Essays* can be found at https://study.sagepub.com/psychologybrilliantessays

Student resources

- **Videos** to talk you through key points from the book and enhance your understanding.
- **Appendix** with supplementary material for further insight into key concepts.

Lecturer resources

- **PowerPoint Slides** which can be adapted and edited to suit your own teaching needs.

Chapter 1

Catch the wave – how to seize the moment, overcome procrastination and write now

Before we start – in order to start – here's a question: *Why not start your essay?* It's all very well feeling panicked and telling yourself, 'Push yourself, because no one else is going to do it for you', but sometimes the essay remains stubbornly unwritten. Before reaching for our list of 115 motivational statements, just take a moment – you have a potential advantage over all the students of other disciplines: *you are a psychologist!* This chapter will support you in using some psychological insights on yourself to help you have a different perspective on your procrastination, to understand why you do it and to find ways that you can charm yourself into your work whatever your reasons for procrastinating.

In this chapter you will learn...

- How you can adopt a different and more empowering perspective on procrastination
- What your reasons for procrastinating may be and how each of them can be addressed
- How you can charm your way into starting your essay

TRY A DIFFERENT PERSPECTIVE

What is the inner dialogue like when you procrastinate? If you try to bully or frighten yourself into working, that may work for a time – at least while the threat feels real and imminent – but what happens as soon as the threat dissipates? Often frightening yourself into working is only effective when the deadline is so close you can almost smell it. The snag is that this can create a cycle where you ignore the threat until it is – once again – the very last minute. Then the cycle starts all over again with your next piece of work.

One psychological concept that is relevant here is reactance. This has different meanings, one of which relates to '*impedance in an AC circuit*', but here we are thinking of *psychological* reactance. Silvia (2005: 277) draws on Brehm (1966) in defining reactance as; 'a motivational state aimed at restoring the threatened freedom'. In other words, if someone tells us we can't do something – depending on how we relate to the person telling us – we may be more inclined to do it, so that we can assert the freedom which we feel is threatened. The message that you *must* do your essay *now*, even if it is coming from yourself or some 'motivational' slogan in font size 72, can work in a similar way – you can feel that it is a threat to your freedom to do all the other things you might want to do right now instead. So, one way of asserting your freedom is to do just what you feel you are being told not to do, just like people who deliberately walk on grass that they are told to keep off, or who speak in a silent study section of a library. Your defiant assertion of freedom is all the easier when the very same screen used for writing your essay can be the gateway to assert your hedonistic independence at two clicks, or three at most, and the essay is left behind as you are wafted up in a flight of fancy.

This is such a big factor in terms of writing – or not writing – essays, that we should stay with it for a moment longer. Before the temptation to flee proves too strong to resist, consider some ideas that might give us another perspective on our essay writing and our procrastination.

Your escape is not so great after all

Most of us would sooner deny or ignore the idea that attempting to escape from our academic work is futile. In fact, if you can read through the next few pages without desperately scrambling towards your habitual distraction, then that is kind of amazing. Most of us have different things we like to do to assert our freedom. It may be obviously hedonistic, or have some semblance of wider value, but it takes us from what we '*should* do' to what we '*want* to do'. Or at least we construct it as a contrast between 'should' and 'want'. Perhaps you can get curious here? What really happens when you get distracted? How long does it last? What do you get from it and what do you lose? Maybe becoming mindful and aware – without becoming harsh or judgemental – will help. Why not acknowledge that you want to be distracted, but carry on working a little bit more than usual – just to see what it's like. You might have got this freedom thing all wrong. Without getting too paranoid, maybe several hundred thousand people want you (and others like you) to be distracted so you can consume whatever they are offering. Maybe staying with your work is a much more potent statement of your independence and freedom.

Your work can actually be fun

This sounds like a prototypical nurse telling you that you 'won't feel a thing', but this time it is true! There is a real satisfaction in getting a task done – if that task has meaning and value. The weird thing is that the other side of the mountain of distraction is where most of the treasure lies. Essay writing is, typically, sufficiently open ended – usually we are not merely completing a pre-set template – that it is both intimidating and *meaningful*. Why deny yourself this freedom? You may want to feel free to *consume* the games, videos and other output created by others, but what about the freedom to create yourself? In this essay, right now, you can create – consuming can be great, but creating can be greater.

You can flip back to work now

Most of us get distracted plenty of times – no matter how perfect we sound when spilling out advice to others. One of the real myths that crushes those of us who know distraction well is this one: 'it's too late now'. I would take this head on. This is the threat to your freedom. Use your reactance on this myth; it is trying to deny *your* freedom to go back to the work you were distracted from. Don't argue with it. *Prove it wrong* by switching back to your work, not after you get to the next level, finish watching this episode or finally work out whether going to sleep in wet socks prevents colds or causes them. The door is open – step back in, don't feel bad, don't tell yourself off, just try a completely non-threatening five or ten minutes of work. Often, in the midst of distraction, we tell ourselves, 'just five more minutes, then I'll start work again'. Use the same method to charm your way back to your work, just committing yourself to five or ten minutes of work can be all that it takes to massively transform your writing. Your essay is not the big, oppressive authority figure; it is your creative freedom. You can enjoy it, so allow yourself to do just that.

ACE YOUR ASSIGNMENT
Your phone and you

If your phone is in a different room from you, what will happen? Will you experience an existential crisis, your thumb poised over the space in your hand where the phone should be? Perhaps your phone will shutdown or explode, never to work again?

You, like me, may find that sometimes it is extremely helpful not to have your phone within arm's reach of you. You can meet up again after this brief separation without any hard feelings or spontaneous combustion on either side. The technology is amazing, but it is also the most potent technology for distraction and delivering you to adverts that has been devised so far.

Why not use that concept of reactance again here? Are you going to let the wealthiest companies in the world determine what you do? Your essay, or your degree, doesn't actually matter to them, as long as you stay hooked on your phone long enough to be delivered to the (increasingly) bespoke adverts.

It is hard to get the happy medium of enjoying our phones as a phenomenally useful and fun tool without paying a heavy price in terms of wasted hours checking social media or seeing videos of someone who claims their parrot is more intelligent than they are. But our day-by-day, hour-by-hour choices, which seem so small in themselves, really do add up to something significant.

If putting your phone in another room frees you up to write, it is worth it. And your phone will forgive you, I am sure.

You've already started

Do you find yourself building up the start of your essay? It is so easy to think I'll start when I… fully understand the title/have completed all the reading/have really understood all of the issues/have got what I am going to write really clear. These are all understandable and sometimes backed up by the guidance that we pick up and pass on. But what really is an essay? An academic essay is a medium for displaying your scholarly, or learned, thinking about the issues identified in the title. If you have these thoughts, if you are reading this sentence, it looks like you have started your thinking which is part of and central to writing the essay. The essay does not start when your word count clocks up a certain number; it starts when we engage with the ideas that are relevant to the essay. So pat yourself on the back and encourage yourself like you would encourage someone you care about – if you are thinking, you are *essaying*. Perhaps you can jot down your thoughts.

Confusion is a friend not an imposter

It is easy to hate confusion – perhaps especially now when Siri, Google and Alexa instantly answer any questions that flit through our minds the moment we voice them. But wait, confusion is good – or at least *constructive confusion* is good. Confusion is constructive if we articulate it and use it to inform our thinking, reading and writing. Look at these three confused reactions in relation to essay titles and take a moment to note that they are actually helpful:

1. **Essay title**: 'Critically evaluate Kelley's Covariation Model of Causal Attribution.'

    Constructive confusion: 'I don't understand Kelley's distinction between distinctiveness and consistency.'

    Why it is helpful: Most people mix these up – identifying the uncertainty is the first step to identifying the subtle difference between these two aspects of Kelley's model. This will guide some of your reading and thinking and will mean that your essay has a clarity and understanding that would not be there if you had not identified this confusion.

2. **Essay title**: Evaluate the strengths and weaknesses of longitudinal methods of investigation in developmental psychology research.

    Constructive confusion: 'How can I critique longitudinal research when I am only aware of its strengths?'

    Why it is helpful: This demonstrates an awareness of the need to consider the research from different perspectives. This constructive confusion will inform the reading and note-taking undertaken (see Chapter 2 for more on this) and lead to a richer, more complete and more genuinely evaluative essay.

3. **Essay title**: Critically evaluate the Social Identity Theory perspective on why people engage in acts of aggression.

Constructive confusion: 'How can I write an essay on aggression when psychologists do not have one simple definition of what it actually is?'

Why it is helpful: You have identified a really great critical point – that it is possible to question how we actually define our terms in psychology, not least how we define aggression (what do empirical studies treat as aggression), and what real-world scenarios (two men fighting, gang fights, drone warfare, riots) are we trying to explain. If this is confusion, try to get more of it. This sort of thinking can really supercharge your essays, informing some of your literature searches: 'How has aggression been defined?', 'Critiquing definitions of aggression', and providing a way of questioning fundamental assumptions in the specific material that you are evaluating in your essay.

UNDERSTANDING WHY YOU PROCRASTINATE

It can be helpful to ask ourselves – as we might ask a friend – why we don't start (or continue) with our essay right now. We should ask this in a sympathetic manner, as if we want to find out, rather than simply admonish ourselves – we probably do too much of that anyway. By identifying the different sorts of reasons why we allow ourselves to become distracted or otherwise procrastinate in our work, we can reach a better self-understanding. Instead of telling yourself off, you could first stop and ask: 'What are the advantages of not writing my essay now?'

STOP
What are the advantages of NOT starting my essay now?

If I delay, I can:

- Make sure that I get it right
- Avoid feeling anxious
- Work (more effectively) under pressure
- Do other things I have to do
- Have fun now
- Come back to it in a better frame of mind

List other reasons you can think of:

MAKE SURE THAT I GET IT RIGHT

This is a core reason for not starting essays. The thought that you want to get it right comes from a good place – it is your inner editor who is keen to ensure the quality of your work. Being keen to do really good work will certainly come in handy, especially when you are editing a draft of your essay, so acknowledge this feeling, but do not let it stop you from starting. It is usually much easier to edit a draft – even if it is far from perfect – than to try to produce high-quality writing from scratch. If this thought is leading you to delay your essay, then you need to start putting words on the page, knowing that later on you will look at it with this more critical, editorial eye.

EXERCISE
Your inner editor

What does your inner editor say to you? What can you say to your inner editor?

_____

_____

_____

_____

How can I get started?

Any start is a much better place than not starting at all. So rather than aiming for perfection, aim for some imperfect start – your inner editor can come into the picture later. Think of the essay that you feel you should be working on. Now, without checking notes and textbooks, journal papers or social media, just write for three minutes on that topic.

EXERCISE
The three-minute challenge

It's only 180 seconds – time yourself and write something imperfect but relevant for the essay you are (or should be) working on. You might write an idea that you have, identify a debate or disagreement, write some name or theory that you can remember, or write a question that you have about the title.

   Bullet points may help right now, as we tend to be less perfectionist when putting down thoughts in this format.

My ideas about my essay:

- _____
- _____
- _____

AVOID FEELING ANXIOUS

You might feel that postponing your essay means that you avoid all the anxiety surrounding your essay. That makes sense, but it's not a great solution; the anxiety doesn't really go away. It's like shoving a dragon under the carpet – it just gets a little more scary each day. Most importantly, we can change the frame for our essay – yes, there can be anxious elements, but let's find a more encouraging way into it. What would you say to encourage a friend or relative who has anxieties about writing an essay? How might you encourage them? Try to encourage yourself in this way.

How can I get started?

Turn it from a chore to something playful. Just play with the ideas. Here are some ideas that might help you to find your own playful engagement in starting to write your essay:

- What are the relevant names or ideas? Do little speech bubbles for them, what might they say?
- What if they were all at a party together – what would they wind up saying?
- Find a supportive environment. Do you work best when others are around you, or perhaps with the background sounds of a café, or the focused concentration of quiet sections of a library?
- Perhaps some sort of background music or ambient sounds work for you, but be realistic about what is genuinely helpful, and don't spend ages trying to find the perfect acoustic accompaniment.
- Think about the times of the day when you are most productive and try to make use of them – perhaps 'chunking' your time into manageable units with short breaks in between.
- When the situation is less than perfect, as it so often is, don't tell yourself you can't – *show yourself that you can work even in tricky circumstances* – this is your Mount Everest that you are climbing.
- Can you draw something that expresses the ideas or how they relate together?
- Can you create a two-minute summary? Perhaps a small podcast of what you know about the topic? This could include some of the things you want to find out, though don't use this to get out of documenting those things that you do know.

ACE YOUR ASSIGNMENT
Try these practical fixes for procrastination problems

- **Work separately from your phone**

  When were you last looking at your phone? If you are like me and find that the phone can be quite a distraction then just ask yourself, who's the boss you or the phone? Your phone won't take it personally if you switch it off, turn it face down or put it (safely) in another room. Afterwards, your phone and you can enjoy a happy reunion.

- **Choosing a target**

  Some writers work to a specific word length (for example, completing a certain number of words per day), others for a scheduled amount of time (for example between 8pm and 11pm). These options are discussed later in this chapter, but see what you find most encouraging and motivating for the essay writing tasks that you need to complete right now.

- **If it's flowing keep going**

  Do you know that feeling when your writing is going well? It is wonderful, it's precious and it can be worth riding that wave for a while. Don't let little distractions knock you off – keep with the energy.

- **If it's not, keep going**

  I'm writing this sentence immediately after a phase when it was not flowing at all. Don't get too ready with the narrative, 'It's gone rubbish today' or, 'I've been hopeless'. The real skill is to transform those times when it's not flowing into something productive. It might mean changing the focus of our writing – but stay on task and be really encouraging to yourself. Getting back on track is a small miracle – well done you!

- **Leave it in a nice state to return to**

  When you need to park your work – leave it so when you come back to it, it is really clear how to carry on with your writing. An easy guide to yourself on what you were working on and what feel you need to do would be great. Be kind to the 'you' of tomorrow who's going to pick this stuff up.

- **Schedule facilitative breaks**

  Some people find that working for short segments of time (perhaps 20, 30 or 60 minutes) punctuated with very short breaks (perhaps 5 minutes) works well. As long as this pattern does not break your flow of concentration, this 'chunking' approach can be a good way of keeping energy and motivation levels high. The idea of chunking (and Cirillo's, 2018 Pomodoro Technique) is briefly touched on in Chapter 12.

I WORK 'BEST UNDER PRESSURE'

Many people feel that they work best under pressure – telling this to themselves and others can help to justify not having to tackle the essay right now. If you feel that this applies to you, it is worth asking whether this pattern really is optimal, or is it – at least partly – a way of avoiding the inhibiting effects of perfectionism? When we leave things to the last minute, we can't afford to be perfectionist and at last we are free just to write. It could be worth acknowledging that working well under pressure is wonderful and can certainly help in many pressurised situations – exams being a key example. However, getting started before the last minute might be even more effective. We can create an imperfect draft and then bring our capacity to work under pressure to spur us in editing this into the final piece of work that we submit.

How can I get started?

- Create a productive pressure environment. Sometimes looking at the schedule of all the work (and other commitments) that you have to do might achieve this sense of imminence.
- Creating exam-like conditions, on your own or with others, perhaps having a time-limited, relatively formal context, can really work in encouraging the intense focused work that you may find facilitative.
- Creating deadlines that are convincing and which you will not simply cheat on may be helpful.
- Getting away from perfectionism may be a key element here – that is often why people experience a freedom of writing at the last minute. See if you can get away from this by writing a far from perfect draft, knowing that you will edit it – perhaps under pressure – later.

LEARN
Time, text or task?

Authors differ between those who work for a fixed time, those who monitor their output in terms of words written, and those who focus on identifiable tasks that can be completed – and many other permutations.

Numbers of words can be really reassuring as you see how your work relates to your target length – not forgetting that you will edit your work later (see Chapter 10 for more on editing). But academic writing is uneven. When you are planning your ideas, becoming familiar with the literature that you will refer to, or drafting a conclusion, your word count will probably increase quite slowly and counting numbers of words can be disheartening.

Another alternative is to see your essay in terms of several discrete tasks, for example: writing a plan, reading up on the topic, checking your notes, writing an introduction, drafting the main body, writing a conclusion, completing citations and references, and editing your draft. This is very output-orientated and usefully maps onto what needs to be done, so we feel that we can measure our progress. However, taking this approach does run the risk of being discouraging when we are working on a task that we find difficult. We might work for a considerable time on our conclusion and feel that we have little to show for it, whereas if we were just working for a fixed time, for example a target of 60 minutes work, we can feel that we have accomplished our task.

(Continued)

Working for a (realistic) fixed time can be good for building a ritual, removing an output target that you might not reach and allowing for the uneven nature of academic writing and reading. However, working for a fixed time may involve a certain degree of faith that we are making progress, even when we haven't some clear evidence (for example, in words written or tasks achieved) that we have done so. Having some sense of how we are progressing can be reassuring.

It may well be that a mixture of these approaches works best. Early on, when we are putting down thoughts and ideas, reading around the topic, writing our initial plans and questions, having a time or an achievable task target may work best. Once we are into our draft essay, we may find an awareness of words works best, and in some cases identifying the discrete parts of an essay to be written (for example, the introduction) may also help. Working on our conclusion and detailed editing may be harder to measure in terms of words written (editing often removes words), so switching to time and/or a task focus may help.

It is best to see time, text and task focus as slightly different orientations to be used at different times so that they encourage and inspire you in your essay writing. When the words are flowing well, having a sense of word output can be really encouraging. When we have a sense of what is needed to finish a section of our essay, a task focus can work well and give a satisfying sense of progress. When we need to get started with plans and ideas or finish with final editing, sometimes it can be helpful to commit ourselves to spending a certain amount of time. Time, text and task of course constantly interweave with one another, so use them sympathetically as an encouragement, and not as a rod to beat yourself with.

DO THE OTHER THINGS I HAVE TO DO

This is usually not just an excuse, as there are many, really valid and important demands on our time. It is sometimes helpful to write down rather than simply mentally recycle all of the different pulls on your time that you experience. In some cases, being honest about the amount of time required for your academic work and the other things you have and/or want to do, and acknowledging how flexible or inflexible they are and when they occur, can be helpful. Taking time to do this can help you schedule your work to some extent.

A second factor to bear in mind is that it is easy for us to tell ourselves – and others – that we need a clear morning, or afternoon, or a whole day to be able to devote ourselves to our academic work, or, more specifically, to writing our essay. This can lead to us under-valuing those smaller pockets of time that we could potentially use, perhaps especially in the earlier phases of writing. Anthony Trollope wrote 250 words every 15 minutes as he sat at his desk from 5:30 to 8:30 each morning – before going to his day job with the postal service. We might not be as systematic and disciplined as Trollope, but we could be missing lots of opportunities for good writing if we are thinking that we need an uninterrupted stretch of a day or a half-day in order to achieve anything.

Sometimes we may actually need to attend to other matters and then come back to our writing. This could be better than being in a state of tense inactivity where we feel unable to get anything done because of the competing demands we face. If there is something else that is time sensitive to do, then perhaps doing that is the right thing, although often we do not need to see our day, or part-day, in either/or terms. We might do *that* and *this* as well.

How can I get started?

- Write down some of the things that you need to do – don't let the list become oppressive.
- Where meaningful, schedule these other activities.
- You may find that having a reasonable minimum number of words or time period for writing each day really helps.
- If you are able to write even a little towards your essay in the morning, it can often be easier to continue – even just dipping into it – later on in the day.
- Sometimes doing the duty or fulfilling the obligation that is on your mind might free you to do other things, such as writing your essay.
- Keep a look out for realistic pockets of time that you can schedule in advance or just identify in the moment. It can be really surprising how minutes scattered across a day or week can become meaningful opportunities for your writing.

EXERCISE
Which of these apply to you?

- Looking after others, perhaps younger or older relatives.
- Paid employment.
- Medical appointments.
- Voluntary work.
- Sporting and other recreational commitments.
- Societies and clubs that you belong to.
- Relationships.
- Other friendships.
- Other time commitments – please specify.

HAVE FUN NOW

We don't only have lots of duties, we have lots of distractions. Wherever we are, most of us carry a device that can enable us to connect ourselves, entertain ourselves and lose ourselves in hundreds of ways at just two or three clicks. A small minority of phones and some simplifying apps are now designed so that we experience less distraction, bright colours are muted, functionality streamlined and, in some cases, the user is required to specify what they are intending to do when they pick up their phone. But it isn't just the conspicuous encroachment of distracting technology, we can readily find and externalise distraction whatever our digital footprint. Perhaps this is a key point – we tell ourselves that distraction is being done to us, but often we are choosing to go from the relative discomfort of feeling we should write our essay to some other place, the more immersive, the better. At the end of a month it is us who have decided to give four days to social media and a day and a half to League of Legends, Subway Surfers or Fortnite, even if it didn't feel like a decision at the time.

We may have to discover what works for us here. Perhaps we should acknowledge the distraction and go ahead with the essay. If we can use this approach it can be really empowering. We might find that some sort of deal works best: for example, we could have a deal that we will be distracted in 10 minutes' time, rather than right now (this is an easier deal to stick to than going for 10 minutes of distraction first, followed by our work).

A key thing to bear in mind here is that it is not too late to change back to writing your essay. We often tell ourselves that we've blown it, that we shouldn't have watched those four episodes of *Game of Thrones*, gone snowboarding on our phone or got hooked into YouTube videos about 'what you can do with a water melon that has no water'. Maybe we shouldn't have – but the idea that there's no way back, or that there's no point in switching back to writing now is far more destructive. If you do get side-tracked – and who doesn't – always allow yourself to switch back. Who is stopping you?

MAKE IT MORE FUN

Let's close the gap between work and fun a little. Why not introduce some light-hearted creativity to your writing. Try the following:

1. Use speech bubbles to identify some of the ideas that are relevant to your essay. This is a really good way of outlining some of the key debates.

    Use the speech bubbles below to get going:

    Essay topic:

    Argument 1:

Argument 2:

Argument 3:

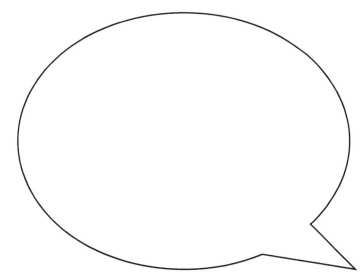

2. Host 'The Psychologists' Party' – expenses are minimal, there are zero health risks and your guests will leave whenever you want. Just imagine which psychologists you can invite to talk about the specific topic of your essay. What will they say and, crucially, how will they each respond to what the others have said?

Essay topic:

Guest list:

Conversation highlights:

Agreements between guests:

Disagreements between guests:

3. Try speed-psyching – this is a little like speed dating with rather less at stake and no need to check where the exits are.

    Quickly write down the names and or ideas that you think are relevant for your essay. Get your timer out. Each name, or idea, has just 60 seconds to convince you that they have something relevant to say about the topic of the essay. Write down what it is they would say in this situation. Don't delay, you haven't got time, just write it down.

    Name:

    Their 60-second statement:

    Name:

    Their 60-second statement:

    Name:

    Their 60-second statement:

How can I get started?

- Acknowledge that you feel like being distracted – being swept away from the bits that feel stressful with the work in front of you. Those feelings are fine, but why not carry on with your work anyway?
- Possibly probe why you have such negative feelings – often stress, anxiety and guilt – associated with your essay writing. Is there a way you can help yourself approach your writing in a spirit of play rather than of stress?
- If it is not simply too depressing, you might calculate how long – in a typical month – you spend on doing things that you slip into in an unthinking way. Social media, video games and TV are all likely candidates, but you can create your own list.

- Consider a deal where you will first do your writing and then go for distraction time. Finding the optimal timing for this is tricky, as the more distractible you feel the more you may have to charm your way into writing with the promise of an imminent break – but that break has to be timed too.

- You may find that certain environments might reduce some of the prevalent distractions that affect you. Writing with another person silently present, working in a café or library, or online study environment may work for you.

- Different times of day can have quite a different energy about them as both we and our environment change quite markedly. I am writing this sentence at 1:57 am. The house and the road outside are very quiet. It's a different feeling from when I was jotting down some words here at 7:30 am yesterday, and different again from writing for a few minutes on a subsequent train journey with my children at 10 am.

- Always allow yourself back. It's not too late. Don't try to kid yourself that you've blown the day and there is no point in starting now. You haven't and there is.

COME BACK TO IT BETTER PREPARED

Often it is easy to put off starting – or continuing – with your essay by telling yourself that it is for the best. A particularly effective argument is that you will be better prepared later on. This can be effective in convincing yourself to wait, not least because you might be feeling sub-optimal right now; perhaps you are tired, hazy or distracted – not like that image of 'the essay writer' that you have conjured up in your head. You might even be able to persuade yourself that you cannot possibly start *that* essay without a bit more reading, more time to understand the ideas or a really clear sense of what to write. If you have experienced this – and many of us have – has it ever really worked out? It may be that sometimes it really has, perhaps in quite special circumstances, but most of the time this is just one of the ways we persuade ourselves to escape for now from the task before us. As we do this, we are in danger of building our essay into something extraordinarily demanding, something which requires us to be in increasingly super-human form to tackle.

Most of the time it is better to even complete a few brief moments of work on your essay than to wait for this time when we are alert, primed for action, free of distraction and full of energy. Probably few of us feel like this most of the time, so don't wait around for this supercharged feeling to descend on you. You don't need it – you can almost certainly write now. The strange thing is that when we start writing – even though we feel tired and uninformed – we can often feel our way into the issues and ideas and make contact with at least some sort of writing energy. It is even more effective for getting in the zone than watching YouTube clips about 24 pets that can talk like humans.

How can I get started?

- Don't wait to feel perfectly informed, perfectly inspired or perfectly energised – that might never happen. Start now – you can do good work right where you are.

- Don't build an oppressive image of how you or your circumstances *have* to be in order to effectively tackle your essay – really effective essays are often written in sub-optimal circumstances.

- Charm your way into starting work – make it fun, simple, engaging and non-threatening.

- Making a start now is usually a much better idea than starting after you have… [fill in your excuse here]. Start now, just as you are. You can read the books, research the area, think around the issues, find your notes, create a detailed plan and do all of this more effectively if you start to engage with your essay now.

- Don't kid yourself that you will come back to 'it' if you haven't done any 'it' in the first place. It is far better to do even a few minutes writing before any break than to start with a break and a good intention to start 'soon'.

THINK
Why not come back to it later?
Listen to yourself

Coming back to it later can work, but usually only if you have been with 'it' in the first place. If you do even a few minutes straight away, it is so much easier to come back to. But don't take my words for it – listen to yourself.

You are wiser than you think. Try having a conversation between the part of you that wants to procrastinate and the wise, caring and encouraging part of yourself. Please note, it is not so helpful to invoke the strict sergeant major/angry parent/red-faced teacher – you have probably already done enough of that. Instead contact the part of you that is perceptive and caring.

Here's how my inner dialogue is going this morning. Have a look – if that helps – and then write out your own:

Procrastinating Paul: 'I am a little tired this morning – I might feel more refreshed later.'

Perceptive Paul: 'If you start in the morning, the first chance you can, it will be so much easier to come back to.'

Procrastinating Paul: 'I don't know, maybe just a really quick break and I'll feel more energised.'

Perceptive Paul: 'You'll feel better once you start putting some words down.'

Procrastinating Paul: 'Yes, but do I need to push myself? Besides, perhaps I should just check my emails?'

Perceptive Paul: 'The emails will be there after you do some writing.'

Procrastinating Paul: 'I'm not sure I am in the mood.'

Perceptive Paul: 'Your mood will probably change within a few minutes of sitting down to write.'

To an extent the Perceptive Paul won the debate and I did start writing, although the tension did rumble on a bit. Perhaps unwisely, I checked my emails just after I had started writing. If these had been more urgent, I may have been derailed early on.

EXERCISE
Fill in your own inner dialogue

Procrastinating part of me:

Perceptive part of me:

Procrastinating part of me:

Perceptive part of me:

Procrastinating part of me:

Perceptive part of me:

WHERE DO I START?

It's all very well feeling that we should start our essay, but where – and how? Do we start at the beginning and push through to the conclusion, or perhaps start reading first, or writing a plan – or should we stop until everything seems a little bit clearer? The best idea is to start doing *whatever it is we can do without any delay* – for example, without having to find notes and references, or read and understand an idea and ..., we will do that *once we have started*. If we delay at the start, we might never start.

It may be useful to think this through with some examples. Below, two essay titles are given, followed by an initial outline of ideas using both speech bubbles and notes, and including an identification of gaps in knowledge. Each of these examples imagines a different sort of gap in knowledge on the part of the student having a first thought about their essay. Note how, despite these gaps, something can be usefully started and the gaps can be better specified as a result.

Example one

Essay title:

'Critically evaluated Piaget's stage theory of cognitive development.'

How you feel about the essay

Roughly aware of Piaget's ideas, but cannot recall the studies in any detail. Aware of certain criticisms regarding Piaget's ideas and some sense of the contrasting approaches, but cannot recall the names and specifics of the ideas.

How you can get started

You have quite a lot of understanding that can inform the shape that your essay might take. You need to clarify a fair amount of detail. Although you could turn to your notes, textbooks and other sources to fill out these details, it is probably best to write first without delay and then you will be less likely to be distracted and more likely to undertake really focused, purposive reading.

What your start might look like

1. **Using images**

Piaget:

Critic one:

I have a problem with how your experiments were conducted. Wording? Difficulty?

Critic two:

I want to challenge your whole-stage approach to development. Perhaps it is more gradual. A different, cognitive-type approach?

2. **Note form**

Piaget ran experiments about children's cognitive development.

Piaget emphasised stage-related progress.

Some people criticised the way that Piaget conducted his experiments – something about the wording and the difficulty.

Some people had a different cognitive approach – something about a more gradual development.

What I need to find out and where:

- What Piaget's experiments were called and what they involved (I have some lecture notes on this).

- What his evidence looked like (the textbook covers this).

- Who raised what specific objections concerning the wording and difficulty of his tasks – and what was their evidence (the textbook covers this).

- Who suggested that instead of stages children developed more gradually – and what was their evidence (the lecture notes give names and the textbook provides more detail on this).

Note: Identifying where you can find the information is super-important. Without this you will stop because you do not have the information you need to continue, or you will look perhaps half-heartedly for sources – secretly pleased that you have an excuse to stop thinking so hard about your essay. Alternatively, you might quickly check the web, just in case, and then... '50 things to do with a water melon – I'll just check that first'.

Example two

Essay title:

'Outline and evaluate the deindividuation account of why people engage in acts of aggression.'

How you feel about the essay

Aware of some ideas about aggression, but not clear on what the 'deindividuation account' is. There was something about groups and aggression and something else about how we define what aggression is and how it can be debated.

How you can get started

1. **Using images**

Deindividuation

One approach to aggression is the deindividuation approach.

Group approach

> Some approaches – perhaps including the deindividuation approach – have not considered how groups are linked to aggression. Weakness of deindividuation?

Definition of aggression

> We could question how aggression has been defined by the deindividuation approach and within social psychology in general.

2. **Note form**

The deindividuation approach is one way of understanding aggression.

Some approaches challenge the deindividuation approach.

Some approaches emphasise thinking of aggression in terms of groups – it might be a weakness of the deindividuation approach if this did not consider the role of groups in understanding aggressive behaviour.

Group approaches to aggression can be used to challenge and evaluate the deindividuation approach.

Another perspective suggests that we can question how aggression has been defined – it might be possible to challenge or question the definitions within the deindividuation approach as well as within social psychology in general. This idea might challenge most of the literature considered in the essay, so it might work best towards the end.

What I need to find out and where:

- What the deindividuation approach is (I have some lecture notes on this).
- What the evidence is and how the empirical evidence and the theory can be evaluated or thought about in different ways, from different perspectives (the lecture notes give some information and the textbook provides more detail on this).
- What approaches challenge the deindividuation approach (I have some lecture notes on this).
- How group approaches to aggression might challenge aspects of the deindividuation approach (not sure of the best sources of information for this).
- What is being argued by the approach that questions how we define aggression and whether this can be used to challenge deindividuation and other approaches to understanding aggressive behaviour approach (not sure of the best sources of information for this).

Note: In this list there is uncertainty regarding the best source of information for the last two points. Be alert, wandering around looking for information is as precarious as Frodo succumbing to the power of the ring as he is about to throw it into the fires of Mount Doom, or facing the zombie-like husks of *Fortnite: Save the World*. It takes a heroic effort not to be side-tracked or lose focus as the procrastination forces are ranged against you. Will you win through? Being aware that you are highly likely to get side-tracked when wondering where to find information can in itself help. You need to get into the mindset of Sherlock Holmes – this is detective work, you are locating and finding out information and you can even do it without a pipe and deerstalker.

RETHINKING 'WHERE DO I START'

In the two examples above, the imaginary student was faced with an essay that they did not fully understand but they sketched out some ideas without delay. These ideas gave a potential shape that their final essay might take, highlighting the possible debate(s) that their essays might develop and showing an awareness of how one idea, perspective or empirical study might be used to evaluate the essay target (Piaget's stage theory and the deindividuation approach to aggressive behaviour). From an unpromising start – with lots of knowledge gaps – a useful plan was developed and more clarity about what needed to be found out was achieved.

If our imaginary students had gone to a search engine to fill in those gaps before they started, (1) the gaps would not be as clearly specified and (2) there would be a real risk of missing the wave – or letting the momentum slip past. How easy it is to transition from a Google Scholar search for information about deindividuation, for example, to distracting YouTube videos about 12 things you can do with an orange that's past its use-by date.

REFLECTING ON THE CHAPTER:
Writing an essay is not like assembling IKEA furniture

Lots of things we do, whether assembling furniture, replacing a phone battery, following a recipe or even watching a film, have a sequential preference – there is (usually) a correct order in which to do these things. Essays are a bit deceptive: they *have* an order with an introduction, a main body and a conclusion; they should usually be *read* in that order, but they are not necessarily written in that order. Essay writing is less programmatic than following a recipe. We start wherever we start and from that we form the substance out of which we will create our work. Forming an essay is a little like being a potter – we will work and rework our words, like the potter shaping their clay. We pull form and beauty out of the mass of words and ideas that we have to work with. The main thing is that we do not delay in starting to write something – from that first step all of the others are possible.

TAKE AWAY POINTS FROM THIS CHAPTER

- You have reasons for not working right now that should be honestly acknowledged.
- You don't need to 'know it all' or 'understand it all' before you start.
- Your questions are great – they can inform your thinking, reading and writing.
- Your writing can be a resource for thinking more deeply about the topic.
- You are already working on your essay as soon as you are thinking about it.
- The smallest of steps is still a step.
- You can find fun in the task if you look for it.

LINKING TO OTHER CHAPTERS

This chapter has touched on a lot of issues that are addressed in much more detail in subsequent chapters. After Chapter 2, which concerns how you can make your essay your own, the chapters that follow are linked to the different components of your essay and, where possible, are structured in the order in which their topical focus is likely to be most relevant in your essay. The first of these (Chapter 3) addresses how to write an effective introduction, the next how to address the essay title (Chapter 4) and the next how to smoothly interconnect your essay (Chapter 5). The following chapters address how to successfully evaluate (Chapter 6) and describe (Chapter 7) in your essay. The next chapters are concerned with coursework essays and outline how you can tackle two very different but often neglected components of a brilliant essay: conclusions (Chapter 8) and references (Chapter 9). We then look at the editing process (Chapter 10) before addressing the specialist area of writing effective essays in exams (Chapters 11 and 12). While each chapter should give you some genuinely helpful guidance and encouragement, you may find it helpful to use feedback from your essays and your awareness to focus particularly on the issues that keep coming up for you. There is no plot that will be spoiled if you move straight to Chapter 9, no mystery character that doesn't make sense if you go straight to Chapter 7. It's your book, your resource, so use it in the way that works best for you. Writing essays is such a great skill to develop – I hope this book helps you to realise your full potential.

Chapter 2

Make it yours – how to use sources effectively and avoid the plagiarism trap

There is a famous quote which appears to praise 'stealing' the work of others. One form of it goes like this: '*Good writers borrow, great writers steal.*' You might instantly think that Pablo Picasso said this, or TS Eliot, or maybe Oscar Wilde. If you attribute the phrase to any one of them, you are right. They all said it – or something very similar – and several others did too, so it's not entirely clear who 'stole' from whom. We could leave to one side what this quote is trying to express – perhaps something about the dangers of trying to sneakily *imitate* others – and dig a little deeper. Is it still theft – or, for our purposes, plagiarism – if Picasso inserts the word 'artists', Eliot 'poets' and Wilde 'writers'? Many students use exactly this technique of word substitution, or versions of it, to try to evade plagiarism detection or in a genuine effort to make the copied passage 'their own'.

This chapter will tackle plagiarism head on – not to simply wag a metaphorical finger at you and tell you what you *really mustn't do*, but by examining all of the key features involved in making your essay your own. Here you will find not only tips on avoiding plagiarism, but also how you can readily become a proactive researcher in locating sources for your essay, how you can create notes that genuinely empower your essay writing and how you can use those sources to make your essay sparkle. This chapter will support your natural curiosity to find out more about psychology and your sense of satisfaction in doing something well – creating something really worthwhile. Your sense of curiosity and creativity is what really matters, so don't let stress, anxiety and time pressure blow you off course.

In this chapter you will learn…

- What is plagiarism and why it matters
- The active-engagement approach to locating and utilising sources

(Continued)

- How to search effectively for information
- Dynamic note-taking
- How to really make it your own

PLAGIARISM: WHAT IT IS AND WHY IT MATTERS

Before we get into dire warnings about plagiarism, the likelihood of being caught and the consequences when you are, let's try and get a sharper sense of what it actually is and then we can work out how to find a much better way of drawing on the work of others. Plagiarism is used to refer to instances where *someone presents another's work as being their own*. It dates to at least 70 CE when one Roman poet (Martial) became aware that another poet (Fidentinus) seemed to be doing just that. It is interesting to note that concerns about plagiarism have risen as the act of committing it has become easier – and right now it has never been easier. It took 10 seconds to go from writing the previous sentence to finding several online essay writing services. But wait, there's more: if I have an essay to do on Piaget, I can type the six letters of his name into Google and get, as I did, precisely 32 million pages. I could create not one, but hundreds of essays by assembling sentences, paragraphs and pages that I find online. It's as if I don't need to think – I just search and find, copy and paste. I might feel bad about the deception involved in getting someone to write my essay for me or cutting and pasting large sections of text, so I could try a more popular form of plagiarism where I just make minor modifications. Perhaps, if I change a few words it will be more authentically mine and harder to detect – a win–win situation.

The Plagiarism Casebook

Look at the following cases in Tables 2.1–2.3. The cases and names (which are from a random name generator) are fictitious, but the incidents are informed by real events. For each case, consider what the student did, what happened and what, in hindsight, they could – or should – have done.

TABLE 2.1
Example from the Plagiarism Casebook: Kylan

The context	Kylan is extremely stressed with his third-year assignments and feels awkward asking his supervisor for help. He has found a website that offers online assistance with completing his academic work. He sees from the reviews that most people are very happy with the service and there is no mention on the site that this is plagiarism.
The decision	After some hesitation, Kylan decides to ask the essay assistance company for help in completing one of his essays.
The consequences	Kylan is identified as having used an essay-writing service, and his case escalates from a departmental level to a university disciplinary committee. The committee finds Kylan guilty of intentional gross academic misconduct. He is failed on the assignment and may be expelled from the university.

| The alternatives | Getting someone else to write all, or part, of your assignment is clearly intentional and premeditated plagiarism. Although it can be awkward, it is important to keep in touch with your tutor. It is best to do so before matters reach a crisis point. Usually there will be someone whom you feel more comfortable about approaching; they may be within the department or part of a counselling, welfare or other support service. Seeking help for the problems that you are experiencing can be extremely difficult but can make a huge difference – don't let awkwardness, embarrassment or anxiety hold you back. |

TABLE 2.2
Example from the Plagiarism Casebook: Ciaran

The context	Ciaran is running out of time to complete her essay on the multistore model of memory, which is due in tomorrow. She has found some websites that seem to have highly relevant material and which discuss some of the literature mentioned in class.
The decision	Ciaran copies over a paragraph into her essay. She is planning to come back to it later and put it in her own words, but because of the deadline she hands in the essay with the paragraph essentially unchanged.
The consequences	Although all of the other paragraphs were written by Ciaran, the paragraph is identified by plagiarism software as being copied. Ciaran is failed on the module and has to re-submit a new essay with a different title. If she passes, Ciaran's grade will be capped at a bare pass, otherwise she will fail.
The alternatives	Even though Ciaran wrote most of the essay, a substantive copied passage has been identified. Don't tell yourself that you can't express things in your own words. This isn't simply a skill that you either have or don't have, it is one that you learn. Start learning this skill whenever you are taking notes, not just when you are writing an essay that is due in tomorrow. Reading and thinking can involve a struggle to make it your own. Try to stay with this struggle – it is worth it. See tips on how to *make it your own* later in the chapter.

TABLE 2.3
Example from the Plagiarism Casebook: Shelly

The context	Shelly is struggling to explain Kelley's covariation model of causal attribution. She has found a textbook which explains it in a clear and succinct way and wants to use it.
The decision	Shelly decides to copy the paragraph but changes as many words as she can without having to change the format of the sentence. Shelly finds the easiest way to do this is to use synonyms, replacing 'rational' with 'logical', 'reasoning' with 'thinking' and 'circumstances' with 'occurrences'.
The consequences	Although Shelly did change many of the words in the passages she copied over, she was judged to have essentially copied the ideas and passed it off as her own work. As with Ciaran, her work is failed. She is required to re-submit a new piece of work and if the work passes, her grade will be capped at a bare pass, otherwise she will fail.

(Continued)

TABLE 2.3   (Continued)

The alternatives	Swapping words in sentences that are essentially lifted from the work of others is still plagiarism. Switching words for synonyms avoids thinking about the actual topic yourself – perhaps out of a fear of getting it wrong. Unfortunately, swapping a few words in this way is wrong in that it attempts to complete the assignment while bypassing your brain. Usually such cosmetic changes to what is essentially someone else's work wind up being a poor copy, weakened by the word substitution, and often in a way that highlights a lack of understanding of the topic itself. For example, using the word 'occurrences' instead of 'circumstances' will probably ruin an attempt to explain Kelley's notion of consistency.
	See tips on how to *make it your own* later in the chapter.

If this chapter is successful, it will stop you from choosing to outsource your essay, to cut and paste another's work or to simply make cosmetic changes to someone else's work. All of these turn a beautiful, human task of creation into an ugly, mechanical chore of simulation. Writing is difficult, joyful and satisfying; copying is easy, shameful and empty. At rock bottom, even if you could 'get away with it', plagiarism is pointless. It is pointless in the sense that it sucks point and meaning, learning and growth, out of your work, and your experience of being a student is diminished. The opportunity to really learn and grow – and you will learn and grow by writing – is just too precious to squander in an anxious bid to complete your assignment.

The tragedy is that most people do not set out to cheat. Even the essay-writing services attempt to appease the consciences of their potential customers, suggesting that their service is 'like having another teacher' and that students can 'learn from the essays' that are written for them. The cut-and-paste passages are often done with the intention to change it, *soon*. Finally, students often make cosmetic changes to a passage not just to evade detection by plagiarism software, but in a genuine attempt to 'make it their own'.

ACE YOUR ASSIGNMENT
Citation and referencing

Chapter 9 addresses the issues of citing and referencing sources using the formatting guidelines of the American Psychological Association (APA) in substantial detail. Here it is worth very briefly touching on some of the implications that these have in regard to plagiarism.

The sources that you draw on in informing your ideas should be cited using the format: Surname (date of publication), for example, Dereckson (2020), within the body of your essay. At the end of your essay, the reference section (arranged alphabetically by surname) should contain the full reference details, enabling your reader to locate that resource (Chapter 9 discusses these issues in more detail).

Where the phrases or sentences are used from a source, these should be given in quotation marks and you should cite the surname, year of publication and page, or pages, from which the quotation was taken (again, Chapter 9 discusses this in more detail).

It is important to realise that citing sources is vitally important throughout your essay, but that doing so doesn't then license you to give up thinking, letting your essay be carried by extensive (cited) quotations. While there is little of the deception usually associated with plagiarism in essays that do this, they are still over-reliant on the thinking of others. Do take into account immediate guidance from those involved in setting your assignment but, in general, quotes should be used to support your intelligent engagement with the essay, not replace it.

THE ACTIVE-ENGAGEMENT APPROACH TO LOCATING AND UTILISING SOURCES

What am I trying to do in my essay?

Before we turn to sources, let's turn to the essay title itself. Thinking about the essay title will guide us as to the sorts of things we need to do in the essay. This will give us a much better sense as to how we can actively use the sources – as resources – in our essay. If we don't do this, we are in danger of being too passive, waiting to get a sense of what to write entirely from what we read, and we will never reach anything like our full potential. When we have an essay title we need to Stop, Look and Think.

STOP
Read the title carefully

If you do not stop, you are treating the essay like a Wikipedia entry – you see the trigger name or idea and immediately reference 'the' material that matches so that you can write 'the' Piaget, Freud or Short-Term Memory essay. This is a terrible idea. The essay is almost never in the form: 'Tell me whatever you know and can find out about Piaget'. Instead, it asks you to *do* something, something much more specific.

LOOK
What is the title asking you to do?

Look *really carefully* at what the essay title is asking you to do (see Chapter 4 for more on how you can address the specific essay title). You may be asked to evaluate evidence or contrast ideas; the essay may be focused on a specific aspect of Piaget, Freud or Short-Term Memory; the essay might be framed in a highly specific way, asking you to explore a particular perspective on the target topic.

THINK
How do I best address the title?

Think not so much about 'what is *the* answer' as 'how can I display relevant scholarly understanding and thinking regarding the issue(s) identified in the title'. The essay is your opportunity to display that depth of scholarly thinking – your reader wants to see the extent to which you serve up something subtle, knowing and sophisticated, rather than simply slop out the usual gruel. Think about the sorts of things you need to do for your specific essay title and the sorts of things you need to find out in order to do these things.

This Stop, Look and Think process is illustrated below.

ACE YOUR ASSIGNMENT
I is for index

We live in a world of i-prefaced words, but what about that amazingly useful but, widely neglected i, namely the index. Some digital search tools are addressed in more detail below but, for now, note that most academic books have not one, but two indexes (for both names and subjects). This means you can search for that psychologist whose work you were interested in, or that special topic – or you can really push the boat out and do both.

It is a real hassle for authors and publishers to compile carefully copy-edited indexes and they do it as some small but precious act of kindness for you. Why not accept their generous gift and save yourself many hours of flicking through texts, wondering if that key name or idea will pop up, and enter the wonderful world of indexes? It's what Sherlock Holmes, Hercule Poirot, Miss Marple and Adam Dalgliesh would do – you should try it too.

Imagine the following essay title:

'Critically evaluate the evidence for the multistore model of memory.'

Stop – this is not asking for whatever you know or what the textbook says about the multistore model of memory.

Look – the essay is particularly focused on an evaluation of the evidence regarding the multistore model. Although the essay refers to the evidence *for* the multistore model, as you are evaluating the evidence it would *normally* (though do be aware of specific tutor guidance) be appropriate to include evidence *for* and *against*.

Think – what do you need to do in this essay and what do you need to find out in order to do it?

What do you need to do? You need to demonstrate:

- An understanding of what the Multi-Store Model is.
- An awareness of empirical evidence relating to the Multi-Store Model.
- A capacity to evaluate the empirical evidence relating to the Multi-Store Model.
- A capacity to think about these issues from different viewpoints.

What do you need to find out in order to do this?

- You need information that will help you to describe the Multi-Store Model.
- You need information concerning the empirical evidence for the Multi-Store Model.
- You need information that both supports the empirical evidence and criticises it – or identifies its shortcomings.
- You need information concerning alternatives to the Multi-Store Model. These can be used to evaluate the Multi-Store Model, but care has to be taken to keep the focus on the Multi-Store Model itself.

Don't let this active orientation to using sources as resources become oppressive. It can be fun. Get into detective mode. You are identifying just what it takes to provide a really strong answer to your specific essay title. The next part of the essay challenge is to locate the information and ideas that will support and stimulate you in writing an excellent essay.

Locating your (re)sources

What do you need to find out in order to solve this essay?

- Start by noting what you know – briefly jot down all the thoughts and ideas that you have regarding the essay title that you are working on.
- Then identify what you need to find out – you might need further details, names and dates, specific bits of information, or it could be more generic, such as 'information that I can use to critique the Multi-Store Model'.
- Note where you can look to find this out – don't just lazily list 'on the web', be precise. Is it in your lecture notes, a textbook or an item on the reading list?
- Make use of your notes, textbook and other material that has been identified as being important on your course, and specifically for this topic and this essay. This is most likely to include key information – do make use of it.
- Identify the potential challenges along the way – there are possibly things that might be difficult to find. Perhaps the hardest are those we are not yet aware of – perhaps there are

excellent reviews of the evidence that we do not know of, which could be invaluable. Try to envisage what *might* exist as well as looking for the bare essentials of what you need.

- Be careful as you enter your distraction zones! Yours might be as you search on the web, or look for your notes, or go to find a textbook. Be aware of where *you* are most likely to be distracted away from your goal and acknowledge the temptation, without giving in to it. Gamify it: give yourself 50 points, a cut-out and keep medal, or some other reward for running three Google searches without suddenly being caught by YouTube videos of a fish that can speak fluent Spanish. All those distractions will still be there later.

- Identify what you could include that might make your essay shine. Would a meta-analysis relating to the issue be relevant? Perhaps there is a recent empirical or review paper, or a paper which details a different perspective on the issue? This can be especially valuable if the topic of your essay has a well-trodden debate (the nature–nurture debate being the most obvious example of this).

This *active–engagement* approach is so different from the 20 or so Google searches we might do each day, which can be unthinking, almost automatic responses, like scratching, simply performed to relieve the inconvenient sense of not knowing. Here we are being strategic: we are thinking and planning before searching. Doing it this way means that we approach sources proactively, strategically – that is, with a sense of how we might use them. Yes, they will suggest modifications to our plans, they will offer something that differs from what we expected, but we have approached them as *mind meets mind* – not *mind meets photocopier*. Adopting this proactive engagement approach is a massive step towards making whatever we find our own.

Finding relevant sources

We all probably develop a default preference for one or two databases. Like our preferred smartphone, we get used to the way it feels, how it works and we feel we are somehow in tune with it. However, this approach could be limiting us far more than we realise. If we visit the same café, order the same snack, drink the same drink, we are at least dimly aware of the alternatives – with databases we tend to almost forget that other options exist.

There are a couple of snags with giving advice of this nature to readers who are associated with different institutions. For one, my ESP is really rather limited, so I don't know the provision at your university. The only compensation here is that you do, or at least you can do. The second is that even if I did have such incredible knowledge, I couldn't keep up with your institution's changing subscriptions, and if I did, this book would be so long and boring that it might become a major intervention for most forms of insomnia. Given these limitations, you need to become familiar with your institution's online and hard-copy resources, and make use of your information professionals' expertise in terms of identifying relevant information and accessing it. Here I will sketch out some key databases, but it is not a complete list (see also Table 2.4). The bespoke information concerning your specific institution will vary and it is really worth investing 45 or even

60 minutes of your life to find out about it. In the meantime, investing just a few minutes right here, right now could help you to avoid simply defaulting to whatever you are most familiar with.

Some recurring terms

Abstracts
Often your search will yield results that include abstracts of publications. These are typically summaries of around 200–300 words which provide the main details of the articles, chapters or books that you have come across to a search. Abstracts are super-helpful in working out how relevant the source might be to your essay, but beware of being sucked into paying for articles unless this has been highlighted as an expectation of your course. Your institution may well have free access to the source and, if not, the source may not be as relevant as it seems. Try to avoid staying with the abstract alone – an abstract provides insufficient information for all but the most passing citation within the body of your essay. An essay populated with information from abstracts will look a little vague and superficial. Usually if an article is worth citing, it is worth reading.

Abstracting and indexing databases
You will notice that some of these databases are primarily for identifying the articles that you want. These will typically provide full citation details (that is, all of the information identifying the article – author, title of article, book, journal or conference proceedings details, etc.) and will often include an abstract, if available. You may – partly depending on your institution's subscription arrangements – be able to access the full text. While abstracting and indexing databases can lead to a two-stage article access process, they mainly help you to identify relevant material rather than necessarily to access it. They often utilise sophisticated and flexible search parameters, giving you a lot of freedom in terms of how you search. Abstracting and indexing databases often draw on a wider pool of journals and may be less limited to particular publishers or organisations than full-text databases.

Full-text databases
Some of the databases do include full-text access, offering you the opportunity not only to identify relevant articles but to access the full text (rather than just an abstract) of them as well. It is worth noting that full-text databases, while convenient, may draw on a narrower range of sources, and in some cases relying on just one full-text database could mean that important perspectives are underrepresented.

Peer-reviewed sources
This is often used as a benchmark of academic quality. When a journal states that it is 'peer reviewed', it refers to the fact that the articles which it publishes go through a process in which

fellow experts (peers) read and review submissions to ensure the quality of all articles that are selected for publication in the journal. The databases listed in Table 2.4 focus on peer-reviewed journals, although more generic platforms, such as Google Scholar, will often include both peer-reviewed and non-peer-reviewed sources. With academic books, the review system is more varied and it can make sense initially to use texts which are recommended, or which are published by reputable publishers. These will be the sorts of publishers which typically pop up in your reading lists and which populate the reference lists of other publications.

ACE YOUR ASSIGNMENT
Search terms and search parameters

The importance of indexes in academic texts was mentioned earlier (see 'i is for index' above), but it is really important to use search terms and search parameters wisely to both identify your articles and to search within them. 'Search terms' include all of the specifying words that you use to locate relevant articles, while 'search parameters' act as a filter, specifying, for example, the date, name or type of publication from which you want your results to be drawn. Practise using different search terms and search parameters *not just when an assignment is due* – perhaps choose a topic that especially interests you, or one that you know well. Honing this skill will really help when it comes to the task of locating items for your assignments.

TABLE 2.4
Brief database overview

Database	Quick summary at the time of publication
Google Scholar	This is a convenient cross-disciplinary search platform which is very widely used, not least because of its ready accessibility whenever you are online. It draws on a massive range of articles but that does not mean that each discipline is comprehensively covered. It offers a multidisciplinary reference tool which can be helpful, but it needs to be checked for accuracy and completeness.
	Searching with Google Scholar, you may find that it is more difficult to limit your search to genuinely scholarly work, including peer-reviewed work. In some cases, links to full-text articles are given, and some of these will take you to a paywall, or another platform which you may need access to (such as Researchgate). You may want to use your institutional resources (such as online journal subscriptions) to access the sources that you identify.
PsychINFO You would usually log in to this via your institution	This is an abstracting and indexing database with more than 3 million records drawn from approximately 2,500 psychology journals. The database is very helpful for finding the abstracts and citation details for articles, and you may be able to link to the full text in some cases, but this will partly depend on your institution's subscription arrangements.
PsychArticles You would usually log in to this via your institution	This is a full-text psychology database of more than 80 peer-reviewed journals published by the American Psychological Association and affiliated journals.

Database	Quick summary at the time of publication
Social Sciences Citation Index You would usually log in to this via your institution	This is an abstracting and indexing database of more than 3,000 social science journals. Similar to other abstracting and indexing databases, the Social Sciences Citation Index is very helpful for finding the abstracts and citation details for articles. Accessing the full text will partly depend on your institution's subscription arrangements.
SocIndex With Full Text You would usually log in to this via your institution	This is a full-text sociology database drawing on more than 600 full-text peer-reviewed journals.
Web of Science/Web of Knowledge You would usually log in to this via your institution	This is an abstracting and indexing database of more than 33,000 journals across the natural and social sciences and humanities. As with other abstracting and indexing databases, Web of Science is very helpful for finding the abstracts and citation details for articles. Accessing the full text will partly depend on your institution's subscription arrangements.
Academic Search Premier You would usually log in to this via your institution	This is a database of more than 3,100 full-text journals and magazines (approximately 2,800 of which are peer reviewed). Disciplines covered include psychology, applied and natural sciences, religion and philosophy.
Scopus You would usually log in to this via your institution	At the time of writing, this is the largest abstract and citation database of peer-reviewed literature. As with other abstracting and indexing databases, Scopus is primarily helpful for identifying relevant articles and supplying their abstract where available. Accessing the full text will partly depend on your institution's subscription arrangements.
WorldCat www.worldcat.org	This is a massive database drawing on a collaboration of more than 72,000 libraries, in 170 countries and territories, that helps you to search library collections locally and globally. You may find links to full texts and downloadable content or just citation information that will identify relevant sources which you can then track down.

SEARCHING EFFECTIVELY

Let's assume that Sophie and Olivia have to tackle the following essay title:

'Critically evaluate the Elaboration Likelihood Model of persuasion.'

Search strategy one: Hope for the best

Sophie sees straight away that the topic concerns persuasion. She gets onto Google Scholar and in 0.03 seconds 904,000 results are identified. Towards the top of the search are some of the most important and highly cited papers, including Hovland et al.'s research into attitudes and one of Petty and Cacioppo's influential papers outlining the Elaboration Likelihood model (Hovland, Janis & Kelley, 1953; Petty & Cacioppo, 1986). There are then disparate papers covering diverse topics, such as persuasion and healing and coercive persuasion. Sophie wasn't expecting to cover coercive persuasion or persuasion and healing, but includes these along with the Hovland et al. and the Petty and Cacioppo articles to add breadth to her essay. Sophie finds that only about a quarter of the articles have full-text versions available free of charge, so she uses summaries of the papers where necessary.

Sophie's search strategy

Databases: Google Scholar only

Initial search term: 'Persuasion'

Variations: None

Parameters: Default – limited options are available with this search tool, but even these (e.g. date) are not used

Follow-on strategy: None

Selection of articles: Four are taken from the first page of results.

Verdict on Sophie's search strategy: Sophie has been reactive and restrictive in her search. She has turned to one database, used one search term and then used whatever emerges from that – rather than really thinking about the title – to shape her essay. This is like essay writing by Yahtzee – whatever turns up shapes the essay (even if it's a brief summary of an article irrelevant to the title). Whatever Sophie does next in terms of her introduction and conclusion, her structure and critical evaluation, her essay is like a boat with a large hole in the hull. It's flawed, compromised and likely to sink. The good news is that it is quite easy to improve this situation, as Olivia demonstrates.

Search strategy two: Proactive engagement

Olivia is faced with the same essay title, but she is more proactive and uses the the Stop – Look – Think approach outlined above. She doesn't rush blindly to search a database and doesn't feel the need to restrict herself to the one that was quickest to use. Looking at the essay title, Olivia sees that it is really centred on the *Elaboration Likelihood Model* of persuasion – not attitudes or persuasion in general – so her initial search terms focus specifically on the Elaboration Likelihood Model. Olivia realises that she probably won't find all that will be best for her essay in one search. She knows that varying the search terms (including Elaboration Likelihood Model, criticisms of the Elaboration Likelihood Model, etc.) and refining the parameters of her search (such as date of publication, journal, authors, etc.) will really help. For example, paying attention to some of the recent literature by refining the date range in some of her searches will ensure that she includes contemporary as well as classic references. Olivia also notices that the essay title emphasises *evaluation* and she thinks about how she needs to find out about the ways in which the ELM has been evaluated. Olivia identifies that there might be *theoretical* or *conceptual* evaluations of the ELM as well as *methodological* ones, and that this could inform her search terms. By using different databases Olivia not only identifies a wider range of citations, but also finds articles that are more relevant for the argument(s) being developed in her essay. Olivia's thinking about the essay and planning of it are happening concurrently with her searching for articles. This helps her to set up a thoughtful, scholarly, argumentative essay. In addition, by using different databases she has found full-text access for the key papers she wants to include.

EXERCISE
Searching the literature

Take a moment to note *your* 'go to' search strategy. What search engines and other tools and reading lists do you use? How long do you spend finding sources for your essay? How effective do you think your approach is? Thinking of the advice in this chapter, what can you change to make your literature search more effective?

Olivia's search strategy

Databases: Google Scholar, Psych Info, PsychArticles, ejournals finder, Web of Science

Initial search term: 'Elaboration Likelihood Model'

Variations: Olivia uses multiple search terms. For example, an initial PsychArticles search 'Elaboration Likelihood Model of persuasion' yielded just six results; removing 'persuasion' increased this to 24. Olivia's search terms included: 'Elaboration Likelihood Model of persuasion', 'Elaboration Likelihood Model', 'ELM', 'Criticisms of the ELM', 'methodological criticisms of the Elaboration Likelihood Model'.

Parameters: Olivia varied the date parameters in some searches to highlight recent developments. Some of the databases offered a wide range of parameters that could be controlled, allowing particular journals and authors to be used as well as control about where the search terms occur (for example, in the title, abstract or body of the article).

Follow-on strategy: Initial searches revealed the term 'conceptual criticisms' which informed further searches, names were identified as authoring evaluative articles and these were used in follow up searches. Attention was also paid to journal titles that contained relevant papers and these informed subsequent searches. It was initially difficult to identify more radical critiques of the ELM so other databases were used and search terms that included reference to discursive psychology and rhetoric (both of which provide a radical critique of classic approaches to persuasion) were used.

Selection of articles: The essay title was inspected again and an initial structure was identified.

Verdict on Olivia's search strategy: Olivia has been proactive and flexible in her search. For Olivia, thinking about the essay title and how she will address it has already started, rather than being deferred until after she has her resources in front of her. This proactive investigative search strategy has meant that Olivia is locating resources that not only are relevant to the essay title, but also enable her to develop a critically evaluative essay as she has specifically identified articles that will support this. Her intelligent use of different search terms to support the arguments that she wishes to develop enables her essay to sparkle with the quality of on-target excellence and critical thinking that is associated with sophisticated scholarship. Using different databases enables Olivia to access full-text articles, but this does not necessarily mean that she reads the full text of every one of these articles. Again *purposively*, Olivia can locate just the most useful and relevant information within them to most effectively develop her essay.

TABLE 2.5
A comparison of two strategies to using resources in an essay

Sophie's essay – driven by casual inspection of immediate results	Olivia's essay – driven by the active construction of an argument
Introduction	Introduction
Outline of attitudes (based on Hovland et al., 1953)	Outline of the Elaboration Likelihood Model of persuasion (ELM)
Outline of the Elaboration Likelihood Model of persuasion (based on Petty and Cacioppo, 1986)	Methodological criticisms of the ELM
Coercive persuasion	Alternative models of persuasion to the ELM that share certain assumptions – for example, a similar understanding of attitudes and/or a cognitive experimental outlook
Persuasion and healing	Radically different perspectives on persuasion and on the ELM – for example, discursive and rhetorical perspectives
Conclusion	Conclusion

LEARN
Tops tips for source searching satisfaction

- **Consult the information professionals at your institution's library (and online guidance).** Databases and access to full-text sources (and how these two are integrated) vary quite a lot, so get on-the-spot advice to become a super-searcher.
- **Vary your search terms and your search parameters**. Be like a really brilliant detective – think Sherlock Holmes, rather than inspector LeStrade. Try different angles to really get at the best information available.
- **Diversify your use of databases**. It is so easy to get locked into one easy-access database – especially as it is likely that the database is very useful. But just think how easy it is to supplement that database with another tool. Just a few additional minutes might make a crucial difference, giving you more access to full-text articles, or more control over your search parameters or access to references that you would otherwise miss.
- **Be proactive not reactive**. You are shaping your essay – what information do you need to make your essay excellent? Be purposeful: 'I am looking for something that will help me evaluate x' is better than simply typing in either the essay title or the general topic area. Don't wait to be 'told the answer' by the sources you find – *interrogate* them to discover information, ideas and perspectives that *you can use in developing your scholarly essay*.

DYNAMIC NOTE-TAKING

When you think of note-taking, what image comes to mind. Are you in a lecture theatre copying PowerPoint slides from a screen? Are you huddled over a textbook copying out passages or is your pen – or finger – hovering, waiting for the best bit, the idea that will really make a difference? Note-taking is the Cinderella of academic study – amazingly potent, genuinely transformative, yet left behind, neglected in the shadows and all but forgotten.

Let's change that now. Mundane, passive note-taking isn't anything to get excited about and most of us have a device within arm's reach right now that can produce a high-resolution photograph of anything we see and a reasonably clean audio recording of anything we hear. If we are passive recorders, then technology has probably superceded us already. But if we are simply writing in an unthinking way, when are we planning to start thinking? Do we do the thinking sometime later when we have to look through our notes to write our essay or revise for our exam? A much more exciting option is waiting, calling us to a different way of note-taking. We could see note-taking as an active, dynamic process, where we bring our ideas, uncertainties and questions to what we are reading and hearing. This dynamic interplay is great – it's where learning happens.

Three aspects of this process will be focused on here. They are all concerned with note-taking as a dynamic process. Dynamic note-taking is a means of capturing how the ideas that you encounter (in lectures, textbooks or articles) relate to: each other; your assignments; and your ideas and questions.

Capturing how the ideas you encounter relate to each other

When you are reading a textbook on a particular topic or listening to a lecture, what are the ideas and how do they relate? This very obviously varies considerably, but think of it in terms of an essay that you are writing or an exam answer that you are preparing right now. As I start to answer this question myself, immediately I get a sense of a complex pattern. Some ideas form an obvious debate, and some a far more subtle relationship. Try using the questions below to guide your thinking.

Can you locate the key debate(s)?

Sometimes this is unmissable. If you are in a lecture on language acquisition, you are very likely to come across the fact that Skinner (1957) and Chomsky (1959) expressed divergent views. Locating the key debate is at its easiest when one article directly comments on another, as with Chomsky's (1959) review of Skinner's (1957) book, or Zimbardo's (2006) response to Haslam and Reicher's (2006) paper on their televised prison experiment. But it can be more subtle. This is the case when we come across ideas that are incompatible, but one does not specifically name and critique the other. In this case, we are looking at one perspective or idea and working out the implications it might have for our target idea, or focus. In doing this we are making the connection ourselves.

Which ideas support others?

It is important to think about how some ideas that we come across might share commonalities. This can be in the form of complete or partial agreement. We may find that one article provides further empirical evidence for another – for example, McArthur's (1972) empirical studies provided empirical evidence for Kelley's Covariation Model of Causal Attribution (Kelley, 1967). When we come across supporting evidence or concurring ideas, we may want to note what this might add to the argument and bring that out in our essay – for example, is there a different type of methodology which yields supporting results. Think about the argument almost as if you are building a legal case, interrogating the sources that you read: 'Does this strengthen one side of the argument?' If you identify something that does contribute to one or other side of the argument(s) in your essay, bring out the way in which it does so when writing your essay.

Which ideas expand on others?

Sometimes an idea expands or modifies another in a certain way. For example, Drury and Reicher's Elaborated Social Identity Model (Drury & Reicher, 2000; Stott et al., 2018) very much built on Tajfel, Flament, Billig and Bundy's Social Identity Theory (Tajfel et al., 1971; Tajfel, 1979). Identifying the nature of the difference, while recognising the common ground, is important in order to demonstrate a clear, sophisticated understanding of this more complex relationship between the perspectives that you are drawing on.

Which ideas reconceptualise the issue(s)?

This gets at more fundamental questioning and can often be used to take your initial notes and your finished essay to a higher level. A lot of critical psychology overtly does this by *questioning the core assumptions and focus of psychology*. Critical psychology challenges: for example, the individualising nature of psychology and its heteronormative and sex/gender binary assumptions. It challenges unthinking use of conventional definitions (of 'aggression' for example) and the neglect of the influence of ideology on what we study and how we study it.

Capturing how the ideas you encounter relate to your assignments

However intricately we grasp how the ideas we come across interrelate, we need to be really clear about what the essay title is asking us to do. If the essay title is asking me to 'Outline and evaluate the excitation transfer model of aggression', then critical material about the way in which aggression has been defined in general may not be directly relevant, or may form part of a concluding conceptualisation towards the end of the essay. By contrast, the title 'Critically evaluate some of the key assumptions inherent in empirical research into aggression' is pitched at an overarching conceptual level, thus material about how aggression has been implicitly and explicitly defined would be key.

There may be more subtle differences in terms of the scope within an essay. The following two titles both highlight Piaget, but the first indicates that attention should be paid to his entire stage theory, while the second points to a series of experiments that relate to the stage theory:

'Outline and evaluate Piaget's stage theory of cognitive development.'

'Critically evaluate Piaget's interpretations of his conservation experiments.'

Think for a moment about the shape of the essay that these different titles suggest. You can probably imagine that a lot of similar material would be relevant – for example, reference to conservation is likely to feature in both. But think on for a moment longer. There are likely to be differences between an essay that gets into the various nuances and critiques of the conservation experiments and a more global contrast of Piaget's stage theory of cognitive development with, for example, information processing perspectives.

Really mastering this neat fit between the literature that we come across, the relationships between these sources and what we need to do in our essay is an art, but both the beginner on their first essay and the expert on their millionth word of psychology have to ask the very same question: 'How does this relate to what I am trying to write?' Even asking this question will help free you from the limiting tendency to simply trot out 'the Piaget essay' (as if there were a singular Piaget essay) whenever you see the name. Further guidance about how to really answer the specific essay title can be found in Chapter 4.

Capturing how the ideas you encounter relate to your ideas

Your ideas have a slightly odd status in academic writing. In a sense they are there, but not in a self-conscious way. Dropping in 'I think' – unless you are specifically required to do so, for example in some self-reflected component of an assessment – does not usually work well in academic essays.

ACE YOUR ASSIGNMENT
Brainstorming and mind mapping

In 1953, Alex Osborn developed the idea of *brainstorming* – an approach to problem solving which facilitates the raising of different ideas and perspectives, however strange or unusual they might first seem. This approach very much encourages thinking around an issue from different perspectives, developing novel 'outside of the box' ideas. In the 1960s Tony Buzan, who was frustrated with traditional note-taking, developed a visual way of connecting ideas which became known as *mind-mapping* (Buzan, 1993). In mind-mapping the core topic or focus is typically placed in the middle of a page with links branching from it to show connected ideas and thoughts. This method for generating ideas and for representing their relationship have been used in education for several decades now and could help you with your essays.

- You may find that brainstorming helps to support you in thinking about the ideas that you come across – perhaps especially with evaluating some of the literature that you draw on in your essay.
- You may find that mind mapping works well in planning your essays and in revision.

(Continued)

These tools can help with our academic work. Brainstorming can provide the permission and context for generative and creative ideas, whilst mind-mapping can enable a fun and visually appealing way of helping to plan our essays and check what we know about a topic for a forthcoming exam. But perhaps they are most effective if we are aware of potential limitations, or misuses. Blue-sky thinking about our essay topic is great – but our essays have to address the precise essay topic and the core literature. Visually appealing representations of ideas are a brilliant idea, but do remember that language itself can often represent much more subtle nuances of how things inter-relate than lines alone can, however multi-coloured they may be.

HOW TO REALLY MAKE IT YOUR OWN

What does it mean to *make it your own*?

This sounds obvious, but it isn't – especially as most of us have never been taught how to take notes from source materials. If we do receive such tuition, it is most likely hurried, obvious and focuses on the practical ephemera (have your laptop ready and organise your digital files) as much as on the intellectual substance of note-taking. But there is an intellectual challenge in note-taking that is easily underestimated – if we don't recognise that, we could be in trouble. If you give note-taking the respect it deserves – seeing it as a challenging and creative part of writing your essay – you will be able to do it much more effectively and this will enhance your essays.

Think of all the online and hard-copy sources of information that you have found to be relevant for the essay you are thinking about right now. Immediately, you may have some notes you took down in class; there may be lecture slides or printed notes; there's probably at least one textbook, and most likely some additional references. If you have read all of these, they won't *form* your essay, but they certainly can *inform* it. Sources, however good they are, will not 'tell us what to write', but they will contain arguments and details that we can weave into our own argumentative essay. You are the Hercule Poirot or the Sherlock Holmes of your essay, marshalling the evidence and weighing up the different interpretations. Don't become less than that. You are the person who can demonstrate *in this very essay* your own intelligent engagement with the complex and contradictory ideas and evidence in front of you.

You may feel that it is all very well being told that you should make it your own and be given a sense of how creative and heroic that can be, but *how on earth is it done?* Use the examples below to help you get a vivid sense of what it looks like when sources are used poorly and effectively. From this you can build an understanding about how you can really have a sense of sources as *re*sources, which are there for you to use in constructing your essay. To do this means that we are being intelligently proactive, coming to the sources with a sense of what we are looking for. We are not so rigid that we fail to learn anything, but nor are we so passive that we are waiting for what we read to dictate what we write.

How to move beyond word substitution

In a famous scene from the US sitcom *Friends* (www.youtube.com/watch?v=B1tOqZUNebs), Joey tries to make his letter of recommendation sound 'smart' by using a thesaurus to substitute words. Using this technique, his original sentence 'They are warm, nice people with big hearts' becomes 'They are human prepossessing homo sapiens with full-sized aortic pumps'. It's unlikely that you would use any form of word substitution quite so blindly, but it is amazing how often intelligent people use word substitution to 'make it their own' – or at least to *look* like it's their own. One problem with taking someone else's writing and substituting words within it is that plagiarism software will detect word matches even if there are word substitutions sprinkled throughout the passage. If you change too many individual words within the original sentence structure, your writing will look odd – nearly as odd as referring to people as having 'full-sized aortic pumps'. Fundamentally, swapping words in other people's writing means that you are cheating yourself out of something really remarkably precious – the opportunity to think, to think about a discipline that you are interested in. Why not give up on word substitution scams – they don't convince anyone – and instead really make it your own? Table 2.6 provides some suggestions for overcoming the main obstacles to making it your own.

TABLE 2.6
Overcoming key obstacles to making it your own

Potential block to 'making it your own'	Strategy
Confidence This is a big barrier. You are not alone if you feel that the source(s) you have come across seem(s) to express it so well, know more about it than you do, or simply sound more intelligent than you do.	Writing a journal article, chapter or book takes a lot of time, benefits from a number of reviewers' comments and typically involves lots of redrafting. When you read any sources for your essay, you are typically looking at a finished product rather than ideas in the process of being formed, so comparing your essay with published work is really unfair on yourself. Don't get intimidated if someone who has perhaps written a million words of psychology across their career and had feedback from over 100 people about their writing seems to express themselves well. You would too – and you can.
Anxiety There is something just plain worrying about 'making it your own', regardless of other sources of information. Doing so feels like a risk – you could stand up, just to get knocked right down.	Linked to a lack of confidence when comparing your work to sources, is the experience of anxiety. You can feel remarkably exposed and vulnerable when it is *your* formulation of ideas that is informing your essay, and it is tempting to hide behind the words of others. Acknowledge the anxiety, because it may help you to take care with what you write. Confident and effective writing – of the best sort – often emerges from a puzzlement and lack of clarity. If you are confused, not clear, unsure of how to make sense of the dissimilar ideas and contradictions, fear not – value that uncertainty and use it to help deepen your writing. Great academic writing conveys a sense that things are 'not all neat and straightforward'. Don't assume there is a problem with you if ideas don't line up neatly, but rather work to reveal the debates, subtleties, nuances and contradictions.
Distraction Looking for information for your essay, especially online, can be dangerous. It is like driving along the notorious 'death road' of Bolivia – you are likely to fall of the precipice into the oblivion of distraction.	You may find that you are less likely to be distracted if you search online using a laptop rather than a smartphone. You should also plan your search rather than casually drift into it. If you are likely to be distracted, plan a return strategy – being too censorial won't help you here. Agree with yourself in advance that if you do get distracted, you'll come back to your work; no drama, no guilt-trip, just back to your essay.

Use the examples below to get a sense of how you can make the source material that you come across your own. For the two examples provided, look at the target passage and then at the attempts of the authors to make it their own. Attempt one relies on swapping words, which is one of the most common ways in which people try, and fail, to make source material their own, whereas attempt two really engages with the ideas.

Example one

Imagine that you need to complete an essay entitled 'Outline and evaluate Kelley's Covariation Model of Causal Attribution'. You would not be alone in finding this model quite technical and, at least in part, tricky to articulate clearly. Then you stumble on the following text:

Target passage

Kelley followed Heider in suggesting that identifying the broad location of the cause – internal to the person or external to them – was a crucial goal of our attribution reasoning. Kelley also subdivided the category of external to distinguish stimulus (a recurring feature external to the person) from *circumstance* (something specific to this instance of the behaviour). For Kelley, we all (ideally) follow a causal analysis that is similar to an empirically orientated scientist … (Dickerson, 2012: 118).

Attempt one: Word substitution

You might think that rather than simply copying these sentences as they are, which you understand is plagiarism, you will change it a bit, but retain the essential sentence structure:

Kelley pursued Heider in arguing that the wide location of the cause – within the person or without – was an essential target of our attribution thinking. Kelley also split the grouping of without to distinguish stimulus (a constant feature without the person) from *circumstance* (something targeted at this example of the behaviour). For Kelley, we all (faultlessly) follow a causal analysis that is similar to an observationally orientated scientist …

The changes above look far-fetched in places, but are, alas, not uncommon. While the paragraph uses several of Kelley's key terms and phrases (stimulus, circumstance and 'location of the cause'), the substituted words, synonymous though they may be, reveal an unthinking process and a lack of understanding, rendering much of the text inaccurate and incomprehensible.

Attempt two: Making it your own

This attempt does not use all of the information in the target passage. The distinction between types of external causes has been left to one side for now. A crucial consideration is what you want to do in the paragraph you are working on and how the information that you come across can facilitate that.

A key feature of Kelley's Covariation Model of Causal Attribution is its emphasis on the importance of distinguishing between internal and external causes of behaviour. From this perspective, the key question driving our causal reasoning concerns the *location* – internal or external – of the cause of whatever we are making an attribution about. For Kelley, we *ideally* locate the cause as being internal (to the person whose behaviour we are trying to explain) or external (to them) by using a causal reasoning process that is like a scientist, logically reasoning from the evidence that they encounter.

This second attempt makes it much more the author's own work. Do you notice there is a sense of confidence in the writing, that the author is not afraid to make well-grounded claims? The assertion that the internal/external distinction is 'a key feature', the reference to the 'location' of the cause and to 'logically reasoning' are informed by the target passage, but certainly not shackled to it. Some of this freedom can come by bringing in a wider understanding, informed by other sources. It also comes from thinking about how you can use the details and arguments that are at work in this passage, what points you want to emphasise so that it is easier to pick them up – perhaps to debate them – later in your essay. Table 2.7 demonstrates how you might think about a target passage, identifying the constituent parts of what is being described and argued, thinking about what is debatable or could be contested (which is great for a critically evaluative essay) and, crucially, reflecting on how you can use these ideas in your essay.

TABLE 2.7
How to use sources that may inform your essay

Essay Title:
Outline and evaluate Kelley's Covariation Model of Causal Attribution.

Original passage	Making it yours
Kelley followed Heider in suggesting that identifying the broad location of the cause – internal to the person or external to them – was a crucial goal of our attribution reasoning. Kelley also sub-divided the category of external to distinguish stimulus (a recurring feature external to the person) from *circumstance* (something specific to this instance of the behaviour). For Kelley, we all (ideally) follow a causal analysis that is similar to an empirically orientated scientist ...	**1. What is being described?** This passage describes Kelley's emphasis on the distinction between an internal and external location of cause and the distinction Kelley made between stimuli and circumstance. **2. What is being argued?** It contains the overt arguments that Kelley followed Heider and that, according to Kelley, in making attributions people reason similarly to a scientist working from available evidence. **3. What is contentious about the content of this passage?** It is possible to debate or question the usefulness of the internal/external distinction and the idea that, when making an attribution, people 'ideally' follow the sort of reasoning processes that an empirical scientist uses. **4. How can I use it?** Given the essay title, some of this passage might be used quite early on in outlining Kelley's covariation model of causal attribution. Reference to the split between stimulus and circumstance might be important, but not necessarily. The emphasis on the internal/external distinction and the idea that people reason similarly to scientists in making attributions could both be picked up in later paragraphs to form substantial criticisms. The word in brackets 'ideally' might be important because it could be used in a counter-argument to criticism of Kelley. From this perspective, Kelley's model was not intended to depict what people *actually* do, but rather what they would, or could, do in fully-informed (*ideal*) contexts.

Break it down, then rebuild it

One of the key reasons that we might struggle to make a passage our own is that we are trying to: (a) reduce time, and/or (b) reduce thinking. If you are short of time, don't start swapping words left and right, turn to Chapters 10 and 12 for clarity about what you should focus on. Alternatively, if you want to reduce your thinking because you do not have confidence in your ideas, stay with this chapter (and the ones that follow); we can really build your well-placed academic confidence together.

To really make the passage your own you will need to do something that might seem crazy, off-putting, pointless – you need to break it from the coherent whole into the constituent ideas so that you can assemble it as your own whole. In this way, you have taken the raw material ideas referred to and made an argument with them – that is, you have used them to do a particular job in your essay. As mentioned above, the skill of note-taking is drastically undervalued, and almost never taught, so if it seems difficult or off-putting, that's hardly surprising. To get started, practise identifying and separating the detail and the argument in the paragraph that you are looking at.

Interrogate the argument

Interrogate the paragraph by asking it: What is being argued here? Is an idea or position being supported or is it being challenged (or perhaps a bit of both)? What idea is being supported, challenged or nuanced? Crucially, ask yourself: How can I strategically use this sort of argument – or a challenge to it – in the essay that I am developing? The focus of your essay and the original context of any specific paragraph are unlikely to be identical. And even if they are, your argument in addressing that essay is, or should be, distinct in some way. In the light of this, understand the argument being made and think how it relates to your argument(s) so that you can deploy it really effectively. In the context of an academic essay that means in a way that displays scholarly thinking – that ability to move between ideas, acknowledging contradictions, debates and syntheses, and to navigate an intelligent path through them to shed light on the specific issues identified in the essay title.

Assemble the details

Once you have a clear sense of what is being argued and how this may relate to the arguments you wish to develop in your essay, it is worth inspecting some of the detail to see how that might be used effectively. If it is an empirical study, what was done and what was found; if it is an idea or theory without empirical evidence, what specific points are being made?

Example two

Now imagine that your essay title is 'Outline and evaluate the Equity Theory of intimate relationships in the light of relevant research.' In addition to describing Equity Theory, you are required to draw in different perspectives.

Target passage

Wong and Goodwin's (2009) qualitative study also raises important questions concerning how relationship satisfaction is thought about by individuals in relationships. In qualitative research across three cultures – the United Kingdom, Hong Kong and Beijing – Wong and Goodwin (2009) found that there was an emphasis on the importance of 'a stable relationship with the spouse', 'spousal support', 'partnership with the spouse' and 'stable family finance'. The cultural differences that emerged included 'companionship' being more important for UK participants and 'harmonious marital relations' being more important for Hong Kong respondents. Taken together, these issues might, indeed, be construable as ingredients that inform equity based calculations, but some of them are suggestive of something slightly different – perhaps a concern with an overarching 'characterisation of the relationship' rather than a calculation of the benefits and costs of its individual constituent features in the light of profit or fairness concerns. (Dickerson, 2012: 97).

Attempt one: Word substitution

Have a quick look through this passage, which merely tries to substitute some of the words, leaving the sentence structure and the organisation of the ideas untouched. To achieve this was easy and quick – the passage was copied over and some of the words that were not in quotation marks were substituted. The sentence structure and order were unchanged. This made it quick, and perhaps reduced the apparent risk of 'getting it wrong' in terms of misunderstanding the ideas referred to. It 'got it wrong' in a more fundamental way, however, by demonstrating a lack of understanding and by being a clear example of plagiarism.

Wong and Goodwin's (2009) qualitative investigation also raises vital interrogatives respecting how relationship achievement is thought about by individuals in conjunctions. In qualitative research across three cultures – the United Kingdom, Hong Kong and Beijing – Wong and Goodwin (2009) discovered that there was a stress on the salience of 'a stable relationship with the spouse', 'spousal support', 'partnership with the spouse' and 'stable family finance'. The cultural divergences that emanated comprised 'companionship' being more important for UK participants and 'harmonious marital relations' being more important for Hong Kong respondents. Taken concurrently, these matters might, indeed, be construable as ingredients that inform equity based computations, but some of them are evocative of something slightly divergent – perhaps a concern with a supreme 'characterisation of the relationship' rather than a calculation of the values and detriments of its individual constituent features in the light of yield or fairness apprehensions.

Attempt two: Making it your own

This second sample, below, is much better. The author has made it their own. It is shorter, but contains several key ideas contained in the original passage. To create this passage took a little bit longer, but not as much as you might think. The original passage was read for detail and argument, in the way a detective might read for evidence and motive. The detail included 'qualitative', 'cross-cultural' and some of the quotes that summarised findings, such as 'a stable relationship with the spouse'. The argument identified that there were findings common to both cultures as well as those which indicated cross-cultural differences and that both *could* suggest (according to Wong and Goodwin) that participants were principally concerned with the overall characterisation of the relationship, rather than separable 'costs' and 'benefits'.

> Wong and Goodwin's (2009) cross-cultural, qualitative study poses a challenge for the Equity Theory understanding of relationships. Across the UK, Hong Kong and Beijing, participants appeared particularly concerned with the *quality of the relationship*, for example 'a stable relationship with the spouse'. Even where cultural differences were identified – such as 'companionship' being rated as more important for UK participants and 'harmonious marital relations' for Hong Kong participants – the emphasis was still on the *overall relationship*, rather than discrete costs and benefits to the individual.

This second attempt is much stronger than the first. You might notice how it is selective in the detail that it uses – who says we have to use *all* of the information in the sources that we consult? Often it's just a key idea, argument or detail that we take up. If you get a clearer sense of what you want to use it for, it is much easier to be in control of the target passages that you draw on, rather than weighed down by them.

To define or not define?

In many forms of writing there is an expectation that terms referred to will be defined. This is particularly the case in technical manuals – mixing up your engine nozzle, docking tunnel and sensing probe could prove really awkward if you are trying to fly your space rocket back to earth. Sometimes – rightly or wrongly – we are encouraged to start essays by defining our terms. This can work well in some cases, for certain types of essays, but it can leave our essay on the launchpad (to stay with the space metaphor), unable to really take off.

One way in which sources are frequently misused is to provide a clumsy, simplistic definition, often right at the start of an essay. Perhaps a textbook is referred to, or worse, a dictionary or a mediocre website, and the definition is given as a truth that cannot be questioned. And that is the problem. The reason to be cautious about turning to sources for simplistic definitions is that it takes that whole area out of what can be debated, discussed, thought about.

Imagine you have this as an essay title:

> 'Critically evaluate empirical evidence of the idea that aggression is best thought of in terms of intra-psychic processes?'

Now, imagine that after an introduction you launch into your definition of aggression:

> Aggression has been defined as: 'feelings of anger or antipathy resulting in hostile or violent behaviour; readiness to attack or confront' (www.dictionary.com).

Quite apart from the clumsy, 'lifted from the dictionary without thought' way in which this is written, this presents as *unnecessary for further consideration* what is actually at the very heart of this essay, which asks us to critically evaluate how aggression has been conceptualised. This illustrates that defining terms sometimes takes them off the table as something to be discussed or debated. If that is required for the specific assessment – an *a priori* definition may be just what is needed – but often it isn't. Our essays might be stronger if we discuss the intricacies of definitions or debate different perspectives concerning how we think about them, rather than treat it as a matter of common agreement right at the start of our essay.

Integrating different sources

A particular issue about trying to make ideas your own can arise when you need to integrate many different sources. It is important to avoid simply noting what lots of different psychologists have said about the topic of your essay. Instead, you should aim to bring a sense of evaluation and debate to your note-taking itself, as this will inform a genuinely evaluative essay and avoid a passive replication of the material that you have found.

Example three

Let's look at a third example. Imagine that this is your essay title:

'Critically evaluate the ways in which attitudes have been understood within social psychology.'

Attempt one
This is how your notes and perhaps your essay plan could look if you are passively noting all of the psychologists that could be relevant.

Billig (1987, 1991, 1996) argued that attitudes are shaped or designed for argument addressing just those issues that are up for debate within a specific culture at a particular period of time.

Wiggins and Potter (2003) show how displays of food preferences can be examined in terms of what the talk might do or accomplish, for example in terms of giving and receiving compliments appropriately.

Greenwald, McGee and Schwartz (1998) developed the implicit attitude measure to address the fact that people might attempt to conceal their 'real' attitudes.

Elliott, Armitage and Baughan (2007) found that self-reported behaviour could be found to differ from observations of the person's behaviour.

Wicker (1969) questioned whether attitudes were in fact a useful construct.

These notes do actually assemble the details to some extent, and provide some basis for overcoming certain forms of plagiarism, but they don't interrogate the argument. Notes of this nature and the essay plans they inform don't quite make it your own, and they clearly underplay issues concerning *structure and critical evaluation* (these topics are further developed in Chapters 5 and 6).

Attempt two

The previous attempt could be a useful stepping stone for something stronger – something that interrogates arguments as well as detailing facts. Attempt two asks questions of the material with the essay title in mind, which informs what should be done in terms of finding other resources and planning the essay itself. By questioning the abbreviated summary that we have, the possibility of something much stronger can be built.

> Billig (1987, 1991, 1996) argued that attitudes are shaped or designed for argument addressing just those issues that arc up for debate within a specific culture at a particular period of time.

This could be developed as a perspective which can be contrasted with alternative understandings of attitudes. To develop this, it is worth considering the sorts of understandings of attitudes that Billig's work questions and critiques. In the essay, it could be worth bringing this perspective in after some other, perhaps more traditional, approaches to attitudes – there seems little on this in these notes so far.

> Wiggins and Potter (2003) show how displays of food preferences can be examined in terms of what the talk might do or accomplish, for example in terms of giving and receiving compliments appropriately.

These ideas form another sort of critique. This may fit with Billig's work. This is at a greater level of specificity and may exemplify an approach or perspective (in this case, that of Discursive Psychology).

> Greenwald, McGee and Schwartz (1998) developed the implicit attitude measure to address the fact that people might attempt to conceal their 'real' attitudes.

This may be relevant if it can be used within an argumentative essay concerning how attitudes have been understood. Care would have to be taken to ensure that the essay does not slide into a discussion of how attitudes have been measured, and that instead all that is included informs our thinking about how attitudes have been understood.

> Elliot, Armitage and Baughan (2007) found that self-reported behaviour could be found to differ from observations of the person's behaviour.

This may be relevant to the essay title but runs the risk of getting into how attitudes are measured. It may be best to place this information on one side for now to see if and how it can really inform an argumentative essay concerning how attitudes have been understood.

> Wicker (1969) questioned whether attitudes were in fact a useful construct.

This might be useful earlier on in your notes or essay planning as it raises a general questioning of attitudes as a construct. This might open up the different ways in which that construct has been developed. While chronology is not king, the fact that this is a relatively early critique does support the idea of considering this point earlier on. Again, it is important to keep your notes focused on evaluating how attitudes have been understood, rather than getting side-tracked into whether attitudes predict behaviour or not.

Thoughts arising from these reflections on the notes

There is some potential critique here – such as the work of Billig – but more is needed on what is being critiqued. The notes, essay plan and essay itself would all be stronger if there was supporting material for different perspectives to inform a genuine debate. It would be good to organise the material by perhaps moving from less radical to more radical and fundamental critique as the essay develops. To achieve this, more material supporting different perspectives on attitudes is needed. Drawing on a mixture of broader theoretical perspectives and specific empirical data would work well. It is easy to get lost in the vast array of research into attitudes – the material has to support ideas and arguments regarding how attitudes have been understood. Forming a sense of how the essay is to be structured around the debate between different understandings of attitudes informs what is searched for, what ideas and findings are drawn on, and how they in turn are used in addressing the essay title.

REFLECTION ON THE CHAPTER:
Painting with finite colours

Imagine the two great artists John Constable and Vincent van Gogh painting whatever you can see from where you are right now. You don't have to know their work at all well to realise that where Constable will bring out a realistic, finely detailed and romanticised interpretation of the scene, van Gogh's interpretation will be highly expressive, his strokes of vividly contrasting colours conveying a sense of the dynamic emotional intensity of the artist. The amazing thing is that the scene and even the pallet of colours can be the same, yet each artist will produce something absolutely unique and unquestionably their own.

When we are writing essays, we have a specific topical focus and a finite range of relevant resources, but through our interrogation of these and our reflection on how to apply the ideas and arguments which arise to our essay, we can create something quite distinct, perhaps even beautiful. This is not suggesting that we make it ours by doing something odd or unexpected in our essay. For some time, I felt I had to read different and unexpected resources to make my essays unique. This can underestimate the relevance of reading that has been recommended for a very good reason. Really good essays have a sense of being the author's own when we see a clarity of thought – a mind at work in the writing. The foundation of this is bringing our questioning engagement with the essay title to the reading, note-taking and planning of our essays. Our essays are probably unlikely to form exhibitions in major galleries around the world, but in their own, small way they can develop and demonstrate a well-formed clarity of thought that has a beauty all of its own.

TAKE AWAY POINTS FROM THIS CHAPTER

- Resources are there to support your thinking not replace it.

- Forget the short cuts. Cutting and pasting (or copying) is not a great idea, no matter how much you tell yourself that you will rework it later.

- Active engagement with your developing argument from the beginning will empower your essays.

- Thinking about your essay title should inform your search strategy and note-taking.

- There should be a creative tension between the essay title, the resources and your thinking.

- Actively interrogating the resources that you use, while still learning from them, builds the resources for a strong, critical essay.

- Your essay will convey a sense of scholarly engagement if that is present from the start.

LINKING TO OTHER CHAPTERS

Some of the issues raised in this chapter are explored in more detail elsewhere. This chapter has touched on a lot of issues that are addressed in much more detail in subsequent chapters. A recurrent focus in this chapter is the importance of keeping the specific essay title in mind in reading, searching for resources, note-taking and planning for your essay. Chapter 4 examines how to address the essay title in writing and editing your essay. This chapter has also argued that all of our preparatory essay work should be informed by thinking about how we might structure our essays. Chapter 5 provides a detailed examination of how we can ensure that our finished essays are well structured and smoothly interconnected. A key idea within this chapter was the importance of interrogating what we read in terms of relevant detail and argumentative, or evaluative, points. Chapters 6 and 7 respectively address how we can ensure that our written essays demonstrate effective evaluation and convey appropriate, clear and dynamic description. The sense of argumentative thinking that this chapter has suggested should be present in searching for resources and taking notes reaches its clearest expression in a well-crafted conclusion, and support and guidance in achieving this is given in Chapter 8. Finally, the issue of citing and referencing material which is touched on here is fully addressed in Chapter 9. Writing an essay can feel like a chore, but it is also a privilege. This is the opportunity for your intelligent engagement with the issues. Seize it – don't waste it.

Chapter 3

Set it up – how to write an effective introduction

They blew out a breath and did the thing all heroes must do – they took that terrifying first step. (Neill, 2016, p. 32)

Introductions can be tough. Let me restart that. I want to introduce this topic properly. If you struggle with introductions, whatever else you are, you are not alone. When we think of our essay – especially if we are thinking of each essay task we need to do (complete the reading, write the introduction, etc.) – we often see the introduction as one of the first bits of actual essay writing. No wonder we sometimes stop so early on, with a sense of frustration and failure. Writing the introduction is not an indication of how tough the whole essay will be and it is often best to come back to the introduction after we have written at least some of the main body of our essay – the sections in between the introduction and conclusion.

This chapter is the first of seven which will examine the actual words of your essay. These chapters aim to clearly demonstrate how you can write an evaluative, smoothly interconnected, crisply written, relevant, well-referenced essay, with a strong conclusion and, as detailed here, an effective introduction. One snag with 'how to' writing is that it varies enormously – recipes, flat-pack furniture instructions, Google travel advice and You-Tube tutorials on how to make a rocket that can go into space are all part of the extremely broad 'how to' family. This chapter attempts to show as well as tell what bad and good writing looks like and to identify some of the steps that can help you to improve your work. It is not quite as step by step as most recipes are, and there are fewer left-over screws than when following most flat-pack furniture instructions, but if you do your bit, practising the suggestions and applying the ideas, I think you will notice a change that you yourself will have brought about.

In this chapter, and those that follow, there are many examples of academic writing. In some cases, these are followed by responses that a reader or marker might have made to the writing. To aid clarity these responses are indicated in italics.

In this chapter you will learn...

- What is special about introductions for student academic essays
- What introductions are and why they matter
- How to write a brilliant introduction – step by step
- How to write introductions like a reader
- How to make sense of feedback concerning introductions

THE SPECIAL CASE OF STUDENT ACADEMIC ESSAYS

Academics often make the mistake of treating good academic writing as synonymous with good writing. There is much that is common across different forms of writing, especially if we narrow down to non-fiction writing. But it can be helpful to be aware of the special case of academic essay writing. A well-written newspaper article and an opening statement in an academic debate may share some similarities with a well-written student academic essay, but you will notice differences. We can think about the different audiences that they are addressing and the different formats they take. *Crucially*, though, they each do a *different* job. Until we get a really sharp, clear sense of the specific thing a good essay should do, we are quite likely to misfire, producing essays that, from the first paragraph, look *journalistic* or *opinionated* when what we are really aiming for is *scholarly*.

> **Newspaper article** – The first paragraph is shaped around a title and byline (or strap line), which is usually composed by the journalist and will summarise the key points – the who, what, where, why and how questions – relating to the article. It needs to both present a summary and hook the reader so that they will want to read more. A good introduction to an academic essay can be similar – in that it indicates the key issues that the essay will address. However, the academic essay is typically more formal in tone and focuses on clearly showing the reader the ideas and debates at the heart of the issues identified in the essay title.

> **An opening statement in a debate** – In order to be effective, an opening statement in a debate will identify some of the questions and issues that will be addressed in the subsequent debate. Furthermore, it will demonstrate an awareness that the motion being considered can be seen from different perspectives. Both of these features – identifying key issues and awareness of different perspectives – are present in good academic essay introductions. However, an academic essay does not declare a position and then marshal the evidence – it investigates the evidence and the issues and draws out the often subtle and complex implications.

Student academic essay – The first paragraph usually orientates to a title that the essay writer has not composed themselves. The essay has to demonstrate a scholarly understanding of the key issues relating directly to a given academic essay title. The first paragraph has to show an awareness of the relevance of the title and outline the sensible, well-reasoned, thoughtful approach that the essay adopts in addressing it.

The comparison above perhaps sets the scene that student academic essays are special – it is quite a niche type of writing, although the skills you learn in doing it are incredibly helpful. In particular, the careful planning and execution of an evidence-based argument can be very helpful, even if you never write an actual 'academic essay' again for the rest of your life. Being able to write in that way means that you can think, talk and read in that way, bringing a critical, evaluative eye to evidence, half-truths and mis-truths, a skill that has perhaps never been more important than now.

What am I doing and for whom?

It is perhaps worth reflecting on a couple of these issues in a little more detail – specifically, what level of knowledge should be assumed on the part of your reader, and what, actually, does an 'introduction' *do*?

The knowledge that should be assumed on the part of the reader of your essay is a tricky one. On the one hand, you have probably been told the importance of defining your terms clearly, which suggests a limited reader knowledge. On the other hand, your principal reader is likely to be someone who has taught you psychology, or at the very least has studied it at postgraduate level. First, a caveat – do take into account the guidance on this that you may receive from your course or module tutor(s). Different essays are designed to test different things, so make use of the on-hand, proximal advice. With that in mind, a useful, if slightly cryptic, rule of thumb is to assume that your reader has sufficient knowledge *to ask the question that is set in the essay title* and that they require a *display of knowledge that is relevant to that title*. Your essay title should – normally – set the parameters of your essay and different titles do suggest different levels of reader (or essay title-setter) knowledge. This issue is addressed in detail in Chapter 4, where the focus is on how to genuinely address the essay title. For now, we can note that the title itself gives a sense of the parameters for framing our essay in the introduction.

If our essay title refers to the *multistore model of memory*, then we will want our essay, from the introduction, to convey a scholarly understanding of that model, an understanding that is *in the service of the essay*, which forms a part of that essay rather than a dictionary definition, an encyclopaedia of psychology or Wikipedia entry. From the very beginning of our essay the reader should get a clear sense of why they are being told what they are being told. The reader should never ask, 'why is this term being defined?', 'why is this being described?' or 'why is this perspective being referred to?'. The introduction, which outlines how your essay will address the title, conveys that rationale, so your reader does not need to ask all of those 'why' questions. Implicitly ('This essay will first address…') or explicitly ('In order to better evaluate the strengths of …, the essay will first address …'), the introduction presents *your rationale* for what your essay covers. Your introduction can get your reader off to the best possible start in your essay by enabling them to get a sense of your scholarly mind at work.

ACE YOUR ASSIGNMENT
What is being introduced to whom?

Although we all talk about introductions, we rarely stop and think about these links, connectors, bridges and the slightly amazing work that they do. In your essay, your introduction does – or can do – something almost magical. It connects the body of your essay with your reader. Wow! That is such an important role. With a strong introduction, your reader will be ready to step into your essay, see your rationale and know where you are taking them. Without an effective introduction, your reader will feel frustrated, possibly slightly cheated. This may settle down if your essay is strong elsewhere, but, equally, it may not. Your writing will create reactions in your reader – why get them in an agitated mood right at the start, when instead you could demonstrate the luminosity of your thinking? A strong introduction is within reach – reach for it, it will make all the difference.

INTRODUCTION: WHAT IT IS AND WHY IT MATTERS

Fiction and non-fiction, books, films, plays and musicals often introduce explicitly or implicitly some of the characters, issues and contexts that will be addressed. Academic introduction writing is one, quite specific, example of that. As has been argued above, introductions really do matter. Done well, they help you to take your reader with you. Look at how it feels to read an essay without an introduction. Below are two brief essay extracts. Imagine that they are the very beginning of an essay. Each shows a first paragraph and then the first sentence of the next paragraph.

Extract one

Point illustrated: Unless directed otherwise – you need a proper *scene-setting* introduction.

Reader's reaction: *Where's the introduction gone?*

Essay title:

'Outline and evaluate Milgram's interpretation of his obedience experiments.'

Sample essay one

Milgram found that approximately two thirds of participants obeyed in his obedience studies. They demonstrated obedience by continuing to administer (what they thought were) electric shocks to a confederate, as prompted by an experimenter in a learning experiment. Milgram interpreted this obedience in terms of a shift to the agentic state. The agentic state describes a change in a person's sense of agency, from feeling responsible for their own actions, to feeling that they are no longer responsible for their actions, but rather that they are following the orders of someone in authority over them.

Another approach to making sense of Milgram's findings was put forward by Reicher and Haslam (2011), who argued that …

Extract two

Point illustrated: Again, you need something prior to the material that actually answers the question – you need an introduction which acknowledges the title with an orientating sentence and includes a statement of intent which outlines how the essay will address the essay title (these are detailed later in this chapter).

Reader's reaction: *This essay has launched into answering the essay – the essay has merit but is not introduced to the reader.*

Essay title:

'Critically evaluate the contribution of fMRI research to understanding psychological processes.'

Sample essay two

One particularly important strand of research has involved using fMRI data to localise psychological function to specific brain regions. An example of this is found in the work of Downing, Liu and Kanwisher (2001), who investigated whether the same regions of the brain were employed in object recognition regardless of the specific object being perceived. A particular interest for Downing et al. was whether different modules of processing were involved in perceiving human bodies as compared to other types of objects. Downing et al.'s fMRI research identified that there was a region within the right lateral occipitotemporal cortex that was associated with the perception of human bodies.

While Downing et al.'s research can be seen as evidence of the use of fMRI to examine functional specialisation, this work and the approach that it exemplifies has been challenged. …

Making sense of the sample essays

Without getting too concerned about content (it really doesn't matter how familiar you are with the right lateral occipitotemporal cortex), think about how reading these two sample essays made you feel. They were both on-topic, and in that sense answering the question, but something didn't feel quite right. You might find that it is a bit like missing the start of a film. Perhaps you feel that you want to rewind – that you have been cheated out of something. Possibly you feel like saying to the writer 'hold on a minute'. Both of these examples launch straight in on the topic but do not really do what is necessary to clearly show how they are addressing the essay title. Not doing this is like the train, ship or plane leaving before the passengers are ready – the reader is left stranded and might never really feel that they are on board with the essay.

You might have noticed something that is emphasised here, which is how writing – in this case, the writing of introductions – makes the reader feel. That could strike you as odd in an academic essay. Surely an academic essay is supposed to be about ideas and evidence, and not feelings. However, the concept of *our reader's experience* of our writing is really key for effective academic writing. Not including an introduction in your essay will produce a reaction in your reader – they will feel that something expected is missing, and that is not the frame of mind you want them to have from the very beginning of reading your essay.

HOW TO WRITE A BRILLIANT INTRODUCTION – STEP BY STEP

To connect to our reader, and to help them to be in the frame of mind that is most able to appreciate our essay, our introduction should really do two things: first, it should orientate to the topic of the essay title, and second, it should outline how the essay will address the essay title. We can think of these two parts of the introduction as the *orientating sentence* (although it could be longer than a sentence) and the *statement of intent*.

Our orientating sentence provides the reader with a sense of how we understand the context of the essay title, for example, conveying a sense of why it is relevant, important or worth considering. Without an orientating sentence, the reader experiences a sudden jolt as they move from the essay title to the essay. We can avoid that by setting the scene for the essay title. Our statement of intent communicates, with some level of specification, a sense of how our essay will address the essay title, signposting the ideas, evidence and debates that will be covered. Without the statement of intent, the reader is left in a strange place without a map or GPS. But it doesn't need to be like that. We can give the reader a sense of where the essay will take them and a sense of the logic to this journey.

Good and bad introductions

The best way to get a clear, useable sense of what a good introduction should look like is to contrast some examples of good and bad introductions, and then to try it yourself. If you practise converting a poor orientating sentence and a poor statement of intent into something stronger and – strange though it may seem – can also do the reverse, you will start to identify very clearly what makes for an effective introduction. Keep writing orientating sentences and statements of intent and you really will improve – don't wait until the crunch time of an assessment to try to work out how to write an introduction.

Look at the essay title below and the orientating sentences. To aid clarity, some of these samples will include the beginning of the statement of intent that would follow on from the orientating sentence(s).

The orientating sentence

Essay title: 'Critically evaluate Kelley's Covariation Model of Causal Attribution.'

Sample orientating sentences
Look through these orientating sentences:

a. Attribution is all around us. We are always trying to work out why things happened. This essay will examine the omnipresent phenomenon of attribution.

b. Human beings are cognitive creatures for whom thinking is crucial. Our social world is a vital part of our lives. This essay will examine attribution, which is a very important part of being human.

c. Your friend blanks you – why? You are making an attribution and you probably do so all the time. This essay will provide the answer to these mysteries of human interaction.

d. Kelley's covariation model of causal attribution outlined the way in which we decide whether a cause is internal or external. Kelley argued that we assess the consensus, consistency and distinctiveness of an event that we are trying to make an attribution about.

e. Kelley's covariation model of causal attribution could be understood as representing a particularly important example of applying a rational framework to understand human cognitive functioning. This essay will first outline the rational, deductive principles which Kelley's covariation model suggests that we use in calculating causality.

Making sense of the sample orientating sentences
Perhaps start by identifying the strongest of these opening sentences. It is extremely likely that you, like I, would choose sample e. But let's dig deeper here. Without getting bogged down in Kelley and covariation, why not characterise what these sentences are actually doing? Try the quick exercise below.

EXERCISE
Characterising opening sentences

Look through the sample opening sentences again. What is each one actually doing?
   Here are some of the ways in which you might characterise what the sample sentences are doing:

1. Launches into a description of Kelley's covariation model

2. Provides a chatty sense of what attribution might look like in everyday life

(Continued)

3. Demonstrates a clear conceptualisation of what Kelley's model means in psychology
4. Tries to emphasise the importance of the topic for humanity
5. Tries to give a very global sense of attribution's relevance

How would you fit these characterisations to the samples that we have just looked at? Please note, some do overlap (for example, 4 and 5).

Sample (a) – I think this _____

Sample (b) – I think this _____

Sample (c) – I think this _____

Sample (d) – I think this _____

Sample (e) – I think this _____

The less effective sample opening sentences could work in other contexts. The chatty style of sample c could be a reasonable opening to a relationship-focused magazine article. Similarly, sample b's emphasis on the importance of attribution could be relevant for introducing attribution to a non-specialist audience who were not previously familiar with it. Perhaps it could work for a very general psychology-orientated website? But the academic essay is a special form of writing. Your reader does not seek the chatty examples or the emphasis on global significance; they want to see your scholarly understanding.

Let's look at reader feedback on the above sample orientating sentences:

a. Attribution is all around us… *This is just so generalised. The essay is about Kelley's Covariation Model, not life, the universe and everything. More precision is needed here.*

b. Human beings are cognitive creatures for whom thinking is crucial… *This is generalised and involves truisms, why should we be told that thinking is important to humans? A more precise focus on the significance of Kelley's work for psychology, not attributions relevance for humanity, is what is needed.*

c. Your friend blanks you – why?… *I can almost see the colour photos that could accompany this text in a magazine article. For an academic essay, you don't need to draw in your reader in this way. Show them a scholarly understanding of the topic of the essay and its relevance for psychology.*

d. Kelley's covariation model of causal attribution outlined the way in which we decide whether a cause is internal or external… *Where is the orientating sentence? Where is the introduction for that matter? This has simply launched in with a description of Kelley's Covariation Model. It is true that it is not over-generalised, but it is also not an introduction.*

e. Kelley's covariation model of causal attribution could be understood as representing a particularly important example of applying a rational framework to understand human cognitive functioning… *This is not perfect, but it does address Kelley's work by conceptualising what it has brought to psychology. This really conveys a sense of a mind at work – there is thinking and understanding about the focus of the essay title and its significance within psychology.*

What makes it good?

A strong orientating sentence provides a sense of really grasping the relevance of the essay topic for psychology. It conceptualises the topic – in this example, Kelley's Covariation Model – showing an understanding of the distinctive contribution that it makes within psychology or a subdiscipline of psychology (such as social, developmental or cognitive psychology) or a field of research within that subdiscipline (neuro-imaging, children's cognitive development or prosocial behaviour). Your orientating sentences are an opportunity to impress your reader straight away with your grasp of the essay topic. A simple sentence or two – if carefully thought out – can convey a real depth of understanding. Your first sentences will *do* something – look through these examples and try to ensure that yours do the job of communicating a focused, clear understanding of the distinctive features and relevance of the essay topic.

The statement of intent

'Statement of intent' is an unusual term, with a somewhat legalistic ring to it. The statement of intent is the programme guide, street map, menu or orientating briefing for your essay. A clear statement of intent improves the reader's experience of your essay and that really is important. With a statement of intent, your reader will know what is coming next and so the essay starts to feel well structured. If your statement of intent is really good, then the reader can see the rationale for what you have included and for the order in which you are addressing different ideas in your essay. A strong statement of intent can even help to convey a sense of critical thinking as it can highlight what you identify as some of the key points of discussion and debate that are relevant for the essay topic.

ACE YOUR ASSIGNMENT
Think about your reader's experience –
from the beginning

Tables 3.1 and 3.2 present a weaker and a stronger example of some introductory paragraphs and how a reader might interpret them. Look at each example first and pause to think how it made you feel before checking the reader's reactions.

(Continued)

TABLE 3.1

Thinking about your reader's experience: Opening sentences and statement of intent – weaker version

Essay title:

Outline and evaluate the use of longitudinal research within developmental psychology.

Your introduction	Your reader's reaction
Longitudinal research has been used by numerous psychologists. Sroufe, Byron and Kreutzer (1990) used longitudinal research in investigating the impact of early childhood experience. A sample of 190 participants took part in this study. Regression analysis was conducted to calculate which factors best predicted subsequent adaptation. The results provided some support for Bowlby's emphasis on the importance of both prior history and present circumstances. Cotter, Burke, Loeber and Navratil (2002) examine the ways in which researchers can improve retention in longitudinal studies.	1. This first sentence is too generalised – anyone could write this with almost no knowledge of psychology. Why not give a more informed sense of the evidence that longitudinal research has been important in developmental psychology? 2. After the first sentence this paragraph does not introduce anything – instead it launches headlong into describing one study. Why not outline what this essay will cover? 3. The second paragraph has some potentially interesting and relevant material but no sense of what it is communicating to the reader in terms of the essay title. This material could be helpful when considering how one of the key difficulties with longitudinal research (attrition – or drop out) might be addressed.

TABLE 3.2

Thinking about your reader's experience: Opening sentences and statement of intent – stronger version

Essay title:

Outline and evaluate the use of longitudinal research within developmental psychology.

Your introduction	Your reader's reaction
Longitudinal research has been a part of Developmental psychology research for nearly a century, with Terman's *Study of the Gifted*, commencing in 1921, arguably forming its beginning. Across the intervening decades, collecting data with the same participants across different time points has been used in numerous studies not only to observe development processes but also to identify factors, including early experience, mass media, social context and concurrent circumstances that may have an influence on development. In order to understand the use of longitudinal research within developmental psychology, it is important to first consider some of the key features of longitudinal research and how these principals are realised in practice. To fully evaluate the use of longitudinal research within developmental psychology it is useful to draw on actual instances of its use to investigate the advantages, the potential shortcomings and the more nuanced understandings that identify the ways in which it is implemented and interpreted as being key to the value that it has within developmental psychology.	1. There is a sense of an informed stance in the opening two sentences – a historical marker is given and there is a broad sense of the different ways in which longitudinal research has been used, which avoids being either too vague or too particular. 2. In the second sentence longitudinal research is defined in passing. This avoids opening up a longer definition in this first paragraph; a more detailed definition might be expected in the second paragraph. 3. This introduction illustrates the way that a statement of intent can be worded so that it avoids the 'this essay will...' format, which some academics are less keen on. 4. The statement of intent conveys a sense of a mind at work. This is particularly evident in the way in which a simple pros and cons approach to thinking of longitudinal research is transcended with more subtle considerations concerning implementation and interpretation. This also hints at themes that might be picked up in the conclusion of the essay.

A strong statement of intent can tick so many boxes, conveying an understanding of the relevant literature, a sense of clear structure and some critical awareness, but a *typical* statement of intent falls short of this. Many essays do not have a statement of intent or have something so generic that it is neither sign-posting a rationale nor demonstrating evaluative thinking. To get a clearer grasp of this, let's return to the sample essay title used above and see how a statement of intent could be written.

Example

Essay title:

'Critically evaluate Kelley's Covariation Model of Causal Attribution.'

Sample statement of intent with feedback

a. This essay discusses Kelley's covariation model of causal attribution and evaluates it.

This is barely a statement of intent at all. It is little more than stating 'This essay will answer the question that was set'. What is needed is a sense of some further detail about how the essay will answer the question.

b. This essay will examine Kelley's model. It will also discuss the evidence for it. It will then critique Kelley's model, it will cover attribution bias, it will refer to work which considers how attributions are communicated and it will end by reflecting on Kelley's contribution.

This provides some further detail about how the essay will address the essay question, so it is a clear improvement on (a) above, but it reads like a list. There is no sense of understanding the different approaches that are covered, limited sense of how they relate to each other and little rationale for why the essay will be addressed in this way.

c. This essay will evaluate Kelley's model first, by outlining its key elements and the empirical evidence relating to it. It will then consider critique from work which has identified various biases as well as research which challenges Kelley's neglect of how attributions are communicated. In doing so, the essay will consider whether the framework which Kelley provided is best thought of as limiting or enabling subsequent approaches to understanding attribution.

This statement of intent could be further improved – it could characterise Kelley's approach, perhaps referring to its emphasis on rational thinking. However, it is nonetheless a strong statement of intent. First, it is reasonably specific, though perhaps further specific names and theories could be identified. Second, it conveys some clear thinking about the approaches referred to, for example, the reference to Kelley's neglect of how attributions are communicated. Third, there is a sense of debate between Kelley's approach and that of other perspectives that will be drawn on. Outlining the debates to be covered provides a rationale for what is included and demonstrates relevant evaluative thinking. Finally, this statement of intent hints at a conceptualisation of the implications of Kelley's work (whether Kelley's framework 'is best thought of as limiting or enabling subsequent approaches').

LEARN

TABLE 3.3
Transforming your introduction: Using editing and redrafting effectively

Essay title:
To what extent can specific instances of 'rioting' be made sense of in terms of Social Identity Theory?

Steps in drafting the introduction	Editing thoughts
1. First draft Social Identity Theory suggests that riots can be thought of in terms of group identity. There are different strands within Social Identity Theory, including Drury and Reicher's (2000) Elaborated Social Identity. Riots have been studied in social psychology for a long time, Le Bon (1896) argued that being in a crowd made people become like 'a creature acting on instinct'.	1. This first draft gets some good ideas down but it looks jumbled, nothing flows and there is no clear indication concerning the direction that the essay will take. 2. Le Bon could be used in an orientating sentence, giving a sense of how long rioting has been examined in social psychology. 3. It would make sense to deal with variations on the Social Identity Theory approach after referring to Social Identity Theory itself.
2. Second draft – getting it in order Riots have been studied in social psychology for a long time. Le Bon (1896) argued that being in a crowd made people become like 'a creature acting on instinct'. Social Identity Theory suggests that riots can be thought of in terms of group identity. There are different strands within Social Identity Theory, including Drury and Reicher's (2000) Elaborated Social Identity.	1. The order makes more sense. 2. There could be more of a sense of how these ideas connect – it seems like a list of separate sentences on the topic of the social psychology of riots. There could be a much clearer sense of why these ideas matter – the reader might ask 'so what?', unsure as to why they are being told these things.
3. Third draft – starting to link ideas Riots have attracted interest within social psychology ever since Le Bon's (1896) book, *The Crowd: A Study of the Popular Mind*. This essay will focus on Social Identity Theory. Particular attention will be given to Reicher's (1984) seminal study of a riot in Bristol. Attention will also be given to the 'Elaborated Social Identity Model' (Drury and Reicher, 2000).	1. The first sentence reads more smoothly now – there is a sense of flow and it is less staccato. 2. There is a more clearly specified sense of what will be covered in places – for example, highlighting Reicher's (1984) key study. 3. There is scope for a richer sense of why the ideas that will be covered are relevant for this essay title and how they interrelate.

Essay title:
To what extent can specific instances of 'rioting' be made sense of in terms of Social Identity Theory?

Steps in drafting the introduction	Editing thoughts
4. Fourth draft – a mind at work Riots have attracted interest within social psychology ever since Le Bon's (1896) highly controversial book, *The Crowd: A Study of the Popular Mind*. Le Bon had argued that when isolated from the crowd, a person may be 'a cultivated individual', yet once immersed within the crowd he or she will become 'a creature acting on instinct'. This essay will focus on a wholly different approach to understanding crowd behaviour – that provided by Social Identity Theory. Particular attention will be given to Reicher's (1984) seminal study of a riot in Bristol, with some attention being given to criticisms and developments of this approach, such as the 'Elaborated Social Identity Model' (Drury and Reicher, 2000).	1. This introduction conveys a sense of thinking and awareness of the ideas that are referred to – Le Bon's ideas are characterised as controversial and briefly articulated, as is Social Identity Theory. 2. There is a more fully articulated sense of how the ideas relate to one another – the contrast between Le Bon's work and Social Identity Theory helps to better define the latter. A contrast is implied, although not fully developed, between Social Identity Theory and the Elaborated Social Identity Theory. 3. A sense of the approach that the essay will take and its structure is conveyed in the introduction. 4. There could be scope for some further sense of the sorts of criticisms and developments, perhaps including some more recent literature and possibly conveying a sense of where the essay will take the reader.

Making your statement of intent sparkle!

The statement of intent is a fabulous opportunity to demonstrate your thinking to the reader. It is more than just dressing up an essay with the right catch phrases – the act of writing a really effective statement of intent forces you to pay attention to what you will include in your essay, the order in which you will include it, how the ideas relate to one another, how you would characterise the ideas that you refer to and where you may arrive at the end of the essay. Let's consider these issues in a little more detail:

> **What you will include** – This is usually the easiest bit of the statement of intent. You need to ensure that you make reference to the key ideas, and possibly some key names, that are relevant for the specific essay title that you are addressing.

> **The order in which you will include these things** – The order may be straightforward but it is worth thinking about. Often essays are ordered chronologically, or in the order in which they have been presented in textbooks or lectures. This may be the best order, but arrive at the order through thought and consideration, such as how can you organise a really effective debate rather than unthinkingly adopting date of publication or order on your lecture slides as necessarily being the best arrangement.

> **How the ideas relate to one another** – This can involve some careful thinking and will inform the order in which you cover ideas in your essay. For many essays it is worth identifying those issues – of relevance to the specific essay title – where there are different views. This is at the heart of evaluative thinking – being able to discuss empirical evidence or

theoretical ideas from different perspectives. Developing your understanding about how the ideas interrelate, where there are differences and debates, and where there are confirmations and clarifications can take time, but will improve the quality of your entire essay.

How the ideas can be characterised – Some further careful thinking and reading may help you to get a clearer sense of what the target approach in the essay is offering. This type of thinking is so helpful that it is worth considering with each key idea that you encounter: 'How can I characterise this perspective?', 'How have others made sense of or characterised it?' and 'What are the different ways of thinking about this approach?' This is an example of how it is not simply that we get ideas clear in our head and then write them down, but instead that there is a dynamic dialogue between our thinking and our writing (see the 'Think' box below).

Where does that leave the reader – A clearly articulated statement of intent communicates that you have thought about what will be included in your essay and the order in which you will do so. If it is really well written and reflective of good thinking in terms of what is included and when and how the different ideas interrelate, then the reader already feels that this is a well-structured essay that addresses the essay title and may anticipate that it will be critically evaluative also. While it is possible that the body of the essay could cause the reader's positive anticipation to be revised, an excellent statement of intent is likely to have come from careful thinking. Even the writing of a strong statement of intent can help the author to improve the body of their essay, and the reader, aware of that, comes to the essay in a positive frame of mind.

THINK
Sculpting not smashing

Think of someone sculpting a beautiful statue, having to work with the clay or other materials, bringing form out of them, with them and through them. The medium used isn't just the passive recipient of the will of the artist; it can inform and shape what happens next. This act of creation is quite different from an act of destruction, where the will to destroy is simply imposed on the outer world with little or no engagement with the target object. Essay writing – *good* essay writing – has that creative quality, working *with* the words and ideas. We take our plans to our writing, but our writing then talks back to us – it highlights problems, offers new ways of seeing things and it suggests things to us.

Our writing helps our thinking which helps our writing

We may struggle with our writing at just the point where we are thinking through different ideas. Our writing can help identify that struggle – for example, that effort to characterise an approach. This develops our thinking as we try to think about the issues we are writing about more deeply. This dynamic interplay is at the heart of some of the best academic writing. The author isn't the font of static, fixed knowledge that they passively convey as if taking down some dictation. Instead, the author is dynamically struggling with ideas and articulating them. In making ideas clear to others, they are simultaneously making them clear to themselves. This dual articulation process involves passages that run smoothly and then hit a snag, but the snag isn't like a blockade in the road ahead; instead, it identifies an issue that can be taken deeper – an opportunity to further clarify, deepen or extend our understanding. Writing and thinking are dynamic, mutually-enhancing processes. That is what makes them creative, fun and worthwhile.

HOW TO WRITE INTRODUCTIONS LIKE A READER

This advice might be best left on one side when you are trying to get words on the page – you certainly don't want your inner editor inhibiting you. But writing is a bit more like speaking than we sometimes realise. When we talk, we often take into account our audience. We sense, or try to sense, how well they are understanding what we are trying to communicate and what they feel about it. We can't get that sort of live feedback when we write, but we can try to think about how our reader(s) might relate to what we are writing. Starting an essay without an introduction is a very clear signal that the writer is not thinking about their reader, but is just keen to cram down whatever they have in their mind connected with the essay topic. By contrast, a thoughtful, intelligent introduction gives the sense of the author relating to their reader in what they write – not with 'witty' messages to the reader in brackets (you know what I mean, don't you?), but with an intelligent outline of what the essay is all about.

The 'so what?' reader

This concept will be returned to in later chapters, but for now let's revisit an abbreviated version of one of the opening examples in this chapter.

Essay title:

> 'Critically evaluate the contribution of fMRI research to understanding psychological processes.'

Sample essay beginning

> One particularly important strand of research has involved using fMRI data to localise psychological function to specific brain regions. An example of this is found in the work of Downing, Liu and Kanwisher (2001), who investigated whether the same regions of the brain were employed in object recognition regardless of the specific object being perceived. A particular interest for Downing et al. …

This looks like it could have been a really good essay – but it has gone wrong from the start. It is not that the content is incorrect or irrelevant – it looks right on target. The problem is that the reader comes to an academic essay with a high chance of asking the two-word question that they (almost) never ask of dictionaries, encyclopaedias or of the instant results to their twentieth

Google search that day: 'so what?' Don't write your essay like a dictionary or encyclopaedia entry or a Google factual search result. These are great for conveying information, but your essay needs to do more than that and your introduction sets the scene.

Starting an essay without conveying a sense of what you will cover and why it is relevant to the essay title means that however relevant and accurate your information actually is, your essay will suffer as you have not demonstrated a scholarly mind at work. Your essay, from the introduction onwards, is a medium for demonstrating your thinking about the title and *showing* that thinking, rather than leaving the reader to try to deduce what sort of thinking there was or wasn't from flimsy and incomplete evidence.

While the reader of your essay is possibly the most wonderful, engaged and enthusiastic person you can think of – it can be handy to imagine that – whatever their many strengths, they have a tendency to ask 'so what?' A well-written essay can meet the 'so what?' challenge and prevail. It can even prevent our dear reader(s) from even asking the question.

To write a good introduction, get a draft down first and then read it through as if you were the reader – perhaps the marker – who does not know what's coming up in your essay, rather than the author, who does. Reading your introduction in this way, ask yourself these three questions:

1. Can you tell from the introduction alone (roughly) what the essay title is?
2. Can you tell (again from the introduction alone) how this essay addresses the title?
3. Can you tell something of the author's understanding of the issues involved – for example, concerning what issues are debated in this topic and how different perspectives can be characterised?

EXERCISE
Interrogate your introduction

Try interrogating your first paragraph with the questions in Table 3.4. You may find it helpful to look at the expanded definitions in Table 3.5.

TABLE 3.4
Interrogation questions for your first paragraph

Do you have an orientating sentence or two?
>Does that contextualise the topic?
Do you have a statement of intent?
>Does that outline what will be covered?
>Does it convey a rationale for what is included?
>Does it convey a rationale for the direction of your essay?
>Is there a sense of characterising the approaches?
>Is there a sense of the essay's destination?

TABLE 3.5
Expanded interrogation questions for your first paragraph: Essay Title: *Outline and evaluate Kelley's Covariation Model of Causal Attribution*

Do you have an orientating sentence or two?	
>Does that contextualise the topic?	Do your initial sentences provide some relevant sense of why the essay topic is relevant or important, how much controversy it has attracted or how long it has been an issue within psychology?
Do you have a statement of intent?	
>Does that outline what will be covered?	First and foremost your statement of intent should identify the key ideas that will be covered. A list of names (Kelley, Jones and Davis, etc.) is less helpful than a sense of the ideas involved (*Kelley's rationalist depiction of the attribution process, Jones and Davis's outline of an important attribution bias*).
>Does it convey a rationale for what is included?	This rational might well be implicit, but could be explicit in places (in order to grasp the full impact of…the essay will address …). Whether implicit or explicit, the content should make sense in terms of the essay title.
>Does it convey a rationale for the direction of your essay?	Again, this might be implicit or explicit but should be mindful, not simply chronological or reflecting the order in a lecture or textbook. Ask yourself: 'In terms of your response to the essay title, what order makes the most sense?'
>Is there a sense of characterising the approaches?	Careful, appropriate characterisation can be really helpful. To stay with the previous example, referring to Kelley's approach as offering a '*rationalist depiction of attribution*' would make sense in the context of an essay that debates this understanding of the attribution process.
>Is there a sense of the essay's destination?	A statement of intent can be nicely rounded off by indicating the sort of position that the essay works towards. The essay's destination can take many forms, one might be that *context is crucial* (as was the case in the longitudinal research example used earlier). For example, 'This essay argues that ultimately the value of … (idea being evaluated) rests largely on the *specifics of its implementation* rather than on some context-free appraisal of its strengths and shortcomings.'

FEEDBACK ON INTRODUCTIONS

Introductions often attract feedback from markers. Let's look at some of the more common forms of feedback that directly and indirectly indicate that changes to the introduction would be a good idea. Some of the feedback will indicate quite precisely the aspect of your introduction that should be improved.

The following feedback is often used in commenting on introductions:

- Include a statement of intent
- Signpost your essay
- Indicate how your essay will address the question

These comments all indicate that your essay should overtly indicate how your essay will address the question. Your introduction needs to identify what will be covered in your essay. This statement of intent should convey a sense that you thought intelligently about what you included and the order in which you included it, rather than it appearing to be the result of unthinking passivity, such as simply following the content and order of a textbook, lecture notes or, much worse, your favourite psychology website.

- Outline how your essay will approach/address/answer the essay question

This is getting at the same idea as the previous comments, but it does usefully highlight that you need to convey a sense of the relevance of what you plan to include for the essay title. A strong statement of intent conveys a sense of not only what will be included and when it will be included, but also why it is relevant for this particular essay.

- Set the context for the essay
- Don't start abruptly
- Don't start so generally

These comments about the first paragraph in your essay indicate that as well as considering your statement of intent, your orientating sentence should be looked at. The first – or orientating – sentence in your essay is a challenge and is often easier to write after you have completed most, or perhaps all, of your essay. Use your orientating sentence to convey an awareness of the relevance of thinking about the domain that is indicated by the essay title. A well-written orientating sentence cues the reader into thinking about the specific aspects of psychology from which the essay topic is drawn. This can vary but might be thought of as the sort of subsection in a textbook in which you could imagine finding this essay title. For example, 'Cognitive development in children has been a key concern within developmental psychology and a focus of substantial debate' could set up a debate between different approaches to children's cognitive development, while 'Piaget's stage theory of children's cognitive development has been a major influence within developmental psychology while simultaneously being questioned in terms of its theoretical scope and its empirical basis' sets up a more specific evaluation of Piaget's contribution. Sometimes an additional sentence may be used to further specify the relevant focus of the essay. In the previous example, adding a sentence such as, 'One aspect of Piaget's work that has attracted considerable debate concerns his series of Conservation experiments', identifies that a more specific focus on evaluating Piaget's Conservation experiments will be pursued. Feedback comments such as these, when made in response to your introduction or first paragraph, can be a challenge to address, but looking at both your orientating sentence and statement of intent (unless another part of your essay is indicated by the comment) is wise. Do bear in mind that your orientating sentence and statement of intent can often be substantially improved if you edit them after you have finished you essay.

EXERCISE
Try to Wreck It! – *The Intro*

The introduction below is not perfect, but it is fairly good. See how bad you can make it with the fewest changes and then compare your best effort to the online version.

For this challenge you are allowed to:

- Change the order of the sentences.
- Swap an existing sentence for one of the alternative sentences below.
- Create your own on-topic, grammatically correct but otherwise lousy alternative sentences (see the alternative sentence pool for ideas).

If you are to make it really bad in as few changes as possible, what are you going to target and why?

Essay title:

'To what extent do Onorato and Turner (2004) critique the claim by Gaertner, Sedikes and Graetz that self-schemas are "monuments of stability" (1999: 5)?'

The introduction

The notion of self-schemas has been particularly important in social psychology, drawing on the substantial body of research into schemas to provide an empirically informed perspective on the often-illusive topic of self. This essay will start by briefly outlining some key work on self-schemas before discussing the challenge provided by Onorato and Turner's (2004) self-categorisation approach, in particular focusing on the argument that self-perception is variable and context-dependent. The essay will also consider some of the challenges to social identity and self-categorisation approaches developed within discursive psychology, which in turn suggest that these approaches themselves have, through focusing on cognitive aspects of self and identity, failed to grasp something of the fluidity of constructions of self.

What makes this introduction good?

For a three-sentence introduction this is reasonably strong, especially if the material referred to really is made relevant in the body of the essay. The introduction provides an informed orientating sentence. It outlines what the essay will cover and demonstrates an understanding of the key focus (Onorato and Turner's criticism of Gaertner, Sedikes and Graetz's claim that 'self-schemas are "monuments of stability"'). It further indicates an awareness of other potentially relevant material against which this criticism can be evaluated, although in addressing this it will have to keep focusing on the precise essay title, making it clear how discursive approaches are relevant for evaluating Onarato and Turner's critique of Gaertner et al.'s claim.

(Continued)

Alternative sentence pool *<and why they are not so great>*

- Who am I? Who are you? What is self? Philosophers and psychologists have struggled with these issues through the ages. *<Admittedly this is more than one sentence, but it reveals important weaknesses. Above all, it is far too vague. Being more specific is both better in itself and also enables relevant knowledge to be drawn in more easily. As it stands, can you even tell that the author of this knows anything about the topic at all?>*

- The self is a key issue in psychology and has been the focus of much empirical study. *<Again, too vague and no real psychological knowledge is evident. Anyone could write a sentence like this without knowing anything about psychology.>*

- Gaertner, Sedikes and Graetz (1999) proved that self-schemas are "monuments of stability" (1999: 5), whereas Onorato and Turner (2004) proved that this was not true. *<Psychology essays are typically much more concerned with evaluating different perspectives than with identifying what has been proved. This example is deliberately bad to vividly show how limiting it is to refer to 'proof'. How could two completely contradictory views both be 'proved'? Views are asserted, argued and suggested, and these are challenged, questioned and contradicted.>*

- Everyone has different views. Gaertner, Sedikes and Graetz (1999), Onorato and Turner (2004) and many others all disagree with each other. *<This recognises that there are different perspectives but gives no sense of direction. It's like asking for directions and being told some of the places on the way in no particular order. You are left wondering how they relate – what leads to what. This sentence also leaves you wondering who the 'many others' are and whether or not you'll ever get to find out.>*

- This essay will examine the claim by Gaertner, Sedikes and Graetz that self-schemas are 'monuments of stability' and Onorato and Turner's critique of it. *<This sentence could have been written by anyone who can even partly comprehend the essay question. There is no knowledge here that isn't entirely contained in the essay title itself. This is like a bogus psychic practitioner repackaging information that a sitter has already revealed to them as if it was evidence of their own psychic powers. A stronger alternative would display an understanding of Gaertner et al.'s position and the critique developed by Onorato and Turner – as well as other relevant perspectives – without being limited to the words of the title itself.>*

REFLECTING ON THE CHAPTER:
The end of the beginning

Introductions can be tough. But they are most tough when we start our essays right there, before we really know what we are trying to introduce. Imagine you were asked to give directions to a place you only vaguely knew and had perhaps been to once when you were half asleep. How much easier, if you had another chance, would it be to give those directions after you had been there with your eyes wide open. That's the great thing about writing essays. Although they are highly directional in terms of how they are supposed to be read, we can *write them* in any order we choose. Let's stay with that thought a moment longer. We can write our essays from the middle, end or beginning, or any mixture of the above. It may well make sense, therefore, to switch off some misquoted voice that tells us to 'start at the beginning'. Why should we? It probably makes sense, at the very least, to edit our introduction in the light of where we get to in our essay itself. That way we at least have a clearer sense of the destination and the route we took.

TAKE AWAY POINTS FROM THIS CHAPTER

- Your introduction conveys your thinking to the reader straight away, so it is worth making a good impression from the start.
- Finding your academic voice can take time, so read good academic writing and keep writing – don't expect the first version to be the best that you can do.
- Drafting a good introduction encourages you to do the sort of thinking that really strengthens your essay, especially its structure.
- A strong introduction conveys a clarity of thinking to your reader.
- An appropriate orientating sentence is a real kindness to your reader, drawing them to the essay and the essay to them.
- A clear outline of your essay (a statement of intent) should convey a sense of what you will address, when you will address it and why it is relevant for the essay title.
- It is often worth editing your introduction once you have completed your essay.

LINKING TO OTHER CHAPTERS

This chapter addresses a specific section of your essay which performs a very specific task – introducing your reader and essay to one another and outlining how your essay will address the specific essay title. A strong introduction addresses the specific essay title given and Chapter 4 provides more detail on how to keep that direct orientation to the title present throughout your essay. Crucial to our thinking about the statement of intent in this chapter was the way in which it should convey a clarity of structure. Chapter 5 outlines how you can ensure a smooth interconnection throughout your essay both between and within each paragraph that you write. The current chapter also noted that a strong statement of intent may convey how and where the evaluation of relevant ideas is tackled in your essay. Chapter 6 addresses how our essays can be more deeply evaluative throughout. Finally, the introduction, as the first paragraph in your essay, has a special relationship with the last paragraph in your essay. Both, in different ways, highlight the key issues at stake for your essay. Chapter 8 addresses how you can create a truly effective conclusion, an ideal bookend to your incisive introduction.

Chapter 4

Keep on target – how to answer the essay question

In this chapter you will learn...

- How to answer the precise essay question – from the introduction to the conclusion
- How to avoid losing marks for less relevant material
- How to keep your reader/marker happy with your essay
- How to transform a less relevant piece of writing into something totally relevant

In the classic UK satirical comedy *Yes Prime Minister*, the Prime Minister (James Hacker) offers the following advice on how to avoid answering the question:

> James Hacker PM: Then if they ask the question again, what you say is: 'That's not the question. The real question is', then you make another statement of your own.
>
> (www.youtube.com/watch?v=UnnY4O3oDpk)

Not answering the question is part of the stereotype we hold (perhaps with good reason) of politicians, and the technique illustrated above – where a *re-specified* question is answered – is *the* classic way in which this is done. While there is indeed a set of rhetorical skills that can enable us to dodge questions, for effective academic essay writing we need another set of skills entirely. We need that special set of skills that will really help us to *identify* and *orientate* to the *precise essay question*.

Answering the essay title is something that is at one level obvious. Apart from people who may be attempting a joke, fulfilling a dare or conducting a bizarre social experiment of their own, everyone who submits an essay thinks that they have at some level answered the question. You might wonder why such a self-explanatory issue is even being addressed in a book on how to write brilliant essays. If that thought is in your mind, you have several options available:

a.   Skip to another chapter

b.   Close the book and empty your mind

c.   Repeat some self-affirmations such as 'I *do* answer the essay title'

d.   Stay with it and surprise yourself

If you are wavering on option (d), bear this in mind – not answering the question is done by students who honestly believe that they *have* answered the essay title. Nobody hands in an essay on the psychology of Fraud when asked to write about the psychology of Freud – well almost no one. Most of us are usually really good at spotting the key name or main topic, but the issue is much more subtle than that. Where it goes wrong is at a more nuanced level – a quick glance at the essay title, followed by a *triggered* response and *Ker Pow*! out comes *the* stock essay for that name or topic and what could have been *really* good will now, at best, be *nearly* good.

ANSWERING THE QUESTION: WHAT IT MEANS AND WHY IT MATTERS

Don't I always answer the question?

To get into thinking about answering the essay title try this thought experiment. Imagine for a moment meeting the world's worst therapist and you are talking about your experience of anxiety. The dialogue goes something like this:

You: 'Well, I suppose I have experienced some anxiety – for example, with my last exams I found…'

Worst therapist: 'Let me stop you right there. Right, anxiety – let me tell you about anxiety. I was anxious just last week. There I was, bidding for an inflatable canoe on eBay, half-certain I was going to be outbid…'

The world's worst therapist does what so many people do when they talk. They react to a trigger word with their own pre-set response, blasting out of the blocks with *their* story and never really stopping to listen to what the other person is saying. In academic essays, something similar often happens and it looks like this:

Example essay title: 'Outline and evaluate methodological criticisms of Piaget's conservation experiments.'

First thought response: 'Great – a Piaget essay. I'll nail this!'

Essay (abbreviated): Piaget was a Swiss psychologist who developed a stage theory of cognitive development (sensorimotor, concrete operations, formal operations) … The stages have all attracted criticism both in terms of the methodological approach adopted and the theoretical assumptions made (sensorimotor, concrete operations and formal operations) … In conclusion, Piaget was a Swiss psychologist who provided a stage theory of cognitive development. There is some debate about his findings and further research is necessary.

The essay isn't as heartless and potentially dangerous as the world's worst therapist's responses above, but it still just trots out a predetermined response to a *trigger* word – in this case, 'Piaget', perhaps one of the most salient trigger names in psychology. When these trigger words and names appear, the eyes become dull, the ears muffled and bang! out pops *the* Piaget/Long-term memory/ Milgram essay. Therein lies the problem – the pre-set for that famous psychologist or theory is bashed out, *regardless of the specific essay title*.

For students making this mistake, the crucially important specific wording of the question is barely noticed. Think about the poor marker in this situation. It's like asking for a *latte macchiato* and getting an *expresso*. Yes, they are both coffee – but you had kind of hoped that the barista would pay attention to the *details* of your request.

EXERCISE
Being triggered by familiar topics

Without sneaking a look, think of the example essay title that we have just considered above. If you were asking someone if they had started this essay, how would you refer to it? Would you call it 'the Piaget essay' or 'the conservation experiments essay'? I think, given the fame of Piaget and our tendency to simplify to crude recognisable categories, most people would refer to this as '*the Piaget*' essay. That could be misleading and is more likely to make us treat it as, above all else, an essay about Piaget and his ideas. From the start, we need to think of each essay in *specific* rather than general terms.

With all essay titles and especially those with trigger names (e.g. Piaget, Milgram, Zimbardo and Freud) and trigger ideas (e.g. attachment theory, Big Five personality traits, cognitive schemata and social identity theory) we need to focus on specifics, not generalities. This means that we need to understand the differentiating focus – that is, what is distinctive about this essay title, and what distinguishes it from other Piaget/Freud/attachment theory essays. In place of the habit of a triggered response, we need to develop a thoughtful response (see Figure 4.1). The first step in doing this is to think of the essay title in terms of *its specific requirements* rather than simply the more generic topic that it refers to.

LEARN
Stay on target

Our gloss on essay titles is actually quite important because we can use that gloss to easily kid ourselves that we are 'on target' when we have in fact actually changed the target – expanding it from something that is highly specific to something that is more all-inclusive. Aim for the bulls-eye, rather than just the general direction of the target area.

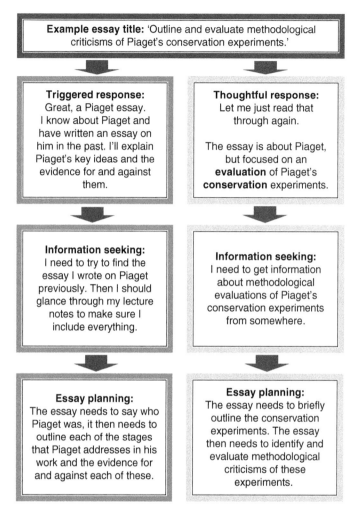

Example essay title: 'Outline and evaluate methodological criticisms of Piaget's conservation experiments.'

Triggered response:
Great, a Piaget essay. I know about Piaget and have written an essay on him in the past. I'll explain Piaget's key ideas and the evidence for and against them.

Thoughtful response:
Let me just read that through again.

The essay is about Piaget, but focused on an **evaluation** of Piaget's **conservation** experiments.

Information seeking:
I need to try to find the essay I wrote on Piaget previously. Then I should glance through my lecture notes to make sure I include everything.

Information seeking:
I need to get information about methodological evaluations of Piaget's conservation experiments from somewhere.

Essay planning:
The essay needs to say who Piaget was, it then needs to outline each of the stages that Piaget addresses in his work and the evidence for and against each of these.

Essay planning:
The essay needs to briefly outline the conservation experiments. The essay then needs to identify and evaluate methodological criticisms of these experiments.

FIGURE 4.1
The triggered and the thoughtful response to familiar topics

If we dig a little deeper, we may find that we are – in part – actually motivated to think of new essay titles in terms of familiar names and ideas. Once we think of an essay as being about 'Freud', nearly all of us will have some relevant knowledge, something to say and quite possibly something that we have previously written. We even know where to find material about this ubiquitous psychologist. 'Great!', we think, so much potential struggle has been dispelled. We may be reluctant to embrace the uncertainty and challenge associated with those less-familiar details – perhaps a specific aspect of Freud's work or a particular critique. However, *it is only by addressing the specifics that we can really demonstrate that we are actually addressing the essay title.*

In Figure 4.1, it is easy to see how a person following the triggered response path might simplify their essay as being 'about Piaget'. They would then seek information and plan an essay 'about Piaget', feeling that they are genuinely answering the question, and not realising that they are actually answering a different essay question. The thoughtful response, by contrast, zooms in on the *specific* features of the essay title.

EXERCISE
How well does your essay address the title?

Use this thought experiment to test how well your essay addresses the title. Reading your essay (but not the actual title), ask yourself: what would a mystery reader guess the title to be? If, in all honesty, they would guess the correct title (or very close to it), then congratulate yourself heartily – and possibly make an occasion of it – because it seems that your essay really does address the title. If, however, the mystery reader would not identify the right title from the essay itself, then you get a gold star for academic awareness and you can experience the warm glow of realising that your essay can be improved quite dramatically.

Note that in Figure 4.1 the thoughtful responder reads through the essay title more than once, looks beyond the trigger name 'Piaget' and *gives thought to the title*, even though this involves a degree of uncertainty.

AVOID LOSING MARKS FOR LESS RELEVANT MATERIAL: SETTING UP YOUR ESSAY

You probably agree that essays should address the essay title. You might also agree that it is best to get into the *specifics* of the essay title rather than stay with a much more general topic focus. But do you also wonder how you can do this from the start, without missing out important contextual details? How can you justify the relatively narrow focus of an essay given all of the possibly relevant material that exists?

Yes, you may think, you could dive in on the specifics of an essay that refers to Freud, Piaget or Milgram, but surely you should acknowledge something of the contribution or context of these super-significant psychologists? Similarly, if the essay title refers to attitudes, personality traits, attachment or long-term memory, surely these are such important and heavily-researched areas of psychology that the importance of them should be acknowledged. Diving straight into specifics and brushing aside or ignoring the broad area might even be seen as showing a lack of awareness of the context in which the specific issue is situated.

You may have slightly different, but related, concerns. Perhaps you feel absolutely fine with restricting yourself to the specifics of the title, but you are aware that even these specifics open up vast amounts of *potentially relevant material*. How can you justify focusing on a very restrictive pool of material?

If you have any of these thoughts, fear not. This is a *desirable dilemma* – it is one of those tensions that can lead to a really great essay. These dilemmas reoccur in essay writing and experiencing them is such a good sign that you should pat yourself on the back the minute you notice one. You will find they pop up when, for example, we try to handle the tension between exploring different ideas while maintaining continuity (Chapter 5), and when conceptualising ideas while maintaining specificity in your conclusion (Chapter 8) – especially if you are doing a really good job. This particular desirable dilemma – the tension between broader context and specific focus – if handled carefully, will help your essay to come across as both on target and well-informed.

Let's stay with that thought for a moment. Out of this tension between wanting to acknowledge the broader context while focusing on the specifics, you will be able to show to the reader that you are aware of the broader context and are selecting to focus on the issues identified as being important in the essay title. In this way, a *brief* acknowledgement of context can actually convey your mastery of the topic. Doing this suggests that you might have taken the essay in different directions, that you are aware of the range of work of the famous psychologist, or the breadth of the topic, but that you are also aware of the specific focus of the title and have chosen to home in on exactly that. Your reader will feel a rush of delight, perhaps even elation, when they come across this in your essay – so spread some joy by developing this skill.

Much of this is achieved in the introductory paragraph of your essay. Your introduction should typically start with an orientating sentence (or sentences), which situates the essay title in the broader context of the topic. Following this, your outline of how your essay will address the essay title (your statement of intent) provides an opportunity to develop a well-justified focus in the light of the broader context. The statement of intent performs a particularly important job in clearly conveying to your reader that the forthcoming essay answers the specific essay title in a thoughtful, well-justified way (see Chapter 3 for more on the introductory paragraph).

Orientating to context in your initial sentence(s)

In order to illustrate the way in which you can provide a very helpful contextualisation, without including irrelevant material, look at the example of weaker and stronger orientating sentences and statements of intent below, annotated with marker comments (see Chapter 3 for more details on producing excellent orientating sentences).

Essay title:

'Critically evaluate the extent to which case studies of brain-damaged individuals have contributed to our understanding of the relationship between brain and behaviour.'

1.   Weak orientating sentence

      The brain has been a great mystery throughout the history of psychology. *<This sentence attempts to set the context, but it is too general in its framing. The fact that it could be used at the start of any essay about 'the brain' suggests that it lacks specificity.>*

2. Slightly improved orientating sentence

There has been a lot of research into the relationship between brain and behaviour, and some of this evidence comes from case studies. *<This is an improvement. It orientates to the broader issue of the relationship between brain and behaviour and it situates case studies within that context. It does, however, fail to indicate how important the issue of brain and behaviour has been (for neuropsychology) and the prominence of case study research in addressing that issue.>*

3. Stronger orientating sentence

Historically, the relationship between brain and behaviour has been a key interest for neuropsychological research, with case studies having been a particularly salient source of evidence since Charcot and Bernard's report on *Monsieur X* in 1883. *<This is quite a strong orientating sentence. The importance of the broad area – research on the relationship between brain and behaviour – is directly addressed and reference is made to the relevant field of 'neuropsychological' research. Case studies are not simply listed, but their prominence or* salience *is referred to. Finally, this sentence demonstrates an awareness of the long period of time in which case study research has been prominent by reference to specific temporal markers – specifically, Charcot and Bernard's famous case study. The potential weaknesses here are minimal. The sentence is arguably a little long. Sometimes the orientating 'sentence' can be spread across more than one sentence. Reference to a specific date does run the potential risk that the reader might think of another (in this case, an earlier) date. But these points are splitting hairs. This is a super orientating sentence that acknowledges the wider context.>*

Statement of intent

The issue of selecting a well-justified, thoughtful focus from the broader context of possibly relevant material is at the heart of the statement of intent. Written well, the statement of intent conveys to your reader not only what is coming up, but also why and, more specifically, why that matters given the precise essay title. A strong statement of intent conveys in a few sentences that this essay will indeed answer the precise essay title.

1. Weak statement of intent

There are several examples of case study research that are relevant to brain and behaviour. *<This is so vague it gives the reader no sense of what is coming up in the essay. Crucial for our current concerns, it does not suggest any intelligent focusing; there is no sense of developing what is being focused on specifically and why that focus is relevant for this particular essay title.>*

2. Slightly improved statement of intent

This essay will examine three key case studies which address the relationship between brain and behaviour. It will examine Charcot and Bernard's (1883) case study work with Monsieur X, Wilbrand's (1892) case study of Fräulein G, and Shallice and Warrington's (1975) report on patient K.F. *<Sometimes it is worth writing out a first draft of what you want to convey – in this case, a statement of intent – knowing that you can edit it down later on.>*

3. Stronger statement of intent (first draft)

This essay will evaluate two case studies from the 1800s: Charcot and Bernard's (1883) study of Monsieur X and Wilbrand's (1892) case study of Fräulein G, both of which share a focus on prosopagnosia. It will also consider Shallice and Warrington's (1975) research with patient K.F., which addresses the idea of separate short-term memory stores. In evaluating the evidence that these case studies provide in terms of evidence for the link between brain and behaviour, attention will be paid not only to the different presenting symptoms of the patients, but also the different methods that each case study employed. Finally, the essay will address the fundamental question concerning the possibilities and limitations of the case study method itself, as a means of understanding the link between brain and behaviour. *<When I wrote this, I thought, at 119 words, that it was a little long, so I edited it down to the 103-word version below. Try to edit your work until it does what you want it to do.>*

ACE YOUR ASSIGNMENT
Edit!

If you do not currently edit your essays, then do it – you're worth it!

Getting into the habit of editing your essays is the single most effective way of transforming your writing. It is almost like having Aladdin's lamp within reach – it is that magical. Almost every published article, book chapter and book you read is edited. Writing often comes out as rubbish at first, even when you have written over a million words of psychology in your life. Why put yourself at a disadvantage? First, write a draft, and then get out your (metaphorical or literal) red pen, start editing and live the dream.

4. Stronger statement of intent (edited version)

This essay will examine the case studies of Charcot and Bernard (1883) (Monsieur X), Wilbrand (1892) (Fräulein G) and Shallice and Warrington's (1975) (patient K.F.). Together, these not only cover different presenting issues, such as prosopagnosia and modality-specific memory impairment, but they also employ different methods and were used to address issues topical at the time that they were conducted. In evaluating the contribution that these case studies make to understanding the relationship between brain and behaviour, attention will be paid not only to the different contribution that each makes, but also to the value and limitations of the case study approach itself. *<The draft statement of intent (above) benefited from editing. This statement of intent ticks a lot of boxes. It goes beyond outlining 'what will be covered' to communicate why it is important to cover these things. This justification or rationale is given in the context of this specific essay title – that is, the reader gets a sense of why the forthcoming essay content is relevant for the specific essay title.>*

A well-written introductory paragraph is vitally important to our concerns with *actually answering the question* – it conveys to the reader that you have:

1. Read the question.
2. Read it carefully, rather than skimmed over it.
3. Understood the question and what it entails.
4. Understood what material should be covered.
5. Discussed material that is directly relevant for the essay title.
6. Understood how and why that material is relevant given *this specific essay title*.

Take time with your introductory paragraph (see Chapter 3 for more on this) as it can be vitally important in not only conveying that you have addressed the essay title, but also in helping you to do so. To really understand this point, let's look at making use of the interplay between thinking and writing.

Making use of the interplay between thinking and writing

It is worth stopping for a moment. You are probably aware of the famous 'Which came first, the chicken or the egg?' dilemma. Here is another one 'Which comes first, thinking or writing?' You might be about to answer 'thinking of course, you idiot!', but just reflect for a moment. Do you ever get stuck trying to express your thoughts in writing? Perhaps we sometimes get stuck because our writing highlights tensions, conflicts and dilemmas (desirable or otherwise) in our thinking.

If we can start to see that many of these 'sticking points' are potential break-through points, then our whole perspective changes. We might not actually find ourselves dancing around the kitchen in a state of ecstasy when we feel stuck with our writing, but perhaps a wry smile will steal across our face as we think 'I wonder where this will take me?' The sense of being at an *impasse* is so much a part of good writing; it suggests we are really thinking. It's like really creating, rather than just dishing out clichéd nonsense. The skill – and it is an amazing skill which you already have but just need to practise – is to work with that feeling of being stuck.

ACE YOUR ASSIGNMENT
Top tip!

When you feel that you can't progress the ideas that you are trying to express, try the following three steps:

1. Quickly write what related ideas you have got clear.

2. Try to specify the detail of what is tricky, or doesn't seem right.

3. See if you have one of these potential dilemmas – or something different – and note the comments for each:

    - A contradiction between different ideas, perspectives or authors

      Great! You have spotted some potential debates. Try to specify and develop these as debates so that they really bring your essay to life. (See Chapter 6 on critical evaluation for more on this.)

    - A contradiction within an idea, perspective or author

      This can help you dig deeper. Stay with the apparently self-contradictory ideas, reading, thinking and noting down your thoughts. Digging deeper may clarify the apparent contradiction, highlight what others take to be a contradiction, or actually confirm a contradictory aspect to the ideas that struck you as self-contradictory. Bringing this into your essay – where it is consistent with addressing the title – can show some great scholarship at work in your essay. (See Chapter 6 on critical evaluation for more on this.)

    - A sense of lots of different ways of ordering your argument or structuring your essay – with uncertainty as to which is 'right' (See also the bullet point immediately below):

    - A sense of confusion as to how on earth you are supposed to order your argument or structure your essay in answering this essay title

      Both of these concerns demonstrate an excellent awareness of the importance of structuring your essay to effectively address the essay title and the idea that you can shape the structure in quite different ways. It can be worth trying out different potential plans for your essay, to see what works best and changing plan where necessary. (These issues are further examined in Chapter 5, which addresses how to structure your essay effectively.)

    - Confusion over what is being argued or suggested by an idea, perspective or author

      What we think of as 'confusion' is really sometimes the very cusp of thinking more deeply about the ideas in front of us. It's as if we are spiralling down ever more deeply into the ideas and each turn takes us through a cloud of uncertainty. That uncertainty and unknowing is the path to greater and deeper knowing. Try to stay with this – try to get a deeper understanding. Can you use the awareness of what is not clear, specifying the uncertainty as clearly as possible so that it can deepen your knowledge? (Chapter 7 on effective description addresses these issues in further detail.)

STOP
You're a psychologist, aren't you?

You may have already noticed that we can actually apply some of our psychology knowledge to help our-selves with answering the essay title. For the sake of simplicity, let's consider two ideas that are particularly associated with the area of social cognition. Even if, like me, you might question some of these ideas, they may nevertheless identify broad patterns of thought and behaviour, such as simplifying and expediting, that capture something of how we perhaps approach a potentially tricky essay title.

See if either of the following hold true in your experience of essay writing:

> **Schema theory** and approaches that emphasise **categorisation** suggest that we order our complex world into more simple categorical units. Could this process be at work in reducing the complexity of a specific title to the more simple, generic topic of that title? Do you sometimes make the essay easier to tackle by thinking of it in terms of the broad name or topic, rather than the complex particulars?

> **Cognitive miser theory** and much of the psychology of **heuristics** identifies that we often seek to save thinking effort and/or look for short-cuts in our thinking. Might we be doing this when we take the essay in a more familiar, less effortful direction than the exact title specifies? Have you found yourself tempted to make the essay more manageable by not making the effort to address all that the title specifies?

In themselves, these ideas don't offer a solution, but they could usefully raise our awareness. If we are aware, for example, that we might be seeking to simplify, or to decrease our effort, then we might stop our-selves, rather than repeat the same old process each time we have a challenging essay title to tackle. Look back on times when perhaps you did not quite address the essay title, or found it difficult to do so. Were these factors at work or was it due to something else. Drawing on your knowledge of psychology, what are you aware of in explaining the times that you did and did not quite answer the essay title?

HOW TO KEEP YOUR READER HAPPY WITH YOUR ESSAY: GOOD AND BAD ORIENTATION TO THE ESSAY TITLE

In this section we look at examples of how good and bad orientation to the essay title can help us to improve our essays. In Chapter 3 we considered what good and bad introductions can look like. If this approach works, it is because it doesn't simply define 'good' and 'bad', but *shows* it. In doing so, it makes *good* writing somehow more attainable. Contrasting good and not so good writing gives you not only a sense of what the good looks like, but also a sense of *what it does* and *how it does what it does*. This can be really empowering, even if you feel that you don't immediately get it. Just getting a sense of what good writing does for the person reading your essay can really transform your written work.

To some extent it is easier to illustrate good and bad writing when the focus is on a particular part of the essay, for example, the introduction (Chapter 3), the conclusion (Chapter 8) or the reference section (Chapter 9). In each of these examples, the focus is on small, self-contained sections of the essay. In this chapter (and Chapters 5–7), the focus is on phenomena that permeate much, if not all, of an essay (such as structure, critical evaluation and description). While it is always helpful to be able to get sufficient sleep each night, giving whole-essay examples through-out Chapters 4–7 could take things too far and have you snoring each time you want to find out about effective structure, description, or – in this chapter – answering the question. In support of your conscious engagement with these ideas, highly truncated essay samples and introductory paragraphs will be used to give a flavour of the qualities of the essay that are being referred to.

Imagine for a moment that *you* are marking an essay. The title is:

'Outline and evaluate Boag's (2006) view that Freudian repression has been substantially misunderstood.'

Your marking burden is very modest, as there are just two submissions which are (unimaginatively) called 'Essay one' and 'Essay two'. Without turning ahead, which do you think better answers the question? You could of course cheat here and no one will know. Although if you do, you may wake suddenly in the night weighed down with the dreadful sense that you dared to sneak a look at the right answer.

Essay one: Outline

Freud is often seen as not only the father of psychoanalysis, but also one of the most significant think-ers of the 20th century. Among all of the ideas that Freud developed, repression has been one of the most enduring and influential. This essay will evaluate several key perspectives on Freudian repres-sion. After briefly outlining Freud's key concept of repression, the essay will address the arguments that repression is scientifically problematic (Nesse, 1990) and that it lacks any empirical evidence (Hayne, Garry and Loftus, 2006). This criticism of repression will be revisited in the light of Boag (2006) and Erdelyi (2006), who argue that the concept has been substantially misunderstood. Finally, the essay will address two important reconceptualisation's of repression, namely, Maze and Henry's (1996) and Boag's (2018) emphasis on neurological aspects of repression and Billig's (1996) rework-ing of repression as rhetoric. The essay argues that a reconceptualisation of repression is necessary for it to retain an enduring relevance.

Essay two: Outline

Freud's development of the idea of repression across his career has had a crucial impact on psycho-logical theory and therapeutic practice. This crucial influence of Freud's developing understanding of repression makes it relevant to question, as Boag (2006) does, the extent to which Freudian repression has been accurately represented and understood and the implications that this has for psychology. This essay will first outline Boag's (2006) key ideas concerning the ways in which Freud's idea of repression has been misunderstood, with a particular emphasis on the ways in which critics of repression have focused on Freud's earliest articulations of repression rather than his subsequent developments of the idea. Boag's (2006) argument will be evaluated in the light of those who concur with this viewpoint (such as Erdelyi, 2006) as well as those who challenge it, and suggest that *proponents* of repression, rather than critics, have carelessly construed it (Kihlstrom, 2006). Finally, the essay will consider the argument that far from misunderstanding repression, it is the critics of repression who best understand it and who have usefully identified that there is no empirical evidence for *any* form of Freudian repression (Rofé, 2008; Hayne, Garry and Loftus, 2006). The essay argues that Boag (2006) usefully identified 'how we define repression' as being crucial to any debate about its efficacy, but that this issue of 'what repression is' is itself far from being resolved.

Comment

This essay title is really tough – it has a very specialist focus in which the arguments in Boag's (2006) paper are the central focus. Furthermore, an evaluation is called for in which attention has to be paid not only to the supporting evidence for Boag's position, but also to the counterarguments and alternative perspectives (which have not been directly specified in the title). As if that's not tricky enough, this essay title has a booby trap built into it and most people will get caught. It has the name of the world's most famous psychologist and most people looking at it will think: 'oh, it's an essay about Freud'.

If you can really answer the question when faced with a super-tough title like this, then, as Kipling once said: 'Yours is the Earth and everything that's in it'. Well, perhaps not the whole earth and maybe not quite everything, but you should get a good grade, which is some consolation.

Which essay answers the question better?

Both of these paragraphs demonstrate the sorts of qualities that are identified in Chapter 3 as being important for a really strong introduction. They have a good orientating sentence, a clear statement of intent and indicate a coherent argument. If you are not sure what these are or how to achieve them, turn to Chapter 3 and experience the warm gentle breeze of understanding. Here the emphasis is on a separate issue: regardless of how well written these first paragraphs are, *how well do they answer the actual question?*

Let's look at each of these in turn with the marker's reactions.

Essay one: Examining the outline

Freud is often seen as not only the father of psychoanalysis, but also one of the most significant thinkers of the 20th century. Among all of the ideas that Freud developed, repression has been one of the most enduring and influential. *<This beginning is on the cusp of being really good – it sets up repression as a relevant issue to think about. So far so good, but the essay title is actually focused on Boag's (2006)* view that Freudian repression has been substantially misunderstood. *Can you see how that is much more precisely focused than 'repression' or 'Freud's concept of repression'.>*

This essay will evaluate several key perspectives on Freudian repression. *<An alarm bell is going off now. Is this going to be an essay about Freudian repression? If so, then the actual title has been partly*

engaged with and partly ignored. Will Boag's (2006) argument about how critics have misunderstood Freudian repression be the central focus of this essay *or not? If not, then the precise essay title has not been addressed. (A frown steals across the marker's usually benign face.)>*

After briefly outlining Freud's key concept of repression, the essay will address the arguments that repression is scientifically problematic (Nesse, 1990) and that it lacks any empirical evidence (Hayne, Garry and Loftus, 2006). This criticism of repression will be revisited in the light of Boag (2006) and Erdelyi (2006), who argue that the concept has been substantially misunderstood. Finally, the essay will address two important reconceptualisation's of repression, namely, Maze and Henry's (1996) and Boag's (2018) emphasis on neurological aspects of repression and Billig's (1996) reworking of repression as rhetoric. *<This looks really well written – if we didn't know the essay title. What a shame that the writer* crucially *misses the bull's eye. This is the beginning of a really good essay about Freudian repression, but the title is about* a *specific idea concerning Freudian repression* developed by Boag (2006). *(The marker slowly and sadly shakes their head.)>*

The essay argues that a reconceptualisation of repression is necessary for it to retain an enduring relevance. *<The conclusion that is indicated here directly addresses an essay about Freudian repression, but it does not link to the precise focus of this essay title. Put another way, what is there* in each sentence *that directly addresses Boag's (2006) argument that Freudian repression has been substantially misunderstood. There is just one sentence in this paragraph that seems on target: 'This criticism of repression will be revisited in the light of Boag (2006) and Erdelyi (2006), who argue that the concept has been substantially misunderstood.' This could have been a useful draft introduction, and the author could have asked of each sentence: 'What does this say about* Boag's (2006) arguments that Freudian repression has been substantially misunderstood?' Such questioning could have led to changes that dramatically improved this introduction. *(A pang of what might have been enters the marker's heart.)>*

Essay Two: Examining the outline

Freud's development of the idea of repression across his career has had a crucial impact on psychological theory and therapeutic practice. This crucial influence of Freud's developing understanding of repression makes it relevant to question, as Boag (2006) does, the extent to which Freudian repression has been accurately represented and understood and the implications that this has for psychology. *<These two sentences might not look like much, but they convey a really good grasp of the issues. Right at the beginning there is reference to the key idea of 'Freud's development of the idea...'. The relevance of the specific, actual essay title (the bull's eye) is referred to here, rather than the much broader area of Freudian repression.>*

This essay will first outline Boag's (2006) key ideas concerning the ways in which Freud's idea of repression has been misunderstood, with a particular emphasis on the ways in which critics of repression have focused on Freud's earliest articulations of repression rather than his subsequent developments of the idea. *<This sentence identifies that the essay will focus not on the general issue of Freudian repression, but rather the specific issue identified in the title, that is,* Boag's view that Freudian repression has been substantially misunderstood. *(A sense of joy enters the marker's heart at this moment.)>*

Boag's (2006) argument will be evaluated in the light of those who concur with this viewpoint (such as Erdelyi, 2006) as well as those who challenge it and suggest that *proponents* of repression, rather than critics, have carelessly construed it (Kihlstrom, 2006). Finally, the essay will consider the argument that far from misunderstanding repression, it is the critics of repression who best understand it and who have usefully identified that there is no empirical evidence for *any* form of Freudian repression (Rofé, 2008; and Hayne, Garry and Loftus, 2006). *<This is great. This promises a debate that draws on relevant literature and focuses not on an evaluation of Freud's ideas concerning repression – which is easier to do, but not directly on target – but instead on Boag's (2006) argument, as identified in the essay title. What a wonderful read this essay promises to be!>*

The essay argues that Boag (2006) usefully identified 'how we define repression' as being crucial to any debate about its efficacy, but that this issue of 'what repression is' is itself far from being resolved. *<This indicates that the conclusion will directly address the essay title. It also conveys a sense of conceptualising the whole debate by suggesting that the issue of 'what repression is' is a key question for the discipline. (The marker smiles broadly, even manically, causing others nearby to edge away awkwardly.)>*

The outline of Essay two indicates a precise – rather than crude 'nearly right' – focus. This outline suggests that the essay is zooming in on *exactly* the issues that the title identified. The outline suggests that the essay will outline *Boag's views*, evaluate them in the light of specific literature and then arrive at a conceptual way of thinking about the issue identified in the essay title. This final step – a conceptual take on the issues – was not specifically asked for in the essay title, but is a feature of the very best academic writing. This is touched on in a little more detail below and extensively in Chapter 8, which examines how we can write really effective conclusions.

The body of the essay

One way of thinking about how the body of our essays can really address the essay title is to see the essay title as similar to a recipe. The title, like the recipe, indicates (in an abbreviated form) what we are to do in our essay and the sorts of ingredients that we should use in order to achieve this. Thinking about titles in this way might help to make sure that from start to finish your essays are really on target in addressing the essay title.

Titles are like recipes – read them carefully!

Have you ever rushed through a recipe, perhaps missing an ingredient or a step in the process? The result might be a disappointing slush. Essay titles are just like those recipes – they tell you the ingredients and the processes that you need to create a really appetising essay. But, and this is key, essay titles are usually brief, a sentence or two, and typically do not have each step laid out for us, so we need to take time to unpack them.

Let's look at the essay title we have just been considering:

'Outline and evaluate Boag's (2006) view that Freudian repression has been substantially misunderstood.'

Read it through just like you normally do. Now stop, take a breath and read it through again. Note down some of the ingredients in the title. We would all spot 'Freudian' – so far so good. But let's be really precise about our ingredients here, because we don't want to use caster sugar when *vanilla* sugar is identified. It's actually 'Freudian repression'.

Reading through again we should pick up 'Boag' – or more specifically 'Boag's (2006) view' – so a specific paper by Boag is referenced (published in 2006) in which he expresses a view about 'Freudian repression' and in particular 'how Freudian repression has been misunderstood'. There are some ingredients that are strongly implied rather than directly specified: evaluation is mentioned and evaluation, like herbs and spices, carries much of the flavour of an essay, so we know that we need some evaluative content.

Our ingredients look like this:

Freudian repression

Boag (2006)

Boag's view that Freudian repression has been misunderstood

Evaluative content

Now we need to ask, what are the processes that we have to follow in creating this essay? It is useful to pull out the command words – those words in the title that are telling us what to do. In the case of this essay title, the command words are: **outline** and **evaluate**. These command words will operate on the ingredients that we have specified above, so what the title is asking us to do with the ingredients looks something like this:

Outline: Boag's (2006) 'view that Freudian repression has been substantially misunderstood'.

Evaluate: Boag's (2006) 'view that Freudian repression has been substantially misunderstood'.

Finally, let us elaborate this so that we are really clear about the steps that will help us fully address the essay title:

1. Read Boag's (2006) paper and outline his arguements about the way in which Freudian repression has been substantially misunderstood.
2. Draw on lecture notes, recommended reading and search tools to identify publications that cite Boag (2006). Identify the arguments that support, challenge or reconceptualise Boag's claims about how Freudian repression has been 'substantially misunderstood'.
3. Create an essay plan so that there is clarity about how the arguments in our essay will be structured (Issues concerning improving essay structure are addressed in more detail in Chapter 5).
4. Develop a conclusion that captures – or conceptualises – the issues that we have identified as really important in discussing the precise issues identified in the essay title. (This is touched on further below and addressed in detail in Chapter 8 on writing effective conclusions.)

Unpacking the essay title in this way can help to make sure that we do not miss key content that we need to address, or key processes (such as evaluation) that we need to engage in. As we look though our essay as a whole, we need to ask, paragraph by paragraph, how it is addressing the question, what it is doing, why it is there. The 'so what?' test below may help with this, but whatever the detail of your process, you need to challenge each paragraph of your essay in order to clarify why it is in your essay, why it is where it is and what it is doing in terms of what the specific essay title requires.

ACE YOUR ASSIGNMENT

Transform your essays with the 'so what?' test

Read through your writing as if you were the reader and ask the 'so what?' question. Interrogate what you have written with the question: 'Why is it important for me to be told this, given the specific essay title?' You can extend the question to include: 'Why am I being told this here, at this point in the essay?', 'What is this sentence or paragraph doing or trying to do within the essay?' However, keep coming back to the idea that you can ask the 'so what?' question of your writing *before* you hand in your essay.

Doing this can help you to spot parts of your essay that need to be amended. You may need to remove a sentence, or perhaps several sentences or paragraphs, or you might need to make its relevance for the specific essay title clearer. Asking the 'so what?' question yourself can help you to modify your essay, making it so directly and overtly relevant to the essay title *that your readers never ask 'so what?' themselves.*

The conclusion of your essay
Most of us have struggled with conclusions at one time or another. Feedback on one of the first papers I had published asked me to clarify in my conclusion what the 'take home message was for the reader'. This is a really good way to think about conclusions – what do we think the informed reader should be left considering after reading our essay?

For our current concerns, our conclusion needs to:

- Be more than a summary of what we have covered in our essay – it needs to conceptualise the issues (see Chapter 8 for more on this).

AND

- Be specifically focused on the issues identified in the essay title.

Let's come back to the guiding concept of the *take home message*. This is not the same as a recap or reminder – we are not assuming that the reader has a problem remembering things and thus sees the conclusion as an opportunity to jog their failing memory, like a list of things to buy at the supermarket. Instead, we write our conclusion to display our deep understanding of the key issues. What key issues, you may ask? The very same issues that are *identified in the essay title.*

Your reader should be able to read the essay title and then turn to your concluding paragraph and think both:

a.   'This essay has been on target'.

AND

b.   'This author has understood the issues and can really think about them'.

These are joyful thoughts to engender in your reader, yet difficult to do without sustained effort. The effort on your part is, however, worth it, for your essay, for yourself and of course for your tired and overworked reader. Why not bring a little sunshine into the world with a conclusion that demonstrates thoughtful, intelligent engagement with the precise issues identified in the essay question.

Key steps for keeping your conclusion on target

- Read some published conclusions – go straight from the title of the piece to the conclusion and see what it is that they do.

- Treat yourself to reading Chapter 8 in this book – this can help to supercharge your conclusions.

- Looking at your essay in progress, start by seeing your conclusion as a part of your essay that you really can improve by editing – something that is actually true of your whole essay.

- In this frame of mind, read straight from the essay title to your conclusion – does your conclusion actually look like it is addressing exactly the issues identified in the essay title?

- If you have a strong conclusion, it will convey that the bit in between the title and the conclusion (the bulk of your essay) has really engaged with the issues that the title identified. If that is not the case, start interrogating the whole essay (not just your conclusion). It is painful to chop out content or change emphasis, but you want not only *relevant* content, but relevant content that is *used to do just what the title asked you to do* (see the section on 'The body of the essay' above).

- If you have a beautiful conclusion it will show that you have not only addressed the issues identified, but have provided a sense of what is at the heart of the issues that have been discussed in your essay. Certain conceptual issues that are often effective in conclusions include identifying:

  o   The ways in which our definitions of the phenomena (for example, how we understand the concept of 'self', 'aggression', 'repression' or 'attribution') we are discussing are important to understanding the different perspectives considered in the essay.

- The sort of evidence (for example, longitudinal research, observational data, clinical case studies or brain imaging data) that may be considered most appropriate or convincing.
- The sorts of theoretical assumptions (for example, whether we understand people as essentially rational, whether articulation of cognitive processes should be the key emphasis in psychology) that account for the debate(s) considered within the essay.

Writing an effective conclusion is a struggle – so are many of the most meaningful things that we accomplish. What will you do with the struggle? Stop, revert to something easier (perhaps just listing what the essay covered) or maybe try to redraft your conclusion until it starts to do justice to the depth of your thinking about the issues identified in the essay title.

TRANSFORMING YOUR ESSAY TO ADDRESS THE ESSAY TITLE: WRITE LIKE A READER

A key to effective communication – perhaps *the* key – is to think of your audience. Spare a moment to reflect on how the marker of your essay will think about your essay (see Figure 4.2). Will they be feeling that yours is yet another essay that does not answer the question, or will yours be one that really *does* address the details of that title? To put it another way, do you write in such a way that any reasonable, knowledgeable reader will conclude that you really do address the detail of the essay title?

Interrogate your essay

In earlier sections of this chapter and throughout Chapter 5 (which addresses structuring your essay) the idea of asking questions of your essay – of interrogating it – is touched on. The key concept is simple: our readers, especially if they are required to form a judgement, will ask questions about our writing. These questions can be divided into:

- Questions arising from external criteria, such as a marking scheme (for example, 'have they included the relevant content for this essay?' or 'have they evaluated the material?').
- Questions prompted by the writing itself (for example, 'why have they included this?' or 'have they understood this correctly?').

You can really empower your essay writing by asking these questions of your writing. If it helps, print out a copy of your essay, view it on a different device, change its font colour, size or style, or simply walk away from your essay and come back to it as a reader/marker. Look at any marking scheme or essay guidance that you have for your essay and ask whether the essay you are writing is doing what these external criteria require. Look also at your actual essay and read it not as a loving parent absorbed in the wonder of their child's first squiggles on a sheet of paper, nor as

1. The student spots a familiar name or topic when glancing quickly at the title.

2. They then write about the broad name or topic and ignore the specific wording of the essay title.

3. The marker then reads essays that do not pay attention to the specific title.

FIGURE 4.2
The unfortunate sequence of not answering the essay title

a vindictive critic, but instead as a professional, perhaps a journal editor who is keen to check that this piece of writing really is on target.

It is worth bearing in mind that if we don't ask questions such as, 'What are you doing here?' or, 'So what – why am I being told this?' or, 'Why is this point made in this location?' as we write our essays, our readers might instead. In other words, if we have not taken the time to challenge and interrogate the extent to which each paragraph genuinely addresses the essay title, then our essay is more likely to contain just the sort of less relevant content that will jar with our reader, causing them to frown and roll their eyes. We should avoid this, for their sakes and our own, and we can avoid it by challenging the relevance of our content ourselves.

As a result of our interrogation of content, we might identify some of the sorts of issues that we could otherwise come across in feedback on our essay (see the following section). This is a key point. If we adopt the gaze (or viewpoint) of the reader (or marker) we can pre-empt their response – we can identify and fix issues before it is too late. Getting into the reader's mindset is the best tool we have for doing that, and it is particularly relevant for the issue of directly addressing the essay title.

What can really help here is creating enough distance from the essay itself. In advice offered on writing, there is the suggestion that we write our draft essay, then take a break for a while – possibly visiting remote islands in the Indian Ocean – and then come back to our essay refreshed and ready to edit. This sounds idyllic in many respects, but it also sounds unrealistic. We are probably writing the essay within a time frame that really reduces our capacity for extended breaks and intercontinental travel. So let's find an approach that can work not only effectively, but also quickly.

One particularly effective way of coming to your essay with a reader's eye and letting this inform your editing is to imagine that the essay was not written by you. Instead, as touched on above, you are a professional with the responsibility for giving a fair-minded assessment of this piece of work. You might be a journal editor, a publisher or an academic involved in marking, but you do not have a positive or negative starting point. Rather, you want to fairly see what is present in this essay and, for our current concerns, ask, 'How well does this piece address the specific title?'

For some it can be really difficult to switch off that inner critic (see Chapters 1 and 11 for more on this). The best way of dealing with this is to acknowledge the inner critic and the useful role that it can have, soon – but not quite now. The inner critic can – if not too manic and foaming at the mouth – help us at various points in editing our work, but it needs to be balanced and constructive and we have to read our essay in a neutral, interested way first of all. By seeing what is actually there, we are in the best position to think about how we can improve and develop it and – in terms of our current focus – ensure that it directly addresses the essay title.

FEEDBACK ON ADDRESSING THE ESSAY QUESTION

Receiving feedback such as '**always address the essay question**' or '**read the title carefully**', '**this is not relevant**' or '**answer the question**' can be disheartening. In some ways, this feedback can often be harder to take than other critical feedback. If there is one thing that you feel you *have* done it is that you answered the question – or at least tried to. The moment you first see feedback that suggests otherwise you may, quite naturally, feel disappointed and annoyed, perhaps feeling that you and your essay have been cruelly misunderstood.

We have all been there and had those sorts of experiences. When you feel able to use the feedback – rather than simply wanting to fight it off – then turn it into a positive by *learning from it*. Look at your essay again, not as someone whose ego is so identified with the essay that they can't have it criticised, but as someone who is open to learning and improving. When you are able to think about your essay and your feedback in this way, then look at your essay and try to identify exactly *where* the issue lies.

Look through your essay in the light of any feedback you have received and from your own re-reading of your essay and ask yourself: '*In what way am I not addressing the essay question?*' and '*Where does the problem lie?*' It is likely to be in one or more of the following five broad areas:

1. **Introduction** – not setting up a relevant approach for the essay title.
2. **Conclusion** – not coming back to the main issues of relevance for the essay title in your concluding paragraph.
3. **Within a paragraph** – citing less relevant work or ideas within a paragraph that contains relevant material.
4. **An irrelevant paragraph** – addressing a less relevant idea or ideas across a whole paragraph.
5. **Across paragraphs** – failing to answer the question by focusing on what is less relevant and/or failing to focus on what *is* relevant for a substantial proportion of your essay.

Let's consider each of these in turn in a little more detail and identify the steps that you can take to tackle them so that you really have *learnt from* your essay and any feedback.

1. **Introduction** – this is dealt with in more detail in Chapter 3 and has been touched on in the section above on good and bad orientation to the essay title. If you have a problem in your introduction, it is very likely that you will have issues elsewhere in your essay.

   To address this issue ask the following simple question that we will return to below:

   Can an unbiased reader work out (fairly precisely) what your essay title is *just by reading your introductory paragraph*?

   Think about the ideas touched on in the section entitled *How to keep your reader happy with your essay: Good and bad orientation to the essay title* above. The introduction has to be so well written that the reader goes beyond thinking that the essay is about say, Freud or even about Freudian repression to realising that it has something to do with *Boag's arguments concerning* Freudian repression.

   Look at the way that you can edit your introductory paragraph. Pay particular attention to your outline of what your essay will cover (your 'statement of intent'). Does this just set up the broad area, OR, does it indicate that your essay will address *exactly the issues identified in the essay title*.

EXERCISE
Look once, look twice

Invest five minutes in making your essay better. Read the title through and look for the *precise* focus, NOT the general topic.

    Make sure that your statement of intent indicates that your essay will address the precise focus.

    Try to make it as precise as possible.

2. **Conclusion** – your conclusion should really address the issue of the precise essay title, not by simply restating 'what has been covered in this essay', but by getting to the heart of the issue. Good conclusions typically conceptualise the key issues of direct relevance to the precise essay title, perhaps distilling core debates and perspectives of direct relevance to the title. There is a real skill to writing effective conclusions, which is worth practising – even when you do not have an essay due. See Chapter 8 for more detailed guidance on writing conclusions that do justice to your thinking about the precise essay topic.

3. **Within a paragraph** – sometimes even 'on target' essays make a diversion to something less relevant. Usually, the author is thinking something along these lines: 'If I include this, I might get a higher grade.' Well, yes – you might. But not if what you are including does not directly address the essay title.

It pays to go through your essay and interrogate the contents. Imagine each cited author and each idea as a person – let's say a miniature person – standing on your desk, table, floor or bathtub. You are Sherlock Holmes, Nancy Drew, Hercule Poirot, Miss Marple, V.I. Warshawski, Dirk Gently or Precious Ramotswe and your job is to interrogate them to find out what they are doing in your essay. Do you spot an imposter? Did one of them crack under your interrogation, or perhaps offer no plausible explanation as to why they are present in your essay?

Unless they can come up with a reason for being in your essay that stands up to scrutiny, then, with regret, you will have to ask them to leave. It can be tough to throw out names or ideas after you went to all that trouble to include them, but imposters in essays are a bad idea. Thank them – if nothing else, they may have helped highlight what your essay *should* focus on. Now guide them gently (yet firmly) to the door.

4. **An irrelevant paragraph** – if putting a red line through a sentence or two is tricky, then slicing through a whole paragraph is positively painful. However, if you really have included a paragraph that shouldn't be there, it will detract from, rather than add to, your essay. That is a difficult concept to really accept. Surely, you may think it is best to include it as it might be relevant? This thinking does not lead to good essays. In fact, many marking schemes specifically identify the 'inclusion of irrelevant' material (especially if it is a substantial amount) as a key feature of essays that merit a low grade.

I have for decades marked essays where a stray paragraph that is not relevant to the essay is included. Usually there is a logic to this – it might have been covered in the same lecture as the target essay issue, or perhaps in the same textbook chapter – so there is typically some sort of association with the essay topic. However, if it is not directly relevant to the precise essay question it shouldn't be there.

5. **Across paragraphs** – essays that are very substantially off target may wind up there for different reasons. Sometimes the author of the essay wants to be different or do something different. This is understandable. Most of us experience something of the dilemma of wanting to be both 'a part of' and 'apart from' – we want to both belong *and* to be special. In the context of our essays, wanting to be special can make us want to approach things differently from others. In my undergraduate essays, I remember my own endeavour to be different made me keen to read things others might not read. That's not completely mad, but it led me to sometimes undervalue key material just because I felt everyone else would turn to those references. I have marked essays that have brought dramatic, journalistic and poetic writing styles to familiar topics, but the essays have suffered as those formats do not typically allow the display of scholarly thinking that academic writing does.

This desire for difference can lead to a different focus, content and/or approach being adopted within academic essays. The difficulty is that this often displaces the focus, content and approach that is more directly relevant for the specific essay title. It might look like the title is constraining you – in some ways it is – but within those parameters there is a lot of freedom for you to display your deep, thoughtful and scholarly understanding of relevant (rather than irrelevant) issues.

Sometimes it is not the desire to be special or different that makes the whole essay go off track, but instead, a genuine misunderstanding of what the title is about and/or a lack of awareness as to what material is relevant for this given title. This problem may be hard to identify in advance, as it centres on a lack of understanding and/or awareness, but it does show how important it is to take the following steps:

i.   Read the title carefully and then re-read it again carefully – out loud (unless this is going to frighten strangers who are in the same lift, bus, train or public convenience).

ii. Pay attention to the detail of the essay title, not just the main name or topic. Those details are crucial, but a little like the chimp paradox – are you going to let yourself be tricked into not noticing them?

iii. Use essay guidance, relevant lecture material and key reading.

iv. Write an essay plan and check it carefully against the title and the guidance that you have (if any) for writing the essay.

v.   Write a draft essay and – if time allows – put it to one side for a short time. Now, ideally, you should achieve a state in which you transcend the ego. That can be tricky, so you may just want to come back to your essay and honestly look at the title and at what you have written.

vi. Edit your work to keep it all on track. Sometimes it is on track but that clarity of argument needs to be made more explicit. At other times you need the courage to chop bits that are irrelevant. Rather than cling to the myth that more inclusion is necessarily a good thing, come to see that relevant inclusion is a good thing, but irrelevant content, focus or approach is a bit like adding tomato sauce and vegemite to your macaroons – it detracts from, rather than enhances, what is already there.

REFLECTING ON THE CHAPTER:
You aren't being marked for showing what you know

Have you, like me, ever found yourself trying to impress others with what you know? If not, perhaps you have noticed others doing just that. Sometimes we have almost the opposite tendency – to hide our own lack of knowledge, reluctant to admit what we don't know. These two tendencies, to show what we know and to hide what we don't, are at the heart of not answering the exact essay question. We show how special and insightful we are with a display of our greatest insights – even if they are not directly relevant – and we side-step difficult, awkward aspects of a question so that we don't 'get it wrong'. When our essay comes back, we feel crest-fallen, dejected and misunderstood. It is a challenge to overcome this and to really answer the essay question, but the first, magical, truly transformative step is to see what we are doing. Looking at your essay, as an independent but kind observer, and asking how each paragraph is relevant can help you make changes to ensure that it really speaks to your reader. That genuine orientation to the precise question is better than a desperate attempt to impress – or hide. Instead, it is authentic communication.

TAKE AWAY POINTS FROM THIS CHAPTER

- Look through your essays and see if you directly answer the question throughout. Try to adopt a fair, rather than a severe or lenient reader perspective.

- Move to a precise understanding of the essay title, rather than a general sense of the broad topic or key names.

- Pay particular attention to your introduction and conclusion. Both of these sections are super-important for setting up the issues of direct relevance to the essay title that are to be addressed (introduction) and providing an intelligent conceptual reflection of the issues of relevance to the essay title (conclusion).

- See whether you have material that does not directly address the essay question. This might be a stray paragraph or sentence. If it looks suspicious, interrogate it. Ask it what it's doing there. If it hasn't a good reason to be there, *given the specific essay title*, then – possibly with regret – it needs to be fired/removed/deleted or sent elsewhere.

- Adopt the perspective of a mystery reader. Can you triumph with the mystery reader challenge? If your mystery reader can fairly precisely work out the title of your essay from reading your essay, then great! If they can't, this is great in another way – it means you are about to really improve your essay by making changes so that your essay more clearly conveys (without restating) the essay title.

- Most essays can be sharpened and they do not typically need a full rewrite. A relatively small amount of work can bring your essay much more sharply on track with the specific essay question, thus spreading joy to all who are lucky enough to read your essay.

LINKING TO OTHER CHAPTERS

This chapter has shown the ways in which addressing the precise essay question is relevant to each part of your essay. Chapter 3 provides further details on how you can develop your statement of intent and other parts of your introduction in order to ensure that your first paragraph frames the issues that you will cover in a way that overtly addresses the precise essay question. Chapter 8 further develops the idea that your conclusion can encapsulate what your essay has covered, ensuring that it is directly relevant to the issues raised by the essay question. Chapter 7's focus on description and your academic voice provides further specification of how you can help ensure that your essay avoids too much – or too little – descriptive detail, keeping the balance and tone just right for genuinely answering the essay title. Finally, Chapter 10 focuses on the ways in which reviewing and editing our essays can be used to really ensure that they are effectively addressing the title – and what to do if they are not. 'Answer the question!' is the constant complaint of academics marking essays, so use these chapters to support yourself in developing the crucial and transformative skill of being able to do so.

Chapter 5

Keep it smooth – how to interconnect your essay

In this chapter you will learn...

- How to make your essay flow smoothly from introduction to conclusion
- How to connect within and between paragraphs
- How to quickly identify and fix interconnection issues
- How to transform poor structure into great structure in your essay

INTERCONNECTION: WHAT IT IS AND WHY IT MATTERS

Most people would agree that writing an essay can be a challenge – but reading one can be also. If you have to read a lot of essays – especially a lot of essays not written by yourself – you may find yourself reacting to what you read. The interconnection (or lack of it) in your writing will help shape how your reader(s) feels as they read your essays. Thinking about how your reader/marker feels as they read your essay is absolutely essential. A smoothly interconnected essay can be a joy to read. It's like listening to a wonderful piece of music, reading a great book or watching a terrific film – there is something satisfying about how it unfolds. Most essays are not quite like that. Elements of connectivity are usually there, but unfortunately there are also jarring *non sequiturs* – or unconnected elements – clanging like discordant notes and making the reader recoil in frustration.

What order – what connectors?

You may find that you have lots of things to write in your essay. You might know some of the points that need to be addressed, and have a sense of what needs to be covered, but struggle with how to structure your essay. Alternatively, you may feel that your essay has included a lot of relevant material but find in your feedback that the lack of interconnection is raised as an area for you to improve. What should you do? Should you order the literature that you draw on by date of publication, by the order they are referred to in the essay title, or in which they were covered in your module? Even if you have the ideas in the 'right' order, how do you join them up so that they do not look simply like a list? Table 5.1 indicates four aspects of interconnection that are especially relevant for our current concerns: we need to find a way of ordering *content* both within each paragraph and between paragraphs, and we need to find a way of *connecting* our content to communicate how it is interrelated.

TABLE 5.1
Interconnection components

Interconnection components	Content	Connectors
Within paragraphs	How the information is arranged within each paragraph.	The words which indicate how ideas within each paragraph interrelate.
Between paragraphs	The order in which the paragraphs are positioned in the essay.	The words, usually in the first sentence of each paragraph, that indicate how the paragraphs interrelate.

GOOD AND BAD INTERCONNECTION

To really develop the interconnection in your essay writing it's no good just having a list of things your essay needs to do – you need to see what it looks like. Even better, it helps if you can contrast an example of good interconnection with an example of weak interconnection. In reflecting on watching numerous plays as part of his own development into becoming an accomplished writer and editor, Stein (1995) argues: 'I learnt more from the painfully bad than the few remarkable plays that kept me enthralled.' Part of this learning is that through exposure to the bad we gain an understanding of how writing makes an audience feel. By contrasting how we feel when reading good and bad writing, we can get a sense of the significant effect that relatively small changes in writing can have.

ACE YOUR ASSIGNMENT
Write like a reader and read like a writer

A key point of the samples used throughout this chapter is to encourage you to approach the reading of these good and bad examples of interconnection with a sense of writing in mind, that is to, as Stein (1995) puts it:

'read like a writer'. Doing so will make you conscious of what does and does not work in the writing that you are looking at and give you a sense of what you can do in your own writing to make it interconnected.

A second aspect of looking at these contrasting samples is to encourage you to keep your reader in mind when you are writing and to write like a reader – or to write the sort of smooth interconnected writing that would give you a good experience as a reader. If you are having doubts about your ability to interconnect your writing, just bear in mind that if some of the samples of writing you read here strike you as better interconnected than others, then you already have the sense for interconnection that is crucial. This chapter will help you clarify more explicitly what it is that makes for good interconnection and how to achieve it in your essays.

Interconnection is such a potentially slippery concept that it is all the more important that we examine examples of poor interconnection – so that we start thinking about the effect that writing has on our readers. It is equally important that we contrast poor interconnection with good interconnection – so that we can clearly grasp what it is that can make our writing smoothly interconnected for our reader. It is worth bearing in mind throughout this chapter that our reader approaches our writing from a different perspective from that which we, as an author, have. Why? Because we have authored our writing, and they have not. This is especially relevant for how interconnected or disjointed our writing is. We may see both gross and subtle connections, but if we do not articulate our sense of interconnection *in our writing*, our reader will have no way of knowing.

Let's move from the hypothetical to some concrete examples. In this chapter we will investigate interconnection by considering essay topics on Piaget's conservation experiments, Milgram's obedience studies and perspectives on language acquisition. Let's start with the first of those topics. Imagine that you have an essay title such as: 'How do constructivist and information-processing accounts explain why younger children fail at the "conservation" task?' Which of the following two abbreviated sample essays is more smoothly interconnected? (These abbreviated samples contain a brief version of what might be the second, third and fourth paragraphs of an essay addressing this essay title.)

Essay title: 'How do constructivist and information processing accounts explain why younger children fail at the "conservation" task?'

First, let's consider how the information is structured within the second paragraph and how that structure is communicated to the reader.

Paragraph two: Smoothly interconnected version

The conservation task was designed to measure whether children would be able to understand that certain properties remain stable despite superficial changes in appearance. **One version** of this task entailed presenting children with two identical glasses of water – one of which is then poured into a shorter but wider container, thereby resulting in the water level being lower within that container than it was in the original glass. **Another version** involved having the same number of items (such as coins, sweets or buttons) arranged in two rows, which first occupy the same width and then are adjusted so that one row – which retains the same number of items – is widened (with greater spaces between the items) than the other. **Piaget found that** Pre-operational children (under 7 years of age) performed less well – believing that these superficial changes meant that there were fundamental differences in the volume of water or the number of items – than those who entered (and subsequently mastered) the concrete operational stage (ages 7–12). *<This paragraph does a good job and is reasonably well organised: sentence one sets up Piaget's approach to conservation, sentence two briefly outlines one version of the conservation tasks, sentence three outlines another version and sentence four succinctly states the findings. Note how the highlighted beginnings of each sentence really indicate what is coming up – overview, one version, a second version and findings. So far, so good, but it is easy to go wrong, even within a single paragraph. How would it read if most of the highlighted connectors above were removed and the order was changed? An abbreviated version of this is given below. (See the companion website for the complete version of this paragraph.)>*

Paragraph two: Poorly interconnected version, abbreviated sentences

Children were presented with two identical glasses of water…

Pre-operational children (under 7 years of age) performed less well…

The conservation task was designed to measure…

Children were presented with the same number of items (such as coins, sweets or buttons) arranged in two rows…

<Even looking at these sentence stems, we can see that there are problems here. The order looks very jumbled and difficult to follow, and reading through it conveys the impression of being a list. Good paragraphs have a clear sentence-by-sentence order and connection – just as good essays have a strong paragraph-by-paragraph order and connection. As you compare examples of good and bad interconnection you may be surprised that sometimes even small changes in order or expression can make very big differences.>

Developing structure throughout your essay

Below are two samples of abbreviated paragraphs. These show how the structure might develop in subsequent paragraphs for the same essay title that we have started to consider above: '*How do constructivist and information processing accounts explain why younger children fail at the "conservation" task?*'. First, let's look at sample one. For now, please focus on how you feel as you read this sample.

Sample one

The information-processing approach argues that younger children fail at this conservation task. They fail because of limited processing capacity. **They fail because** of biological constraints. **There are upper limits** to the processing speeds for different ages. They focus on only one aspect. They have limits in working memory. Case (1998). That is why older children are more successful.

Coming back to Piaget, he argues from a constructivist perspective. **Younger children cannot complete the conservation task. They are at a different stage of cognitive development. Centration is the problem.** Younger children only focus on one aspect, they do not take into account the height *and* width of a liquid when comparing volume, for example. As children develop, they are able to perform mental operations on, or transform, the physical stimuli they see and reverse these processes to understand that the volume or number of the item being considered has not changed despite a manipulation of their appearance.

The way in which the experiment is conducted can affect the results as well. If children are told that the naughty teddy has changed things, then they will answer differently. That proves that the experiment was flawed. Donaldson and McGarrigle (1974) proved this point. **When the 'naughty teddy' was introduced** and appeared to mix up the physical stimuli being asked about, children were more likely to believe that the volume or numbers were the same. They knew that the teddy had made things look different. They knew that really things were the same.

Next, information processing argues that social aspects can be important as well. Scaffolding can help (Kail, 2000).

STOP AND THINK
Micro pause

- How do you feel when reading sample one above? See if you feel differently when you come to sample two below.
- How do you think a reader would feel? What effect would there be on the marks and comments?

Now contrast sample one with sample two below. Once again, note how you feel as you read this sample.

Sample two

Piaget developed a constructivist account for the findings arising from his conservation experiments. Piaget emphasised the limits in terms of how younger children thought about the stimuli that they were presented with. **Key to this is the concept of** *centration* **– the idea that younger children are only able to focus on one aspect of the stimuli at a time**, for example, just the height (but not the width) of the water in the two containers, or the total width of (but not the spaces in between) the coins laid out in front of them. **For Piaget, pre-operational children (under the age of 7) are at a different stage of development.** As they enter the concrete operational stage (7–12) they are increasingly able to perform mental operations on, or transform, the physical stimuli that they see and reverse these processes to understand that the volume or number of items being considered has not changed despite a manipulation of its appearance.

The information-processing approach, by contrast, offers a perspective that emphasises limitations in *processing capacity* – such as working memory and processing speed – as key to understanding why younger children fail at conservation tasks. **Case (1998) argues that it is these processing limitations – partly due to biological constraints regarding processing speeds for younger children – that mean that children are not able to solve the conservation tasks. Others adopting an information-processing perspective support the idea of biological constraints yet also note the importance of social factors. Kail (2000), for example,** notes that task performance can be improved with external scaffolding as this can help to direct the child's attention as they attempt to solve tasks that are on the cusp of their ability.

EXERCISE
Your response

How does it feel to read the above sample answers?

    Before going any further, note down here the feelings that came to mind as you read the two samples above.

    Reading sample one, I felt:

    Reading sample two, I felt:

Comparing the two samples of essay writing

(i) Your thoughts and feelings about the samples of writing

Both of the sample answers are clearly incomplete, representing a brief example of what might follow the first two paragraphs of an essay. It is fair to note that the differences between them are not absolute – it is not the case that one approaches perfection while the other is the worst imaginable sample of writing. However, stop and think how reading each made you feel. Did you find sample one a little less clear in terms of where the essay was going?

    Did you feel that reading sample one was frustrating? It's a little like getting in a taxi to catch a train and having it alter its route several times – just as you think you are getting somewhere there is a sudden change of direction. Sample two did not include each of the different ideas that were in sample one. For example, the interesting reference to 'naughty teddy', who is introduced as the reason why the physical stimuli might *look* different, is absent. However, while it might be relevant to include such additional material at some point in the essay, *from an interconnection perspective*, sample two is significantly stronger. Let's get out our microscopes and investigate what makes sample two better at interconnection. The best way to do this is to articulate the reader's thoughts as they read through sample one and sample two (see Table 5.2 below).

(ii) The reader's reactions to the samples

Table 5.2 captures the reader's reaction to samples one and two above. For brevity, the samples are represented in the table by using brief extracts, which appear in bold in samples one and two above. The reader's reactions in Table 5.2 refer to both the brief extract itself and (in some cases) to the surrounding text found in samples one and two. For the complete reader's comments on the two samples please see the companion website.

TABLE 5.2

Summary of the reader's thoughts in response to the two samples

Sample one	Reader's reaction	Sample two	Reader's reaction
The information-processing approach argues that younger children fail at this conservation task.	*Several problems here, including that a proper source should be cited (see Chapter 9). This paragraph should come later and should highlight the different interpretations that are offered.*	**Piaget developed a constructivist account for the findings arising from his conservation experiments.**	*This paragraph comes at the right place and the first sentence neatly characterises Piaget's approach (constructivist) before expanding on it.*
They fail because ... They fail because ... There are upper limits	*This section within the paragraph is disjointed. The sentences should be rewritten to form a coherent argument rather than a disjointed list.*	**Piaget emphasised the limitations in terms of how younger children thought about the stimuli.**	*This is a really helpful conceptualisation of Piaget's approach – the detail to come will be contained within this framework.*
Coming back to Piaget ...	*'Coming back' has all of the hallmarks of being a paragraph that is out of sequence. Try out a different order for your paragraphs – find an order that is really logical.*	**Key to this is the concept of centration – the idea that younger children are only able to focus on one aspect of the stimuli at a time.**	*Again, this essay maintains and develops a conceptual overview. This demonstrates a grasp of the fundamental principles at work.*
Younger children cannot complete the conservation task. They are at a different stage of cognitive development. Centration is the problem.	*These sentences contain some very important ideas but they are disjointed. This passage reads like notes that need to be edited into a coherent argument for the essay.*	**For Piaget, pre-operational children (under the age of 7) are at a different stage of development.**	*This nicely encapsulates Piaget's position and the stage is set for a contrast with researchers who adopt an information-processing perspective.*
The way in which the experiment is conducted ...	*This paragraph is out of sequence in terms of the essay title. It could make sense to bring these ideas in at some point, but first the debate between Piagetian and information-processing perspectives needs to be developed.*	**The information-processing approach, by contrast, offers a perspective that emphasises limitations in processing capacity**	*This sentence beautifully addresses the essay question and also conveys to the reader how what is coming up in this paragraph relates to what has been considered previously.*
When the 'naughty teddy' was introduced ...	*Empirical detail should be succinct and carefully positioned. Here it comes abruptly rather than smoothly, illustrating the empirical basis for Donaldson and McGarrigle's (1974) position. This would work better: 'In their empirical investigation, Donaldson and McGarrigle (1974) found that...'.*	**Case (1998) argues that it is these processing limitations – partly due to biological constraints regarding processing speeds for younger children – that mean that children are not able to solve the conservation tasks.**	*This writing demonstrates an awareness of how information-processing researchers share ideas about processing speeds, which contrasts with Piaget's constructivist approaches. It also shows a nuanced understanding of the different emphasis within information-processing approaches.*
Next, information processing argues that	*'Next' – like 'another point...' – works to suggest that there is a list (where connection is relatively unimportant) rather than an argument (where how ideas relate to one another is key).*	**Others adopting an information-processing perspective support the idea of biological constraints yet also note the importance of social factors. Kail (2000), for example,**	*This is a great piece of connective writing. The writing articulates a partial agreement, noting both where there is common ground and a contrasting emphasis.*

EXERCISE
Try it out

Find some essays that you have written and look at them not for content, but for interconnection.

- What are the key sentences or phrases that do the connecting work in your essay? Highlight them if possible.
- Is there an order to the content that would make sense if you had to explain to someone else why you placed each paragraph where you did?

(iii) Reflecting on the reader's reactions to the two samples

As you look at the reader's reactions in Table 5.2 above, bear in mind that the more your writing can take into account the reader's thoughts the better it will be. You are writing to make contact with the reader; they do not see the intricacies of your thinking *unless you have conveyed them in your writing*. If you can start to imagine your reader's reaction to your academic writing, your essays will be more smoothly interconnected. The reader in Table 5.2 above is a human, like you. Note how they seem to get frustrated at times, as they try their best to engage with the writer's ideas and to make sense of what is being argued, but the lack of smooth interconnection is making it difficult for them. In Table 5.2, the reader's comments are unedited so that you can really sense how the reader is reacting to the writing. If the reader were to give official feedback on the essay, the tone would (most likely) be considerably more measured.

Sample one left our poor reader feeling frustrated. The direction of the essay within and between paragraphs was unclear. There were two distinct facets to the poor interconnection in sample one: first, the way in which the material was arranged (the order in which various points were addressed), and second, the explicit connection of the material, or lack of it, (for example, the first sentences of the new paragraphs that link what is coming up to what has previously been addressed). Note how the reader seems far less frustrated and much more impressed as they read the imperfect but much more smoothly interconnected sample two.

STOP
Essay health check – interconnecting your essay

Let's look again at your own essays. Ignoring your introductory, second and concluding paragraphs for a moment, look at the first sentence of each paragraph in the main body of your essay and ask: 'Does this link what *is to come* (in that paragraph) to what *has been considered* (in the paragraph above)?'

The *link, or connecting, sentence* for each paragraph can be written in a number of ways but needs to help the reader understand how what is coming up links (perhaps being a contrast, a further example, an alternative conceptualisation, a refinement or a more complex relationship) to what has gone before.

(iv) What – why – how

Reflecting on the two samples of bad and then good interconnection above, you might find that you have several questions:

- **What** was it that made sample two better than sample one?
- **Why** is there better interconnection in sample two?
- **How** is it possible to unlock the secret of that interconnection so that it can be applied across psychology essays?

STOP AND THINK
Micro pause

What advice would you give to the author of sample one that might help them to improve the interconnection in their writing?

Let's first consider some answers to these questions and then examine another sample to more clearly see what these ideas look like in practice.

- **What** was it that made sample two better than sample one?

  In sample two the material referred to was better organised and more clearly interconnected.

- **Why** was there better interconnection in sample two?

  In sample two the ideas were coherently organised within and between paragraphs, and related ideas were grouped together in a logical manner. Connection was explicitly developed: for example, the first sentence of the third paragraph makes it clear that there is a contrast between what is addressed in that paragraph and the approach developed in the previous paragraph.

- **How** is it possible to unlock the secret of that interconnection so that it can be applied across psychology essays?

  You really can develop this skill. Part of the process is reconsidering how thinking and writing relate to each other. Instead of a simple one-way arrow from thinking to writing, there is (or should be) something much more mutual going on. Your ideas guide your writing, but – *just as importantly* – your writing makes you ask questions of and think about the material that you refer to. Your desire to smoothly interconnect your writing leads you to ask specific questions about the ideas in your essays, such as:

  o   What point am I making in each paragraph?

    ○   How can the component parts of each paragraph be ordered effectively?

    ○   What is it about these points that makes it sensible to treat them together?

    ○   How does this point or idea relate to the one that I have previously mentioned?

    ○   In what ways do these ideas relate to others that I raise and how can I express that relationship in my essay?

TRANSFORMING THE INTERCONNECTION IN YOUR ESSAYS

Taking the position of the reader

To really start to interconnect your essays, first, try to put yourself into the position of the reader. Read through sample three below. This example comprises seven (very brief) paragraphs from an essay entitled: 'Evaluate Milgram's idea that obedience to authority is best understood as due to a shift in agentic state.' The essay has a number of problems, including the introduction (see Chapter 3 for more on writing effective introductions), the lack of critical evaluation (see Chapter 6), the treatment of description (see Chapter 7) and the extreme brevity of the paragraphs. Here the focus will be on features of the essay that are directly relevant to interconnection. As you read this example, note down how it makes you feel.

EXERCISE
The reader's perspective

See if you can develop a detached eye on your own writing. It may be easiest to do with an essay that you wrote some time ago. Rather than judging your essay or getting absorbed in the content, try to imagine how the reader would feel.

    More specifically, ask these questions:

- Would the reader know which direction the essay was going in?
- Would the reader sense that the ideas were interconnected well?
- Would the reader sense that I (the author) had really understood how the ideas relate to each other in all of their intricacies?

Sample three

Milgram's obedience studies have had a profound impact in social psychology, providing both an insight into the extent to which people obey those in authority and an understanding as to the possible underlying mechanisms. This essay will address the ways in which agentic state is important for understanding why people obey those in authority and will evaluate it.

Milgram's participants did not realise that the shocks were not real. The participants obeyed the experimenter's instructions to continue even though they wanted to stop. Milgram understood this as being due to the agentic state.

Ethical issues concerning Milgram's experiment are worth considering. The participants were told that they must continue even when they expressed that they wished to withdraw from the experiment.

Gibson (2013, 2019) examined the rhetorical aspects of obedience.

Reicher and Haslam (2011), focusing on the variation of results across the different experimental conditions, emphasised the idea that the findings could be understood in terms of the group – or social – identity of the participants.

Agentic state is a psychological state in which one no longer considers oneself to be responsible for one's own actions but rather as responsible for obeying the authority figure.

Milgram's participants arrived at the lab and were greeted by the experimenter, who allocated them – ostensibly on a random basis – to be either 'teacher' (the one administering the shocks) or 'learner' (the one receiving the shocks).

EXERCISE
Your response

How does it feel to read sample three? Note your feelings here.
  Reading sample three, I felt:

Did you feel frustrated reading this passage? Was it like listening to someone going on and on, wondering where they are going, what it is they are trying to say and when – if ever – they are going to stop? When we are reading (and often when we are watching a film or listening to music) we typically like a sense of direction. It is true that some authors, directors and composers deliberately challenge our expectations, but to try to do so in our academic writing would typically result in it being impenetrable, confusing and frustrating for our readers.

Thought experiment

Try your own version of the 'naughty teddy' thought experiment for a moment.
  Imagine that you have the example draft of an essay on your laptop and that you leave the room. While you are out, naughty teddy starts playing on your laptop – not changing any words,

but shuffling around the order in which the paragraphs are written. Could you (or even better, a friend) put them back into the correct order?

Let's switch the thought experiment around. Your friend has this same draft essay on their laptop, and their mischievous younger brother cuts and pastes the paragraphs into a different order. Could you put those paragraphs back in the right order?

Your essays should be written so that even if a 'naughty teddy' and a mischievous younger brother teamed up to rearrange your paragraphs – and even your sentences – you (or, ideally, someone else) could tell *from how it is written* what the correct order should be.

ACE YOUR ASSIGNMENT
Make it better – make it worse

If you haven't done so already, grab a pencil, pen or digital equivalent and try the following challenges on a piece of your own work:

1. Ignoring the first paragraph, which is obviously some form of introduction, can you re-order the paragraphs to make them worse?

    Reflection – if you cannot obviously make the paragraph order worse, then the order really does need fixing.

2. Ignoring the introductory paragraph again, can you come up with a better order for the paragraphs, one that flows more logically?

    Reflection – if you can re-order your paragraphs to make them flow better, then you should do so without delay.

3. As well as improving the order of content by rearranging the paragraphs, it is important to look for the use of connectors, such as the first sentence of each new paragraph. Once your paragraphs are in an improved order, can you find some sentences that could link what will be covered in any given paragraph (ignoring the first, second and concluding paragraphs) with what has been addressed in the preceding one?

    Reflection – it can be helpful to ask of your new paragraph: 'How do you relate to the previous one?' Then consider how you could express that connection in a linking sentence at the beginning of your new paragraph. Connectors are addressed in further detail below.

Making it better

Let's work on sample three to improve it. Try following the steps outlined below, identifying what content to include and the best order for it, as well as how connectors can be used and how these principles can be applied to the whole essay. As you look at these improved abbreviated paragraphs, why not quickly ask yourself if you feel that the suggested changes really improve sample three and, if so, how?

(i) Identify what to include and where to include it

Getting order and inclusion right is key. Look at the comments on sample three to see how what is included and where it is placed have been improved.

Milgram's obedience studies have had a profound impact in social psychology, providing both an insight into the extent to which people obey those in authority and an understanding as to the possible underlying mechanisms. This essay will address the ways in which agentic state is important for understanding why people obey those in authority and will evaluate it. *<The introduction needs a more detailed sense of how the essay will address the essay title – see Chapter 3 for more detail on effective introductions.>*

Agentic state is a psychological state in which one no longer considers oneself to be responsible for one's own actions but rather as responsible for obeying the authority figure. *<This paragraph works well fairly early on as it provides a provisional understanding of the topical focus for the essay. It should probably come after Milgram's empirical evidence has been briefly outlined.>*

Milgram's participants did not realise that the shocks were not real. The participants obeyed the experimenter's instructions to continue even though they wanted to stop. Milgram understood this as being due to the agentic state. *<This paragraph does not offer a great deal in terms of this specific question, although it does at least mention agentic state. See Chapter 4 for more on addressing the specific essay question.>*

Ethical issues concerning Milgram's experiment are worth considering. *<This may not be relevant for this essay and might be best deleted, although do note that specific guidance relating to the essay might indicate whether it is expected that ethical issues are covered.>*

Gibson (2013, 2019) examined the rhetorical aspects of obedience. *<It may be best to include this approach after both Milgram's agentic state and Reicher and Haslams' (2011) social identity theory, as it has a radically different focus on language in interaction. Positioning this paragraph after agentic state and social identity theory enables it to be used to critique or question each of these alternative explanations.>*

Reicher and Haslam (2011), focusing on the variation of results across the different experimental conditions, emphasised the idea that the findings could be understood in terms of the group – or social – identity of the participants. *<This could be considered after the agentic state idea has been addressed.>*

Milgram's participants arrived at the lab and were greeted by the experimenter, who allocated them – ostensibly on a random basis – to be either 'teacher' (the one administering the shocks) or 'learner' (the one receiving the shocks). *<This paragraph, or some of its content, probably has some place in the essay, but would be better as the second paragraph. See Chapter 7 for guidance on making description effective.>*

(ii) Add a clear and logical statement of intent

A clear statement of intent expresses the logic of what you have included and where you have included it – which was considered above. Look at the ways in which a statement of intent conveys not only what is coming up but also a sense of how the ideas relate to each other and how they are all relevant for the precise essay title.

Milgram's obedience studies have had a profound impact in social psychology, providing both an insight into the extent to which people obey those in authority and an understanding as to the possible underlying mechanisms. **This essay will first briefly detail what Milgram's experiments entailed before outlining how Milgram developed the notion of agentic state in explaining the results of his empirical studies. The essay will then evaluate Milgram's 'agentic state' interpretation by contrasting it with alternative frameworks for making sense of his empirical results, including Reicher and Haslam's (2011) Social Identity Theory approach, Russell's (2011) identification of Milgram's 'strain reducing mechanisms' and Gibson's (2013, 2019) focus on the role of rhetoric.** *<A clear sense of what will be covered in the essay is conveyed in this statement of intent, see Chapter 3 for more on this.>*

(iii) Add connector sentences

Well written connector sentences are key to really well-structured academic essays. Your reader – and especially your marker – will focus on connectors as these express your understanding of how the ideas you refer to relate to each other. Look at how connector sentences (in bold) are used in the abbreviated paragraphs of the improved sample three.

Milgram's participants arrived at the lab and were greeted by the experimenter, who allocated them – ostensibly on a random basis – to be either 'teacher' (the one administering the shocks) or 'learner' (the one receiving the shocks). *<Effective description is addressed in detail in Chapter 7. Here it is worth noting that the level of detail should be just that which is needed to inform the arguments that are developed in your essay. There is quite a concise tone here, which is good. >*

Milgram's own understanding of the results of his empirical work focused on the inner psychological state of the participant in their role of teacher acting under the instructions of the authority figure, 'the experimenter'. In developing this account for his findings, Milgram was placing the emphasis not on some empirical failing (the 'unrealistic' experimental set up), not on the vicissitude of his participants (such as the characteristics of Yale University students or the personality traits of participants he recruited outside Yale), but rather on a psychological state brought about by particular features of the external environment. 'Agentic state', as Milgram uses the term, refers to a psychological state in which one no longer considers oneself to be responsible for one's own actions but rather as responsible for obeying the authority figure. *<The beginning of this paragraph now offers a lot more to the reader in terms of interconnection. Agentic state is introduced as the framework that Milgram used to make sense of his findings, linking the key focus of the essay title to the brief overview of Milgram's empirical work in the previous paragraph.>*

Reicher and Haslam's (2011) understanding of Milgram's findings does, to an extent share with Milgram a focus on certain intrapsychic changes that the environment brings about. However, for Reicher and Haslam it is changes in the individual's identity, specifically in their shared, or *social, identity*, that are key. They consider how – for the participant – a group, or social, identity might be made salient in a physical environment and a task format that groups together the participant and experimenter and separates – both physically and in terms of the task – the 'learner'. Reicher and Haslam, focusing on the variation of results across the different experimental conditions, emphasised the idea that the findings could be understood in terms of the group – or social – identity of the participants. *<The first two sentences articulate the way in which the material in this paragraph relates to what has been considered previously. You may note that it is positioned as being a complex relationship rather than straightforward agreement*

or disagreement. Really good connecting sentences like these actually show the reader the writer's understanding of how ideas relate to each other.>

Whilst the explanations for Milgram's findings considered above differ, they could both be understood as, to some extent, focusing on intrapsychic phenomenon; 'agentic state' and 'social identity' respectively. By contrast Gibson's (2013, 2019) rhetorical approach, examines the ways in which *rhetoric* played a key role in Milgram's experimental findings. Drawing on transcripts of Milgram's experiments, Gibson highlights that acts of disobedience and obedience under duress were typically accompanied by challenges to the experimenter. *<The first two sentences of this abbreviated paragraph draw a contrast not only with the immediately preceding paragraph, (covering Reicher and Haslam's Social Identity Interpretation of Milgram's findings), but also with Milgram's own (agentic state) interpretation. In this way the connectors are used to relate what is developed in this paragraph to more than one preceding idea – which makes the essay even more well structured and on target for this specific essay title.>*

STOP AND THINK
Organising and Connecting Ideas in Your Essay

Think about the way in which sample three was improved. The modifications to sample three involved the better organisation of ideas – there was thought about what to cover and where to cover it. There was also a much clearer sense of connection, this was evident in both the statement of intent in the introduction, and the clearer connections between ideas throughout the essay. Note that the ideas to be addressed in the essay are not simply listed in the statement of intent, e.g. Milgram, Reicher and Haslam, Russell, etc.; instead, they are are *characterised* as Milgram's '*agentic state*' interpretation, Reicher and Haslam's '*social identity theory*' approach, etc. Throughout the abbreviated paragraphs of the improved sample three above, connective sentences (in bold) make the essay stronger by linking what is about to be covered with what has been covered. Relatedly, there is cohesion within each paragraph, which now develops a clear point. Having a first sentence that links to the previous paragraph, then sentences that develop the new point being considered, enables both between and within – or inter- and intra- – paragraph interconnection.

To improve your essays so that the ideas are well organised and smoothly interconnected you have to bounce between your writing and your thinking. This really strengthens the organisation and interconnectivity of your writing. Sample three was improved by interrogating the paragraphs to find out how they interrelate – asking what relevance the ideas to be included in the essay have for each other (and for the essay title). Repeatedly asking; 'how do these ideas relate to one another?' gives a clearer sense of what to include, how to order it and what the nature of the relationship between those relevant ideas is. You can then articulate your understanding in a clear statement of intent in your introduction and in connecting sentences throughout your essay. In this way your reader will vividly *see your understanding* of how the ideas you refer to interrelate, rather than simply inferring that poor understanding has resulted in poor structure.

FEEDBACK REGARDING INTERCONNECTION

Putting the principles of interconnection into practice can be a challenge no matter how experienced you may be in essay writing. Let's now look at some further specifications that may help.

Thinking about feedback

My essay is described as 'disjointed' or 'list-like'– what does that mean and why does it matter?

A list does not necessarily require any sense of how or why one item relates to another – think of a typical list of things that you plan to buy. You could order them by location within the store, type of item, for whom they are intended, level of necessity or price, but you probably don't need to. A good essay, however, is not a list. In a good essay, a crucial issue concerns *linking* – that is, addressing the question 'how do these ideas relate to each other?', so that your readers never have to ask that question themselves.

Links don't always pop out automatically; they sometimes require us to interrogate the ideas we want to link and to ask them: 'What do you have to say to the other ideas in this essay?' When we have the order of our points mapped out, we can ask the more specific question: 'How do you relate to the other ideas that I have just discussed?' See the section on 'Finding connecting phrases' for advice about expressing – in writing – the relationship between the ideas that we raise.

My essay is described as having 'non sequiturs' – what does that mean and why does it matter?

In some – especially humorous – writing, non sequiturs (or things that do not follow) are not only present, they are often celebrated. The extract below is one example of this device being used to comedic effect. It comes from an episode of the satirical chat show-based comedy *Knowing me, Knowing You with Alan Partridge*. The extract occurs after a prolonged sequence in which the chat show host (Alan Partridge) expresses to his literary guest the firm conviction that Sherlock Holmes was a real person who should be admired not only for solving crimes, but also for writing them all down afterwards.

> Literary guest: If Sherlock Holmes were real, how is it that he was able to describe in intimate detail the circumstances of his own death?
>
> (Long pause)
>
> Alan Partridge: The Nobel Prize for literature – you never won it – what went wrong?

In academic writing, though, non sequiturs are a problem rather than a resource. They should be avoided.

My essay receives feedback comments such as 'What direction is this essay taking? and 'What is your line of argument?' – what does that mean and why does it matter?

The direction that your essay is taking (and has taken) can be understood as relevant in three different places within your essay: in the introduction (this is addressed in further detail in Chapter 3), in the conclusion (this is addressed in Chapter 8) and in the main body (this is addressed in Chapters 4, 6 and 7). It is worth noting:

- Your **introduction** should outline what your essay will address and the order in which these features will be addressed, and it should characterise the approaches to be covered where possible.

- The **main body** of your essay should interlink in the ways outlined in this chapter, with particular attention to the job that first sentences of new paragraphs do in relating ideas addressed in a new paragraph to those discussed in previous ones.

- Your **conclusion** should conceptualise the issue or issues that lie at the heart of your essay.

Finding connecting phrases

It is really helpful to have a sense of some of the tools, and particularly the language, that you can use to explicitly interconnect your writing. If you scan through good, published academic writing, you will find some of the different phrases that do this important job.

Try thinking about the three 'Cs' of interconnection – concurrence, contrast and complexity. Most of our academic writing will be connected in one of these three ways. Let's first get a sense of what these three ways of connecting look like. To help with this, consider the classic debate between Skinner (we learn language through a process of reward and punishment – *operant conditioning*) and Chomsky (we have an innate ability to acquire language – the *language acquisition device*). Imagine your somewhat predictable essay title was: 'Critically evaluate Skinner's argument that we acquire language through the process of operant conditioning.'

Concurrence – The ideas you wish to connect are in agreement, or concurrence, with each other, that is, they are making the same sort of point. *Pop-up example: 'Bartlett, Ora, Brown and Butler (1971) provide further support for Skinner in their study examining the efficacy of operant conditioning principals…'.*

Contrast – The ideas you wish to connect are different from each other, that is, they are in disagreement or they contrast with each other. *Pop-up example: 'Chomsky, by contrast, fundamentally opposes Skinner's concept that language is simply learned from the environment, instead arguing that…'.*

Complexity – The ideas you wish to connect cannot be simply categorised as being in a relationship of concurrence or contrast with each other. Here, the ideas relate in a more complex way, partly concurring and partly contrasting. *Pop-up example: 'Bruner's language acquisition support system incorporates elements that stress the importance of the environment, while also retaining an emphasis on an innate dimension missing in Skinner's approach...'.*

Phrases that help to interconnect paragraphs

Concurrence

Here are some phrases that help when the new paragraph makes a point that is aligned or in agreement with the point in the preceding paragraph or paragraphs. These connectors position what is coming up in the new paragraph as concurring with what was mentioned previously. For simplicity, let's consider that the previous paragraph concerned the ideas and research of X and the current paragraph concerns the ideas and research of Y.

- *Empirical evidence for X's [name X's idea, approach or interpretation] is found in the work of Y...*

- *Y's empirical research provides further evidence for X's notion of...*

- *Y similarly argued that...*

- *X's perspective on [topic] is endorsed by Y, who argued that...*

- *X's perspective on [topic] is endorsed by Y, whose empirical research found that...*

Let's consider how this looks within the structure of an essay:

Paragraph outlining a particular point *<For example, Kelley's Covariation Model of Causal Attribution.>*

Empirical evidence for this is found in the work of... *<the paragraph then develops further evidence for the point outlined in the previous paragraph. For example, it might outline McArthur's (1972) experiment, which provided some experimentally based empirical support for Kelley's Covariation Model of Causal Attribution.>*

Why does it matter? It matters because:

The reader experiences a smooth sense of how this new paragraph connects to the preceding one.

The reader who is marking your essay sees not just a good writing style, which is valuable in itself, but also *the writer's grasp of how the ideas that they refer to relate to one another*. Here the reader/marker sees that the author understands that the material in the new paragraph relates in a specific way to the preceding paragraph(s) – in this example the relationship is that the current paragraph *provides evidence* for the point that was referred to in the previous paragraph.

Contrast

Often you will find that psychologists don't just agree with each other, they keep arguing. This is actually great news for writing an essay that has a real sense of debate and critical evaluation (see Chapter 6). The fact that you are aware of or uncover disagreement and debate means that you can show how you *can examine the topic of your essay from different perspectives*, which is an absolutely key element of most strong academic essays. However, clearly you can't use connectors such as those above if your current paragraph is critiquing or standing in contrast to the preceding one. So, here are some illustrative connectors for the first sentence of a paragraph that disagrees with the previous one(s):

- *While X emphasised [...] Y emphasised...*
- *However, Y disputes X's argument that [...], instead suggesting that...*
- *Z offers an interpretation that differs from that of both X and Y. While X focused on [...] and Y emphasised [...], Z explains [...] in terms of...*

Let's consider how this looks within the structure of an essay:

Paragraph making a particular point *<For example, Skinner's ideas regarding language acquisition being explainable in terms of operant conditioning.>*

While Skinner emphasised the role of the environment, specifically the importance of environmental re-enforcement of language attempts, Chomsky explained language acquisition in terms of an innate language acquisition device. For Chomsky... *<The paragraph develops Chomsky's language acquisition device and contrasts its emphasis on the innate propensities of the language learner with Skinner's emphasis on environmental re-enforcement.>*

Why does it matter? It matters because:

This not only conveys the author's sense of how the ideas interrelate, it also demonstrates the critical ability to examine an issue – in this case, language acquisition – from different perspectives. This writing helps to convey that the author has understood something of the debate between perspectives that they are drawing on.

Complexity

Let's be honest, it is easier and more straightforward to link paragraphs when the current paragraph agrees with your previous one(s), or when it starkly contrasts with what has gone before. However, sometimes the relationship is more complex, with the ideas to be addressed in your current paragraph *partly endorsing and partly disputing* previous arguments that your essay has addressed. But here is the incentive for working on this tricky connection task: if you can do it, your essay will start to sparkle like a diamond in the sunshine. When you read an essay that accurately depicts the complexity of how the ideas being raised relate to those already addressed you think: '*Wow! This author knows what they are talking about.*' So here are some illustrative connectors for the first sentence of a paragraph that partly agrees and partly disagrees with the previous perspectives addressed in your essay:

- *While Y endorses X's notion of [...], they critique the emphasis on...*
- *Y endorses X to a point, agreeing that[...], but whereas X emphasises [...], Y by contrast focuses on...*
- *Y's research provides partial support for X's notion of...*
- *Y's interpretation of X's work concurs in terms of [...], but differs in that Y, in contrast to X, argues that...*
- *Z's research shares certain seemingly contradictory features found in the work of both X and Y...*

Let's consider how this looks within the structure of an essay:

Paragraph making a particular point *<For example, Chomsky's approach to language acquisition, having previously outlined Skinner's approach.>*

<u>While Skinner and Chomsky represent the two polar extremes of environmental determinism and innate capacity, Bruner's approach draws on the interplay of both person and environment in developing an interactional account of language acquisition...</u> *<The paragraph then outlines Bruner's approach to language acquisition paying attention to the ways in which it relates to the accounts offered by both Skinner and Chomsky.>*

Why does it matter? It matters because:

It not only demonstrates a smooth interconnection between ideas, it also conveys a subtlety of thinking. This suggests that the author can grasp something of the complex way in which ideas interrelate, which can go beyond mere concurrence or disagreement. Grasping these subtleties gives a scholarly feel to the writing.

STOP AND THINK
Organising your ideas

Never mind linking phrases, what if my ideas are all jumbled?

It is a really difficult task to read ideas, understand them, express them accurately and introduce relevant evaluation all within a well-structured, smoothly interconnected essay. If you want to make it even more difficult for yourself, try doing so without an essay plan and without a draft of your essay.

To help with the complex multifaceted nature of the essay writing task, it is a good idea to separate out the task of identifying the ideas that you want to address in your essay from organising the structure of your essay. Putting down the points to be made in your essay first of all, without worrying about connections, can then let you consider the different ways of ordering those points more carefully.

You will want to form paragraphs that cohere in making a point. This might be describing an empirical investigation, outlining a theoretical approach, evaluating ideas and interpretations or some combination of these. Once you have a sense of what each paragraph is trying to say, you can look again at how they relate to each other.

Carefully considering what order works for the smooth interconnection of ideas, you might, for example, place your paragraphs which outline different perspectives at an earlier point in your essay than your paragraph critiquing these perspectives. Similarly, if you outline an approach (which is relevant to the essay title) that poses a radical rethink of most of the research in the area, then it would probably work best later in your essay. Take time to think about the order – and don't be afraid to try out alternatives.

Connecting ideas within paragraphs

Table 5.3 demonstrates how paragraphs in the main body of your essay can be more clearly structured. (Chapters 3 and 8 address introductions and conclusions, respectively.) The table distinguishes three broad types of paragraph (or passages within paragraphs): those that are primarily focused on describing experiments (that is, empirical description), those outlining theory and those raising critically evaluative points. Let us assume that the essay title is one that we used earlier in this chapter: 'Evaluate Milgram's idea that obedience to authority is best understood as due to a shift in agentic state'.

Using your imagination

It can be helpful to imagine that the ideas that you are to include in your essay are people and that they have been invited to some sort of party – admittedly a slightly stilted and unusual one. For example, you might have invited Skinner, Chomsky and Bruner to your language acquisition party. First, think about what would be the key idea or point that they would each want to get across. In a speech bubble, imagine what Skinner wants to say about his ideas, and then do the same for Chomsky and Bruner. It can be useful to do this exercise even when you feel you haven't read all that you need to. Get the party (and the debate) started and then bring in relevant literature and refine your points in the light of that.

(a) Articulating what psychologists have said about each other's ideas

Now – and this is the interesting bit – just bear in mind that these guests are really not the sort of people to just listen without comment to what the others have said. They will all have something to say about the others' ideas. Try to think what each guest would say to the others. You will find that it is easier to do this in some cases than in others. For example, Chomsky commented directly on Skinner's ideas about language acquisition, but Skinner did not comment on Bruner (who developed his ideas a number of years after Skinner). It is clearly good practice to note what one researcher has directly said about the perspective of others, so it is best to do that first.

What the guest at your party might say:

Chomsky: 'Skinner, you have completed ignored the innate capacity of the child to identify rules – such as grammar – from the language that they are exposed to.'

TABLE 5.3

Improving the structure of the main body of your essay

Original paragraph sample	What is wrong and how to improve it	Revised paragraph sample
Empirical description Each experiment involved three people. There were 24 variations. Experiment five was the new baseline. The confederate, the experimenter and the teacher. The teacher was the naïve or real participant. The experiment began when the naïve participant was apparently randomly allocated to be the teacher. The learner was then sat in a separate room and connected to electrodes. The teacher administered electric shocks to the learner. The teacher was in the same room as the experimenter. The learner was in a separate room. Each time that the learner…	*The sentences are very disconnected.* *Try to step back from the detail and think what it is that is important to convey. Don't worry, the paragraph is useful – but as a first draft. Now it needs editing (see Chapter 10 for more on editing your writing). Part of the trick is identifying the sort of information that might be useful later on (see Chapter 7 for more on effective description). It can help to first list the absolutely vital information and then to try different ways of combining it. Note how this consideration has informed the revised paragraph, with the reader being given a good sense of several key features of the experiment described.*	**Improved empirical description** Milgram undertook 24 variations of his obedience experiments. The baseline, which is focused on here (experiment five), entailed the participant being allocated to play the role of teacher, delivering electric shocks to the learner (who was a confederate of the experimenter). In this baseline experiment, the teacher and learner were in a separate room from the learner, who could be heard but not seen.
Theoretical outline Milgram interpreted his results in terms of the agentic state. Because of this, we obey those in authority. The agentic state argues that people no longer see themselves as being responsible for their actions. The agentic state means that we see ourselves as being responsible for following the authority figure's instructions. The opposite to the agentic state is the autonomous state. The autonomous state argues that we act as if we are responsible for our actions.	*The sentences are again disconnected.* *With theoretical detail it is useful to have the different points outlined in the original sample, but we need to conceptualise the material. This involves not only finding ways of summarising or pulling points together, but also considering ways of capturing the essence of the approach that will be useful later on, where we may contrast different approaches.* *In thinking about Milgram's approach, consider if there are ways of characterising it in relation to other approaches – perhaps one idea here is its intrapsychic focus, with its emphasis on processes within the head of the individual. This stands in contrast to approaches that consider the rhetorical aspects of obedience or the ideological justification of 'doing science'.*	**Improved theoretical outline** Milgram's interpretation of his findings focused on the effect that the authority figure had on the sense of agency – or agentic state – of the subordinate. This approach suggests that within an authority–subordinate environment, a person in the subordinate position may shift from being in a self-directed *autonomous state* to an *agentic state*. Milgram characterised the agentic state as a condition in which the individual no longer feels responsibility for their own actions, but rather for following the instructions given by an authority figure.
Critical evaluation Milgram's experiment can be criticised for not being realistic. It should have been conducted on females also. Also, Reicher and Haslam saw the intergroup processes as explaining the results. Gibson argued it was rhetoric. Russell said it was strain-reducing mechanisms, such as the ideology of science.	*These sentences are disjointed and touch on points like a butterfly, swiftly moving from flower to flower. What is needed here is the separation of different lines of critique – the material should not be compressed into one paragraph.* *To improve this super-condensed note form of potential critique, separate out the key points to be developed:* • *A methodological critique (check for accuracy, for example, Milgram's experiment number eight involved female participants).* • *Reicher and Haslam's (2011) intergroup critique.* • *Gibson's (2013) rhetorical critique.* • *Russell's (2011) reference to strain-reducing mechanisms and specific reference to the ideology of science.* *In the context of the essay question (and depending on the length – here, let's assume a length of approximately 1000–2000 words), one might expect to give a paragraph to each of these points.*	**Improved critical evaluation** While Milgram emphasised an intrapsychic shift concerning the individual's sense of agency, Reicher and Haslam (2011) developed an approach that examined how the social, or group identities, of participants shaped the results. Noting the different levels of obedience across Milgram's conditions, Reicher and Haslam (2011) considered how differences in group identities could explain this variation. <After this perspective has been outlined, others can be introduced as separate (but interrelated) paragraphs.> For example: *In contrast to both Milgram's emphasis on agentic state and Reicher and Haslam's social identity account, Gibson develops a perspective that moves the focus from intrapsychic phenomenon, such as agency and identity, to rhetoric in interaction.>*

How you could word this within the context of an academic essay:

From Chomsky's perspective, Skinner has focused on re-enforcement to the exclusion of alternative understandings that may better fit the observable facts of child language acquisition. *<The essay could then go on to outline Chomsky's contrasting perspective.>* For Chomsky, the data suggest that children have an innate capacity to detect regularities or rules of languages which they are exposed to and to use those patterns in their production and comprehension of language. *<The essay might then detail and evaluate the evidence for Chomsky's perspective, for example, the occurrence or 'virtuous' or 'logical' grammatical errors as evidence for the acquisition of language rules.>*

(b) Articulating what *could be said* from the perspective of one psychologist

In addition to voicing what different psychologists have said about each other's ideas, it is also useful to be able to occupy the point of view of your different psychologist guests and to think *from their perspective*. So, to illustrate this idea in practice, you could think about how, from Skinner's operant conditioning perspective, comments could be made about Bruner's emphasis on the scaffolding of language. Note that, in the essay version (in the second paragraph below), some of the language that is used (which is underlined) makes it clear that the author is not saying that Skinner made these claims, but rather that this is a critique that could be developed from Skinner's perspective.

What the guest at your party might say:

Skinner: 'Your emphasis on scaffolding is good. But it is good because it echoes exactly the point that I have been making – that the environment shapes and facilitates language development. If we were to look at the detailed mechanism of scaffolding, we would find that there is, in essence, a reward in terms of attention and tone of voice from the parent to the child for their attempts at language, and particular praise for the best attempts that the child produces. These are the principles of operant conditioning that I outlined.'

How you could word this within the context of an academic essay:

From the perspective of operant conditioning, some of the features found in Bruner's approach can be seen as echoing the very concern with the role of the environment that Skinner emphasised. Indeed, the similarity may run deeper. Bruner's emphasis on the scaffolding of language could – at least in part – be seen as involving certain operant conditioning mechanisms, with positive, child-focused responses to imperfect attempts by the child providing rewards that encourage further and more accurate language production on the part of the child… *<To develop this point, it might be worth considering counter-arguments, such as some of the important ways in which Bruner's work differs from that of Skinner. Being able to adopt different perspectives like this reveals a sophisticated understanding, and citing relevant literature to support this would be great.>*

(c) Articulating the counter-arguments that psychologists have raised or could raise

You can imagine that there may be some tension in your party. If Skinner starts trying to claim that key features of Bruner's ideas merely echo Skinner's own original concept of language acquisition Bruner might counter-argue as illustrated below. Again, note the text underlined in the essay version and see how this handles the ideas in a smooth and interconnected way:

What the guest at your party might say:

Bruner: 'You have created a false characterisation of my approach. I avoid the extremes of your myopic focus on the environment alone and Chomsky's attention to the child without regard for a supportive language environment. My whole approach and my specific reference to scaffolding argue that language acquisition is a genuinely interactive phenomenon arising from the interaction between the child and their language environment. Both elements (child and environment) are important and the interaction between them is key.'

How you can word this within the context of an academic essay:

However, for Bruner scaffolding depicts a mechanism that is quite distinct from and not reducible to the principles of operant conditioning. From Bruner's perspective, scaffolding forms part of his articulation of a genuine interaction between the environment and the child in facilitating language acquisition and avoiding the narrowly focused emphasis on either the environment or the child, which typifies the work of Skinner and Chomsky respectively. *<The essay could now detail Bruner's perspective and evaluate the relevant evidence pertaining to it.>*

EXERCISE
The psychologists' party

Think of the essay that you are working on. Now write out a guest list of the psychologists who really need to be at this party. This might include some whose work is the focal point of the essay title and others who have perhaps developed contrasting perspectives.

The party might be a little bit awkward given that the guests don't all agree with each other, but what would they say, first, about their own take on the essay title and, second, on each other's ideas?

Treating your essay like this can be a great way of focusing on the key debates and making it easier to get started with your essay. You can start to do this task even if you feel you have no time, energy or inclination because you don't need to wait until you have read or thought more in the topic. Start now and fill in further details later.

Troubleshooting some common problems

Here some sample responses to frequently asked questions about essay writing are outlined. These questions pick up on some of the ideas developed throughout this chapter.

How to interconnect
Issue:

I understand the idea of using linking phrases, but I still can't interconnect the ideas I want to include in my essay.

Response:

That concern is probably a good thing. It shows that you are aware that it's no good just pasting in connectors without thinking about the material that you are covering. Smoothly interconnecting involves this bouncing between finding the best connecting words to use and looking at the ideas to be covered in your essay, and asking of them how they connect. In this way, our thinking informs our writing and our writing informs our thinking.

How to structure

Issue:

I haven't yet mapped out the structure of my essay. I do not know the order in which I should cover the different things I need to write in my essay.

Response:

Try to identify the different points that are to be made. Think of the ideas and people that you refer to as being in a room together. Imagine that they have a few seconds to summarise their point. What do you hear them say? Treat this task – of identifying points – as a separate process from arranging the points, drafting your essay and then editing your essay.

How to link ideas

Issue:

I know some of the points that I need to make in my essay, but how do they link?

Response:

That is a great question. The skill here is using that question to unlock the interrelationship between the ideas that you refer to.

Issue:

That sounds a bit vague. Can you give an example?

Response:

If you had Skinner and Chomsky in the room together talking about language acquisition, it is easy to imagine that Chomsky wouldn't simply describe his approach, but rather he would say something about how his ideas differ from Skinner's ideas. In your essay, this may mean that you use a connecting phrase such as:

'In contrast to Skinner's emphasis on the way in which environmental reinforcers lead to the development of language, Chomsky emphasised our innate capacity to detect the rules that govern the language that we are exposed to.'

Like all of the examples given in this chapter, this isn't 'the right' form of words. Different ways of expressing this can, and should, be used. Essay writing and interconnecting your ideas is a genuinely creative and stimulating activity.

How to connect complex paragraphs

Issue:

I want to connect my paragraphs, but the paragraphs I am trying to connect are saying different things.

Response:

Try to identify the ways in which they differ. Think of how you can characterise the key point of each paragraph and the key differences between them. If the paragraphs are making several points, ask yourself what is the key purpose of the paragraph within the context of this essay? Make sure that each paragraph clearly and coherently fulfils its own unique key purpose (e.g. outlining a theoretical approach or examining critiques of that approach).

How to structure each paragraph

Issue:

I want to connect my ideas within my paragraph, but I don't know how best to arrange them.

Response:

Try to see each paragraph as doing a specific job in your essay. The introduction needs to address the question and outline the direction of your essay (see Chapter 3), the conclusion needs to conceptualise the key issues at the heart of the essay (see Chapter 8), but the paragraphs in the main body of your essay are also doing specific jobs relating to the essay title. One paragraph might be outlining empirical evidence in support of a theoretical perspective, another might be introducing an alternative way of making sense of that evidence, yet another might be critiquing the methodological approach used in the key experiment, or experiments, referred to. Once you have decided on the key point that the paragraph is making, it can be easier to structure the paragraph to make that point effectively.

In essence: Think of the reader and think like a writer

Many different ideas to help you to interconnect your essay have been addressed in this chapter. These are like different keys that can help to unlock your various interconnection issues, such as: identifying problems, fixing issues within paragraphs and fixing issues between paragraphs. However, there is also a magic key that can help you. Much of what goes into making smooth interconnected writing comes down to being able to adopt the perspective of the reader, who comes to your essay trying to see into your understanding of the essay topic through the imperfect window of your essay. If you can start to think about *how the reader experiences your essay*, you really do hold the magic key – and you are already well on your way to genuinely interconnecting your work. This is done both in terms of how you structure your material within each paragraph and the order in which you position each paragraph. It is also achieved through the phrases and sentences that you use to connect your ideas throughout the essay – expressions that indicate not only clear-cut relationships of agreement and disagreement, but also far more subtle ones.

Alongside this concept, as a twin pillar of smooth, interconnected writing, is the idea that you should *think like a writer*. This is true when you are reading – look not only for content (though, of course, that is often crucial) but also at the way in which the material is connected and how the author displays their grasp of these interconnections. Thinking like a writer is also an injunction to see writing and thinking as intimately and productively bound together. Our very best writing entails not only putting down what we think and understand, but also struggling with those ideas – letting our writing raise questions for us about how ideas relate to each other and then letting that thinking revise and refine what we express in our words. This might not be as simple and mechanical a task as we might sometimes want it to be, but it becomes as creative and intellectually satisfying an activity as we could hope for.

REFLECTING ON THE CHAPTER:
Smooth interconnection is like music to the marker's ears

Some people really do like music that has no predictable structure at all, but across all forms of music (apart from atonal music itself) there is some sort of structure. The tunes we listen to might be innovative and unusual, but in the end they typically make some sort of sense, and the ones we like best are somehow satisfying. Reading a good essay brings to the reader a similar sense of having been taken through a sequence (in this case a sequence of ideas) that is somehow satisfying. Your essay can do a lovely thing – it can make the reader sigh with contentment. And structure is the key to making that happen. You don't need to master anything as complex and intricate as music theory to achieve this; just take your essay and look at the connection across paragraphs and the coherence within paragraphs. Using the ideas in this chapter to make each paragraph coherent in itself and connected to each other will sometimes throw up issues we need to think about: 'Do these authors agree or disagree?' or 'How can I best depict the partial agreement and disagreement between these ideas?' But these questions then inform our writing, taking it deeper and making it smoother. Use the guidance in this chapter and you will almost hear the sigh of delight from your reader.

TAKE AWAY POINTS FROM THIS CHAPTER

- Separate out the task of identifying the points you need to make from thinking about the order in which they should occur.
- Think of each paragraph as doing a specific job in your essay – for example, detailing empirical work, outlining a theoretical approach or identifying a contrasting approach to the essay topic. Check that your paragraphs do this job with clarity and coherence.

- Look at the first (or connecting) sentence of the paragraphs in the main body of your essay – try to make each one of them communicate your understanding of how the current paragraph relates to the previous one(s).

- Scan through your essay and consider whether there is a better, more logical order in which this material could be placed – if so, change the order.

- Check your essay and ask yourself: if your paragraphs were shuffled around, could someone put them back in the right order? If not, then check the order of your paragraphs and the clarity of your connecting sentences.

LINKING TO OTHER CHAPTERS

Interconection is so absolutely vital to writing a briliant essay that it links to nearly every other chapter in this book. Some of the key links are detailed here so that you can deepen your understanding and sharpen your skills in this most crucial area. The statement of intent in your introduction is absolutely key to giving your reader a sense of clear structure from the very first paragraph, and further guidance on this can be found in Chapter 3. Your concluding paragraph can accomplish a more conceptual, overarching sense of struture for your essay and Chapter 8 can support you in developing a genuinely powerful concluding paragraph. A key focus within this chapter concerned how you can most effectively express the relationship between different ideas across paragraphs, Chapter 6 addresses this issue, as the essence of critical evaluation is the relation of one idea to another. Cohesion within paragraphs and descriptive writing, is an important aspect of interconnection and this is addressed in detail in Chapter 7, which provides guidance on sharpening this neglected aspect of great academic writing. Developing a great structure has to be done with one thought above all else in your head: 'the essay title'. Making sure that your struture really stays completely and fully relevant for the specific essay title is covered in further detail in Chapter 4. Finally, one of the straightforward and amazingly effective things you can do in reviewing and editing your essay is to look at your structure. Chapter 10 provides guidance on how to do exactly that. Structure really is like magic fairy dust – if you can bring structure to your essay, then before you can even say 'abracadabra!', your essay has magically transformed into something beautiful.

Chapter 6

Keep it critical – how to develop your critical evaluation

In this chapter you will learn…

- How to understand what critical evaluation is
- How to feel empowered to actually do critical evaluation
- How to plan your essay to make it more critically evaluative
- How to develop critical evaluation even when you cannot find any
- How to build and use critically evaluative ideas in your essay
- How to find the language for critical evaluation
- How to review your essay to maximise its critical evaluation

CRITICAL EVALUATION: WHAT IT IS AND WHY IT MATTERS

Writing an essay that will be graded can be a risky business. It can feel reasonably safe describing what others have said, as you can fact-check your statements against your notes and textbooks. But how can you 'evaluate' what these famous psychologists have said? What does this evaluation even look like? How are you supposed to 'evaluate' when you are told not to put your own opinion into your essays? When you are told to 'critically evaluate' is it the same as 'criticising'?

There is a secret about critical evaluation that you might not be aware of. Should I even let you know this secret? OK, I'll risk it, but I'll just whisper. Here it is: *you can do it*. Students sometimes think that critical evaluation is a knack that they somehow haven't got, but I think you really can start to do it now. How 'now' do I mean? This very moment – try the next exercise.

EXERCISE
Critical evaluation is a little bit easier than I realised

Here are your ingredients:

Perspective one: Kelley (1967) argued that when we make an attribution (find a cause of something we are trying to explain) we use a rational process.

Perspective two: Ross (1977) argued that we are biased towards making internal – person-blaming – attributions, which Ross referred to as the 'fundamental attribution error'.

Now write a sentence that captures how Ross's perspective differs from that of Kelley. Here is how it might start:

In contrast to Kelley's (1967) rational account of our attribution process, Ross (1977) argued that...

Critical evaluation is just the ability to write sentences like that. It is the capacity to bring one perspective to another. In this case, it is contrasting one specific, named perspective with another specific, named perspective.

In order to unlock the secret power of critical evaluation in your essays it is worth noting that critical evaluation is probably a bit broader than you may realise. Which of these do you think demonstrates critically evaluative thinking?

a. X's methodological approach was questioned by Y…
b. X's theory was endorsed by Y…
c. X's approach could be criticised on the basis that it…
d. X's approach could be seen as depicting our thinking as…
e. All of the above.

I don't want to sway you too much, but I really think it is 'e' – all of the above. 'a' looks like indisputable critical evaluation, citing another psychologist, 'Y', to challenge the work of 'X'. But even when we cite other perspectives that support the work we have previously referred to (see 'b'), that is still an evaluation, albeit a positive evaluation.

We can take this further. Is it still evaluation if we do not have a name to refer to (see 'c')? Yes, it is. This is still bringing thoughts from another perspective to bear on the work of X. True, if we can cite sources who have made this point, that would be even stronger, but making the critique in itself is valuable. More controversially, I would argue that even 'd' is evaluation and that it can actually be among the best evaluation that we might produce. 'd' conceptualises the target of our evaluation (X). This would be even stronger if it was followed with some contrasting conceptualisations that depict our thinking in different ways. The next exercise illustrates this further.

EXERCISE
What is critical evaluation?

Take a moment to come up with your own definition of what you think critical evaluation is – just the first thing that pops in your head.

Critical evaluation is...

Now try to think of all of the different situations where you have used this skill. You can include academic writing of course, but try to think of other contexts also.

I have used critical evaluation when I...

UNDERSTANDING WHAT CRITICAL EVALUATION IS

If you have read the preceding pages, you should have a snapshot picture of what critical evaluation is and, most importantly, a sense that you can develop this skill. But let's dig deeper into this idea of critical evaluation. As we get a sharper sense of it, we will be further empowered to actually put it into practice.

There is a danger that academics can act like wizards. This often involves taking words that are familiar (we've all heard of 'critical' and 'evaluation') and putting them together in slightly strange and unexpected ways ('critical evaluation'). This particular form of alchemy makes sense at one level – for example, it can try to specify a special type of evaluation or a particular purpose for the critique – but it has a downside. When a much less familiar technical term is used, for example, 'redaction criticism' or 'form criticism', then coming to it as a student we could learn it as a new concept, without all of the baggage of partial familiarity. But 'critical evaluation' sounds half-familiar. It brings to mind 'criticising' and 'evaluating', so we have a fuzzy sense that it probably involves pointing out all of the problems with an idea or piece of research. It is actually quite tricky to move past our own existing associations with the words so that we can really hear what is actually meant by 'critical evaluation'.

A useful way of thinking about critical evaluation is to use the idea of perspective. You might recall that in Piaget and Inhelder's (1956) famous 'Three Mountains' experiment, Piaget was interested in whether children could mentally adopt the perspective of someone looking at a model of a mountain from a different visual perspective (for example, standing on the opposite side of the model mountains). To succeed at Piaget and Inhelder's Three Mountains experiment, children needed to be able to think about how the model mountain looked, not just from where they themselves were standing, but from – literally – *other points of view*. When we are really engaging in 'critical evaluation' we are looking at, or thinking and writing about, ideas and empirical research from different perspectives. It is that amazingly useful skill that is at work.

Right now, you might be thinking: 'Is it such a big deal?', '*Why* is it such a big deal?' and '"*Amazingly useful*"? – really?'

'Critical evaluation'? Sounds familiar

You may find that critical evaluation is often referred to in an academic context. Here are some of the places where you are likely to come across it in relation to essay writing:

Essay titles – often your essay title will explicitly ask you to 'evaluate', for example, 'Outline and evaluate…' or it may use some other form to explicitly request critical evaluation. Even when there is no specific request for you to do so, it is usually – unless otherwise guided – relevant to evaluate in most forms of academic writing. You are quite likely to encounter essay titles such as:

'Evolutionary Psychology provides the best explanation for understanding human attraction. *Critically discuss* this assertion in the light of relevant evidence.'

'*Critically evaluate* the evidence for the functional-network account of cognition.'

'*Evaluate* the idea that self can best be thought of as a discursive achievement.'

'*Critically review* the evidence for the Big Five personality dimensions.'

Look through *your* assignment titles and see if there are explicit requirements to critically evaluate.

Essay guidance – where essay guidance is provided, it will often refer to the need to go beyond merely describing and to 'evaluate', 'contrast perspectives', 'critically evaluate' or 'critically discuss' ideas and findings that are relevant to the essay title. The guidance might also indicate that consistent, relevant evaluation is a key feature of a strong essay.

Marking criteria – you may or may not actually see the marking criteria for your assignments, but they will guide markers as to what they should look for and how this will relate to grades. Critical evaluation is typically explicitly associated with essays that should be awarded higher grades, often being *the* key feature that distinguishes stronger from weaker essay answers. Markers will usually be made aware that they should reward students who demonstrate the ability not just to *describe* relevant ideas and research findings, but also to *evaluate* them.

Grade templates/guides – you might see an outline of the characteristics of essays that are awarded different grades, or 'what you need to do' to achieve specific grade categories. Critical evaluation is usually one of the key criteria you will find in the essays that receive a higher grade.

Essay rubrics – rubrics, which identify relevant features of an essay, often as scalable criteria along which an essay might be judged, will typically feature critical evaluation in some form as one of the major criteria along which the essay is judged.

Essay feedback – this will very often refer to the presence – and the absence – of critical evaluation in an essay. Note that for a moment, even when critical evaluation is not present in an essay it is likely to be mentioned in feedback as a feature that is expected to be present in most academic writing. In this way, we can't avoid the issue of critical evaluation; it is no use kidding ourselves that if we are not confident with critical evaluation, we should leave it to one side. Our essays will be judged on the criterion of critical evaluation whether we do it well, badly or leave it out altogether. The issue of feedback is addressed in more detail below.

The amazing skill of critical evaluation

There are many different manifestations of critical evaluation. At its broadest, it can include all of the aspects of being able to see things from different perspectives and asking questions from those perspectives. Doing this – in admittedly very different ways – across different contexts has an importance and relevance that we might not immediately expect. A few examples are listed here, but you will be able to add to and amend these.

LEARN
Manifestations of critical evaluation

'Fake' news

It's a cliché to say that we live in a complex world of information overload, but there is some truth there. We also live in a world of contested claims, where one side will argue that the other is uninformed, selective with the truth or deliberately misleading, and we are stuck with competing and incompatible claims. Being able to look at the evidence from different perspectives, and interrogating it, might not solve this dilemma, but it can certainly help – if only to identify what we do not know and what is difficult to ascertain.

(Continued)

Democracy

The capacity to question power, those in power, those who seek to use power, and institutional processes that establish, exercise and maintain power, is incredibly important. The skill of being able to ask questions and to hold power to account isn't one that we can simply let others do for us, but is the very means through which social progress is made. Think through history about how adopting a different perspective and raising questions from those perspectives has been core to the abolitionist, suffragist, civil rights, anti-apartheid and LGBTQ movements.

Relationships

How many times in relationships do issues arise from a failure to be able to see things from the other person's point of view? While it is best not seen in isolation from other aspects of a relationship, think how transformative it is to be able to really think how things are for the other and the impact that such thinking can have on the relationship.

Decisions

How do you decide where to go and how to get there or what to buy, from where and when? There are lots of sources of information we can turn to but, used uncritically, they might not help us make the right decision. Perhaps, like me, despite the information available, you sometimes find yourself making a decision that you subsequently regret. An (admittedly trivial) one of mine involved buying the largest paddling pool I had ever seen, so large that it took days to fill with water and covered most of the garden. If only I had thought about this purchase from different perspectives rather just followed some mad impulse not to be outbid. You can avoid bidding for outsized water-based fun items like this by bringing that capacity to think from a different perspective into your decisions.

Consuming and communicating information

More generally, critical evaluation is a skill that is relevant for (almost) all times when we are taking in or or giving out information. Being critically evaluative means being more able to see things from different points of view, and consequently to be more aware of alternatives. To really appreciate this, imagine the opposite – for example, a person who uncritically believes everything they come across (perhaps online, or from a favourite media source). We would see them as gullible and not intelligently engaging with information. We might wish that such people would think for themselves, weigh up the evidence and consider a different point of view. We can wish the same for ourselves too whenever we are aware of our own uncritical consumption (reading, hearing, watching) and communication (speaking, writing) of information. Maybe we too can relate intelligently to the information that we encounter and the information that we refer to. Critical evaluation is that very process of relating to information (or what purports to be information) in an intelligent way.

The importance of critical evaluation in your writing

As we have seen in other chapters in this book, academic essay writing is much more than an information dump from writer to reader. Instead, a strong essay conveys to the reader a way of making sense of all of the conflicting information, debates and diverse perspectives that are relevant to the essay title. The strong essay demonstrates an understanding of different relevant perspectives and an awareness of the questions and implications that these perspectives raise for thinking about the target issue. Such an essay is like the gift of clarity, from the writer to the reader. What a lovely present!

Critical evaluation is the key facet of writing academic essays that most easily distinguishes 'mediocre' essays from 'good' ones. While the mediocre essay typically reports potentially relevant facts, the good essay is critically evaluative; it conveys the writer's *thinking about the issues* that the title raises. The person reading and marking a critically evaluative essay gets a sense that they are not being given a load of facts – we can find that almost everywhere anyway. Rather, they are being shown ways of making sense of the target issue(s) from different perspectives.

These lovely-to-read essays don't lazily leave the business of finding coherence and order to the poor reader – that's like inviting someone around to your place and expecting them to tidy up while you relax. My own experience suggests that this domestic arrangement seldom works out. Instead, the critically evaluative essay shows how ideas cohere around different perspectives and draws out what these perspectives have to say in terms of the issues identified in the essay title.

ACE YOUR ASSIGNMENT
Your chance to shine!

Try to look at your essay as a series of opportunities to do the thing that markers really want you to do – that is, to demonstrate intelligent, scholarly thinking about the issue(s) identified in the essay title. Critical evaluation is a major component of this. By bringing critical evaluation into your entire essay, you are sprinkling it with gold-dust or, if you prefer something with fewer flowery metaphors, you are giving the reader the scholarly, intelligent writing they are hoping to see.

GOOD AND BAD CRITICAL EVALUATION

Getting fired up with a desire to 'do' critical evaluation in our essays is great. But because critical evaluation is *so* important, it is worth getting it right. To get a clear sense of what we are aiming for, let's contrast some examples of good and bad critical evaluation.

Imagine that your essay title is the following:

'Outline and evaluate Latané and Darley's (1970) concept of the bystander effect as an explanation for the absence of prosocial behaviour in particular circumstances.'

Now let's assume that you are marking two essays and you come to a passage, roughly 90 words in length, where the same information is drawn on. *The paragraph occurs just after evidence for Latané and Darley's idea of the bystander effect has been presented*. It is worth noting that the paragraph *refers to a different perspective that is relevant for evaluating Latané and Darley's concept of the bystander effect.*

As you look at these two essay snippets, ask yourself the following:

1.   Which one of these conveys – even in these few words – a sense of critical evaluation and which one fails to do so?
2.   In the critically evaluative essay snippet, can you circle the words that really make the difference? What are these words doing? What do they show you, the marker, about the author's thinking?

Essay one

Latané and Darley's emphasis on the potency of the situation for determining behaviour has been challenged by work that has argued that stable personality traits are far more likely to determine behaviour than situational circumstances. Jayawickreme, Meindl, Helzer, Furr and Fleeson (2014) argue that it is *internal* individual difference – in terms of what they refer to as 'virtuous' personality traits – that account for whether or not someone engages in helping behaviour, not the external contingencies, such as whether or not other potential helpers are perceived as being present.

Essay two

Jayawickreme, Meindl, Helzer, Furr and Fleeson (2014) argue that individuals differ in terms of personality traits, some of which remain stable across situations. An individual's stable personality traits will result in their acting in a consistent manner even though their external circumstances may be different. Individuals who are high on what Jayawickreme et al. (2014) refer to as 'virtuous' personality traits are more likely to engage in helping, or prosocial, behaviour. By contrast, individuals who are lower in such 'virtuous' traits are less likely to exhibit prosocial, or helping, behaviour.

The verdict

What is your verdict having read these two samples? You may find it worth reading them through more than once, perhaps switching the order as you do so. There are lots of issues that could be focused on, including the inter- and intra-paragraph structure (Chapter 5) and orientation to the essay title (Chapter 4), but here the focus is on the extent to which the paragraph demonstrates meaningful critical evaluation. To help think our way into this, below is an essay marker's take on the two paragraphs. Let's take them in reverse order.

Essay two

Jayawickreme, Meindl, Helzer, Furr and Fleeson (2014) argue that individuals differ in terms of personality traits, some of which remain stable across situations. *<So what? This might be relevant to the essay title, but the writer isn't showing me **how** it is relevant. This seems like a list which is unconnected to previous material (remember this passage comes 'just after evidence for the bystander effect has been presented'). There is no sense of how this perspective relates*

to – challenging or supporting – previous ideas in this essay.> An individual's stable personality traits will result in their acting in a consistent manner even though their external circumstances may be different. Individuals who are high on what Jayawickreme et al. (2014) refer to as 'virtuous' personality traits are more likely to engage in helping, or prosocial, behaviour. By contrast, individuals who are lower in such 'virtuous' traits are less likely to exhibit prosocial, or helping, behaviour. *<How frustrating! All of the ideas are here to make a great critically evaluative point, but the author is not connecting one idea to another. By commenting on one idea from the perspective of another (bringing it to bear on the other), real, joyful critical evaluation is present. This was so close – how depressing, I need a cup of tea.>*

Essay one

Latané and Darley's emphasis on the potency of the situation for determining behaviour has been challenged by work that has argued that stable personality traits are far more likely to determine behaviour than situational circumstances. *<Ah! There is a real sense of debate here – the writer has shown how this paragraph relates to (specifically, contrasts with) ideas touched on earlier in the essay and identified as key in the essay title. This sense of debate gives me a warm glow inside.>* Jayawickreme, Meindl, Helzer, Furr and Fleeson (2014) argue that it is *internal* individual difference – in terms of what they refer to as 'virtuous' personality traits – that account for whether or not someone engages in helping behaviour, not the external contingencies such as whether or not other potential helpers are perceived as being present. *<This is great! Here there is a more focused identification of how this clash between an emphasis on personality traits and situational determinants of behaviour relates to the specifics of the essay title, concerning the bystander effect. What a wonderful world this is!>*

ACE YOUR ASSIGNMENT
Interrogate your ideas

Writing and thinking really do develop best in tandem. Ask questions of the ideas that are in your essay: How do they relate? What is at the heart of the differences? How can they be characterised? When your writing gets tricky, questioning your ideas in this way is invaluable, so don't be afraid to start interrogating them. Doing so can then give depth to your writing as you return to it. Allow yourself to move from thinking to writing to thinking in a creative way – getting deeper each time.

TRANSFORMING YOUR CRITICAL EVALUATION

If you find that critical evaluation doesn't simply flow from your fingertips, then join the (extremely large and always open to new members) club! Most us have to work at evaluation in our writing, and sometimes it can be quite a struggle. But here's the thing, you *can* strengthen your critical evaluation and you often experience a struggle on the threshold of a really excellent point.

EXERCISE
The psychologists' party

It can be tricky to get at the core debates that are relevant to your essay and even more of a challenge to conceptualise your material. These ideas can help:

1. Use drawings of different psychologists who are relevant for your essay. You may find that it makes sense to adopt perspectives (for example, social identity theory) rather than named individual psychologists in some cases, or you might use a combination of names and perspectives (for example, Zimbardo versus social identity theory). Make speech bubbles and see what they say about their own ideas and each other's ideas.

2. Pay particular attention to both: (a) the different evidence that these psychologists offer regarding the topic of your essay, and (b) the different ways in which the same evidence is interpreted by different psychologists.

3. Try to list points of agreement (between two or more perspectives) and points of debate.

4. Try to identify where there is a more complex relationship – where one perspective partly supports and partly challenges another. This is trickier to articulate than straightforward agreement and disagreement and tends to be found in the best essays.

Critical search strategy

If you like watching or reading about crime scene investigations or detectives, if you like solving puzzles or riddles, if you like games of tactics or strategy, and even if you don't like any of these, you can get a real buzz out of this. You have a challenge: to build critical evaluation into your essay. The clock is ticking, the hunt is on – can you find what you need to solve this challenge in time?

Start by using search tools to help develop your critical evaluation resources. Many search engines and databases will allow you not only to identify what other papers are cited in a specific publication, but also to find out who subsequently cites that very paper (see Chapter 9 for more on this). Using subsequent citation to inform your critical evaluation of a particular publication is an incredibly useful tool as it enables you to examine what other literature has to say about the publication that you are currently reading. While many citations will be relatively undeveloped (perhaps being one of a list of cited sources with little discussion), some will be much more developed and will identify how the subsequent author(s) makes sense of the paper which they cite.

These subsequent publications can enrich your essay with a scholarly awareness of what the published literature has to say about the paper that you are trying to evaluate. You may find that some of the subsequent publications offer support for the paper they are referring back to, perhaps providing fresh empirical evidence, or possibly extending the potential evidential basis for the ideas in the original publication. You may find instead that some subsequent publications critique the previous work, identifying methodological weaknesses, reporting contradictory findings or providing a different interpretation of findings or an alternative theoretical perspective.

Perhaps a useful caveat here is that some of the most well-known publications are inevitably the most widely cited, so some sensible parameters are needed when investigating the subsequent citation of papers that have received several thousand citations – your degree might be over by the time you turn to publication number 12,993.

Let's consider these two points in turn: *reading through your work* and *struggle as being potentially positive*. In regard to the first, you can strengthen your critical evaluation by editing your work with critical evaluation in mind. Try to read through your essay as if you are a marker who is almost obsessed with asking these sorts of questions:

- 'Where's the debate?'
- 'Is there a real sense of the different perspectives or the different ways of thinking about the issues that are relevant to the essay?'
- 'Is this writing just describing or does it demonstrate thinking about what is being discussed?'
- 'Is the thinking that is present academic, or merely the writer's own opinion?'

If you do not look through your essay with these sorts of questions in mind, you can be pretty sure that someone else will – *the person who marks your essay*.

Why leave it to your marker to read through your essay like this? If you would like to avoid higher marks and are keen to accumulate an impressive collection of critical feedback on your assignments, then sure, don't read through your essay in this way. For everyone else who would like to achieve better grades, looking at your work *like a marker will look at your work* will enable you to spot and improve on the very same issues that the marker themselves will otherwise identify as weaknesses in your essay.

In regard to the second point, can struggle really be positive? Yes, it can! The struggles that you experience are often an indication that you could be about to achieve a breakthrough in your understanding and writing. Please don't be put of by struggle in your writing – stay with it, work through it and reap the rewards.

STOP AND THINK
Using struggle productively

When we experience struggle in our writing, we are often on the cusp of a breakthrough. Try to treat that sense of struggle as a welcome guest, rather than eject it as if it were an unwelcome intruder.

The issue of struggle is relevant across several chapters in this book. For now let us consider the specific issue of struggles regarding how to find 'critical' points and what to do when we have them. Rather than doing what we all tend to do when we are struggling – run away, avoid or deny – you could work through your struggle to achieve a new understanding. The following thoughts might express our sense of struggle:

- What 'critical evaluation' can I develop in this part of my essay (or throughout my essay)?
- How can I make sense of the apparent contradiction between the different perspectives that I am drawing on?
- What can I do when one perspective does not simply agree or disagree with another? Can it still be used in developing a critique?

ACE YOUR ASSIGNMENT
Commit to critical evaluation

Get committed to critical evaluation as you are checking out sources and ideas for your essay and as you plan your essay. You can (and often should) add critical evaluation in a final edit, but give yourself the best chance by thinking about how you can build it in to your essay from the very beginning.

Bearing in mind the above discussion, look at the passage below (or, if you have an essay that you are soon to submit, turn to a page of that). It is probably best to focus on the main body of the essay for this exercise – that is, the sections between your introduction and conclusion. Critical evaluation is still important in our introductions and conclusion, but these sections do quite a specific job and are dealt with in detail in Chapters 3 and 8 respectively.

Imagine that you have the following essay title:

'Critically evaluate Kelley's Covariation Model of Causal Attribution.'

This essay title explicitly asks us to 'do' critical evaluation – but remember, critical evaluation should be the default position; we should always critically evaluate in our assignments unless particular pieces of work specifically ask us not to do so.

I could bore you, me, and anyone else passing by, with a 1000- or 2000-word essay response to this title, but life is short and it seems a bad idea. Besides which, someone skimming past Chapter 2 might wind up plagiarising it anyway. So let's zoom straight in on a section of the essay where our dear author is referring to work on attribution bias. Get yourself a comforting beverage (unless that breaches the terms and conditions of your current location) and look at this minor metamorphosis.

An important area within the field of attribution is that of attribution bias. One particularly prominent bias, associated with Ross (1977), is the Fundamental Attribution Error. Ross (1977) suggests that individuals making attributions tend to attribute the cause of the behaviour to be explained to factors within the person rather than to external factors.

EXERCISE
Remember to use the 'so what?' question

Right now, read the paragraph above and ask this simple but transformative question (which was introduced in Chapter 4): 'so what?'

Asking that question, did you get a clear and convincing answer from the paragraph? If not, then we need to fix the paragraph so that no reasonable reader who is aware of the essay title would ask 'so what?' again.

Let's consider the reader's stream of consciousness as they read this paragraph, given the essay title – 'Critically evaluate Kelley's Covariation Model of Causal Attribution.'

An important area within the field of attribution is that of attribution bias. *<Uh oh! Looks like a list is coming on. Why am I being told about attribution bias? Is the author of the essay doing this having thought about the issues, or simply because attribution bias was mentioned in the same lecture as Kelley?>* One particularly prominent bias, associated with Ross (1977), is the Fundamental Attribution Error. *<And this is relevant to thinking about Kelley because...?>* Ross (1977) suggests that individuals making attributions tend to attribute the cause of the behaviour to be explained to factors within the person rather than to external factors. *<Accurate, but what is this – build your own essay night? I can see how this could link to the essay title, but I do not know if the author of this essay can. As the author has not demonstrated an awareness of how the perspective of Ross relates to Kelley's Covariation Model, I have to assume that they do not have a strong grasp of the implications that Ross's work has for thinking about Kelley's model.>*

Are you ready for some writing magic?

Let's sprinkle some critical evaluation fairy-dust on this poor paragraph and see how it looks. To make the point a little more vividly, pretty much the same information will be used – it is the thinking, rather than the information that has been seriously upgraded. The reader's stream of consciousness is given below in italics;

Kelley's emphasis on causal attribution as being – potentially at least – a **rational** process, has been challenged by a range of research into attribution biases. *<Great, I like this! This communicates that the writer is about to refer to attribution bias and, most importantly, it tells me why they think that is relevant for this title. I will not be asking my favourite 'so what?' question.>* One exemplar of this work is research into the **Fundamental Attribution Error**. Developing this important area, Ross (1977) argues that rather than making a rational attribution informed by empirical evidence, individuals making attributions tend to attribute behaviour to factors **internal** to the individual actor rather than external to them. *<This author has demonstrated that they are aware of the perspective of Ross and touches on how it contrasts with the rational reasoning depicted in Kelley's Covariation Model of Causal Attribution.>* This perspective challenges Kelley's concept that we are – or can be – like naïve scientists in making attributions and that instead we often short-circuit Kelley's hypothesised causal reasoning process and default to a person-blaming (or person-attributing) account for someone's behaviour instead. *<This is really super – it has brought me joy just to read these fine words. Here the challenge that Ross's work potentially raises for Kelley's model has been developed more fully. It conveys a real sense of debate between the image of the causal reasoner that Kelly suggested and the one that is implied by Ross's work on the Fundamental Attribution Error.>*

HOW TO BUILD YOUR CRITICAL EVALUATION FROM THE START

We can start critical evaluation even before we feel that we have 'started writing' the essay. We do this by working from the title to think about how we might address it so as to maximise relevant critical evaluation. Notice that this involves actively looking for the opportunity to evaluate from the start, rather than dreading it, avoiding it and only slipping critical evaluation in because you feel you absolutely have to.

Your starting point

Chapter 2 deals with finding useful source material and Chapter 4 discusses how to make sure that you address the essay title, so for now let's focus on how we can ensure that we are alert to the possibility of critical evaluation from the very start of the essay.

When do you think you should start thinking about critical evaluation?

   a.   After you receive feedback on your essay.
   b.   When you are redrafting your essay for submission.
   c.   At those points where it comes up in the essay.
   d.   As you are drafting your essay.
   e.   From the moment you first see the title.

Well, most likely, you have guessed that the correct answer is (e), although, at least some of the time, you may act as if one of the other answers applies.

   a.   After you receive feedback on your essay.

       Do you think about critical evaluation mainly when the marker leaves some feedback comment about it? Feedback is considered later in this chapter, but for now we can note that we could bring that orientation to the marker to the very start of our essay writing, rather than wait for their comments as a sort of post-mortem on our submitted essay.

   b.   When you are redrafting your essay for submission.

       This has potential. Someone treating critical evaluation in this way is right in thinking that we should create an essay draft, read it through and edit it BEFORE submitting it.

They would also be quite insightful in recognising that when we read through a draft of our essay, we should think about how critically evaluative it is and consider how that might be enhanced. But it is best not to leave all of our critical evaluation to this late stage.

c.   At those points where it comes up in the essay.

This response shows an awareness that critical evaluation might be relevant at places throughout the essay. The only problem is that this is a little bit passive. It pays to be more proactive with something as important as critical evaluation: we should actively look for ways to bring it into our essay rather just wait for when the situation seems right.

d.   As you are drafting your essay.

This response demonstrates a sensitivity to the potential relevance of critical awareness throughout your essay. This approach is certainly to be encouraged, especially if a proactive stance is taken towards looking for ways of engaging in critical evaluation throughout the essay. However, we could go one step further still and think, as answer (e) indicates, about the ways in which we can switch to critical evaluation mode *from the very start*.

When you receive your essay title you can start to ask: What have different psychologists contributed to thinking about this issue and how do the ideas generated relate to each other? It is the process of bringing one idea or perspective to another that is at the heart of critical evaluation. Every time we draw on other viewpoints to question, challenge or confirm:

a methodological approach

a research finding

an interpretation of findings

a theoretical perspective

then we are engaged in critical evaluation. Remember, critical evaluation is the action of thinking of one argument in the light of another, which might be confirmatory, contradictory or a mixture of both.

Can we evaluate without a publication to back us up?

Often students have a point which might be a relevant critical evaluation of a methodology, or interpretation of findings, or a theoretical construct, but there seems to be no paper to back it up. All too many of these points are lost, like a sandcastle taken by the tide. But fear not – there are two key thoughts to bear in mind:

1.   Find relevant sources where you can.
2.   Make a relevant *argument* rather than airdrop an opinion.

Find relevant sources where you can

Imagine you are writing a developmental psychology essay and the well-known issue of language acquisition comes up. Your title is something like this:

> 'Critically evaluate behaviourist approaches to language acquisition in young children.'

After outlining Skinner's work, you start a paragraph on these lines:

> 'Skinner's work, however, could be challenged as it doesn't take into account logical or virtuous errors. Young children are often found to make errors that are understandable, such as adding an '-s' to a noun (such as sheep) or '-ed' to a verb such as 'run' when these words are exceptions to a prevalent rule in English. These 'errors' – of over-applied rules – suggest that in the process of language acquisition children are acquiring underlying grammatical rules rather than learning behaviour from whatever has been observed in the environment, or reinforced by adults (such as parents and teachers).

Do you sense that there is a name missing here? Poor old Noam Chomsky. Why did he get no credit for all of his ideas that are paraded in the above paragraph? The take home message here is simple: if you spot a critical point, well done, note it down straight away, but do be alert for those who may have made that point previously. Showing that awareness is part of good scholarly writing.

Make a relevant *argument* rather than airdrop an opinion

Imagine that your essay title is:

> 'Critically evaluate Moscovici's research into minority influence.'

Let's assume that you have some useful thoughts about this topic and your essay includes the following:

You are aware that a lot of the research into minority influence, including several experiments conducted by Moscovici, involved perceptual judgements. You know that in some experiments, for example, participants had to judge whether a slide they were shown was green or blue and researchers investigated how participants' responses were impacted by a majority, or a minority, of experimental confederates. You reflect on the idea that asking participants what colour a slide is might tell us how people are influenced in perceptual tasks, but it could be quite different if it is an issue that they care about. You consider that someone might be happy to start calling the blue slide green, but not to change their opinion about climate change.

That's a great start, but then another thought strikes you. Perhaps, you think, when 'real-world' issues are used to look at social influence (such as attitudes towards an important social issue) other problems arise. Some of the issues relevant to this essay might be more widely discussed, but maybe you spot something that is acknowledged rather less frequently. Perhaps, you think that the manipulation of majority and minority opinion in such research is problematic. Perhaps, for example, you read of experiments in which participants are informed that a majority (in one condition) or a minority (in another condition) of fellow students hold a particular attitude. In one experiment, this was attitudes about gay individuals being part of the US military. Participants were informed that either a minority, or a majority, were opposed to 'homosexuals being allowed to serve in the military'. In addition to ethical concerns about this experiment, you think that the participants might have their own stance regarding whether a majority or a minority of fellow students do actually hold such views. You may suspect that the manipulation of the minority/majority variable (simply telling participants that the view is held by a 'minority' in one condition and a 'majority' in another) is especially problematic when it comes to real life issues. For the sake of simplicity, let's look at what you can do with that second thought – that participants might have their own view as to whether or not a majority or minority of fellow students hold the attitude that they are being told about in the experiment. This point is not just a random observation, but is directly relevant (unless indicated otherwise by the essay guidance) because it evaluates research (which uses 'real world' attitudes) which itself raises methodological issues for some of Moscovici's key research centred on physical perception.

If you can't find a reference for a publication that develops this point you might:

a. Abandon it.
b. Airdrop it in like this: 'What I think is that this research has got problems too. Students are likely to know whether a majority or a minority of students hold a view on an important social issue.'
c. Develop it as an integrated argument, rather than a jarring 'opinion': 'While such research has arguably overcome the issue of the real-world applicability of perceptually-based experiments, it may have raised other potential problems. For example, it could be argued that when participants are informed that an attitudinal position is held by a majority or minority of other students in their university, they may well have their own stance on whether that is likely to be the case. In this way, the 'majority'/'minority' manipulation is compromised by the fact that participants may not take the experimental assertion of majority/minority prevalence at face value.'

Do you see how response (c) makes the point as a clear argument that shines a light on the research at hand. It brings a different perspective to bear on the research being considered – but it makes a skilful argument, rather than a 'you know what I think' type of assertion.

THINK
Your essay is more like a chemistry set than a jigsaw puzzle

When I was young, I got several chemistry sets as presents. I always preferred these to what I saw as the more static and less creative features of the jigsaw puzzle. I loved the dramatic reactions achieved when certain chemicals were mixed together. That is what critical evaluation is like: you mix together two or more perspectives and – alakazam! Look at the beautiful, effervescent critical evaluation that comes out.

State how they relate!

To develop your critical evaluation, you should also ask: How do these different findings and ideas *relate to each other*? What does one imply for the other? Some of the ideas explored here relate to Chapter 5, which addresses essay structure – a key component of good structure in an essay is the clear articulation of how ideas relate to one another. For example, you may look for and find research that confirms previous findings or that contradicts them – both of which can be used in critical evaluation.

Finding confirmation of empirical findings is evaluative when it is argued like this:

> X's finding that [insert relevant finding] is further confirmed in Y's research which examined [identify the confirming research, including relevant details].

Where relevant (in terms of the essay title and the space available) expand to clarify the extent to which Y confirms the work of X and any limits on this confirmation. For example, does Y only partially confirm X's work? Can Y's research be challenged? Is it limited in some way? It may also be relevant to consider limits in terms of the combined evidence of X and Y. Perhaps they have conducted research which even together is limited in some way? Maybe their findings can be interpreted differently, or perhaps their theoretical model or ideas concerning the topic of the essay can be questioned?

Sometimes we may have the relevant papers to equip our evaluation, but something goes wrong when we write it down. Our writing is not (demonstrably) evaluative when it is argued like this:

> X found ... Y found that ...

The problem with this approach, which millions adopt (but they really should stop it), is that the two approaches are listed, *but they never actually meet*. This approach does not bring one idea to another. There is no meeting here, as the writing does not bring one idea into genuine contact with another. We never really get to see what perspective Y offers on X's work. We need to convey *how these two approaches relate to one another*. This might involve a sentence along these lines:

> While X argued that we should understand [topic of the essay] in terms of [X's theory], Y argued that [Y's contrasting perspective].

Do you see how much stronger this is – even though it is working with the same material as the 'X found... Y found that...' sentence. How we handle that content and specifically how we show an understanding about the relationship between different perspectives is at the heart of critical evaluation. Always try to convey how the different studies, findings, theories, sources and ideas that make up your essay relate to one another.

Remember the mantra – 'state how they relate' and you will be on the right track!

Putting it all together

Let's look at the mechanics of building critical evaluation into your essay.

Imagine that this is your essay title:

'Evaluate Block's idea that affect is the fundamental driver of personality in the light of alternative perspectives.'

Let's look at the steps that you might go through in answering this question in a way that ensures that you maximise relevant critical evaluation.

1. Identifying the relevant content for your essay

It always makes sense to use the recommended reading, essay guidance and notes relating to your essay title. In this case, imagine that you have an indication in your lecture notes that DeYoung (2010) provides a critique of Block's idea that 'affect is the fundamental driver of personality'. One of our tasks will be to locate DeYoung's publication(s) that address this issue and to use them to start to build one strand of the critique of Block's work.

2. Clarifying the relevant perspectives for your essay

Knowing that we are going to use DeYoung (2010) can be quite straightforward – especially if reading lists, lecture notes and essay guidance indicate the relevance of this work. The second step involves not just locating but *thinking about* what they have to say that is directly relevant for this specific essay and, crucially, how what they have to say relates to what others (in particular Block) have argued.

If DeYoung (2010) provides an alternative perspective on Block's argument about the fundamental driver of personality, can we identify what that different perspective is? What would DeYoung say to Block at a (perhaps slightly awkward) party where the two met and started chatting about drivers of personality? By bringing DeYoung's perspective to what Block has argued we can build an important strand of our critical evaluation.

3. Deepening our understanding of how different perspectives characterise the target idea

It can be really useful to identify how different publications make sense of the core idea or argument that the essay title identifies as the focus (in this case Block's idea that affect is the fundamental driver of personality).

At this point, we might read DeYoung's (2010) publication and zoom in on sections where DeYoung (2010) *characterises* the work of Block:

'Block (2002) described personality as 'an affect processing system,' with its main task being to avoid anxiety by successfully constraining and channelling impulses or drives emerging from within and successfully comprehending the environment perceived without.' (DeYoung, 2010: 26)

These passages can be useful in understanding the way in which the target paper or idea (in this case Block, 2002) has been interpreted, or made sense of, by subsequent work.

Writing that: 'DeYoung (2010) characterised Block's approach to personality as "an affect processing system", which he interpreted as particularly focused on the task of "avoiding anxiety"…' can be used to good effect, especially if we can subsequently contrast this with other characterisations of the target idea or argument.

Even when we do not open up a discussion regarding how research has been variously characterised, identifying the source of characterisations that we come across – especially if these are primary publications (such as journal papers, specialist books and book chapters) rather than textbook summaries – is good practice and shows our awareness that there may be other ways of characterising the idea or argument being referred to.

ACE YOUR ASSIGNMENT
Acknowledging difference

Really excellent scholarly academic writing doesn't only stay locked into stating what a particular idea or argument is, as if that is entirely consensual; it considers how the idea or argument has been understood. We may become sensitive to the idea that different psychologists don't simply have a different answer concerning the topic of our essay; they might think about the issue itself in a different way. Thus, psychologists may be tackling a different aspect of prejudice, implicitly defining aggression or prosocial behaviour in a different way, or perhaps working from a different understanding as to how we should think about self or attribution or relationships. Acknowledging these (slightly or radically) different stances to the issue that they are addressing is a sign of real scholarly work.

4. Deepening our understanding of how different perspectives contrast and critique the target idea

For now, let's read on and look for *contrastive comments*, that is places where, in this case, DeYoung (2010) contrasts Block's approach with his own. Here we are seeing how DeYoung does some critical evaluation – in this case, contrasting previous work (Block, 2002) with his own research. Here is a relevant passage:

> 'Whereas Block emphasized affect as the fundamental driver of the personality system, my colleagues and I view personality, first and foremost, as a goal-directed or cybernetic system…'

This is great in terms of planning our essay so that it is critically evaluative from the start. We now have something to work with. We can – and should – follow this up in DeYoung's (2010) paper to clarify what is meant by both his characterisation of Block's work and of his own perspective, which understands personality as 'a goal-directed or cybernetic system'.

5. Drawing out the implications of the different perspectives

So far, we have a really cool starting-place for this essay – we have some critical evaluation in that we have DeYoung's (2010) paper, in which he contrasts his work with that of Block. We may – or may not – be able to develop something in terms of how DeYoung characterises Block's work, but we can certainly fully exploit the great critical resources we find in DeYoung's paper. In doing this, we want to make sure that our essay does not become a list. Right now, how many people are writing a list? Perhaps 700,000 people? Don't join them when you are writing your essay. I have seen thousands of essays with paragraphs that are something like this:

> Block argued that the main driver of personality was…
>
> DeYoung argued that the main driver of personality was…
>
> Someone else argued that…

You've got the picture. It's not much more interesting than reading my shopping list for later today:

> Buy some cereal for breakfast
>
> Get some new colourful socks
>
> Buy some oat milk

Let's think how we can really maximise our critical evaluation by drawing out the implications. What implications? The implications of one perspective for another – not just DeYoung's for Block's, but also Block's for DeYoung's. Your essay is capturing a magical debate as if the two were talking. This is part of the wonder of writing an essay – we can bring different theorists and researchers together and reflect on what they might say to one another. We can even do this if the psychologists we want to bring together are no longer alive – how amazing is that!

If DeYoung critiqued Block, how might Block respond. Often, we can find publications that help us think this through (for example, DeYoung commented directly on Block's work), but whether this is or is not the case, it is helpful to develop our own capacity to think of the implications of one set of ideas for another.

Staying with the ideas that we are exposed to and letting them become part of us – digesting them if you like – provides a means by which we can start to think from that point of view and note what we see. How do differing perspectives on personality, relevant research findings and the social world look from the perspective that the main driver of personality is affect? How different do these things look from the perspective that personality is, first and foremost, a goal-directed or cybernetic system? In approaching this level of thinking, we may well be driven back to clarifying our understanding of these different approaches. We are not going back to square one; we are spiralling down – or spiralling up – coming back to the place at a deeper or, if you prefer, a higher level than the last time we thought about this.

6. Identifying further relevant content and clarifying the different perspectives offered

To really develop the critical evaluation within our essay we may have to go beyond the ideas of Block and DeYoung. We could investigate whether there is another perspective which might endorse or challenge either or both of the perspectives we have considered so far. Depending on the sort of guidance we have had regarding this topic, or this essay assignment in particular, it may be relevant to ask more fundamental critical questions, perhaps about the very construct of a 'driver of personality', or, indeed, the idea of personality itself.

These latter questions move more into a critical perspective that questions assumptions – often fundamental assumptions – in psychology. Academics, programmes of study, modules and even specific pieces of work vary enormously in terms of whether it is seen as relevant or appropriate to question 'axiomatic' assumptions within psychology, and it is wise to be guided by lecturers and tutors regarding this.

EXERCISE
Write once – write twice

It may help to start with a form of words that is not especially conceptual but maybe captures something that you want to express. For example, try out the following three different approaches:

1. *The key approach being evaluated has been critiqued in lots of ways* – ask in what ways and how you can express this. For example, 'lots of criticism of Milgram' might be conceptualised as *both methodological* and *theoretical* criticisms.

2. *The approach being evaluated is good in some ways, but has limitations too* – don't give up with this. It is a little trickier, but when it is developed it is really impressive, conveying a sense of magical scholarly engagement. This is one format it can take: *Whilst there is evidence that [the approach] contributes to an understanding of [what it contributes to], questions remain concerning [specification of limitations].*

3. *There are lots of differing views on the essay topic* – again, this is tricky, but it gives a real opportunity to impress. You can tackle this by starting to specify the different approaches and then conceptualising the essence of the key differences. Think about the different approaches that are relevant to your essay (for example, an essay evaluating Milgram's research into obedience might include ideas about agentic shift, social identity theory and strain-reducing mechanisms (among others). Think about how these are similar to (and different from) each other, and then try to characterise these differences at a more abstract or conceptual level: agentic state focuses on '*intrapsychic*' phenomena, social identity theory highlights '*change in identity*' and work on strain-reducing mechanisms highlights the potential role of '*ideology*'. Doing this demonstrates an awareness of how these perspectives relate at a deeper, more fundamental level and really communicates a sense of a mind at work in the essay.

FEEDBACK ON CRITICAL EVALUATION

There is usually not much to decode in comments about critical evaluation. In signalling an issue with our critical evaluation, markers will typically comment that our essay as a whole, or specific parts of it, should be 'more evaluative', 'more analytic', 'more argumentative', include 'more debate' or be 'more critical'. Sometimes the feedback will identify what there should be *less of*, with comments that our essay should be 'less descriptive'. Yet, while this may be suggesting that we need to be more concise in our descriptive writing, it is also suggestive that we need to *increase* the extent of critical evaluation in our essay.

'Cite relevant sources'

Sometimes it is not simply the presence or absence of critical evaluation in our essay, but rather the way in which we have handled critical evaluation that has been questioned. We might, for example, be asked to attribute our criticism to a relevant source (locating sources is addressed in Chapter 2, citing them in Chapter 9), and where we can find a relevant source that makes an evaluative point, it is always good to cite it in our essay.

'Don't just put in your own opinion'

Another issue that might be raised, which has been discussed earlier in this chapter, is the way in which we attempt to critically evaluate. Lots of essays will have tell-tale phrases, such as 'in my opinion' or 'I think', where an attempt at critical evaluation is made but it ends up being an unthought-out opinion: 'I think the research into prosocial behaviour is limited and not like real life', rather than a carefully thought through argument: 'It could be argued that research into prosocial behaviour has been narrowly focused, concentrating on a very small segment of altruistic behaviour, specifically ad hoc, low-investment help of strangers.'

   Do you see how, when we airdrop an opinion, it does not read well (it jars the poor reader). It is also often associated with an under-argued or under-developed point. The improved version could be strengthened by citing a relevant source, but nonetheless it reads more smoothly and it develops a clear, specific and relevant point.

EXERCISE
Putting the theory into practice

Look at an assignment that you have handed in and any feedback you received on it. This can seem painful, especially if it didn't get the grade you were hoping for. But this can also teach us about how we can make better use of critical evaluation and can really help transform our future essays.

THINK

Use the 'Implementing Critical Evaluation Strategy' below and see how you can build more critical evaluation into that essay.

LEARN

Now take this thinking forward to your future essays. From the moment you look at the title, through to planning, writing and reviewing your essay, keep in mind just what you have learned about developing critical evaluation and *put it into practice*.

Increasing our use of critical evaluation

Much of the time the feedback we receive – sometimes the mark itself – indicates that we need to increase our critical evaluation. This whole chapter has addressed that issue, but let's pull some ideas together in considering how you can incorporate critical evaluation into your essay. It is time to unveil the 'Implementing Critical Evaluation Strategy'.

Implementing Critical Evaluation Strategy

If your feedback suggests that you need to incorporate more critical evaluation, then fear not – the Implementing Critical Evaluation Strategy is here to help you.

1. Look at your essay title.

    Refer to lecture notes, recordings, slides and relevant key textbook material and **look out for different perspectives**. Specifically, you want different perspectives regarding the focus of the essay title that you are tackling. Note down some of these different research findings, arguments, theories, definitions or assumptions. You are looking for things that these psychologists would disagree on if they met (some of them are going to meet in your essay). Note those that seem to endorse one another as well – they could also have an important role in your essay.

2. Start sketching out an essay plan that builds in a strong sense of how the research and ideas that you refer to relate to one another.

    You may find you go through several versions of this and when you start writing you may further adjust your plan. The target is a smooth, coherent and critically evaluative response to the specific essay title.

3. In drafting your essay look at the different research, findings and ideas and state how they relate.

That is, with each element you bring into your essay (for example, a new psychologist) articulate how their ideas, research or findings relate to the one(s) you have already referred to. Doing this may also lead you to consider re-ordering or re-structuring aspects of your essay so that your argument is as smooth and logical as possible (see Chapter 5 for more on this).

4. Try to find phrases that capture the nature of the relationship between the different perspectives that you are drawing on.

    Think of these different relationships, for example:

    o   Named perspective directly critiques the target

        Y's research involving [brief detail regarding Y's research] provides a critique of X's perspective. Whereas X argued [brief summary of X's argument], Y found that [brief detail of what Y found] and interpreted this as [an aspect of Y's interpretation that is relevant to critiquing X's argument].

    o   Named perspective directly supports the target

        Y's research involving [brief detail regarding Y's research] supports X's argument that [brief detail of X's argument]. Y found that [brief detail of what Y found] and interpreted this as [an aspect of Y's interpretation that is relevant to thinking about X's argument].

    o   Named perspective partially supports the target

        Y's research involving [brief detail regarding Y's research] provides some support for X's argument that [brief detail of the aspect of X's argument that Y supports]. Y found that [brief detail of what Y found] and interpreted this as [an aspect of Y's interpretation that is relevant to thinking about X's argument]. However, Y did not support X's argument that [an aspect of X's argument that Y did not support], arguing instead that [Y's alternative argument].

5. If you have critically evaluative comments to make and really cannot find a relevant source, then carefully word your critique.

    Try to avoid the personal pronoun here (unless specifically directed otherwise). 'You know what I think…' might work well in some situations, but not in an academic essay.

    These sentence stems work reasonably well:

    o   'These findings suggest that…',
    o   'This perspective can be seen as depicting (human cognition) as…'
    o   'The research considered so far conceptualises (aggression/prosocial behaviour/ relationships) as being essentially…'
    o   'This perspective could be questioned in terms of (methodological underpinning/ theoretical assumptions/implications)…'

6. Think about the method, theory, definitions and assumptions.

You may be able to develop further material to support your critical evaluation by thinking about the following issues:

o What sort of research was conducted with whom?

o How did the research measure the variables it was interested in (often dependent and independent variables)?

o Are there any working or operational definitions (those found implicitly, or explicitly, in any empirical study) that can be questioned? For example, a large number of empirical studies have measured 'prosocial behaviour' in terms of ad hoc, low investment behaviour such as whether participants would pick up something that a stranger dropped. Operational definitions across many empirical studies might appear relatively trivial, narrowly defined and in other ways as providing a limited view of the vast area – in this case prosocial behaviour – being considered.

o Are there any broader definitional assumptions? For example, is it possible to question how research has defined the broader issue it seeks to investigate (perhaps we can ask 'What is "self"?' Or 'How should we conceptualise "aggression"?'

o What is the implication for understanding the aspect of human behaviour which the approach addresses? This requires a little expansion. For example, we might question the rational emphasis found in Kelley's Covariation Model of Causal Attribution. We might raise an issue concerning whether calculations found in the Equity Theory of Relationships and (in a different way) in the Arousal–Cost Reward Model of prosocial behaviour really do shape our relationship satisfaction and likelihood of helping – or do these calculations merely justify our position *post hoc*?

7. Be a superstar and review your essay prior to submission!

Isn't it wonderful! Even if you are reading this and you have to submit your assignment in a couple of hours' time, you can still check through what you have done to see if you can develop your critical evaluation. Look through your essay. Do you state how your ideas relate? Is there a sense of looking at one piece of research, finding or idea from another perspective? Even taking a few minutes to review your work can add some critical evaluation and that can make all the difference. Good luck with your mission – and try to enjoy it.

LEARN
Show your *mind at work* in your essay

Your essay marker is trying to judge how well you can think about the issues identified in the essay title. They are asking 'what sort of mind is at work in this essay?' The most obvious indicator of this is how much and how well you use *critical evaluation* in your essay.

EXERCISE
Expand your evaluation

1. Look through a previous essay that you have written. Have you done some critical evaluation? Can you locate those specific sentences that show your critical evaluation?

2. Is there a bit more critical evaluation that you could do? You may have feedback that identifies where you may develop this.

3. Look for some idea or finding in your essay that could be questioned or looked at from another perspective. For example, you might have a criticism regarding the methodology of some research that you refer to, or an observation regarding a theory that you cover.

4. Try to write one or two sentences that capture that evaluation. You may have differing perspectives within your essay already – just bring them together. Let's suppose that your essay title is: *Outline and evaluate Kelley's Covariation model of causal attribution*. A sentence developed along these lines may work:

    Describe how Y [your new perspective – perhaps research findings or a theory or a simple direct critique]: provides further support for, questions, challenges or partially supports X [your previous perspective].

    Detail this relationship: for example, whilst X [Kelley] argued that we can think of attribution as a rational process, Y [Ross] suggests that our causal reasoning is subject to bias.

    Here is how the sentence might look:

    Ross's (1977) concept of the Fundamental Attribution Error challenges Kelley's (1967) Covariation Model, arguing that our attribution process is not as rational as Kelley suggests. The Fundamental Attribution Error suggests that rather than rationally weighing the evidence, we are biased towards making internal or person-blaming attributions.

5. Here's one I did earlier – I'll tackle the slightly more challenging issue where we have a potential critique but no name to go with it. Imagine that you are writing about prosocial behaviour. You spot that the dependent variable (helping behaviour) in many experiments involves quite trivial behaviour (posting a letter, helping with shopping or picking up a dropped pen). You also notice – because you are on a roll now – that the Arousal Cost–Reward model of prosocial behaviour suggests that we calculate the costs and rewards of helping *before* our decision to help. You could develop critical evaluation like this:

    (Please note, only indicative sentences are given here, rather than complete and interconnected paragraphs).

    These experiments can be questioned in terms of how they have measured 'prosocial behaviour', focusing on one-off, ad-hoc, relatively low-cost helping behaviour. …

    …

    This approach assumes that our calculation of the costs and rewards of helping precedes our decision to help or not. It could, however, be argued that such a calculation takes place afterwards – as a justification for why we did (or did not) help. …

REFLECTING ON THE CHAPTER:
Yes, you can (critically evaluate your essay)

Critical evaluation is one of those features that every academic wants to see more of in nearly all academic writing, from first-year undergraduate essays to completed PhD theses. I have never seen or given the following feedback on any of the many thousands of essays that I have marked and moderated: 'Try to reduce the amount of critical evaluation in your essay'. We all want it, we all want more of it – so what is the problem? A key factor in holding back the glorious sunlight of critical evaluation from lighting up all of our essays is uncertainty: 'What should I evaluate?', 'How should I evaluate?' and 'How can *I* evaluate?' This chapter tackles the first two of these in some detail.

That third issue, 'How can *I* evaluate?', reflects a self-doubt. Should you, *dare* you take on these published psychologists? If you have this doubt – perhaps buried deep beneath some surface confidence – bear in mind that critical evaluation is simply thinking about how one idea relates to another. Yes, it is as easy and profound as that. What are the implications of this idea for another idea? It may be that you yourself are raising the idea or that you are articulating the ideas of others. The important thing is that you are considering the implications of one idea or perspective for another. This is the sort of thing we do in our everyday life – when we are deciding what to buy, where to go or what to do, and, similarly, when we are involved in a (reasonably thoughtful) argument or discussion, or when we are hearing about (or resolving) an argument between others. We think about contradictory ideas all the time and find a way through them. Likewise, we think about the implications that one idea (or perspective) has for another, so we are doing critical evaluation just to get through daily life. This chapter has attempted to support you in deepening the *skills you actually already have*. It is a brilliant skill for essays and a great skill for life.

TAKE AWAY POINTS FROM THIS CHAPTER

- Don't treat critical evaluation as an optional extra. Unless indicated otherwise in your essay guidance, critical evaluation will be expected in your academic writing.

- Get into critical mode immediately! When you read through your essay title is the time to start thinking about how you can develop a critically evaluative approach to writing your essay.

- Take a proactive approach to critical evaluation. Don't just see what turns up – actively look for ways of bringing critical evaluation into your essay.

- Critical evaluation may take different forms – and it is not always 'critical' in the conventional sense of the word. We are critically evaluating whenever we are thinking about how an idea, a piece of research, or a perspective may relate. We can critically evaluate by considering how different empirical studies, interpretations and theories support, critique or have a complex relationship with each other.

- Developing the implication of one perspective on another is at the very heart of the art of critical evaluation. Learning to relate one idea, finding, perspective or argument to another is an amazing skill to develop and will make your essays dazzle.

- Where possible, draw in the publications that make the critically evaluative points that you wish to refer to. You might not immediately be aware of all of the relevant ideas that have been developed in publications, but you can actively search for the comments on previous research that have been made (using search tools to help you, see Chapter 2 for more on this).

- If you cannot find publications which make a critically evaluative point that is relevant to your essay, then make the point as a relevant and integrated argument rather than as an opinion that you just drop into the essay.

- Before you submit your essay, edit it. One thing on your editing agenda should be the extent to which it develops effective, relevant critical evaluation (see Chapter 10 for more on this). Critical evaluation is a key skill and you can start to develop that skill right now!

LINKING TO OTHER CHAPTERS

Critical evaluation is so important to academic essays that, perhaps even more than 'answer the essay title', it is the recurrent plaintiff cry of undergraduate markers throughout this world – and quite possibly other worlds too. In this chapter, the key feature of critical evaluation has been identified as bringing one idea or perspective to another and articulating the implications it has for that idea or perspective. The handling of this in the context of how our essays contain different ideas within an interconnected whole is directly addressed in Chapter 5, which looks at how to achieve a smooth, interconnected essay. Really good, evaluative essays typically convey a sense of argument that is evident from the introductory paragraph (see Chapter 3), which sketches the broad perspectives that will be considered in its statement of intent, to the conclusion (see Chapter 8), which conceptualises the debate that has informed the essay. The evaluation in your essay should be relevant to the precise essay question (see Chapter 4) and should be a key focus of your reviewing and editing of your essay prior to submission (see Chapter 10). Critical evaluation is like the holy grail, the elixir of youth and the magic lamp all rolled into one – as writers, readers and markers we all want it. The good news is that we all have it, even if it has been locked away in a dark cellar for a while. Try to use the ideas in this chapter to unlock your full and fantastic critical potential – you won't regret it!

Chapter 7

Keep it dynamic – how to develop your academic voice and describe effectively

In this chapter you will learn...

- How to find your academic voice
- How to describe in just the right amount of detail
- How to deal with definitions and assumed reader knowledge
- How to handle your own ideas in an essay
- How to write in an effective and scholarly tone
- How to identify and fix problems with your academic writing

EFFECTIVE WRITING: WHAT IT IS AND WHY IT MATTERS

This chapter will address how we can develop an appropriate academic tone for our essay, with a particular focus on the descriptive aspects of our writing. To some extent, piling on hours of extra writing can really help us to improve. An academic who has perhaps written 30,000 words of academic essays as an undergraduate and who has completed a 100,000-word PhD thesis and perhaps 300,000 words of published books and papers, may have a smooth academic style, in part, merely by virtue of having spent so many hours writing. But it is worth bearing in mind that the idea that 'hours of practice equates with expertise' oversimplifies the issue.

You may have heard of the idea that 10,000 hours of practice makes someone an expert. This notion is a misreading of the idea popularised in '*Outliers*', where Gladwell (2008) argued that the magic number of 10,000 hours of *deliberate practice* makes someone an expert across almost any field. A meta-analysis by Macnamara, Hambrick and Oswald (2014) has questioned inter-pretations of deliberate practice research which suggest that *quantity of practice alone* helps to lead to improved performance in any field. One of the key points that Macnamara et al. make is that the more clearly structured and predictable a domain is, the more closely hours of practice are associated with improved performance. Many hours of practice may really help our chess – perhaps especially our opening game, with its predictable starting point – but with education, and more specifically academic writing, some other ingredient may be especially necessary. A partic-ular point raised in deliberate practice research is that it is vitally important to distinguish *mere* practice (just doing what we want to improve), from *deliberate* practice, which focuses in on the specific skills we need to develop in order to enhance our performance. Focusing on developing and practising *specific relevant writing skills* – especially those that our feedback suggests we need to focus on, will really lead to significant improvement.

Each of the chapters in this book endeavours to help you with your journey to writing brilliant essays by trying to crystalise what it means to write a good introduction or conclusion, or to be critically evaluative or to directly address the essay question. This idea of getting a really sharp sense of what excellence looks like is especially important when we are addressing the more general issue of 'what is good academic writing'.

If you have had concerns about your academic writing in general, how you express yourself, the tone or style that you adopt, then try out the ideas in this chapter. Writing lots of words for lots of hours will certainly improve your writing, but a sharply focused sense of what you are aiming at will act as a catalyst, inspiring you to reach your full writing potential.

'Academic writing', what does it mean to you?

Do you find yourself thinking any of the following when it comes to writing an essay?

- I need to develop something unique and different in my essay for it to stand out.
- I don't know how to do 'academic writing'.
- I don't know what is even meant by an 'academic' writing style.
- I can't put my own ideas in an essay.
- I must put my own ideas in an essay.
- I must assume that the reader knows nothing.
- I must assume that the reader has relevant expertise.
- I should define my terms.

These ideas reflect how the whole process of academic writing can be a barrier for us. We may feel that we are going to trip over because we can't make our essay special or that we don't know what 'academic writing' is exactly, or how to do it. We can find ourselves feeling as if we are sinking in quicksand as we think we should (and yet perhaps *should not*) include our own ideas and that we should (or is it *should not*?) assume that our reader is knowledgeable.

LEARN
Mindset is key

Getting the right mindset for academic writing is a challenge, not least because it is so easy to be held back by quite prevalent myths and dilemmas. Check whether any of these relate to you and see how they need not mislead or block you any more:

I need to develop something unique and different in my essay for it to stand out.

Keep the emphasis on providing a strong scholarly answer to the specific essay title, demonstrating mastery of the key material. Seeking uniqueness for its own sake is less productive than developing a scholarly engagement with the key material.

I don't know how to do 'academic writing'.

That awareness is a really good sign. Yes, academic essay writing is different from most other forms of writing that you have experienced. Work with the ideas in this chapter as they will help you to focus on developing your academic 'voice'.

I don't know what is even meant by an 'academic' writing style.

I think you are right if you feel that the phrase 'academic writing' is a little odd or obscure. The best way to define this is by looking at the examples that are present throughout this book, including in this chapter. Getting a clear sense of what good academic writing looks like (when we read it) and feels like (when we write it) is one of the best things you can do to supercharge your own academic writing.

I can't or must put my own ideas in an essay.

When we split our essay between 'my ideas' and 'other people's ideas' we are making things difficult for ourselves. If you can pick up an essay and quickly spot 'the author's own ideas', the essay has probably got some problems. Good writing is outwardly engaged with whatever topic it is addressing. Don't airdrop in 'what I think is...' as that is unlikely to be properly integrated into your essay, it does not suggest a scholarly engagement with the relevant material and it gives your reader an unpleasant jolt. Your treatment of the ideas that are relevant for your specific essay title is what matters – that is, how you connect ideas, evaluate them and develop their implications.

I must assume that the reader knows nothing or has relevant expertise.

You may receive specific guidance on this in relation to your essay, in which case please use it! For most essays, this issue is best addressed by keeping this question in mind: 'What is relevant to the specific essay question?' In other words, provide the details that are relevant for advancing your engagement with the specific essay title. If your essay asks you to 'Critically evaluate Piaget's conservation experiments', a brief outline of the experiments is necessary to advance your evaluation of them, but a biography of Piaget or a definition of developmental psychology would not normally be relevant.

(Continued)

I should define my terms.

This will vary considerably with the particular essay that you are writing and the approach it is encouraging you to take. A collection of approaches, which are often referred to as 'critical psychology', question many of the working assumptions and definitions within psychology, so starting an essay on 'self' or 'aggression' as if the definition is without problem would demonstrate a lack of critical awareness from this perspective. However, for some essays, it may be expected that definitions, in particular 'working definitions' covering how phenomena are defined for your particular essay, will be present. Making use of specific guidance on your essay will help enormously. Try to identify whether definitions are expected for your essay, whether any critical treatment of definitions is desired, or if no definition focus is seen as most relevant for the essay you are working on.

GOOD AND BAD ACADEMIC WRITING

In this section let's try something really tricky – let's try and get a vivid sense of what it feels like to read and to write good academic writing.

Imagine that this is your essay title:

'Critically evaluate Milgram's obedience experiments and his interpretation of their results.'

Now think about a paragraph (appearing just after the introductory paragraph) that seeks to describe the experiments as a basis for later evaluation. From the brief samples below, which do you think is the most promising?

Sample A

Milgram's studies of obedience can be considered among the most famous work conducted in psychology. Milgram's research was very much inspired by his reflections on the Nuremberg trials. He agreed with Hannah Arendt that the perpetrators seemed in many respects disarmingly 'ordinary'. Milgram concurred with Arendt's idea that evil is often different from our common conceptions of it, frequently having a 'banality' to it that is captured in the recurrent, bureaucratic defence, 'I was only following orders'. Arendt (1963) referred to the war criminal Eichmann as being 'neither perverted nor sadistic' but rather as being 'terrifyingly normal'. That idea of being 'terrifyingly normal' was interesting to both Milgram and Arendt in terms of how we can understand the worst of human behaviour. For Arendt the idea that people who commit war crimes could be 'normal' is terrifying because it suggests that any ordinary person might – in a particular set of circumstances – engage in evil acts.

Sample B

Fred looked awkwardly up at the tall angular figure of the experimenter. Should he ask more about the 'punishment' in the experiment? The other guy seemed anxious, beads of sweat formed on the brow of his round face and his voice seemed unable to hide tell-tale traces of tension. The experimenter thrust out a hat with slips of paper in it. This was it. Those slips of paper would determine his fate – 'teacher' or 'learner'. He grabbed a slip and held his breath. What if he was a learner and got 'punished' – just how painful was it? He turned the slip over, staring at it defiantly. 'Teacher'. He let out a long slow breath, shooting a furtive glance at the 'learner'.

Sample C

Milgram was keen to get to the bottom of how seemingly normal people could find themselves committing atrocities – in some cases, even war crimes. His solution was to research the matter. Unknown to the real participant, Milgram used an actor to convincingly portray the role of being another participant, pretending to receive electric shocks each time the real participant pressed what they thought was an electric shock generator. This deception enabled Milgram to test just how far participants would go in administering electric shocks. Would they keep obeying the experimenter in charge all the way up to the maximum 450 volts, or would they stop as soon as they heard the learner protest? Milgram's series of experiments provided the opportunity to investigate exactly that issue – how far would people go simply to obey someone in authority?

Sample D

Whilst Milgram conducted some 24 variations in his series of obedience experiments, for the purposes of this essay the procedure in experiment number five, which Milgram treated as his new baseline, will be briefly outlined. Other experimental variations will be referred to where relevant in order to help evaluate Milgram's ideas. In experiment number five, Milgram recruited participants from the local community via a newspaper advertisement. On arrival at Yale, participants were apparently randomly allocated to being either a 'teacher', who was to administer punishments, or a 'learner', who was to receive them. The allocation was arranged so that a confederate, who was an actor, would always be the learner, and the real (naïve) participant the teacher. The experimental procedure entailed the teacher reading word pairs to the learner and then testing their recall of the pairs. Each time the learner made an error, the participant, as teacher, was instructed to administer what they were led to believe was an electric shock. The level of shock administered was increased for each new error that the learner made and was used as the measure of obedience. Total obedience was operationally defined as administering the highest level of shock (450 volts) that the experimenter required the teacher to deliver. Milgram manipulated several variables in different experimental conditions, including the extent to which participants, as teachers, heard, saw and felt the learner to whom they believed they were administering electric shocks.

STOP AND THINK
Facing your dilemmas

Before going any further, stop and think of a time when you have struggled with that outlining paragraph – the one that details an experiment that you need to critique. What were the dilemmas that you faced? Were you struggling to contain different ideas? Was there too much detail to handle? Did you find yourself slipping in and out of an academic tone or register?

Which of the above passages works best and which ones are problematic? Let's consider each one in turn.

Critique: Sample A

Can you see what is happening here? It looks like the author has read Arendt's (1963) book and while a brief reference to this in a sentence or two could work out well, they just can't let Arendt go. The acid-test here is whether a reader could work out the essay title (more or less) from reading this paragraph. If I read this paragraph not knowing the essay title, I would guess that it was about the influence of Hannah Arendt's work on Milgram's ideas concerning obedience to authority. Drawing on other ideas is great if it enhances our answer to the exact essay title, but not if it replaces or substitutes material that you should be focusing on.

Critique: Sample B

I suspect that you quite easily identify B as not good academic writing. This form of writing does offer something, imaginatively entering into the subjective world of the participants in Milgram's experiment, but its focus seems to be to build drama rather than to explain the basis for evaluating the experiments and how they have been interpreted. Sample B is worth bearing in mind just to remind us that academic writing is a sub-genre of writing, a highly specific one that constitutes a very small percentage of all writing. If you find yourself struggling with academic writing, don't start feeling negative about your abilities. You are trying to tackle a very particular form of writing that most people, most of the time, have little to do with – it is not surprising that you might find it a challenge to master. Don't give up.

Critique: Sample C

This is probably the easiest way to write for many people. It's a natural sort of style for many people and might reflect how we might talk about a set of occurrences to someone. If you write like this, your feedback will probably refer to your essay being 'chatty', 'journalistic' or 'not academic'. If this is close to your style, keep comparing it with the much more formal style of Sample D. Sample C (in contrast to D, which you probably already realised was the best of the bunch) uses lots of questions, doesn't it? There are some more common (or colloquial) expressions, such as 'get to the bottom of' and 'just how far', but these lack the precision of more formal academic expressions, such as 'investigate' and 'the extent to which', and illustrate that sometimes changing a word or a phrase can improve academic writing (see below for more on this issue). There is nothing wrong with colloquial expressions, chattiness or journalistic writing, but once again we see that academic writing is a special type of writing that differs from what we might ordinarily read, hear or say.

Critique: Sample D

If you're not sure that this is the best paragraph (as a piece of academic writing for the essay title given), where have you been? I see this as pretty good writing, especially if the essay length is about 2000–3000 words. For a short essay, though, this might want to be trimmed a little bit (see the section 'What it looks like in practice' under 'Transforming your descriptive writing' for a much more succinct version of a similar paragraph). If I read a paragraph like this as a marker, I would appreciate the fairly skilful way in which a potentially tricky issue – the many variations of Milgram's experiments – is dealt with, and a clear rationale is given for focusing primarily on one experiment (the one Milgram treated as his baseline). I also like the way in which the level of shock is conceptualised as the operational definition of obedience (that is, the definition used within this experiment). Finally, the last sentence succinctly sums up some of the key ways in which Milgram's other experiments differ. This is particularly helpful as it sets up ideas, such as the participant being seen or not seen, touched or not touched, that will probably be referred to later in the essay in a detailed examination of the results. If I needed to trim this essay, I would keep in these stronger elements if possible and take my axe, scythe or nail clippers to the sentences that detailed how participants were recruited, how teacher and learner roles were allocated and perhaps the second sentence, which simply notes that other experimental variations will be reported on as appropriate. Sample D is not perfect (and something like the succinct version we include later in this chapter may be better suited to a shorter essay), but it does adopt an appropriate tone – it is clear and scholarly in style and that should be what we are aiming at.

EXERCISE
Experimenting with styles

Take your assignment title and try to write two or three sentences using different styles. Can you write in a way that deviates from the essay title or that sounds like a novel or a magazine feature? Sometimes trying out these different 'voices' can help us to see more clearly what our 'academic voice' looks like. Warning: try to make sure that the assignment that you actually hand in uses your *academic voice* – the other versions might help with that screen play or feature article you always intended to write.

We all know what good academic writing is, don't we?

What do you think are the ingredients of good academic writing?

- Using clever words or phrases
- Going outside the reading list
- Including unexpected material
- Being very creative
- Writing in an obscure or difficult-to-understand way
- Including your own insights and ideas

To get a clear sense of what good academic writing involves, it is worth doing a spot of not exactly myth-busting, but 'myth-modifying'. Let's take some of the ideas from the bullet points above and think them through, noting how they have a bit of truth in them, but can also lead you astray in your essay writing.

LEARN
Words in context

Books on academic writing often try to separate the wheat from the chaff, identifying 'good' words that you should welcome like a favourite relative and 'bad' words that you should cross the street to avoid.

Mewburn, Firth and Lehmann (2019) suggest that English words that are derived from Latin (for example, principal, advantageous and extensive) can convey a more scholarly tone than those derived from German (such as main, good and big). This is an interesting observation, although of course German provides many technical, scholarly and conceptually rich words that are used in English and are particularly relevant for psychology (such as *zeitgeist*, *weltanschauung*, *angst* and *gestalt*).

Using the 'good word' hypothesis effectively

Some lists of good and bad words actually raise more questions than they address. One list that I found identifies these words as good (for social sciences):

Assess

Deduce

Prove

And these as much weaker words:

Assert

Characterise

Construct

Generalise

Reading this makes me keen to assert that whoever characterises 'prove' as being better than 'construct' should assess what they deduce and how they generalise. But – parody to one side – such lists can be useful, although I would assert that the word 'prove' has almost no place in academic psychology essays.

Lists of 'good' words can help if we use them intelligently. We need to leap beyond blind faith in the individual word to think of what our words are doing, and particularly what they are doing in the context of our essay.

Using clever words or phrases
The concept

Throughout much of my education, including as an undergraduate, I have been told that a sophisticated use of language is associated with intelligence, expertise and/or scholarly writing. Surely, therefore, deliberately seeking to use words or phrases that are less commonly used, more technical or, at the very least, longer will show my intelligence, expertise and scholarship.

Thinking it through

There is a good point here – some words or phrases can be effective – but this can easily go wrong. The issue is that it is the action (what you want the words or phrases to do in your essay) and the context (where they are situated) that really matter. What matters is not the stand-alone 'clever' word or phrase, but rather how we use our words or phrases intelligently. The sections that follow further develop this point.

Going outside the reading list
The concept

We have probably all, quite rightly, been encouraged to read around topics that we are studying. As acknowledged elsewhere, when I was an undergraduate I often felt that items outside of the reading list would have much more impact in my essays than those on the list. You might also have this sense that including material outside the reading list will make your work seem special, distinctive and possibly unique.

Thinking it through

This is an idea that again has some potential, but bear in mind the ideas covered in Chapters 2, 4 and 9: we need to address the essay question and draw in references that are relevant to that specific task. Usually it will be expected that you will draw on material from the reading list as the core basis of your essay. Anything additional to the core reading may enhance your essay *as long as it doesn't displace the key material* that you need to cover or take you away from directly addressing the essay title.

Don't assume that including non-reading list material in your essay is like a magic charm. It does not *inevitably* improve your essay. Look at the material you are planning to draw on and interrogate it. Include it only if it really helps your essay to directly and thoroughly address the specific essay title. If your potential material does not help you in answering the specific essay title, then you have a good reason to leave it out – and it is probably the same reason that it was not on the reading list in the first place. An important caveat here is that it is very well worth making sure that you are clear about the specific guidelines and expectations regarding the use of literature for your specific essay.

Including unexpected material
The concept

Sometimes the impulse to be different in our essays takes us even further than going beyond the reading list. If everyone is using the names and ideas that are expected, or which could be anticipated, then why not really make our essay stand out by including material that is totally unexpected and will really take the reader by surprise?

Thinking it through

Have you ever been reading a sentence that you think is about, say, how to write a brilliant essay and suddenly it tells you that the batter-frying technique in all 'fritter'-type food was invented in Japan. Let's hope that never happens to you. Often when I am marking a large number of essays, I will find quite unexpected material popping up like some magician's bunch of flowers produced in a flourish as the climax to a trick.

In cultures that really prize 'individualism', 'standing out from the crowd' and 'unique selling points', it's easy to understand the temptation to do this sort of thing. But producing something unexpected is a bit like making someone a birthday cake with surprise pickled onions inside – it might work out less than 1% of the time, but usually it will lead to disappointment, despair and dyspepsia. Your brilliance should be present in how you interconnect, evaluate and conceptualise the key material that is directly relevant to the essay title. In doing this, you might not make your reader jump with surprise, but you can achieve something much more special: you can connect with your reader in such a way that they can really see the depth of your thinking about the topic. Leave the magic tricks and pickled onions to others and go for this joining of minds – it's much more special.

Be very creative
The concept

If I develop novel ideas, connections and even approaches to writing, then I am surely operating at a more advanced level than essay writers who are more conventional in their focus and approach?

Thinking it through

This touches on similar issues to those considered above – it comes from a desire to be unique and also to be unconstrained by the conventions of academic writing. I think it's great to encourage creativity, and in taking notes, revising, planning essays and trying out ideas, creativity can be brilliant. Within an academic essay, unless your guidelines or relevant tutor indicate otherwise, it is worth being creative within the formal format of an essay. This whole book is geared to a relatively formal type of academic essay – the one you will most typically encounter on most undergraduate and postgraduate courses. But despite the many requirements regarding academic tone, the writing of introductions, conclusions and references, and the need to address the essay title, interconnect your essay and critically evaluate, there is considerable creative scope. The sort of creativity that will enhance your essay might look different from what you may have in mind. It won't be a 'look at me, see how creative I am' sort of creativity; instead it is present in how you manage your interconnection, evaluation and conceptualisation. Yes, there are potentially restrictive parameters to an academic essay, but the more familiar you are with these the more you will be like a musician not trapped by the musical scale, but empowered by it to make beautiful essay-music.

Writing in an obscure or difficult-to-understand way
The concept

Lots of published academic writing can be difficult to understand. This is perhaps linked to the complexity of the ideas expressed. If my writing is too simple, then perhaps my ideas are too, so complex and obscure writing may indicate that I am being more scholarly.

Thinking it through

Your essay really should be about communication not obscuration. Try to communicate your ideas as clearly as possible. A tightly argued essay gives your readers the best opportunity to see your scholarly thinking at work, and is so much better than needless obscurity, which may result in them assuming that the confusion is in you, rather than them.

STOP AND THINK
Including your own insights and ideas

Put your hand up if you don't want to get something of yourself into your essays. I see no hands, so I will assume that you, like me, want to write partly out of some desire for personal expression. That makes absolute sense. One of the many reasons to keep clear of plagiarism is that it is deadening, turning the essay writer into a second-rate photocopier or 'cut and paster'. People are much more than that; you and I are much more than that. Our own ideas and insights should be in our essays, but not like a stereotypical cab driver, giving forth on what they think is the matter with the world. Airdropping in 'what I think is…' into an essay almost never works – unless the essay specifically requires that you engage in reflection of this nature.

The skill is to take your desire to have your own stamp on your essay and use it productively. Use that good impulse to clearly show your scholarly mind at work on the issues raised by the essay title. Your readers and markers do want to see your thoughts – but it is your thoughts enagaged with the relevant issues that they want. That sense of relevant, on-target, scholarly engagement is much more impressive than any number of creative, obscure and unexpected detours.

HOW TO WRITE PERSONAL REFLECTION

Some essays or other written assignments do require an element of personal reflection. Here – more than all the other times I have mentioned it – you really have to pay careful attention to the way in which you are required to handle this for your specific assignment. Below are a few tips for some common forms of personal reflection.

Personal reflection without additional specifications

In an assignment – or part of an assignment – of this nature you are required to reflect on your experience. In some cases the reflection might be explicitly linked to an academic topic (e.g. 'Reflect on your experiences of cross-cultural communication issues'). You may be asked to reflect on your experiences of undertaking some academic assignment (e.g. 'Reflect on your experiences of researching students' perceptions of "legitimate" and "illegitimate" immigration'). Alternatively, you may be asked to reflect more generally on something you have experienced (e.g. 'Write about your experiences of transitioning to university').

How to approach it

Usually reflections of a highly general nature (for example, 'I felt a bit stressed out when I started my first year') are much less insightful than more specific and thoughtful reflections ('When I first came to university, I had a desperate need to "belong". I joined societies that I wasn't even interested in out of what I think was a need to feel connected, to the university and to other students.').

Being asked to be reflective sometimes unleashes all sorts of responses, so check exactly what is being looked for with your specific assignment. It is important to think of the criteria that will be applied to judge your reflective writing. Don't suddenly move into a novel, poem or play format – or even unrestrained introspection – unless that really is what is being looked for. When the format changes like this – from academic essay to personal reflection – it is so easy to lose all sense of structure, coherence and criteria, but the more clearly you incorporate those criteria into your writing the more effective you will be.

Personal reflection in terms of ideas, theories and findings addressed in the course/module

In this sort of writing, you are required not only to reflect on your experiences but to discuss them in the light of ideas that you have encountered in your course/module. This sort of task really helps you to see the applicability of those ideas to make sense of issues that you have experienced. An example of this might be to use research relating to the experience of stress on performance to make sense of how you have experienced exams.

How to approach it

An assignment of this type can be tricky as you need to mobilise two skills that you usually keep quite separate from each other: personal reflection and a critical engagement with academic literature. It is easy to go wrong by making this either a personal reflection *or* a review of the literature, when the challenge is to integrate the two. You may find it helpful to split your physical (or digital) page into two large columns and see if you can jot down personal reflection in one column, perhaps using bullet points with plenty of space between each item. Using the same format, note down a potentially relevant theory in the other column. This approach enables you to:

a.   Use one set of ideas to inform the other – noting the theory may make you think of relevant experiences (and vice versa).

b.   Link the ideas in one column to related ideas in the other.

This process can then inform your plan, where you can start to think about the theories and reflections that are most relevant for your assignment and how you can most effectively order them.

Personal reflection on the application of ideas, theories and research findings you have encountered to real-world examples

For an assignment of this nature, the task is to show your understanding of theories and research that you have encountered by drawing on them to make sense of real-world examples. A specific example of this would be to apply what you have learnt concerning theories about why people commit multiple murders to make sense of a specific case that has been reported in the media.

How to approach it

This will, of course, vary with individual assignment stipulations, expectations and marking criteria – the clearer you are, the better. Assignments of this nature may involve a search for a particular real-world example or case study. If so it is probably worth sketching down potentially relevant theories, perhaps, again, placing bullet points of relevant theories in one column on a page and potential applications in the other column. If you are given the application or case studies, or have a list of them, then you could work with theories first, applications first, or both together. As much of the skill is finding the best fit of theory and application, an arrangement that enables you to summarise each and look for connections (such as the two-columns approach) can really free you to consider different combinations of theory and application, find the best combination and then plan your assignment around that.

LEARN
Top tip

With reflective writing, editing is often seen as being less important when it can actually be even more important. We may have less experience of writing reflectively for our assignments, so we need to read through our first draft with the criteria in mind to really do ourselves justice.

'Look at me, I'm clever!'

Some of the oversimplified beliefs about good academic writing (touched on above) arise from the writer's attempt to 'be clever' – or to appear to be clever. If you are tempted in this way, then you are far from being alone. Immanuel Kant is sometimes attributed with advocating (and to an extent practising) obscure writing, and Heidegger, Lacan and Derrida are also seen as writers who were (perhaps intentionally) obscure. But before you join these philosophers and start agitating for obscurantism, think about what, at heart, your essay is.

Your essay is, or should be, a communication with your reader, a communication in which you show with clarity your directly relevant engagement with the precise issues identified in the essay title. Don't write to draw attention to your own writing; write to bring real clarity of thinking to the debates and perspectives relevant to your essay.

STOP AND THINK
Confusing 'difficult to understand' with cleverness

The idea that obscure = clever is partly fuelled by our experience of encountering ideas that we ourselves struggled to understand. These might (or might not) have been clever or insightful. If we then start to equate 'difficult to understand' with 'clever', we are likely to become someone who is deliberately obscure (an obscurantist). Go for incisive clarity in your writing. Be more like the radiant sun on a bright spring morning than the fog on a rainy Monday in November.

TRANSFORMING YOUR DESCRIPTIVE WRITING

Imagine that your essay title requires you to outline and evaluate Piaget's conservation experiments. After your introduction, you produce a paragraph along these lines:

> In Piaget's conservation experiment, children were presented with two identical glasses of water, one of which is then poured into a shorter but wider container, thereby resulting in the water level appearing lower within that container than it had in the original glass. Pre-operational children (under 7 years of age) performed less well – believing that these superficial changes meant that there were fundamental differences in the volume of water – than those who entered (and subsequently mastered) the concrete operational stage (ages 7–12). …

Can I just ask, did you even manage to read it all the way through? How does it strike you as a piece of writing? Perhaps you, like me, find it hard to read such turgid writing. This writing raises some issues concerning within-paragraph structure and critical evaluation (Chapters 5 and 6 address these important issues), but right now let's see if we can find a key ingredient that enables us to perform some sort of alchemy, transforming this base writing into pure gold.

STOP AND THINK
Be purposive – not passive!

Read as much of the above sample as you can without turning to stone and note what it makes you feel about the person who wrote it. What sort of energy is expressed in this writing – what sort of purpose? For me, the writing has some level of accuracy, but is extremely passive, not in a grammatical sense, but in that the author is not marshalling their material, they are not drawing on the information to develop a point. The author is being passive, not purposive.

The following passage is perhaps not quite gold, but can you sense something different in the writing? You get the sense of a *mind at work* – you can sense that the author is using the information in constructing a clear overview of Piaget's conservation experiments, rather than passively reporting 'the facts'.

> Piaget developed a constructivist account for the findings arising from his conservation experiments. This account emphasised the limits in terms of how younger children think about the stimuli that they were presented with. Key to this is the concept of *centration* – younger children are only able to focus on one aspect of the stimuli – for example, just the height (but not the width) of the water in the two containers, or the total width (but not the separating spaces) of the coins laid out in front of them. For Piaget, pre-operational children (under the age of 7) are at a different stage of development from children who enter the concrete operational stage (7–12). Children at the concrete operational stage are increasingly able to perform mental operations on, or transform, the physical stimuli that they see and to (mentally) reverse these processes. It is, according to Piaget, this cognitive understanding that enables children at the concrete operational stage to realise that the volume or number of the items being considered has not changed despite a manipulation of their appearance.

You're a psychologist!

Do you remember the way in which Milgram explained obedience to authority in terms of 'agentic shift', where participants no longer felt responsible for their own actions, but merely for carrying out the commands of the authority figure? It may seem a bit of a stretch, but sometimes poor academic writing reflects a similar lack of agency – students feel they need to convey the facts others have produced: the lecturer, the authors of books and articles and the textbooks. Rather than actively think about how they can use the different ideas and information in their essay, they treat it almost as a form of dictation, passively conveying what was done, how it was interpreted and what others have said.

Imagine strumming a guitar, assuming that it will somehow sound musical, or throwing the ingredients for a dish you are cooking into a pot and hoping that, somehow, it will turn out well. Both of these images capture something of the essay writer who does not approach their essay with a real sense of agency. Simply referring to the key facts and citing relevant authors does not create a successful essay, because that dynamic quality of engagement, where material is *marshalled*, or used in a purposive way, is missing.

It is worth noting that what appears to be the opposite extreme of this, such as an essay that conveys a sense of 'it's my show' or 'make yourself comfortable, here come my ideas', is often even worse. When essays are almost entirely focused on the ideas of the author, while they may avoid appearing passive, they run the risk of not demonstrating an appropriately targeted active engagement. That is, these essays are active in terms of a target that they themselves have deemed to be relevant, rather than that which the essay title and essay guidance have identified. Taking an active, agentic stance is successful when it is brought to the material that the essay title and guidance indicate as relevant.

ACE YOUR ASSIGNMENT
The process of transforming your essay with seven sensational steps

It is quite possible that you can see the differences between good and bad academic writing in general, and description in particular, that have been identified in this chapter. It is also quite possible that you under-stand *in principle* what active, agentic, good writing entails. But *putting it into practice* can still be a barrier. If this is where you're at, then don't panic, try these tips:

1. Write something of relevance to the essay title. As the introductory paragraph is quite a different form of writing (see Chapter 3), it would make sense to tackle the second paragraph as an example.

2. Read through what you have written and then read your essay title again and see if the *'so what?'* *question* – that is the question as to why the material written is relevant (see Chapters 3 and 4) – arises at any point in your draft essay.

3. If it does, then try to articulate *what it is that your essay is doing or trying to do*. What do you want it to convey to the reader in relation to addressing the essay question?

4. Try to use a form of writing that conveys the ideas and concepts that are relevant to your essay. For example, rather than stating 'In Piaget's conservation experiment, children were presented with two identical glasses of water...', you could provide a sense of Piaget's approach and why he developed these experimental tests of conservation. Note how reference to Piaget's ideas works in the micro extract below (see above for the expanded extract). This makes the descriptive elements meaningful, situating them as relevant to addressing the essay title, (in this case 'Outline and eval-uate Piaget's Conservation Experiments').

    '...(Piaget's) account emphasised the limits in terms of how younger children think about the stimuli that they were presented with. Key to this is the concept of *centration* – younger children are only able to focus on one aspect of the stimuli – for example, just the height (but not the width) of the water...'.

5. Look through your work as if you were the marker and ask 'Does this give me a sense of an engaged, thinking, mind at work on this essay topic, or does it convey a sense of someone not really thinking about what they write and how it relates to the essay question?'

6. If your essay does not convey a sense of really thinking about the material – well done for spotting it. Now see if you can answer the 'so what?' or 'why is it relevant?' questions by making notes of why, or how, any part of your essay is relevant or what it tells us.

7. Now try to stop your reader from asking 'so what?' without having to write '...this is relevant because'. You need to show the reader the relevance of what you have written for thinking about the issues raised in the essay title.

What it looks like in practice

Imagine that this is your essay title:

'Critically evaluate Milgram's argument that 'agentic shift' explains why we are likely to obey those in authority.'

And here is a paragraph that you have written:

Milgram conducted 24 variations in his obedience experiments. These studies investigated whether participants would obey those in authority. In experiment five (his new 'baseline' experiment), he recruited people from the local community via a newspaper advertisement. Once they arrived at the laboratory, they and another person were invited to draw lots. This would determine who was to be the teacher and who was to be the learner. It was arranged so that the real participant would be the teacher. The other person was to be the learner. They were a confederate. The experimenter showed the teacher and learner the equipment, including the shock generator, which was the machine that would produce electric shocks. The participant received a small, real electric shock to convince them that the shock generator really would deliver shocks. The experimenter explained the procedure which would be that the teacher would administer shocks to the learner each time they got a question wrong. It was basically a memory test. The learner explained that they had a heart condition and the experimenter reassured them. The experiment was ready to begin. The learner was strapped into the chair for receiving shocks while the teacher went to a nearby room where the shock generator was located. The teacher read word pairs to the learner. After reading the word pairs the teacher tested the learner's memory of which words went together. The teacher would read out the first word of each word pair and invite the learner to provide the word that was paired with it. The learner indicated their answer by choosing a letter corresponding to the word that they thought went with the first word that the teacher mentioned.

Read the paragraph through – it may even help to read it aloud, unless that will unsettle people around you on the bus, plane or pilgrimage. How did you find it? I find it painful to read – and I wrote it. Let's see how we can fix this paragraph. First, let's note that there is some good knowledge that is present here – the author is aware of different experimental variations and has a detailed knowledge of what took place in experiment number five. Second, use the Stop–Think–Learn procedure detailed below.

STOP

With each paragraph, as you plan it and when you edit it, take a moment to read through your notes (if it is a planned paragraph) or the actual writing (if you have completed the paragraph). If you see it is going well, that can really energise the rest of your writing and keep it on the right track; if it has gone wrong in some way, you can correct it rather than spinning further off track.

THINK

Ask each paragraph 'What are you doing in my essay?' You need to interrogate the paragraph: what is it doing, or trying to do, to contribute to your answering the essay title? Should it do something else? Should it do it in a different way? Can it do what it is trying to do more effectively? Should it be shorter or longer?

LEARN

Think about the answers that you got from interrogating your paragraph. Use that to inform your editing of the paragraph. Write what each paragraph *is* doing when you review your essay. Try to bring this into how you begin future essays. Write what you want each paragraph to do in your essay plan: for example, 'briefly describe the experiment that is the focus of the essay and what was found'. Noting what you want each paragraph to do *before* you start writing and what each paragraph actually does *after* you have written it will really supercharge your writing.

Let's apply the Stop–Think–Learn technique to this paragraph.

STOP

As we stop and read through this sample paragraph, it feels like it has gone wrong. It feels terrible to read. It is 280 words long and does not even report the findings.

THINK

If we ask: 'What are you doing in my essay?' of this paragraph we probably get a sense that it is trying to provide the empirical details of the key series of experiments that are relevant to the essay title. But let's see if we can characterise this writing a little more. This paragraph does the following: it provides a huge amount of detail, in a somewhat disjointed style, much of which seems unlikely to be relevant *for this particular essay*.

LEARN

In the light of interrogating this paragraph, we need to take action. Don't worry, this is kind of fun and cathartic. Let's write what we actually want the paragraph to do and see if we can bring it back into line. We need the paragraph to concisely describe Milgram's experiment(s) in a fluent way and to report the findings. So let's do that now.

It is really helpful to break this long, listless, laborious, paragraph down and see if we can come up with a crisp, concise and coherent alternative. Try to get to the gist and express it clearly.

Milgram conducted, depending on how one counts them, at least 24 variations in his obedience experiments. These studies investigated whether participants would obey those in authority. In experiment five (his new 'baseline' experiment), he recruited people from the local community via a newspaper advertisement. Once they arrived at the laboratory, they and another person were invited to draw lots. This would determine who was to be the teacher and who was to be the learner. It was arranged so that the real participant would be the teacher. The other person was to be the learner. They were a confederate.

Getting the gist – Milgram conducted 24 (or more) variations of his obedience experiments. In experiment five (his new 'baseline'), he recruited participants from the local community to take part in what was said to be a 'learning' experiment. A confederate, posing as a participant, played the role of being the learner.

> The experimenter showed the teacher and learner the equipment, including the shock generator, which was the machine that would produce electric shocks. The participant received a small, real electric shock to convince them that the shock generator really would deliver shocks. The experimenter explained the procedure which would be that the teacher would administer shocks to the learner each time they got a question wrong. It was basically a memory test. The learner explained that they had a heart condition and the experimenter reassured them. The experiment was ready to begin. The learner was strapped into the chair for receiving shocks while the teacher went to a nearby room where the shock generator was located. The teacher read word pairs to the learner. After reading the word pairs the teacher tested the learner's memory of which words went together. The teacher would read out the first word of each word pair and invite the learner to provide the word that was paired with it. The learner indicated their answer by choosing a letter corresponding to the word that they thought went with the first word that the teacher mentioned.

Getting the gist – The procedure entailed the naïve, or 'real', participant playing the role of the 'teacher' and reading pairs of words for the learner to try to remember. Each time the learner made an incorrect response the teacher was required, by the experimenter, to administer an electric shock to them, with the voltage increasing for each error that the learner made.

Using the Stop–Think–Learn technique the following changes were made:

1. Detail that really doesn't matter for this essay at this stage was removed. This can be difficult to gauge and is something you can easily change. For now, we need to convey the essentials of Milgram's research.

    Easy edits of irrelevant information:

    It was easy to remove some of the less relevant information, for example, about drawing lots and being shown the 'shock generator'. Some sentences seemed to convey no information, such as '…the experiment was ready to begin'. These were also easy to chop. Asking, 'What does this contribute of relevance to this essay?' made it easy to identify and remove these unnecessary sentences.

    Removed for now:

    Details about a real electric shock being administered to convince the participant that the shock machine actually gave electric shocks might be used later on in addressing the criticism that perhaps participants were not convinced of the reality of the experiment.

Similarly, the confederate talking about his heart condition might be drawn on later, perhaps when considering how findings varied across different experimental conditions or maybe to make the point that the participant may well have assumed that the 'learner' had been killed. However, these details didn't seem vital right now, so were left to one side.

2. Details that do matter were smoothly integrated. The more you can practise this the easier it will be for you to do.

    Example edit:

    The experimental procedure was described in a lot of short separate sentences. Reading it through feels like riding on a bumpy road with no suspension, so we need something much smoother. Some connecting ideas within a small number of sentences can help to do this. Quick warning: this is not a suggestion that you go for long sentences, but instead thoughtful, intelligent ones. This sentence, for example, pulls together ideas about the roles of the naïve participant and the confederate and what task they were orientating to in the experiment:

    > The procedure entailed the naïve, or 'real', participant playing the role of the 'teacher' and reading pairs of words for the 'learner' to try to remember.

    The following sentence integrates information about what happened when an incorrect response was given, what the experimenter did in the experiment and when the voltage administered would be increased. Handled in separate sentences these different descriptive components would be very staccato to read, but they can be integrated into a smooth, clear sentence that is not too long and cumbersome:

    > Each time the learner made an incorrect response the teacher was required, by the experimenter, to administer an electric shock to them, with the voltage increasing for each error that the learner made.

3. Missing components, crucial to what the paragraph *should be doing*, were added.

    It is worth mentioning that no shocks were actually delivered by the participant in their role as 'teacher' in Milgram's experiment. It's best to do this in a single sentence and I wouldn't at this point get into too much detail about what the participants may or may not have believed – that can be handled latter. For now, we want the key features of the experiment and the main finding. Something along these lines would do the job:

    > The participant did not in fact deliver any electric shocks to the learner, but both the experimental setting and the learner's reaction gave the impression that they had done so.

    We need to mention the key findings. Milgram tended to focus mainly on the percentage of participants who 'shocked to the limit' (STL). Here is a sentence that succinctly conveys that:

    > The key finding that Milgram reports is that 63% of participants showed full obedience, administering 'shocks to the limit' (STL), the maximum of 450 volts, in response to prompts by the experimenter.

We now have something much better to work with and have used 170 words, rather than 280. That's more than 40% off – it's like a Black Friday sale. See how we have lost 110 words and wound up with a paragraph that is not only more concise, but also more coherent and complete:

> Milgram conducted at least 24 variations of his obedience experiments. In experiment five (his new 'baseline'), he recruited participants from the local community to take part in what was said to be a 'learning' experiment. A confederate, posing as a participant, played the role of being the learner. The procedure entailed the naïve, or 'real', participant playing the role of the 'teacher' and reading pairs of words for the 'learner' to try to remember. Each time the learner made an incorrect response the teacher was required, by the experimenter, to administer an electric shock to them, with the voltage increasing for each error that the learner made. The participant did not in fact deliver any electric shocks to the learner, but both the experimental setting and the learner's reaction gave the impression that they had done so. The key finding that Milgram reports is that 63% of participants showed full obedience, administering 'shocks to the limit' (STL), the maximum of 450 volts, in response to prompts by the experimenter.

ACE YOUR ASSIGNMENT
Editing

Editing our own writing can seem like we are just going over the same ground again and we might not even be sure we are making it better. But go for gold here. Read your paragraph and your whole essay – out loud if possible – and I bet you will spot things you can change within five minutes.

What would you prefer:

a.   You spot problems with your essay and fix them before submission.

OR

b.   Your marker spots problems with your essay after submission.

(Hint: Choose a. if you want to start writing brilliant essays.)

FEEDBACK ON THE QUALITY OF YOUR ACADEMIC WRITING

'Check for grammar and/or typographical errors'

Poor grammar and typographical errors are an extremely common point of feedback. These issues might reflect that we made some slips, perhaps as we rushed to complete our essay on time. If this is the case, do yourself a massive favour. Finish the essay a little early, so that you have time – even if it is just one hour – to check through the essay and quickly correct those errors

(Chapters 10 and 12 have more detail on this). Sometimes these comments can identify more persistent issues, perhaps concerning our grammar. Here it can help to read your essay aloud, which will alert you to the bits that don't sound quite right and allow you to rework them. The more you read well-written English the better your use of grammar will be. Also note that most universities will have various forms of writing support available that can directly help with these issues.

'Too chatty, too journalistic'

First, a quick caveat. When essays are accused of being 'journalistic', it is usually a popular magazine form of journalism that markers have in mind, rather than top-quality investigative journalism. This issue was addressed earlier in the chapter (see Sample C in the section on good and bad academic writing). It is such an easy style to fall into, partly because a lot of what we read (and write) takes this form. If you receive this feedback, try to see if there are sections in your essay that are less problematic and compare them. Look back at the section on good and bad academic writing and compare the 'chatty' journalistic and stronger academic samples (C and D respectively). Once you can sense how the styles differ, you can develop and tune in to your academic voice. Go for it – it's worth the effort.

'Write in an academic style'

Many academics produce feedback such as this and it is not always clear what they (or we) have in mind. Again, if there are specific sections in your essay that this applies to, it can be easier to compare paragraphs and identify what the issue is. Maybe you have slipped into a style that lacks the sense of intelligent, scholarly, third-person reflection on relevant perspectives that is at the heart of most really good academic essay writing in psychology. Try to see if your writing is falling into any of the errors identified in samples A–C above, or double-check the subsection entitled, 'We all know what good academic writing is, don't we?'. If all else fails, ask these questions of your writing:

- Is there a sophisticated understanding of relevant ideas? (That is, is it scholarly?)
- Does it demonstrate an awareness of different perspectives?
- Is it written in the third person, unless you are required to do otherwise?
- Reading it, can you sense an intelligent mind at work?
- What does the section you are writing now actually do in your essay?
- What should it do?

'Too descriptive'

Writing can be described as 'too descriptive' for different reasons. It may be that critical evaluation needs to be developed (see Chapter 6 for more on this). However, 'too descriptive' can mean that the descriptive passages are actually too long. Bear in mind that, depending on the specific requirements for your essay, you usually want to provide only the descriptive detail that is necessary in order to address the essay question. Check the subsection entitled 'What it looks like in practice' in the section 'Transforming your descriptive writing'. This provides an illustration of how you can rework your writing so that your descriptive passages become smoother and more succinct.

Feedback on 'academic writing'

Any essay feedback that is not in praise of how wonderful we are can be a bit like biting into a chocolate and tasting garlic – it can be (for many of us) unpalatable and unexpected. It seems especially painful when the feedback becomes as personal as 'attacking our very writing'. That feels so fundamental that we may well find it the most difficult criticism to take on board, especially if the marker, perhaps working through 100 essays, seems a bit abrupt or curt in their comments. But do yourself a huge favour – after you have got over the shock to your ego, try to see the feedback as something that can help you.

Even feedback that does not suggest *how we can make things better* may usefully identify *what* we should work on and *where* this is a problem in our essay – that in itself is helpful. Use that feedback along with the ideas in this chapter to help to address your writing issues. Put your ego (and perhaps indelicate marker comments) to one side and see this as one part of a roadmap for producing a great essay.

Look at feedback on your academic writing in this way: yes, it may feel depressing because the marker has identified an issue that is likely to be relevant across your assignments, but that is what makes it hold such potential. Investing in improving your academic writing is going to be relevant for improving *all of your written assignments* and is perhaps the most transferable skill for further study or professional work after your degree. Don't let your ego blind you to this. If your writing is about to get better, a little dent to your pride is a tiny price to pay. See comments and feedback as scaffolding – these comments, the techniques we have considered and, above all, your latent ability can work together like a magic triangle, enabling you to reach your full potential.

REFLECTING ON THE CHAPTER:
Communicating with your audience

Academics often make a major assumption – perhaps helped by a certain amnesia – when it comes to writing essays. We tend to (mis)recall ourselves as not really having a problem with writing academic essays and infer that others shouldn't either. This is particularly the case with descriptive writing and (to some extent) academic voice. But in reality, most of us have written our share of dodgy essays and learnt the

(Continued)

skill of academic writing gradually, rather than merely channelling a genius of which we cannot speak. If you want to transform your descriptive writing and find your academic voice, don't forget this amazingly important secret: *your essay is a form of communication with a reader*. You have the secret now – so use it wisely.

Look at how the authors of the books and journals that you read achieve (or perhaps fail to achieve) effective communication with their reader. Don't think vaguely: 'It's not very clear'. Get specific: 'They describe the key features of the experiment in a sentence'; 'They contrast different interpretations of the data'. By reading other academic voices, you can start to find your own academic voice. But above all else, keep reminding yourself that the essay is *a communicative act* – you submit it and someone reads it. It takes time for us to find the best way of communicating with others across any medium, including the academic essay, but you really can do this. Your academic voice might be shaky at first – and that is absolutely fine. The great thing is that you have embarked on a journey to become a better academic writer and, above all, this means that you will be increasingly effective at communicating. It's like you can do a bit of magic that transmits your thoughts and understandings from the privacy of your mind to others – in a way that they can grasp and appreciate. That is an amazing skill and it is within arm's reach.

TAKE AWAY POINTS FROM THIS CHAPTER

- Be clear about what your writing needs to do. Your writing should show your scholarly engagement with the issues raised by the essay title.

- Look (in this chapter and elsewhere) at good – and bad – academic writing. Develop your increasingly astute sense of what good academic writing actually is.

- Check that you are not side-tracked into thinking that your writing has to be 'clever', different, full of surprises, or obscure.

- Get a clear sense of what each sentence and paragraph of your writing is doing in your essay (e.g. outlining empirical details, evaluating the target theory, contrasting different perspectives).

- To keep your descriptive writing concise, use the amount of description needed to support your scholarly discussion of the issues raised in the essay title.

- Take time to look through your work and to make changes that will strengthen your writing.

- Overcome any negative reactions you may have to feedback on your writing and use it to your advantage, seeing it as a key tool for your improvement.

- We don't expect to be virtuoso musicians the moment we first pick up a banjo, bass guitar or piccolo and we should allow ourselves time to become expert academic writers too.

- Writing regularly and reflecting on your writing will empower you to develop your academic voice and reach your full writing potential. Your essay is worth it – and so are you.

LINKING TO OTHER CHAPTERS

Sometimes not finding your academic voice can lead to procrastination, as you put off starting to write your essay until you feel you have a clearer sense of what to say or how to say it. As Chapter 1 notes, this underestimates the role that just writing can have in helping us to find the what (to say) and how (to say it) of our essays. Description can be a particularly tricky (and under-discussed) feature of effective essay writing, and handling this so that it still enables us to critically evaluate (see Chapter 6) and stay focused on the question (see Chapter 4) really helps our essays to communicate clearly and effectively to our reader. An important aspect of both finding our academic voice and handling description effectively is the way in which we structure both within and between paragraphs. This is dealt with directly in Chapter 5. Finally, Chapter 10's guidance on reviewing and editing essays (and Chapter 12's guidance on take-away exams) can help ensure that we can identify and address writing issues before we submit our essays (even when we have limited time left). We have a latent ability to achieve so much in our academic writing – soaking up good academic writing and looking (in a kind-hearted way) at what does and does not work in our own essays can help us to realise something of our own considerable academic writing potential.

Chapter 8

Sum it up – how to write an effective conclusion

In this chapter you will learn…

- How you can identify and avoid problem conclusions
- How to transform a weak conclusion into something much stronger
- How to make your conclusions more thoughtful, scholarly and conceptual

CONCLUSION: WHAT IT IS AND WHY IT MATTERS

We have all had the experience of reading a book or watching a film and feeling really cheated out of a good ending. The 'it was all a dream' ending to the wonderfully creative *Alice's Adventures in Wonderland* might have struck you as dull and unimaginative. Perhaps you found that in both *Huckleberry Finn* and *Little Women* the endings were inconsistent with the rest of the book. Or, maybe you think that the ending of *Harry Potter and the Deathly Hallows* is a little too neat or, in the case of *In the Woods*, a bit too unresolved. We can all think of endings that don't quite satisfy us; it is usually because they matter – we really care about where we wind up at the end of a book, film or TV show. We have given our time and attention, we feel invested and we do not want our expectations to be disappointed by a lazy, inconsistent, unrealistic or unsatisfying ending.

As noted in Chapter 4, a particularly useful piece of feedback that I received was given by an editor on one of the first papers I published. I had struggled to find a way of ending the paper effectively and the editor pinpointed this issue, suggesting that in my concluding paragraph I should give the reader a sense of the 'take home message'. This idea of a 'take home message' simply, but effectively, captures how we should deal with endings in the conclusions of our academic writing. We need to convey to the reader a sense of *where we are* on the issues outlined in the essay title, having discussed all that we have in the body of our essay.

Depending on the format of your writing – and especially, your specific assignment guidance – your conclusion is typically one or two paragraphs in length, though often longer in the case of certain extended essays. It is the final taste that you leave your reader with. As your reader tries to see the depth and sophistication of your grasp of the issues that are relevant to the essay title, your conclusion plays a vital role, encapsulating the essence of your understanding and conveying the extent to which you can conceptualise the material that you have discussed.

STOP AND THINK

Can you identify in your own essays some stronger – and weaker – conclusions?

What features were present in the strong ones that were absent in the weaker ones?

What do you feel could be done to transform the weaker conclusions into stronger ones?

The unfortunate thing, given how vital good conclusions are, is that they are quite rare. Often even well-informed, well-structured and critically evaluative essays fail at that last hurdle, seeming to run out of steam on that final test of their understanding. If you feel unsure about what to write, hesitant about how to voice your own conceptualisation of the issues or confused as to whether new material should be introduced, then you may find that this opportunity to really shine is missed, and, rather than enhancing your essay, your conclusion diminishes it.

The good news is that while good conclusions are often a challenge to write, if you start to develop your craft, the effort is well worth it. If you can't cope with any more good news, please skip the rest of this paragraph. Some further good news for those still reading: you really can learn to write better conclusions.

- You can come to more clearly spot how and when you are going wrong with your conclusions.
- You can get a very clear sense of what makes a really good conclusion.

AND

- You can learn the techniques that will help you to achieve this yourself.

STOP AND THINK
Do you have any baggage?

We probably come to our essays in general and our conclusions in particular, with all sorts of past experiences, ideas about what our writing *should* be like along with hopes and fears about what it *will* be like. It is helpful to acknowledge your own feelings about conclusions, so complete the exercise, 'How do you feel about conclusions' below, to help you do that.

Getting your conclusion right has a significant impact in terms of what your essay contributes, how you experience writing it and how it is judged. It would be misleading to say that this is a quick fix, but thinking through the issues we address in this chapter can genuinely transform your writing. Having the understanding, perspective and technical skill needed to end your essay effectively is like having a superpower. Perhaps you cannot fly, walk up walls or make yourself invisible at will, but you can become 'Conclusion-person' with the special power to create effective conclusions across essay formats and topics!

ACE YOUR ASSIGNMENT
Practising conclusion writing

Start to prioritise your conclusion-writing ability. If you can write good conclusions, you have a superpower for all of your essays. Practise writing conclusions – perhaps drawing on some notes that you have from a lecture and trying to write a conclusion that captures a key debate. You can check how conclusions are written in papers that you are referring to as a part of your degree, or you can look at a (preferably non-empirical) paper, read it through and cover up the conclusion, and then think about what it might include, or write one yourself. You can then have fun comparing your conclusion to the published one. At the very least, write the conclusion for the essays you submit more than once – it is perhaps the most challenging essay-writing skill and practising develops this superpower in you.

IDENTIFYING YOUR THOUGHTS ABOUT CONCLUSIONS

This super-skill is partly separate from the other aspects of good writing covered in this book, but it is strongly linked to them. It is rare, really rare, to find someone who can write great conclusions but has a poor introduction, weak structure and almost no critical evaluation in their essay. In cracking the issue of writing effective conclusions, you are simultaneously engaging with ideas at a deep and profound level. Your struggle with writing an excellent conclusion will in itself encourage you to spiral ever more deeply into the issues at the heart of your essay. Your writing and your thinking can, and will, inform each other. Each time you feel stuck writing your conclusion, the issues to do with how deeply you understand your essay are made more vivid. Right then and there, you have the opportunity to gain a deeper, more profound grasp of the issues. Don't expect a quick fix with writing conclusions – even experienced writers can find them a challenge – but the process of wrestling with your ideas to create a good conclusion is academic thinking and writing at its very best.

EXERCISE
How do you feel about conclusions?

Which of these statements best describes how you feel about writing a conclusion?

a.   I am hesitant about putting my own ideas into an essay.

b.   I don't think I am sufficiently qualified or expert to put my ideas into a conclusion.

c.   I feel that I can put down what others have done and said, but I am not sure what else to write.

d.   I feel that I have done the essay and am not sure what to write now.

e.   I think this is where I am expected to evaluate the work that I have covered.

f.   Conclusions require me to think about the literature in the body of my essay.

g.   Conclusions require me to outline what future research should do.

h.   I think this is a chance for me to share my own ideas.

You have probably selected more than one option. Now look in the text below for some quick responses relating to what possibilities and problems might arise from these different sentiments regarding writing a conclusion.

There are many different ways in which we can approach writing conclusions. Here we discuss some of these key approaches to writing conclusions.

Hesitation and self-doubt about essay and conclusion writing (if you selected a, b or both, this may apply to you).

You may have doubts and uncertainties about writing an essay at all, and a conclusion in particular. This is understandable and is not, in itself, a bad thing. A curious mixture of confidence and self-doubt can really help with good academic writing. It's partly a question of using these two feelings positively. Self-doubt – in moderation – can be great for enabling us to listen, learn, change approach, edit and rewrite. Confidence – in moderation – can liberate us to start writing, encourage us to keep writing and enable us to conceptualise the task as doable rather than overwhelming.

Hesitation is understandable, but the conclusion needs you to be able to identify the essence of the debates covered in the essay. That way you can show your thinking and understanding of what the key debates in your essay hinge on, and how we can conceptualise the relevant critique. Your mind is at work as you read, think and write – the conclusion is a space where all this good work can be made especially visible.

Uncertainty regarding the specific task of writing a conclusion (if you selected c, d or both, this may apply to you).

Essays can so easily become about ideas out there, and when we have outlined these what else is there to say? The conclusion has the scope to offer a framework for making sense of what we have covered in our essay, identifying the key issues at the heart of debates and grouping together the overarching types of critique that have been raised concerning theory and/or research. This reveals your sense-making at work – however tenuous that may feel. Reading this sort of conceptualising conclusion gives the reader much more than just a list.

Associating conclusions with critical evaluation (if you selected e or f, this may apply to you).

These points show a recognition that the conclusion should do more than list what has been covered. The thinking and evaluation referred to should be present throughout your essay, but be at a more conceptual level in your conclusion. The conclusion moves from particular studies to categories or types of study, overarching issues and the essence of key debates.

Associating conclusions with thoughts about future research (if you selected g, this may apply to you).

On its own, this would not be enough. The conclusion needs to provide some framework for making sense of the ideas raised in your essay. If done with specificity and in a way which relates to the key issues already identified in your conclusion, outlining the specific contribution of future research can be a valuable addition.

Associating conclusions with sharing one's own ideas (if you selected h, this may apply to you).

Your own ideas are best thought of as quite different from the 'you know what I think…' format. Rather than a chance to share your thoughts as opinions touched off by the essay topic, the conclusion is an opportunity to display the subtlety and sophistication of your sense-making of the material covered in your essay. Harnessing your desire to 'put yourself into the essay' can be a challenge, but doing so can enable you to achieve something much more impactful than simply dropping thoughts and opinions in – it can give a more learned, scholarly sense to your conclusion.

GOOD AND BAD CONCLUSIONS

In order to get a sense of a good and a not-so-good conclusion, compare the two samples below. The two conclusions are not at the absolute extreme ends of a quality continuum – I don't think either would (ordinarily) be associated with an essay that fails – but one is significantly stronger than the other. In these samples I want to show that a very different quality of conclusion can be written despite being the same length, so both conclusions are exactly 146 words in length.

Guiding thoughts

To get the most from looking at these samples, try to think yourself into the essay title for a moment. If the topic is a little unfamiliar to you, don't worry too much – the focus here is on what is done, not what the content is. Some brief orientating thoughts are also given, but feel free to read these or skip past to look at the sample conclusions without delay.

The title that these sample conclusions are addressing is:

'To what extent does Social Identity Theory account for why people engage in riots?'

A reasonable attempt at this essay should convey an understanding of the way in which Social Identity Theory accounts for riots (this should include reference to the idea that our social, or group, identity is relevant to understanding behaviour that is often glossed as a 'riot'). Some sense of the evidential basis for this theory should be present in the essay. A good essay might well contrast this Social Identity Theory approach with that of Le Bon (who emphasied a form of group consciousness, or 'group mind', and the release of destructive impulses) and also Zimbardo (who emphasised a reduced sense of self as an individual, or deindividuation, and the release of destructive impulses).

Now, without seeing the rest of the essay, let's zoom straight into the conclusion. First, remind yourself of the title and then read each sample conclusion through twice.

Essay title: 'To what extent does Social Identity Theory account for why people engage in riots?'

Sample one

In conclusion, this essay has shown that people riot for lots of different reasons. Le Bon's 'group mind' approach suggested that, when isolated, a person may be a very cultivated individual, but in a crowd he or she becomes a creature acting by instinct. Zimbardo conducted experiments showing that when people are made anonymous, they become deindividuated and that this gives rise to the release of destructive impulses and aggression. In the St Paul's area of Bristol, Reicher found that people engaging in the riot were not like a 'mad mob', but they directed traffic in a responsible way and confined their rioting to the geographical area of St Paul's. The Social Identity Theory account of riots makes sense of the behaviour in the St Paul's riot. Much more additional research is needed in different cultures to provide further information about why people engage in riots.

Sample two

Social Identity Theory has challenged previous accounts of social unrest, including those of Le Bon and Zimbardo, drawing on data from real-world riots to emphasise the role of group, or *social*, identity and to argue that such behaviour may be *purposive*, rather than merely impulsive. Methodological challenges to Social Identity Theory have identified that a reliance on participants' accounts of taking part in riots may inevitably lead to findings that emphasise rationale over impulsivity, while theoretical challenges have argued that the approach has perhaps under-theorised the link between identity and the broader social and ideological context in which social unrest is situated. The continuing significance of Social Identity Theory within social psychology and beyond may depend on how effectively it incorporates diverse empirical evidence and whether it can convincingly articulate the ways in which identity and ideology interrelate in accounts of why people engage in riots.

EXERCISE
Reflecting on the sample conclusions

Take a moment to reflect on how you felt reading the two sample conclusions?

Reading sample one, I felt:

Reading sample two, I felt:

Now note what impressions you formed of the author of each sample. How strong was their grasp of the issues do you think?

Sample one:

Sample two:

Dissecting the stronger and weaker conclusion

Let's go through each of these conclusions and try to identify what the author is doing. Identifying what the author is doing can be quite a challenge when we are not used to it – we are usually so focused on the content of what is being communicated – but it is a great skill to develop. The extracts below are annotated with a brief summary of what is being done.

Sample one

In conclusion, this essay has shown that people riot for lots of different reasons. *<A very vague summary of the whole essay is given here.>*Le Bon's 'group mind' approach suggested that, when isolated, a person may be a very cultivated individual, but in a crowd he or she becomes a creature acting by instinct. *<One of Le Bon's key arguments is summarised here.>* Zimbardo conducted experiments showing that when people are made anonymous, they become deindividuated and that this gives rise to the release of destructive impulses and aggression. *<A key idea of Zimbardo's is given here, with an indication of the empirical basis (experiments).>* In the St Paul's area of Bristol, Reicher found that people engaging in the riot were not like a 'mad mob', but they directed traffic in a responsible way and confined their rioting to the geographical area of St Paul's. *<An outline of what Reicher found in a specific piece of research is given here.>* The Social Identity Theory account of riots makes sense of the behaviour in the St Paul's riot. *<The St Paul's findings are cited as evidence of the Social Identity Theory account of riots.>* Much more additional research is needed in different cultures to provide further information about why people engage in riots. *<The conclusion ends with a very vague sense that additional research is needed and that this should include cross-cultural work. While the mention of further cross-cultural research has potential, it is undeveloped and reads like something that could be, and probably is, used in almost any essay.>*

Do you notice that this weaker – though quite common – form of conclusion has these two key features:

- Much of it is written in the sort of way you would expect the main body of the essay to be written; it appears to recap exactly the phrases that one would expect to find throughout the rest of the essay. This is evident in how both theoretical positions and empirical evidence are handled. Note how this extract fails to conceptualise the theoretical perspective it is referring to: 'Le Bon's 'group mind' approach suggested that, when isolated, a person may be a cultivated individual…'. And this passage focuses on empirical detail at the expense of a thoughtful reflection on (or a conceptualisation of) the state of the evidence: '… they directed traffic in a responsible way and confined their rioting to the geographical area of St Paul's…'.
- In other places it leaps from giving far too much detail to being extremely vague! In the first sentence, reference to 'lots of different reasons' is not very helpful. This could be written without any knowledge or thinking about the issues. Similarly, in the last sentence, the argument that 'Much more additional research is needed in different cultures to provide further information about why people engage in riots' reads like it might be airdropped in to just about any conclusion that this author writes, rather than arising from genuine thought about this specific topic.

EXERCISE
What's it doing?

See if you can work out what these concluding sentence components are doing by matching the indicative sentence stems to the types of error (a–e) listed below:

Sentence stems

1. In my opinion...

2. As this essay has shown, X argued that..., Y argued... and Z argued...

3. More research is needed involving larger sample sizes.

4. In addition to [the material covered in the essay], Z conducted a study which found...

5. Psychologists have lots of different opinions about this issue.

Common errors

a. Vagueness

b. Unspecified future research

c. Listing of ideas covered in the essay

d. Own opinion added

e. New material dropped in

Sample two

Social Identity Theory has challenged previous accounts of social unrest, including those of Le Bon and Zimbardo, drawing on data from real-world riots to emphasise the role of group, or *social*, identity and to argue that such behaviour may be *purposive*, rather than merely impulsive. *<This conclusion starts by conceptualising both the empirical basis ('drawing on data from real-world riots') and the theoretical emphasis ('emphasise the role of group, or social, identity') of Social Identity Theory. It is conceptual because it conveys a sense of the fundamental essence of the approach rather than very specific individual details. It also provides a contrast – at a conceptual level – between Social Identity Theory's purposive account for why riots may occur and Le Bon and Zimbardo's emphasis on impulsivity.>* Methodological challenges to Social Identity Theory have identified that a reliance on participants' accounts of taking part in riots may inevitably lead to findings that emphasise rationale over impulsivity, while theoretical challenges have argued that the approach has perhaps under-theorised the link between identity and the broader social and ideological context in which social unrest is situated. *<Critique of the Social Identity Theory approach is given and it is conceptualised as 'methodological' and 'theoretical' criticisms. A sense of the key underlying argument is given (for example, 'under-theorised the link between identity and the broader social and ideological context...') without repeating details that would be more suited to the main body of the essay.>* The continuing significance of Social Identity Theory within social psychology and beyond may depend on how effectively it incorporates diverse empirical evidence and whether it can convincingly articulate the ways in which identity and ideology interrelate in accounts of why people engage in riots. *<This really effectively sums up the underlying ideas, or deep essence, of what the essay itself would have discussed in further detail. This is precise: it is particular to this essay rather than being applicable to lots of different psychology essays. And it is conceptual: it is appropriately abstract ('the ways in which identity and ideology interrelate…') rather than restricted to concrete particulars.>*

TRANSFORMING YOUR CONCLUSIONS

As you read through the examples of good conclusions in this chapter, it is important not to become disheartened. It is almost impossible to write a really good conclusion straight off, but it is also almost impossible not to get better if you take a little time.

Using the perspective of the reader

As mentioned in other chapters in this book, spare a thought for your dear reader. Picture them, late at night, the moonlight reflecting off their laptop, foxes yelping in the distance as midnight marking beckons. What will your reader think as they read *your* conclusion? What does your conclusion communicate to them and, crucially, if you were the marker, what would you think of your conclusion?

If you can imagine being the reader (the moonlight and foxes are optional), it can really help with your conclusion writing. So try not to think of yourself as the author for now. What comments would you give as feedback for your conclusion? Write down the feedback that you would give. Look at your feedback and see if you can use it – along with the checklist and other ideas developed in this chapter, to really improve your conclusion.

Using the interplay of writing and thinking

Good conclusions make you think. They make the reader think with their specific, relevant, conceptual insights into the issues at the heart of the essay. Good conclusions also make the author think *in the very process of writing them.* As you spiral deeper into the issues at the centre of your essay, you really are faced with questions such as:

How can I conceptualise key debates in this area?

What is the essence of the target perspective or idea in this essay?

How can I conceptualise the critique that has been raised?

What thoughts should the intelligent reader be left with in relation to the essay title, having read the essay?

Don't run away from these thoughts or feel disempowered by them. These thoughts are like golddust; they are the vehicle for taking your conclusion deeper. They do not have easy answers, but staying with these sorts of questions and attempting to address them will make your conclusion stronger.

Using the golden key of editing

It can be disappointing when the answer to our problem is both mundane and – well – kind of hard work. I remember my PhD supervisor once saying, as a throw-away observation, that the key thing that limited most undergraduate work was a lack of editing. It's not the sort of answer we are usually looking for. It's not exotic or mysterious and, even worse, it's not a zero-effort fix for us.

How much nicer if merely chanting the essay title backwards twice while listening to Mozart's *Requiem Mass* meant that we suddenly wrote conclusions like angels. Now that backward chanting may work – I haven't tried it – but it's unlikely, so we are left with something that really will be effective but requires *us* to work: (cue subdued drum roll) *editing*. The importance of editing has been emphasised a lot throughout this book. I have edited most of the sentences in this book, all of the examples of good writing and, most laboriously, each of the examples of *good* conclusions. If I hadn't edited them, the 'good' conclusions would be long, rambling and very boring – in short, not so convincingly good after all. The process has, however, made me more sympathetic to what a challenge good conclusion writing is. It is hard work – but you really can do it and editing provides the key. Write your conclusion, read it, look at the 'Ace your assignment' checklist (below), use the thoughts that are developed in this chapter and *rewrite* it.

ACE YOUR ASSIGNMENT
Conclusion checklist

Use the specific questions and the free-text response boxes to check your conclusion. The aim here is not to sign your conclusion off as 'A' OK, but instead to identify if there are ways in which it can be further improved. Spotting issues is a cause for celebration – yippee! – rather than castigation. If there is scope for improvement, you are on the cusp of making things better. Well done!

Specific questions

Can someone reading your conclusion tell what the essay title is, or would they just get a very vague sense of the broad topic?

Does your conclusion conceptualise or does it restate concrete essay content?

Does your conclusion convey a sense of academic reflection or personal opinion?

Does your conclusion provide specific thoughts about the ideas discussed in your essay or does it rehash general clichés that could be used for most conclusions?

Would someone reading your conclusion get a sense that you, the author, had a knowledgeable academic understanding relevant to the specific essay, or had simply run out of things to say?

(Continued)

Free-text response: What does your conclusion say, do and reveal?

What is your conclusion really *saying*? Ignoring the specific content, try to work out what your conclusion is telling your reader.

What is your conclusion *doing*? Again, moving away from specific content, is your conclusion describing, evaluating, conceptualising or generalising? How would you describe the sorts of things it does?

What is your conclusion *revealing*? What does your conclusion reveal about you the author in terms of your thinking about the specific issues identified in the essay title?

Dissecting a strong conclusion

It really is worth getting a sense of the shape, style and approach of a well-written conclusion. The example below is designed to support this process. First, read it in its entirety twice. Try to identify what features make this a strong conclusion. Having done this, look at the line-by-line analysis of the conclusion.

There is a technique here. There are features that are common across well-written conclusions. You can learn these and transform your conclusions. However, developing these skills, like learning to play the mandolin, takes time and applying them to your writing takes patience, as to do so will require that you write and then rewrite your conclusion.

The idea of writing a draft conclusion (and indeed a draft essay) and then editing it to create a stronger essay can be off-putting. Which of the examples in this chapter do you think were written without editing and which were edited? If you think that it is the stronger examples that required the editing you are correct – beam with pride. The first draft of sample three, below was initially very long (319 words) and not as specific as I thought it should be. The redrafted version is shorter (154 words) and draws on more specific ideas that help to keep the focus more firmly on the essay title. Taking time to redraft your conclusion is amazingly effective – try it!

Essay title: 'To what extent does Executive Functioning Theory provide an adequate understanding of Autistic Spectrum Disorders?'

Sample three

Since its emergence in the 1980s, Executive Functioning Theory (EFT) has offered a cognitively-based framework for understanding deficits associated with Autistic Spectrum Disorders (ASD). While the theory has been understood as accounting for some symptoms long associated with ASD (including repetitive behaviour and a limited range of interests), it has been challenged in terms of its explanatory scope for 'less obviously cognitive' features of ASD (such as emotion regulation and communication). More fundamentally, questions have been raised concerning whether EFT has actually identified deficits directly linked to ASD, or has instead highlighted Executive Function deficits associated with co-morbid neurodevelopmental disorders, particularly ADHD. These different perspectives suggest that the potential contributions of EFT should be understood in the light of the complex and heterogeneous profile of individuals on the Autistic Spectrum and the particular issues that this raises for attempts to develop overarching theories that meaningfully account for the varied experiences and manifestations of ASD.

EXERCISE
Your response

How does it feel to read the sample answer above? Note your feelings here.

Reading this conclusion, I felt:

Sample three

The extract below is annotated, identifying what it is that the conclusion is doing and what makes this conclusion so strong.

Since its emergence in the 1980s, Executive Functioning Theory (EFT) has offered a cognitively-based framework for understanding deficits associated with Autistic Spectrum Disorders (ASD). *<This is directly relevant to the essay title and provides a **characterisation** of the target theoretical approach: 'a cognitively based framework...'. Characterisations such as these demonstrate that you can conceptualise the type of idea or theory that you are writing about in your conclusion.>* While the theory has been understood as accounting for some symptoms long associated with ASD (including repetitive behaviour and limited range of interests), it has been challenged in terms of its explanatory scope for 'less obviously cognitive' features of ASD (such as emotion regulation and communication). *<This section doesn't vaguely refer to different opinions, nor does it simply list what was covered in the essay. Instead, it **conceptualises the scope of the target theory**, highlighting that it has been challenged regarding its capacity to account for 'less obviously cognitive' symptoms associated with ASDs.>* More fundamentally, questions have been raised concerning whether EFT has actually identified deficits directly linked to ASD, or has instead highlighted Executive Function deficits associated with co-morbid neurodevelopmental disorders, particularly ADHD. *<Another critical point is raised here, but it is not simply offered as one more item on a list: 'and another thing...'. This critique is identified as differing in kind from the issues already touched on, in that it raises questions of a fundamental nature. This sense of **conceptualising the different types of critique** really strengthens the conclusion.>* These different perspectives suggest that the potential contributions of EFT should be understood in the light of the complex and heterogeneous profile of individuals on the Autistic Spectrum and the particular issues that this raises for attempts to develop overarching theories that meaningfully account for the varied experiences and manifestations of ASD. *<This is a really nice 'take home message' for your reader. It conveys a sense of the issues that the intelligent reader should be considering in the light of the issues that would have been discussed throughout the essay. It has a particularity that addresses the specific essay question – this could not be lifted and used for any old psychology essay. It also, in a*

nutshell, conveys key concepts that provide a framework for thinking about the issue of the adequacy of EFT for understanding Autistic Spectrum Disorders. It really is worth reading this through several times to get a sense of how language is used here to do this complex conceptual work. As you immerse yourself in good conclusion writing, you are – by a sort of osmosis – acquiring an intuitive skill-set that you can draw on to make your conclusions focused, conceptual and insightful.>

EXERCISE
Catch the concept!

If you want to really improve your conclusions, learn to move from concrete to conceptual thinking and writing. This means moving to a more abstract form of expression.

Try this super, fun – and potentially addictive – game for yourself. If you get really good, you can invent your own examples for the amusement and edification of everyone you meet.

From the list below, see if you can identify the conceptual and the concrete version of each idea pair. These sentences illustrate the conceptual/concrete distinction – a distinction that can help when you are writing your conclusions.

1. (a) In the riot which occurred in the St Paul's area of Bristol, Reicher found that participants were not like a 'mad mob' of destructive individuals as others had claimed. In fact, in the riot, some participants were involved in redirecting the traffic.

    (b) Reicher's account of a riot in the early 1980s emphasised the idea that the behaviour observed was consistent with the participants' social identity and could thus be understood as purposive rather than merely impulsive.

2. (a) Skinner emphasised the ways in which rewards for the child's best attempts at speaking – often involving praise and attention from the parent – would lead to ever more proficient speech on the part of the child. Chomsky argued that there would have to be constant rewarding (and withholding of reward or even punishment) in order for the child to master the complexities of language and that the evidence, including the existence of logical or virtuous errors, demonstrates that children have a capacity to acquire the rules of language.

    (b) Chomsky's emphasis on language acquisition taking place through active, innate mechanisms within the child – whatever the environment – stands in direct contrast to Skinner's conception of a relatively passive child acquiring language via a highly responsive external environment.

FEEDBACK ON CONCLUSIONS

Writing conclusions can be a challenge, so having a really clear sense of what to aim for is important. Before examining the features of a strong conclusion in detail, it is worth thinking about some recurrent feedback concerning conclusions and how the problems identified in the feedback can be addressed.

'Always include a proper conclusion'

What it looks like:

The essay ends without a paragraph that reflects on the totality of the issues identified in the essay title.

What are the key features of this?

The key feature is that the essay ends abruptly. Instead of reflecting on issues discussed in the preceding body of the essay, the last paragraph deals with just one specific part of the essay.

Why is it a problem?

The reader wants to see what you make of the totality of the issues addressed in your essay and what, if any, framework for making sense of it you can provide.

How can I fix it?

Think about the essence of the debates and critique that are present in your essay. What are the factors on which these debates hinge? In what ways can you organise the critique that you cover? Show the reader your mind at work in structuring this material. You may find it helpful to look at the examples of good conclusions in samples two and three above once more to see how these identify the essence of the key debates and conceptualise the material covered, providing a framework for thinking about different types of critique.

'Don't introduce new material in your conclusion'

What it looks like:

Imagine that this is the essay title:

'What challenges, if any, has research raised for conventional understandings of actor–observer differences?'

And this is the conclusion:

In conclusion, actor–observer research has been understood from different perspectives. Some have emphasised the importance of visual perspective and others of empathic understanding. In addition to the literature already referred to, Malle, Knobe and Nelson (2007) have provided important evidence arising from a meta-analysis of actor–observer difference studies. Their research shows that there is enormous variation in terms of the measured actor–observer effect across studies and much of this might be accounted for by significant differences in the methodological approaches adopted in the different studies.

What are the key features of this?

A citation appears in the conclusion that does not appear in the main body of your essay. Although this can sometimes be done to further clarify your conceptualisation of the material, usually it does not work like that.

Why is it a problem?

Your conclusion should be conceptualising the totality of the material that you have covered in your essay. If you start to unpack additional literature, for example empirical research findings not previously discussed, then your conclusion loses coherence, has less conceptual focus and starts to look much less like a proper conclusion.

How can I fix it?

If a reference is worth including in your essay, bring it into the main body of your essay. This is especially true for any literature that is elaborating part of the argument (for example, reporting on relevant empirical findings) rather than conceptualising the totality of what has been discussed.

EXERCISE
Try it out

Locate a conclusion you have written or drafted and read it through. Reflect on what your conclusion actually does (e.g. lists essay content, makes vague assertions, gives own opinion, conceptualises etc.). If you had to characterise what your conclusion does, what would you say? If you find this difficult, you may find ideas touched on in the exercise 'What's it doing?' above help with this.

It can also help to be a little humorous and irreverent in doing this exercise, we probably find it easier to change our writing when we don't take ourselves too seriously. Without getting drawn into the content of your conclusion ask; 'What does it tell the reader?'

Do any of these apply or can you come up with your own characterisation?

- In conclusion let me list all (or some) of the major points in my essay
- Here are some citations that I thought I'd surprise you with
- I have run out of covering what others have said so let me tell you what I think
- I can't think of what else to say but future research might solve it

'Avoid being too vague or general in your conclusion and try to be more specific'

What it looks like:

Imagine that this is the essay title:

'Critically evaluate the contribution of attributional semantics to our understanding of the causal implications of our talk.'

And this is the conclusion:

This essay has argued that attributional semantics has indeed contributed to our understanding of the causal implications of our talk. *Psychologists differ*, with some arguing that attributional semantics makes an important contribution to understanding the causal implications of our talk and others disagreeing with this. The essay has shown that *there are significant problems with the research. Further research is needed* in order to fully address this question.

What are the key features of this?

This conclusion touches on potentially relevant points, such as the differences between psychologists, the problems with research and the need for further research, but without specifying any of them.

Why is it a problem?

Without specific details, the points made in the conclusion are truisms that could be applicable for almost any essay – of course psychologists disagree, research has problems and future research could contribute. It would be much more surprising if any of these were not the case. This vague conclusion conveys no useful insights into this particular essay topic.

How can I fix it?

This vague conclusion is, in some ways, a step in the right direction. The author has realised that conclusions should not just repeat what has been covered in the body of the essay. But in the effort to summarise, too much has been lost and the essential conceptualisation has been avoided. It is easier to become vague than to really get to the underlying essence of the issues being discussed.

Look at the tell-tale problem phrases: 'Psychologists differ', 'there are significant problems with the research' and 'Further research is needed', and interrogate your understanding of each by asking questions such as:

- In what ways and on what fundamental issues do psychologists disagree?
- What, in essence, are the problems with the sort of research that has been conducted?
- What types of research would overcome these problems and contribute to informing the debate between the psychologists you have referred to?

'Avoid truisms or obvious statements in your conclusion'

What it looks like:

Imagine that this is the essay title:

'Critically evaluate psychological perspectives on why people engage in crime.'

And this is the conclusion:

Having considered the different perspectives on why people engage in crime, it is important to note that *every personality is different* and will behave differently. Also, *cultures differ* – so ideas about behaviour will vary across cultures. Things change across time also – *people in one era may differ from those in other eras.*

What are the key features of this?

> Conclusions that contain truisms are often playing it too safe. The author is typically so concerned that their answer might be judged to be 'wrong' that they make assertions that are almost impossible to reasonably dispute. Variations of 'people are different' is a commonly used truism in conclusions: it is, at one level, difficult to dispute and is self-evidently true.

Why is it a problem?

> If things are self-evidently true, why do we need to state them? To develop this point we could ask: 'what do truisms tell the reader about the author's understanding of the issues identified in the essay title?' The reader of a truism will think: 'the author has shown that they are aware of this basic, obvious point, which does not reveal any depth of understanding and could probably be arrived at without studying psychology at all'. Inserting a truism does not add to the strength of a conclusion, it is actually not even neutral – in most cases, it actively detracts from the conclusion, causing the reader to question the author's depth of understanding.

How can I fix it?

> After you have written the first draft of your conclusion read it through carefully. Imagine that you are tired and bored (some of us can slip into this form of method acting more quickly than others) and that you are slightly inclined to say: 'well that's obvious, isn't it?' You need to be careful not to overdo this. You want to assume the identity of a partially jaded reader, not an out and out cynic. You want to challenge and possibly remove only that which is really redundant, adding nothing to your conclusion – not the good bits. If something seems obvious take the following steps:

> a.   Ask 'why is it here?' What were you trying to do by including it? Try to be as honest, specific and fair to yourself as you can with this. You might have wanted to convey an understanding of the wider context, introduce some critique or bring all of the different ideas discussed together in some way.
>
> b.   If you feel it is important to include it, see if you can re-word it so that it is makes a valuable, specific point.
>
> c.   If you can't re-word it but still think it is attempting to do something important, then remove it into some form of notes document for now and, in its place, write what you wanted to do: for example, 'I need to identify the types of criticisms that have been made of the key idea identified in the essay title.'

'Try to avoid talking in terms of what has been "proved"' and 'Try to reflect on the different perspectives that are relevant'

What it looks like:

> Imagine that this is the essay title:

> 'Critically evaluate Milgram's interpretation of the results of his obedience studies.'

And this is the conclusion:

In conclusion, Milgram proved that people obey those in authority. *Reicher and Haslam showed that* group identity is relevant to how people behave in obedience situations such as Milgram's obedience experiments. *Russell showed that* the behaviour of participants in Milgram's experiments was brought about by factors such as the influence of doing something for 'the good of science'.

What are the key features of this?

In addition to listing what was covered without reflection, this conclusion has a problem with how it treats the material being referred to. Reading this conclusion is like hearing the author say: 'Case proved – end of discussion'. This conclusion does not treat the different perspectives outlined in the essay as *perspectives*, but rather as proof, facts and demonstrations.

Why is it a problem?

The issues at the heart of most academic essays in psychology have features that can be thought about much more critically. That is, most of the relevant material covered in an essay comprises *ways of making sense of* empirical findings, theories and the phenomenon identified in the essay title.

How can I fix it?

There are several problematic phrases in this conclusion, and each of them fails to position the idea referred to as a *way of making sense of* obedience or Milgram's findings. Look at each of the problem phrases:

- In conclusion, Milgram proved that…
- Reicher and Haslam showed that…
- Russell showed that…

There is some real potential here – good, relevant ideas are referred to and there is a potential for developing a sense of critique and debate. Now look at the indicative transformations suggested below:

- *In conclusion, Milgram proved that…* → Milgram interpreted his empirical findings in terms of a phenomenon that he described as 'agentic shift'…
- *Reicher and Haslam showed that…* → Reicher and Haslam's Social Identity Theory perspective suggests that group identity can account for Milgram's findings…
- *Russell showed that…* → For Russell, it is the 'strain reducing' features designed to make the experiment more acceptable for participants – such as using a scientific rationale – that best account for Milgram's findings…

These suggested changes (a) position what is proposed as interpretations and perspectives (though they do not necessarily need to use those very words) and (b) provide some sense of what each position represents.

This fix, on its own, provides an incremental improvement on the conclusion. It would still be worth checking that the conclusion does not simply list what has been covered in the body of the essay.

'Don't list what you have covered in your essay, but try to develop a proper conclusion rather than a recap'

What it looks like:

Imagine that this is the essay title:

'Critically evaluate Milgram's interpretation of the results of his obedience studies.'

And this is the conclusion:

Milgram interpreted his empirical findings as indicating that people obey those in authority because of a shift to the agentic state. *Reicher and Haslam's* Social Identity Theory perspective suggests that group identity can account for Milgram's findings. *For Russell*, it is the 'strain-reducing' features designed to make the experiment more acceptable for participants – such as using a scientific rationale – that best account for Milgram's findings.

What are the key features of this?

Conclusions that make this mistake may have strengths, but they do not reflect thoughtfully on the discussion that has taken place in the main body of the essay. In the example here, the conclusion has some fairly strong features – note how the approaches are characterised, providing a sense of what each of the different approaches suggests. However, there is little sense of how the ideas touched on relate to one another and the conclusion therefore reads like a list.

Why is it a problem?

The conclusion should convey thinking about overarching issues and fundamental relationships between the approaches covered. If it merely lists what has been covered, it does not convey the author's understanding of either what the fundamental issues are or how the different perspectives relate to each other.

How can I fix it?

Interrogate the ideas that you refer to. Look back at the specific essay title. In this case the essay asks you to *critically evaluate Milgram's interpretation* – this indicates that your essay and your conclusion should centre on that focal point. What are the fundamental differences in perspectives at work here? Bear in mind that there is no singular, correct format. One framework could be to contrast the *intrapsychic shift in agency* brought about by the specific authority–subordinate relationship, with the situationally invoked and situationally dependent *change in identity* that Reicher and Haslam refer to. Russell's approach could be seen as still more distinct, introducing as it does *an ideological* dimension not directly addressed by the other two perspectives. Notice how these ways of characterising the research referred to are both more conceptual (intrapsychic, identity, ideological) and also highlight differences more vividly than the illustrative segment we started with.

EXERCISE
Try it out

Try using these questions to guide your thinking *even if you cannot immediately answer them*.

- What are the key debates concerning the precise issue identified by the essay title?
  - Mapping out some of the key debates can really help shape your conclusion.

- Are there overarching concepts, frameworks, meta-theories or approaches within which these debates can be situated?
  - There might be methodological or theoretical issues at the heart of the key debates that you identify.

- Are there different levels of conceptualisation at work?
  - Some ideas will be more remote and conceptual – these often work better towards the end of your conclusion. Others might be closer to the work of specific sources that you have cited in your essay and might work best before the still more fundamental conceptual issues are addressed.

- What are the ways in which I can express the key ideas?
  - Try out different ways of expressing some of your key ideas and their interrelationship. Conclusions can be conceptually challenging so give yourself the opportunity to try writing an effective conclusion and then to try again.

'Try not to give your own opinions in your conclusion'

What it looks like:

Imagine that this is the essay title:

'Critical evaluate the idea that positive psychology principally operates to maintain the status quo.'

And this is the conclusion:

Having looked at the debate between different perspectives on this issue, I think that positive psychology can make an important difference in people's lives. While I recognise that some argue that making people more positive can stop social change from happening, in my opinion, making people more positive is a positive social change in itself. Therefore, I think that positive psychology makes an important contribution and does not just protect the status quo.

What are the key features of this?

This essay announces opinion rather than reasoning through different perspectives. Opinionated conclusions such as this often involve use of the personal pronoun (for example, 'I think that…') but sometimes vary (for example, 'Clearly it is the case that…'). It is possible to be just as opinionated even when our conclusion does not invoke 'I', 'me' or 'my'.

Why is it a problem?

For most forms of academic writing this is problematic, although sometimes personal reflection is specifically required (see Chapter 7 for more on this). It is a problem because it typically short-circuits actual thinking. Think how in an argument between two distant family members personal stance might be invoked. Imagine the offended relative, on the edge of tears, blurts out, 'Well, that's what I think anyway'. When we hear this, we get the sense that the person uttering these words wants to close down the discussion.

In a conclusion (and indeed anywhere in your essay), declaring your stance in this way gives a similar sense of not wanting to discuss things any further. If you declare your final position, then you appear to convey that there is nothing further to discuss or think about. How can your conclusion convince the reader of your intellectual engagement with the issues if you pre-empt thoughtful, conceptual reflection with a declaration of your opinion?

What is worse is that a declaration of opinion might be – and often is – given without conveying the reasoning process that led to this view. Even if there was a careful process of reasoning through the evidence, hoisting up the flag of your opinion runs the risk of looking like there was no careful thinking on your part at all, just a belief that you held, perhaps before you even started thinking about the issues of relevance to the essay.

How can I fix it?

First, try to spot it. As indicated above, it might not be quite as easy as you would expect, because opinionated conclusions are not always littered with personal pronouns.

Second, once you have spotted it, don't be too hard on yourself. Of course, we all have stances, perspectives, opinions and positions. It is simply that in our essays we should be displaying to our reader our careful thinking through of the issues, and opinionated writing looks like we are not thinking much at all.

Third, try to work out the reasoning and/or evidential basis for your stance. Cross-examine your position: Where's the evidence? Are there any counter-arguments?

Fourth, be prepared to change your mind or be less opinionated. Focus instead on displaying the perspectives that are relevant to the issues that your essay is addressing. Think about how these debates can be made sense of: how can we conceptualise them? What sorts of different perspectives on the fundamental issues – or on the evidential basis – do they suggest?

Fifth, convey to your reader a sense of not only your sensitivity to the debate(s) covered in your essay, but also of your intelligent awareness of what may lie at the heart of the different perspectives that you have addressed.

The interesting thing is that you might be reading about these steps precisely because strong opinions often intrude into your conclusions. However, following them, doesn't just 'remove a problem', it can lead to a supercharged conclusion, whether your opinion stays the same, changes or recedes from relevance. It is a fascinating, intellectual journey – I hope you enjoy it.

REFLECTING ON THE CHAPTER:
Give your reader a 'takeaway' message

Have you ever missed the end of a TV show, film or book, or maybe you have experienced an ending that was not convincing or satisfying? Think how it feels for the poor marker. Lots of essays do not have a conclusion at all, some look like they do, but the last paragraph simply restates what was covered in the essay or goes for some vague claim that 'Psychologists disagree on this issue and further research is necessary'. Writing a good conclusion is like scaling the trickiest part of a mountain, but although it can be a challenge, you can do it – and do it better than you might think. Look at good writing to see what a good conclusion looks like (use the examples in this chapter to start with). Reading these and seeing how they differ from poor conclusions starts to seep in after a while. Once you get a picture of what that critical, conceptual conclusion looks like, you really can start to write better and better conclusions. The fact that they are tricky to write makes them the most potent part of your essay – if you can pull off a really good conclusion, then that one paragraph will weigh strongly in your favour. What is more, you will be giving your reader/marker joy in their heart – that satisfying experience of a really good ending of a film, TV show, book and favourite piece of music all rolled into one. Absorb good conclusion writing, practise and give yourself time, and your final paragraph will sparkle with clear, conceptual, critical clarity. 'What a conclusion!' your reader will say – and they'll be right.

TAKE AWAY POINTS FROM THIS CHAPTER

- Conclusions are, typically, a challenge to write. Acknowledging this and looking at examples of good and bad conclusions can help you to clearly identify what you are aiming for.

- Don't be hard on yourself, identifying the sorts of problems that occur in your conclusions can be a brilliant step forward. From this you can work out how to avoid recurring conclusion pitfalls.

- Looking at your conclusions as if you were the reader/marker can help to guide your process of writing – and rewriting – your conclusion.

- Edit your first draft to make this difficult job of writing an effective conclusion actually possible.

- It is important to always ask questions of your conclusion. For example: What does it say?, What does it do?, What does it reveal? The answers to these questions should inform the editing of your conclusion.

- It is helpful to really embrace the yin and yang of conclusion writing. It is difficult, but your conclusions need to be precise and conceptual. This takes time to acquire, if you read conclusions and practise writing them, you will make real progress.

- Realise that writing conclusions is challenging and, because of that, it is creative and satisfying.

LINKING TO OTHER CHAPTERS

Partly because it comes last in the essay – and mainly because it is perceived as being difficult – conclusions tend to be delayed and deferred more than most paragraphs (apart from the introduction, which is often linked to starting the whole essay in the first place). The tips in Chapter 1 on overcoming procrastination are relevant not only for starting your essay, but also for completing it, and they have a particular relevance for starting and finishing your conclusion. Even when the essay is complete, the conclusion is a section that should be looked at in reviewing and editing your work (see Chapter 10). A strong conclusion is much easier to write when the essay has a sound structure (see Chapter 5), and it should embody the essence of that structure in a way that addresses the essay title directly (see Chapter 4). Writing an effective conclusion involves being critically evaluative at a conceptual level (which is addressed in Chapter 6) and finding your academic voice (which is the subject of Chapter 7). Bringing these qualities together can take time, but the contrasting examples in these chapters can help you to find not only your *academic* voice, but also your *critical and conceptual conclusion voice*.

Chapter 9

Make it professional – how to ensure high-quality presentation and referencing

---

In this chapter you will learn...

- How to ensure the appearance of your essay communicates positively to the marker
- How to identify issues with your essay from its appearance
- How to use in-text citations correctly, following APA guidelines
- How to produce a reference list that is complete and which follows APA guidelines
- How to give your essay a professional makeover when time is short

PRESENTATION AND REFERENCING: WHAT THEY ARE AND WHY THEY MATTER

Imagine that you get an interview for a job or programme of study that you are really interested in and that they want to see your undergraduate essays. In this thought experiment, do you see your essays as a deal maker, clinching their decision to offer you a place, or a deal breaker, with the interviewer shuffling you to the door with wishes of 'every success for your future, wherever that may be'.

I think many of us would see our essays as not always showing us at our best, not just in the content issues considered elsewhere in this book, but also in the look and feel of the essay. What would that hypothetical recipient be holding in their hands as they were handed a hard copy of our essay? Would they nod encouragingly as they saw what a carefully researched, properly referenced, neat and professional-looking essay we had presented to them? Or would they be struggling to suppress a look of disgust and disdain, wondering whether they should put it in the bin now or later?

This chapter will help you to ensure that your essay is a piece of work that you can genuinely be proud of. It will empower you to write essays that have a professional look and feel to them and, in so doing, will not only give you something to show future employers or course admission tutors with pride, but will also be honing some important transferrable skills that are likely to be highly relevant for professional careers and postgraduate study. What are we waiting for? Let's open this Aladdin's cave of essay excellence and see how we can develop our essays in ways that help us to reach our potential both now and in the future.

COMMUNICATING POSITIVELY WITH THE MARKER

Your essay starts to communicate with your reader before they actually start reading it. That sounds vaguely supernatural, but it's a bit more mundane than that. Whether digital or hard copy, your essay conveys a story to your reader even before they read the first word of your introduction.

Look at the samples below and imagine that you are the marker. What impression do you get? Try to note down your first impressions honestly. Are these notes confirmed when you read the essay? Do you think your first impressions could affect your judgement of an essay?

In all of the cases below, this is the essay title:

'Critically evaluate Anderson et al.'s (2010) argument that exposure to violent video games is a causal risk factor for decreased empathy and prosocial behaviour and contrast it with two other perspectives on prosocial behaviour that have been important within social psychology.'

Look at these snapshots of essay responses as if you were the marker. Look at each essay separately and be slow and mindful in your process. As you approach each one of the three samples, take sufficient time so that you can note the following:

1. What were your immediate impressions from your first glance, before you began to properly read each of the abbreviated essays?
2. What were your feelings, and what did you expect to find, in each shortened essay at the very second that you were about to start reading?
3. Do you think that your first impression shaped your judgment, or could potentially do so?

Sample one

Critically evaluate Anderson et al.'s (2010) argument that exposure to violent video games is a causal risk factor for decreased empathy and **prosocial behaviour and contrast it with two other perspectives on prosocial behaviour that have been important within social psychology. The issue of the determinants and influences of prosocial behaviour has been an important focus for social psychology, particularly since the work of Latane and** Darley, which became associated with the concept of 'the bystander effect'. Anderson et al.'s (2010) work contributes a contrasting perspective to this, with their meta-analysis identifying violent video games as having an important role in negatively influencing both empathy and prosocial behaviour.

This essay will first outline and evaluate Anderson et al.'s (2010) meta-analytic review before contrasting it with two particularly prominent perspectives within the social psychology of prosocial behaviour, the classic 'bystander effect' paradigm, with particular attention to Fischer et al.'s (2011) meta-analysis, and Decety et al.'s (2016) emphasis on the evolutionary-based, biological mechanisms that attempt to explain empathy and helping behaviour. In doing so, this essay attempts to provide both context and perspective against which the assertions of Anderson et al. (2010) can be carefully assessed. Anderson et al. (2010) present a meta-analytic review of… <The essay continues by first outlining and then evaluating Anderson et al. (2010), before contrasting this approach with the alternative perspectives of the 'bystander effect' and Decety et al.'s evolutionary perspective.>

EXERCISE
First impressions (sample one)

My first impressions of sample one:

When I was about to start reading, I felt and anticipated:

The potential impact of my first impression on my judgment of the essay:

Sample two

Prosocial behaviour – are violent video games to blame for its decline?

Introduction

Violent video games have long been investigated in terms of their potential impact on aggressive behaviour. Anderson et al. (2010) have taken things one step further by examining the impact that they may have on prosocial behaviour. This essay will examine the evidence that Anderson et al.

(2010) present and evaluate the evidence for and against the claim that violent video games are a causal risk factor for empathy and prosocial behaviour.

Main body

Evidence for Anderson et al. (2010)

Anderson et al. (2010) present the results of a large meta-analysis of research concerning the possible impact of playing violent video games. <Anderson et al., 2010, and research supporting this is referred to.>

Evidence against Anderson et al. (2010)

<Here the essay outlines in brief paragraphs evidence that critiques Anderson et al, 2010.>

Penultimate paragraph

<Here the essay considers in brief paragraphs more recent research that has referred to Anderson et al.'s (2010) paper.>

Conclusion

<Here the essay reflects on the evidence for and against Anderson et al.'s (2010) argument that playing violent video games can be a causal risk factor for empathy and prosocial behaviour.>

EXERCISE
First impressions (sample two)

My first impressions of sample two:

When I was about to start reading, I felt and anticipated:

The potential impact of the first impression on my judgment of the essay:

Sample three

What causes prosocial behaviour – an investigation? This essay investigates the causes of prosocial behaviour, if you want to find out about what makes people tick – read on! **Prosocial behaviour is all around.**

People help each other but sometimes they don't. Psychologists have found why. Anderson et al. (2010) blamed it on violent videos.

If you watch a violent video you have less empathy and less likely to help.

This was measured and tested. *Anderson et al. (2010)* investigated this question with a meta-analytic review.

EXERCISE
First impressions (sample three)

My first impressions of sample three:

When I was about to start reading, I felt and anticipated:

The potential impact of the first impression on my judgment of the essay:

TRANSFORMING PRESENTATION PROBLEMS

Presentation tends to become a feature when it is problematic. In such cases, it is just as the marker turns to your essay to see your mind at work that poor presentation intrudes. It barges the essay content out of the way, drawing attention to the presentation instead. The combination of chaotic layout, awful and inconsistent fonts, arbitrary use of paragraphs and errors even in copying over the essay title itself, sets precisely the wrong tone. Would you attend a formal interview dressed as a clown and splatting custard pies into the faces of the interview panel? If not, then why submit a formal essay that acts just like that clown? Poorly presented essays make the marker recoil. 'Urgh!' they say, as the weird alignment, doctored essay title and comic sans font hits them between the eyes. There is enough suffering in the world, don't make the poor marker feel irritated, agitated and paranoid. Reassure them with something neat, consistent and well judged. Hand in essays that you would be happy for a future employer or admissions tutor for a postgraduate programme to see – an essay that you are proud of.

There is some good news – fixing poor presentation (which is further addressed in Chapter 10) can be quite swift and it has two benefits:

1.   When you hand in your essay your marker no longer experiences an unnecessary barrier between themselves and the ideas in your essay.
2.   Before handing in your essay, addressing poor presentation issues can sometimes help you to identify content issues that need to be addressed, making them more visible to you.

To further illustrate these points let's consider the three sample essays referred to above.

Sample one

Sample one looks terrible. How did the erratic font, weird spacing and reliance on a single paragraph strike you? Was it enough to put you off? It could well be. If, however, you were able to look beyond the abysmal appearance, you would see a really good piece of writing. This is like the story of the ugly duckling – there is a beautiful, swan-like essay behind a scraggy, off-putting appearance. Poor presentation not only loses marks in itself, it also detracts from the real strengths that are there. Sample one is an easy fix, use the font size and style that your course recommends. If there is no advice at all, avoid obviously problematic fonts and keep the style and font size consistent. Clearly, the introduction (and conclusion) should each have their own paragraph. In longer work they may occupy more than one paragraph. Generally, paragraphs (which might typically be between approximately 150 and 350 words) should each represent one key job (for example, introducing, outlining and evaluating, drawing on different perspectives, concluding) that is being addressed in the essay (see Chapter 5 for more on using paragraphs effectively). Neatened up in this way, see how much more clearly the good thinking – already present in sample one – is visible to the reader.

Sample one: Don't let your presentation create a barrier

Take a quick look at how better sample one starts to look when we remove its glaring presentational issues: Critically evaluate Anderson et al.'s (2010) argument that exposure to violent video games is a causal risk factor for decreased empathy and prosocial behaviour and contrast it with two other perspectives on prosocial behaviour that have been important within social psychology.

The issue of the determinants and influences of prosocial behaviour has been an important focus for social psychology, particularly since the work of Latané and Darley, which became associated with the concept of 'the bystander effect'. Anderson et al.'s (2010) work contributes a contrasting perspective to this, with their meta-analysis identifying violent video games as having an important role in influencing both empathy and prosocial behaviour. This essay will first outline and evaluate Anderson et al.'s (2010) meta-analytic review before contrasting it with two particularly prominent perspectives within the social psychology of prosocial behaviour, the classic 'bystander effect' paradigm, with particular attention to Fischer et al.'s (2011) meta-analysis, and Decety et al.'s (2016) emphasis on the evolutionary-based, biological mechanisms that attempt to explain empathy and helping behaviour. In doing so, this essay endeavours to provide both context and perspective against which the assertions of Anderson et al. (2010) can be carefully assessed.

Anderson et al. (2010) present a meta-analytic review of… *<The essay continues by first outlining and then evaluating Anderson et al. (2010), before contrasting this approach with the alternative perspectives of the 'bystander effect' and Decety et al.'s evolutionary perspective.>*

Sample one illustrates how a good essay can be hidden behind terrible presentation. It is not always as obvious as this, but it is worth checking that presentation errors do not disguise or detract from the strengths in your essays. The good news is if you spot a presentational problem you can almost certainly fix it.

Sample two

If you look carefully at sample two, you will notice that, although it is more neatly presented than sample one, it uses lots of sub-headings, has short paragraphs (the complete introduction is given above to illustrate this brevity) and has not used the exact essay title. The issue of sub-headings is slightly tricky to address as guidance varies considerably across continents, countries, universities, departments, programmes of study, modules and individual assignments. Follow your guidance. If there is no guidance and no advice, then, for shorter essays (perhaps 2000 words or less), be cautious about the use of sub-headings as they make for a choppier and less smoothly interconnected read. Putting sub-heading dilemmas to one side, sample two illustrates the way in which addressing presentational issues can help us as we are writing our essay. These presentational problems relate to two potential issues with this essay:

1. The essay appears not to develop the issues touched on fully – this is evidenced in the very brief paragraphs including the introduction.
2. The precise essay title has been abbreviated and the essay actually answers a slightly different question.

Let's consider each of these briefly, in turn.

Just noting that the paragraphs are short can make us question why they are short and identify that we may not have developed the points that we have touched on sufficiently. Looking through our draft (or emergent) essay and noting short paragraphs can be a powerful tool in guiding our editing (see Chapter 10) and can encourage us to develop the points that we touch on all too briefly in our very short paragraphs.

Doctoring the essay title is an amazingly common and often fairly subtle problem, as is the case with sample two. Look at the original title and how it was simplified and changed in sample two:

Original title:

> 'Critically evaluate Anderson et al.'s (2010) argument that exposure to violent video games is a causal risk factor for decreased empathy and prosocial behaviour and contrast it with two other perspectives on prosocial behaviour that have been important within social psychology.'

Title changed to:

> Prosocial behaviour – are violent video games to blame for its decline?

This might seem irrelevant, or needlessly pedantic, but when essay titles are not used word for word (unless you have been invited to adapt, change or use your own), then it encourages a deviation from the precise essay title given. This common problem is illustrated in sample two where the introduction identifies that the essay will 'examine the evidence that Anderson et al. (2010) present ...' but makes no mention of any contrast with other psychological perspectives (which the title refers to). It is also evident in the conclusion which is described as reflecting 'on the evidence for and against Anderson et al.'s argument ...', again a different remit to that which the essay title itself indicated.

Sample two: Problems spotted and lessons learned

The lesson from sample two is that identifying presentational problems such as using short paragraphs and adapting the essay title, can be clues that we, like a first-rate detective, can use. Paying attention to what we are doing in terms of presentation can help us to identify ways in which we can improve not only these presentational symptoms but also underlying content issues with our essay prior to submitting it. If we think our paragraphs are too long, we can check for the coherence of the point(s) that we are making (see Chapter 5 for more on this). If they are too short, we can develop the ideas that we have touched on, perhaps too briefly. If we adapt an essay title, this is like finding a corpse, a hastily rewritten will and a butler trying to throw the murder weapon into the moat at night. There is something very fishy going on. Changed essay titles are usually matched with essays that do not focus on all of the details of the original title. If you spot that you have done this, well done! You got there just in time. Now address the actual essay title (see Chapter 4 for help with this) and start that process by writing down the exact essay title without changing a single word.

Sample three

What was your impression of sample three? Was it 'urgh!'? Looking at sample three, you are probably struck by the chaos, the different fonts and font sizes, the mix of styles, the organisation of the paragraphs and sentences, the brevity of the sentences, the disjointedness, and the fact that the tone seems wrong. With sample one we focused on the way that poor presentation prevented the marker from seeing the good work that was hidden beneath the poor layout. Sample two demonstrated the way in which presentational issues (such as short paragraphs and a changed essay title) can reveal deeper problems with the essay. Sample three suggests that presentational issues can also work to simultaneously reveal and conceal issues with the essay, and how we, like a good analyst or a good detective, need to go beyond the surface to locate the heart of the issue.

To start our analysis of the essay, first, put the entire abbreviated essay into a consistent font. The multiple fonts have concealed some of the chaotic content so it is difficult to come to the actual writing when we are faced with such mixed formats. However, they have also hinted at something very disjointed. In a consistent font we can see this more clearly.

Sample three: Finding salvation in the chaos

> What causes prosocial behaviour – an investigation? This essay investigates the causes of prosocial behaviour, if you want to find out about what makes people tick – read on! Prosocial behaviour is all around.

> People help each other but sometimes they don't. Psychologists have found why. Anderson et al. (2010) blamed it on violent videos.

> If you watch a violent video you have less empathy and are less likely to help.

> This was measured and tested. Anderson et al. (2010) investigated this question with a meta-analytic review.

In addition to the title having been changed quite radically, which was discussed in the context of sample two, this abbreviated overview reveals thinking that is very underdeveloped. This is the thinking of hash tags and headlines; it is as if each sentence works as a stand-alone phrase, designed to grab your attention, before you switch off or turn to something else. One of the great things about academic writing is that it isn't like that – and perhaps we need this radical, thinking alternative that academic writing offers, now more than ever. Partly hidden and partly revealed through the chaotic presentation of sample three is an absence of a clear academic voice (see Chapter 7 for more on developing your academic voice). The author seems to have adopted the position of a passive announcer of how the world is and what psychologists have found, but there is no sense of a mind weighing the evidence and assessing the argument (see Chapter 6 for more on developing your critical evaluation skills). On top of this, the author does not appear to answer the essay title, or even to demonstrate relevant knowledge which pertains to it (see Chapter 4 for more on answering the essay title). The list of problems could also highlight the introduction, structure and – even though it is not here – the conclusion (addressed in Chapters 3, 5 and 8 respectively).

Sample three suggests an essay that may well be heading towards a fail grade. There is very little knowledge or thinking revealed across its short, disjointed sentences. However, despite these limitations, there are hints at some potential, including an awareness that Anderson et al. (2010) conducted a meta-analytic review. If the author of this abbreviated essay can find and develop their academic voice, they may quite quickly see improvements in their assignments. You may tell yourself that you cannot change, and it is easy to find others who will reinforce that particular message. Change can be uncomfortable for us and others, and it may involve hard work and genuinely experiencing failure and disappointment. It is easy to live with failing if we tell ourselves and others that we don't care, and so much harder if we admit that we do care. But there is potential for something quite beautiful here. We can (if we want to) start to tentatively find our academic voice, perhaps stumbling like an infant finding its feet, but growing in our academic confidence and our ability to express our ideas. If it wasn't so wonderful, I wouldn't recommend it – but it is and I do. That first step might come from looking at the presentational surface of your essay in order to see beyond, into the limitations that you may have hidden from or denied – and that awareness is the golden key to change.

OTHER PRESENTATIONAL ISSUES THAT CAN TRANSFORM YOUR ESSAYS

The three samples above do not address all the issues we need to consider in transforming the presentation of our essay. So let's look at some other presentational issues that can have a big impact on how your essay is perceived.

Essay length

Length is a crucial consideration of our essays. Handing in an essay that is too long is best avoided, as it may attract specific penalties in terms of the grades awarded. It may only be marked up until the stipulated word length is reached, with the 'over-length' portion being ignored, or it may more generally be marked down for not being concise. If, on the other hand, your essay is too short, then, regardless of penalties, you are very likely to lose marks because your essay will probably have less content, clarity and critique than it would if it was the correct length. If your essay is too long (above the upper length allowed) or too short (below the lower length required), then it is not quite finished.

If your essay is too short, you should lengthen and strengthen. Don't just bulk it out with longer sentences or aimless descriptive detail. Look hard at that essay title and ensure that you have all of the relevant content, that the ideas you touch on are clearly developed, smoothly inter-connected and appropriately critiqued. It is not merely a question of adding words, but rather of adding value. Make those extra words that are needed really enhance the quality of your essay by giving more of the relevant content, cohesion and critique that your marker is looking for (use the editing tips in Chapter 10 to help with this).

If your essay is too long, then look at how you can be concise. Are you really on target for the precise essay title throughout your essay (see Chapter 4 for more on this)? Can you rework your descriptive elements to make them more concise (see Chapter 7)? There is a skill to being concise and some of this skill hinges on overcoming the worry that we will lose marks if we leave something out. However, like a much-loved room, trying to keep a bit of everything winds up making for a cluttered environment. The key here is the essay title. Use this to ensure that each paragraph and each sentence is genuinely contributing to answering that specific question.

Ask each paragraph and each sentence: 'What are you doing here?' If the sentence or paragraph can justify itself (for example, 'developing a critique of the theory just outlined') then good; if not, then it may need to go. Using this method, if nothing 'needs to go', then it becomes a matter of expressing more concisely the key, focal point that is being made.

It can take time to make your writing fit what might seem an arbitrary length requirement, but it is a great skill that you can develop. Just as you can give a short, medium or long account of why you like reading Anna Maria Ortese's novels or listening to Fela Kuti's music, so you can shape your essay to fit the required length. Essay length issues are easy to spot for both you and the marker – get your essay to the target length or you really are posting your marks down the drain.

STOP AND THINK
Improving your presentation

Stop for a moment and think about the essay that you are working on or thinking about. Think about the presentational issues we have identified above and how you can apply them to your own work.

Fonts

Much of the detail regarding permissible font sizes and font styles will be clarified by your tutor and/or your essay guidance literature. I would suggest that you do not try to be too inventive here – this isn't the time or place to start a Comic Sans revival, or to try to submit an essay using Wingdings. Such fonts may have their following, and indeed their place, but it isn't in your essay. Neat, consistent, readable and not too insane is a good maxim for thinking about how you use fonts within your essay, but as this is often specified within modules or programmes of study, it is important to be familiar with what is specifically required for your assignments.

Left, right or centre

How you present your essay on the page will probably be guided by your specific assessment or, more generally, by the expectations of your programme of study regarding how assignments should look. Try to keep your alignment of margins consistent throughout your essay. Ideally, as with fonts, the less the reader notices such things the better. Alignment and margin width are tools that help you to convey your written work clearly and are not an end point in themselves.

Pagination

It is surprising how often page numbering is absent from essays. The more pages your essay has the more important it is to number them. Unless instructed otherwise, it is usually worth getting into the very good habit of page numbering your work.

Paragraphs

Paragraphs, don't you just love them! Actually, I am quite fond of them. They help to structure my writing and my reading, and they provide the pace, perhaps even the heartbeat to academic essay writing. I regularly mark essays that have a single paragraph that is one, two or even three pages long and those that use a new paragraph for each (relatively short) sentence. Surely, there is a middle way?

Paragraphs make (or should make) a coherent, identifiable point or, perhaps even more so, they should do a particular job within the essay (for example, outlining the empirical procedure and the results of an experiment that is to be evaluated in the essay). Essays with very short paragraphs tend to have less clearly integrated ideas (or convey that impression). They often have a staccato feeling to them, leaving the reader queasy as the author jumps from one idea to another in a series of fleeting paragraphs.

Essays with long paragraphs often lack a really clear, logical structure to the ideas. This approach conveys that the writer thinks that all of the material they put into their one (or two) super-paragraphs is about the essay topic and there is no real need to structure it in a clear, coherent and logical way. Paradoxically, by going for the all-inclusive 'super-paragraph', the ideas contained within it are typically less well connected and poorly integrated.

Paragraphs are not only a nicety for your reader – saving them verbal indigestion – they also facilitate your writing by allowing you to properly structure your ideas. When you are creating an essay plan it is helpful to think about how you will structure your paragraphs – with each one developing one single idea, or doing one specific task in your essay. Using a sensible number of paragraphs (approximately two per page, depending on specific guidance, font size and line spacing) can really help you to structure and clearly interconnect your work.

Essay title

Last, but by no means least, if you are expected to use the given essay title (rather than creating your own title), then ensure that anytime you write the essay title (this is often required at the beginning of an essay or on a separate title page) that you use the *exact* essay title with no deviation in wording or punctuation. As has been illustrated above, changing the essay title is often linked to a failure to address the precise essay title. While Chapter 4 addresses this in depth, here it can be noted that tampering with the essay title is a presentational symptom of a potentially serious flaw. Always use the exact title. If you have deviated, then you must use your detective skills to see whether your essay content has also deviated. Check it and correct your essay so that someone reading it can work out the exact title as it was given, not your adapted version of it. Unless otherwise instructed, always use the precise title from when you first begin to when you finally submit your essay – it is so hard to stay on track if you put up the wrong signposts to begin with!

STOP AND THINK
Presenting your essay effectively

I once had an interview which began with the interviewer holding up my CV and saying it was the worst pre-sented CV they had received. I uttered an awkward 'thank you' at the time, but since then, as I have marked numerous essays, I have sometimes wondered 'what if a future employer or admissions tutor saw this?'

Reflect on the essays you have completed. Would you see them as an asset or a liability in terms of securing a job or a place on a postgraduate course that you're interested in? Would you be pleased to have the oppor-tunity to show a portfolio of your work, or would you regret that you were going to be judged on something so flawed? A large proportion of our sense of shame about our essays concerns how professional they do, or do not, appear to be. Think for a moment about any professionally-produced publication – this could include non-academic publications, but for simplicity, let's stay within the academic world. With a book, such as the one you are now reading, as the acknowledgements at the beginning indicate, considerable care is taken to think about all aspects of the presentation – including headings, font size, arrangement of paragraphs, length of sections, citation and referencing. You could take a professional pride in the presentation of your essay too.

Try to show that you really care about your essay, by paying attention to its presentation. See your essay as being a piece of work you can be proud of. Perhaps you'll be bringing it out on special occasions for years to come as friends and relatives look on in wide-eyed wonder. Even if this Hollywood version of your essay's future doesn't hold true, your marker's immediate impression is likely to be that you cared about the essay that you have submitted. That's a great first impression to make. Reading a well presented essay – as com-pared to a poorly presented one – the marker will also appreciate that there is no unnecessary barrier in between them and the thoughts you are trying to express in your essay. You want the best, so for the sake of yourself, your marker and your essay – why not invest the small amount of extra time needed to make your essay look like you really do care?

CITING SOURCES CORRECTLY

Citing and referencing guidelines, such as those produced by the American Psychological Association (APA), are more than a finicky set of rules designed to trip you up – they are actually incredibly democratic. When we cite sources in our essay, for example, 'Milgram (1963)', we are not only attributing ideas to a particular source, we are also providing all the details the reader needs to find that source for themselves. We cite sources that have informed our essay and rather than leaving the reader to wonder, 'When did they say that?' or, 'How can I find that?', we pro-vide the surname and date in our essay and an alphabetical list of those references in a section at the end of our essay, and leave our reader with a sense of joy and well-being.

Why just the surname and date?

Many students will want to put in more than the surname and date when they refer to a piece of research in their essay. Thus, why not write 'Stanley Milgram', rather than 'Milgram (1963)', or perhaps we could provide details of the publication: 'Stanley Milgram's paper entitled "The Behavioural Study of Obedience"'. In order to see why this is not a great idea look at the following sentences:

> In his paper entitled 'The Behavioural Study of Obedience', published in 1963 in the *Journal of Abnormal Psychology* (volume 67, pages 371–378) Stanley Milgram reports on one of his earliest experiments into the study of obedience conducted with 40 participants, 26 of whom demonstrated total obedience. In subsequent publications, such as Stanley Milgram's 'Issues in the Study of Obedience: A reply to Baumrind', published in the *American Psychologist* (volume 19, pages 848–852) ...

I could carry on with this example, but I think you get the point and have probably given up reading the above paragraph anyway. Do you see how using this method would involve either (a) being very inconsistent, just citing the full reference some of the time and using a shorter citation the rest of the time, or (b) torturing your poor reader with overwhelming detail that detracts from the point you are trying to develop. Both inconsistency and overwhelming the reader are poor options, so the convention of 'Surname (Date)' makes your essay *more consistent and readable*. Your reader knows that to find out publication details they can turn to your reference section, find the surname in the alphabetically arranged list and kerpow! – there are all of the details they could ever wish for. Don't force publication details on your reader within the body of your essay, unless you want to make it more difficult for them to read it, or you want to bore them into early retirement.

Your reference section also needs to be consistent and readable, and different conventions of citation and referencing have been developed to achieve this. In psychology, the conventions of the American Psychological Association (APA) are favoured because they are simple and effective: 'Surname (Date)' within the body of your essay and reference details, organised alphabetically by surname, in your reference list. This sense of crisp citation has been developed further in the 7th edition of the APA style guide, which indicates, for example, that, where there are three or more authors, only the first author's surname should be used. For example, Downing, Liu & Kanwisher (2001), becomes Downing et al. (2001).

To quote or not to quote?

When you quote, you are normally expected to provide the page number of the quote that you use. The simple logic here is that you are enabling your reader to check the quote if they want to.

Your quote should be in quotation marks and followed in brackets, immediately after the quoted passage, by the author's surname, date of publication and page number.

For example:

> Jung argued that 'Sooner or later nuclear physics and the psychology of the unconscious will draw closer together as both of them, independently of one another and from opposite directions, push forward into transcendental territory...' (Jung, 1959, p. 261).

In the reference section, which is covered in detail below, this would appear as:

> Jung, C. G. (1959). *The Collected Works: Volume 9, (Part 2), Aion: Researches into the phenomenology of the self*. Routledge and Kegan Paul. http://dx.doi.org/10.1515/9781400851058

If you are citing from an online source, use the page number if it is available; if not, then give the paragraph number. For example:

> The National Robotics Network argues that it: 'supports the development and champions the industry end user, supply chain and academic requirements to help promote the adoption of robotics in the UK.' (National Robotics Network, 2020, para. 1).

In the reference section this would appear as:

> National Robotics Network. (2020). *Heritage*. http://www.nationalroboticsnetwork.org/?page_id=217

Do bear in mind that for most essays very extensive use of quotations is not seen as desirable and may actually border on a certain subset of plagiarism. Imagine an extreme case where I use quotes throughout my essay to such an extent that more than 50% of my essay is comprised of quotations. Even though I have not passed off someone else's work as my own (I am citing the sources and page numbers of my quotes), I am still letting these sources do my thinking for me. Quotes are like a chilli powder that is near the top of the Scoville scale: unless otherwise directed, use very, very sparingly.

CITING CONVENTIONS: HOW TO WRITE WHEN YOU CITE

It is worth thinking about how you use the citation conventions in the body of your essay. In order to think about this issue, consider the ways in which someone who tends to cite at the end of sentences, especially if multiple citations are clustered together, has limited what they can do with these citations. Citations like this have been treated as a mere identifier – like a brand label or a price tag, as if there is little to discuss.

By contrast, bringing the cited source into the foreground of your sentence enables and even encourages you to articulate much more about the position that the cited sources have adopted. Foregrounded sources (for example, A argues that…, a position partly supported by B, who argued that…) enable you to address how your cited sources relate to the ideas you are discussing and to the views of each other.

EXERCISE

Bearing in mind the above, which of these samples do you think uses sources more effectively in their essay?

Sample one

> The idea that attitudes can be thought of as measurable, quantifiable, individual evaluations of an attitude target can be contrasted with rhetorical and discursive approaches (Billig, 1987; Edwards and Potter, 1992).

(Continued)

Sample two

> The idea that attitudes can be thought of as measurable, quantifiable, individual evaluations of an attitude object has been criticised by Billig's (1987) rhetorical approach and Edwards and Potter's (1992) discursive approach.

The difference between these two is quite subtle, but by placing the cited sources *earlier in the sentence*, sample two allows the author to identify more clearly which source developed which approach to attitudes.

Samples three and four further exemplify this point. In sample three, the references are bunched at the end of the sentences, giving little scope to consider the different perspectives represented by the cited sources. Sample four brings the sources to an earlier point in the sentence, enabling more clarification of the specific point each source makes.

Sample three

> It has been argued that Milgram's findings in terms of agentic shift could be reinterpreted in the light of other, differing, perspectives (Reicher and Haslam, 2011; Gibson, 2013; Russell, 2011). Some of these perspectives are more radically critical of Milgram's interpretations than others and there is some degree of overlap between certain perspectives, but less so with others (Reicher and Haslam, 2011; Gibson, 2013; Russell, 2011).

Sample four

> Milgram's interpretations of his findings in terms of agentic shift have been challenged by several other perspectives. Reicher and Haslam (2011) developed a Social Identity critique, interpreting the participants' obedience in Milgram's experiments in terms of their sense of group identity. Gibson (2013), by contrast, offered a perspective that was less committed to an articulation of intrapsychic processes than either Milgram or Reicher and Haslam, arguing that the rhetoric used played a crucial and largely unacknowledged part in the participants' 'obedience' and 'disobedience'…

Did you notice how much more freedom there is in sample four to articulate not only the critique offered by the cited sources, but also something of how they relate to one another? Lumping our sources together is like putting all of our favourite food (I'm choosing biryani, dhal, paneer majestic, masala dosa and kulfi) into a blender – it just comes out as a mush and you can't enjoy the different flavours.

LEARN
Top tip

Give your sources some respect. Draw out the particular contributions that they make. That way you can really demonstrate the precision and scholarly depth of your thinking about them.

STOP

Don't toss your citations into your essay like pine nuts into a salad. How you position them in your essay can be crucial.

LOOK

Look at what you are arguing in your essay: the points you have made, are going to make and are trying to make in the part you are currently working on. What role do your citations have right here. Are you wanting to describe a study that was conducted, examine an interpretation or contrast different perspectives on an issue? Get clear about the job that you want this part of your essay to do and use your citations to support and enhance that.

THINK

When you are clear about what you want this part of your essay to achieve, think about how your cited sources can be used to accomplish that. Do you want to cite one key source, for example, to outline what was done or what was found in an empirical study? Do you want to draw on one source to develop a critique or contrast with another source, or to support it? If you are tempted to collect sources together in parenthesis at the end of a sentence, think about the alternatives first. Can foregrounding your sources enable you to show your understanding of what they have each argued, how this fits into the argument of your essay and how the different sources relate to one another? Where possible, avoid lumping all of your sources together – draw them out skilfully in your essay and use them to showcase your scholarly thinking about the issues identified in the essay title.

Referencing sources correctly

In the overview of citing sources correctly, did you notice how the key information was the author's surname and then the date of publication? That same emphasis on surname(s) and date of publication is the key to the order in which your references should appear. First, look at the surnames and arrange them alphabetically by first author. If your first author occurs more than once in your reference list on their own – arrange this author's publications chronologically, earliest publications coming before subsequent ones. Where the same first author occurs with different second (and subsequent) authors – the alphabetical order of second (and subsequent) authors should be used. For example, Smith, M. and Atkinson, R., (2020) would appear *before* Smith, M. and Fry, S. (2000) because 'Atkinson' appears before 'Fry in an alphabetically organised list of surnames. Having ordered alphabetically by surnames, you should then order chronologically with earlier publications appearing before subsequent ones.

You may notice in the examples below, that the paragraphs are 'hanging'. Each reference in your reference list should have a first line that is aligned with the left margin, with subsequent lines being indented by 1.27cm, or 0.5 inches.

LEARN
Top tip

You should have a one-to-one mapping between the sources that you cite and those that are in your reference list. Each cited source should be in your reference list and – wait for it – nothing else. Make sure each citation appears in your reference list – it creates such heartache when names are cited and left stranded, cruelly omitted from the reference list. Perhaps more surprisingly, you should not add books and journal articles to your reference list that you intended to read but didn't get around to, nor those that you did read but did not cite. If it's cited, put it in the reference list; if not, don't.

Think of the reference list as sharing some features with most directories of names, such as phone books, registers and staff lists – the key principle is that they are organised alphabetically by surname and then by date. Alphabetical organisation is such a widely used format for arranging surnames because it is so effective. If we know the name, we don't need to check where it occurred in the essay, we can turn to the references and zoom straight to it and find the necessary details so that we can access the publication ourselves.

Understanding the logic of APA formatting

If you find it hard to remember the details of APA referencing format, it is worth thinking about its underlying logic. Within the body of your essay, surnames and dates are prioritised, therefore the reference section is arranged by surname and then date of publication. The layout details are provided here in step-by-step format, with a schematic example (showing where the name, date, etc. would appear) and an actual reference example. You may find moving between these examples provides maximum clarity.

A quick caveat

APA conventions do change periodically, and they are vast, especially when (as with the full APA style manual) all likely permutations are considered. The guidelines here are a useful starting point rather than being 'the definitive guide to APA formatting'. They will address several of the most common types of citation and reference issues that you will encounter. Guidance provided within your course will indicate what is expected of you in the specific context of your study. The latest APA manual, at the time of writing the 7th edition, American Psychological Association (2020), is impressively clear and comprehensive and is *the* definitive guide to correct citation and referencing in psychology. A quick reference to the latest APA style guide (American Psychological Association, 2020), can be found at: https://apastyle.apa.org/instructional-aids/reference-guide. pdf – the guidance offered in this chapter identifies several key elements of citation and referencing, rather than attempting to cover all eventualities.

Using Digital Object Identifiers (DOIs)

DOIs are increasingly important in the latest APA style guide, which reflects the growing importance of both online sources themselves, and online search tools for locating sources. It is important to note that undergraduate programmes do vary in their emphasis on the use of DOIs in reference lists, so do be aware of and up to date with the referencing requirements that apply to you. DOIs are particularly valued as providing stable and persistent links to sources and source location information.

1. Wherever the DOI is available use it. Even if you use a print copy of the source you are referencing, you should endeavour to supply its DOI. From the 7th edition of the APA style guide the DOI is required to be hyperlinked, starting with 'http://' or 'https://', so http://dx.doi.org/10.1037/a0023304 which is a hyperlink is correct, whereas doi: 10.1037/a0023304, is in the previously acceptable format.

    The DOI appears straight after your reference as follows:

    > Enoksen, A. E., & Dickerson, P. (2018). 'That proves my point': How mediums reconstrue disconfirmation in medium–sitter interactions. *British Journal of Social Psychology*, *57*, 386–403. http://dx.doi.org/10.1111/bjso.12241

2. You can locate DOIs from publications directly, in books they are sometimes included with bibliographic information. In articles they might appear on the first or last page or in headers or footers. Many DOIs can be looked up using an official DOI Registration Agency such as Crossref: https://www.crossref.org/guestquery/. You may find that it is often somewhat easier to locate DOIs for contemporary journal articles than for books and older publications – but it is important to endeavour to identify the DOI whenever you can.

3. Be aware of the strong preference for the more reliable and permanent link of the DOI as compared to URLs – see https://apastyle.apa.org/style-grammar-guidelines/references/dois-urls for more details:

    *   For print works and online works that have a DOI only, use the DOI; if they have both a DOI and a URL, again, just use the DOI.
    *   For print works that have a URL but not a DOI – do not use either a DOI or a URL.
    *   For online works that have a URL but not a DOI – use the URL, if that link will work for readers. However, for works without a DOI from most academic research databases, do not include a URL, these are normally widely available references.

- URLs for example for ebooks from other websites would normally be included where no DOI is available.
- No full stop is to be added after the DOI or URL.

Referencing books (not-edited)

To understand how a book should appear in your reference list, first ask yourself the following question: what ingredients would you need to locate a book that has been cited in an essay?

At a minimum, you would want to know: the author's surname, the year the book was published and the title of the book. It is also useful to know who the publisher is, so add that to your list, if you haven't already done so. Additionally, in APA formatting, we need to add the author's initials (not their full first names). This is especially helpful for more common surnames. Finally, we might want to be able to reliably locate the source digitally, if possible, with a reliable identifier that we can copy into an address bar to identify, locate and possibly retrieve the source; a DOI helps us to do this.

Warning – reading this could make you drowsy. Please do not attempt to drive or operate heavy machinery while reading the following reference format details.

Referencing books (not-edited): Step-by-step guide

1. Surname, followed by a comma and a space.
2. Initial, followed by a full stop and a space (if there is more than one initial, then initial, full stop, space, initial, full stop, space, etc.).
3. If there are two authors, then add a comma straight after the full stop following the previous author's initial and then '&' (ampersand), then a space and then the second author's surname and initial (as above).
4. If there are three or more authors, add a comma directly after the full stop following the first author's last initial, then give the second author's details (as above) using the '&' before the final author's details.
5. Copyright year in parenthesis (brackets), followed by a full stop and a space.
6. Title of the book *in italics*, followed by a full stop and a space. Note that upper case is used for the first word of the title, or proper nouns only. If the book has an edition or volume number you place that in parenthesis, e.g. '(7th ed.)' or '(Vol. 12)' followed by a full stop and a space. If it has both an edition and volume number then give edition number, followed by a comma and then volume number, e.g. '(7th ed., Vol. 12)' a full stop appears after the parenthesis and a space before the publisher's name is given.
7. Name of the publisher, followed by a full stop. The American Psychological Association (2020) stipulates that place of publication, which was previously required, is not to be included in the reference list.
8. If available, add a space and then include a DOI (Digital Object Identifier), see above for details on using DOIs and URLs. No full stop is to be added after the DOI or URL.

Schematic examples
Single author:
Surname, Initial(s). (Copyright Year). *Title of book*. Name of publisher (edition number, volume number). DOI

Multiple authors:
Surname, Initial(s)., Surname, Initial(s)., & Surname, Initial(s). (Copyright Year). *Title of book*. Name of publisher. (edition number, volume number). DOI

Real examples
Single author (with DOI):
Block, J. (2002). *Personality as an affect-processing system: Toward an integrative theory*. Lawrence Erlbaum. http://dx.doi.org/10.4324/9781410602466

Multiple authors (with no DOI):
Potter, J., Stringer, P., & Wetherell, M. S. (1984). *Social texts and context: Literature and social psychology*. Routledge and Kegan Paul.

Referencing a chapter in an edited book

An edited book is different from single- and multiple-author non-edited books in that it contains contributions from different authors (some, but not all, of whom may be the editors themselves). A chapter in such a book is a bit like a mixture of a book and a journal article: it is contained within a book (often a single volume), yet the volume it appears in typically includes different contributions from a variety of authors. These characteristics mean that we need some detail about the title and authorship of both the specific chapter and the edited volume itself.

If you are not seated, please make yourself as comfortable as possible and remain calm. We have a big task here. We need to get the details of our target authors and the title of the chapter they have written and then situate this in the edited volume in which it appears. This will have editors (who may or may not be the same as those who wrote the chapter) and it will have a title, which is likely to be different from the individual chapter title.

Referencing a chapter in an edited book: Step-by-step guide

1. Steps 1 – 4 above (detailing how surnames and initials are handled) apply here, the details given relating to the *authors of the specific chapter* which we are referencing.
2. Copyright year in parenthesis (brackets), followed by a full stop and a space.
3. Title of *the book chapter*, (not the book in which the chapter is found), followed by a full stop and a space and the word 'In'.
4. We now need to mention the editors, after 'In', (and space) insert the initial(s) of the first editor, followed by a full stop and then the surname of the first editor, if there is more than one editor we would follow the procedures outlined in step 4 for non-edited books above, except

that for editors their initial comes before their surname. This would be followed by '(Ed.)' for one, or '(Eds.)' for more than one editor.

5. After a comma and a space give the title of *the book in which the chapter is published* in italics.

6. After the title of the book itself (and a space) you need a left-hand bracket. As noted above, if the book has an edition or volume number you place that in parenthesis, e.g. '(7th ed.' or '(Vol. 12'. If it has both an edition and volume number then give edition number, followed by a comma and then volume number, e.g. '(7th ed., Vol. 12'.

7. Within the same parenthesis you need to identify the pages of the chapter being referenced using 'pp.' to indicate 'pages' and a space, then the start page–final page, followed by a close bracket, a full stop and a space. If there was no edition or volume number this would appear as '(pp. 42–99).', with an edition and volume number '(7th ed., Vol. 12, pp. 42–99).'.

8. Name of the publisher followed by a full stop. The APA style guide in the 7th edition stipulates that place of publication is not included in the reference list.

9. If available, include a DOI (Digital Object Identifier), see above for details on using DOIs and URLs. No full stop is to be added after the DOI or URL.

10. After this get yourself a lovely warm cup of tea.

Schematic example

Surname, Initial(s)., & Surname, Initial(s). (Year of publication). Title of the specific chapter referred to. In Initial(s) of first editor and surname of the first editor & initial(s) of second editor. and surname of the second editor '(Eds.)' [or '(Ed.)' if there is a single editor], *Title of the book* (Edition number, volume number [where available], pages indicated by 'pp.' start page–final page). Name of publisher. DOI [where available].

Real example (with no DOI):

Fiske, S. T. (2010). Interpersonal stratification: Status, power, and subordination. In S. T. Fiske, D. T. Gilbert, & G. Lindzey (Eds.), *Handbook of social psychology* (5th ed., Vol. 2, pp. 941–982). Wiley.

LEARN

Top tip

To become a referencing Grand Master, pay attention to the precise details required (e.g. initials rather than full first name), the order in which these details should appear, the punctuation used (commas, full stops and colons all have specific roles in referencing – check what is used where) and the use of emphasis (italics is used in a very specific way in a reference list).

The APA style guide does an amazing job of outlining numerous possible contingencies of referencing. Referring to this guide and extracts from it can help you deal with conundrums. To illustrate, consider you have a repeated surname in your reference list. If multi-authored, look at the second (and subsequent surname), if the reference has a single author, look at the intials – in both cases arrange alphabetically. Bothered by the same author with more than one publication? Arrange by year of publication (earliest first). If the same author publishes more than one work in the same year then arrange those publications alphabetically by title and assign a letter (starting with 'a') after the year, e.g. Depak (2019a), Depak (2019b) etc, in both the reference list and in the in-text citation.

Referencing journal papers

If you want to access a journal paper, it is very helpful to know: the author's surname, the year it was published and the title of the paper/article. But, similarly to edited books, it is helpful to know the title of the publication in which it appears, in this case the journal title. As journals are typically organised into volumes, which might appear on a more or less yearly basis, information concerning the volume number of the journal is also needed. It can be helpful to know where in the journal the specific paper/article appears, so page numbers are given to help with this. Finally, the DOI offers a persistent, reliable link enabling the source to be located and, or, accessed.

APA conventions for psychology do not typically require that details of an issue number are provided, although there is some variation on this matter (the issue number is sometimes found in brackets after the volume number and indicates in which issue or part of that volume the target paper appears).

Referencing journal papers: Step-by-step guide

1. Steps 1–4 for referencing non-edited books above (detailing how surnames and initials are handled) apply here, the details given relating to the *author(s) of the journal article* which we are referencing.
2. Year of publication in parenthesis (brackets), followed by a full stop and a space.
3. Title of the journal article/paper followed by a full stop and a space.
4. Name of the journal, or periodical, *in italics*, followed by a comma and a space.
5. The volume number of the journal in which the paper appears *in italics*, followed by a comma and a space.
6. The first page of the article/paper, then a short dash, or en-rule, and then the last page of the article/paper, followed by a full stop.
7. If available, include a DOI (Digital Object Identifier), see above for details on using DOIs and URLs. No full stop is to be added after the DOI or URL.

Schematic example

Surname, Initial. (Year). Title of the specific paper. *Journal name*, Journal volume number, first page of paper–last page of paper. DOI [where available].

Real example (with DOI):

Holyoke, T. T., & Brown, H. (2019). After the punctuation: Competition, uncertainty, and convergent state policy change. *State Politics & Policy Quarterly*, *19*, 3–28. http://dx.doi.org/10.1177/1532440018788564

LEARN
Top tip

You will readily come across countless automatically generated references (for example, via searches in Google Scholar) as well as dedicated reference creating software. While these can be helpful tools, it is always worth double-checking them for accuracy, as although they often contain some useful information, they are very frequently inaccurate and incomplete.

EXERCISE
Ordering your reference list

Example X

In this example, we have three single authors with similar names which need to be put into the correct order. For simplicity, here we are considering the surname, initial and date of publication only (as that is all that is needed to order most reference lists). First, let's ignore the initials of the respective authors and put to one side thought about the year of publication – these will be relevant when you have two or more identically spelt surnames.

Try it out. Can you put these publications in the order in which they should appear in your reference list?

Davis, A. (2012)

Davis, M. (1980)

Davies, M. (2019)

Answer to Example X

Davis, A. (2012) <This should go second, because of its spelling – the fifth letter of 'Davis' being an 's', as compared to the fifth letter of 'Davies' being an 'e'. It also comes before 'Davis (1980)' because the initial 'A' comes before 'M'.

Davis, M. (1980) <This should be third, because of its spelling – the fifth letter of 'Davis' being an 's', as compared to the fifth letter of 'Davies' being an 'e' and as, the initial 'M' comes after 'A', it comes after 'Davis, A. (2012) above.>

Davies, M. (2019) <This goes first, because of its spelling – the fifth letter of 'Davies' being an 'e', as compared to the fifth letter of 'Davis' being an 's', the surname comes earlier in the alphabet than the other two and thus goes first.>

Example Y

These references were retrieved from Google scholar after choosing the APA referencing format. Can you first identify what is wrong or missing and then correct them using the information we have covered in this chapter?

Haslam, S. A., Reicher, S. D., & Van Bavel, J. J. (2019). Rethinking the nature of cruelty: The role of identity leadership in the Stanford Prison Experiment. American Psychologist.

Freud, S. (1913). The interpretation of dreams (AA Brill, Trans.). New York: McMillan (Original work published 1900).

Answer to Example Y
1. What's wrong

Haslam, S. A., Reicher, S. D., & Van Bavel, J. J. (2019). Rethinking the nature of cruelty: The role of identity leadership in the Stanford Prison Experiment. American Psychologist. *<The journal name should be in italics. The journal volume number and page numbers are missing (requiring a further online search). These details should be present after the journal name is given.* The DOI is missing and should be added at the end of the reference. If it can't be found from the article itself then using Crossref for an *article search* would usually help to locate the DOI: https://www.crossref.org/guestquery/>

Freud, S. (1913). The interpretation of dreams (AA Brill, Trans.). New York: McMillan. (Original work published 1900). <There is some useful information here, including the identity of the translator and the date of first publication. The book title should be in italics, in line with the 7th edition of the APA style guide, (American Psychological Association, 2020); place of publication is not needed. Finally, the DOI should be included whenever it is available, even if the source was not accessed digitally. You should make an effort to locate the DOI, using relevant resources such as *Crossref*, https://www.crossref.org/guestquery/ . Also note that where cited works have two dates as in this case, both should appear each time there is an in-text citation, e.g. Freud (1900/1913).>

Both references should be formatted, so that they are 'hanging' with an indentation for the second and subsequent lines of 1.27cm , or 0.5 inches.

2. Correct references

Haslam, S. A., Reicher, S. D., & Van Bavel, J. J. (2019). Rethinking the nature of cruelty: The role of identity leadership in the Stanford Prison Experiment. *American Psychologist*, *74*, 809–822. http://dx.doi.org/10.1037/amp0000443

Freud, S. (1913). *The interpretation of dreams*. (A. A. Brill, Trans). MacMillan. (Original work published 1900). https://doi.org/10.1037/10561-000

HOW TO GIVE YOUR ESSAY A PRESENTATIONAL MAKEOVER (AND MORE)

However much we hope to allow ourselves plenty of time, many of us often wind up having a last-minute rush as deadlines approach. Earlier in this chapter we considered that sometimes presentational issues not only create a barrier between the marker and the good ideas in our essay, they can also indicate issues of substance with our essay, such as under-developed thoughts, a failure to address the precise essay title and a lack of connection between the different elements referred to in our essay. These underlying issues require more time to address than the presentational issues themselves, so it is helpful to imagine two scenarios: a quick-fix makeover and a longer, focused reworking. Regarding the latter, it is worth referring to Chapter 10 for more details on editing your essay below the focus is on quick presentational fixes.

ACE YOUR ASSIGNMENT
The quick-fix makeover

If you have even just 30 minutes before you need to begin the process of submitting your essay, in addition to the time needed for printing, binding, delivery or electronic uploading (see Chapter 10 for more on this), then you can still make a significant change to the appearance of your essay. The following check list (with extremely approximate timings) can help you to remove some of the potential presentational problems that might otherwise create a barrier between your marker and your essay:

1. If you are required to write your essay title (for example, at the beginning of your essay or on a separate title page), then check that you have used *the precise essay title given* (unless you have been specifically directed to adapt it or create your own title). Don't just use the broad topic or something close to the title; use the precise essay title, without any changes at all. None. Time to fix = 1 minute.

2. Check that your essay has an introductory paragraph at the beginning (see Chapter 3) and a concluding paragraph at the end (see Chapter 8). Time to fix = checking takes a couple of minutes, writing an introduction could take perhaps 15–30 minutes, (though quite possibly more), writing a very basic conclusion might be similar, a strong conclusion is likely to take significantly longer.

3. Ensure that you correctly cite sources that you refer to throughout your essay. Time to fix = checking takes perhaps between 5 and 15 minutes (depending on essay length), correcting details (for example, adding missing dates for citations) might take 10–20 minutes per 1000 words (if all the details are immediately to hand). If you need to search to find the names of missing sources or missing details, this makes the task much, much slower.

4. Ensure that your essay has a reference section, which follows the appropriate formatting rules (usually APA). Time to fix = carefully checking takes perhaps 10–20 minutes for every 20 references, correcting a reference might take 1–2 minutes per item (if all the details are to hand). If you need to search for details, this will take much, much longer.

5. Check that your essay is within the word length range for the essay. Time to fix = checking should take a minute, but fixing it if you are substantially over-length and (especially) if your essay is too short and key information is missing is likely to take a long time. You might be able to trim, or add, perhaps 200 words in an hour, but this varies enormously. The more you need to read and understand in order to edit your word length, the longer it takes.

6. Check for consistency of font style and size. Time to fix = 1 minute to check, perhaps 5–10 minutes to address.

7. Check for your use of paragraphs. If your paragraphs appear to be too long (perhaps over 300 words) or too short (less than 100 words), then it is usually worth seeing if you can make them work more effectively in your essay. Time to fix = perhaps 2–5 minutes per 1000 words to check, but the time to fix will depend on whether rewriting is required. If your paragraphs are too short because you have not fully developed the point that you briefly touch on, then you have done well to identify an important issue, but if you need to read and/or think about your content further, you have a longer process ahead. If, however, you have separate paragraphs developing essentially the same broad point, you may more easily and quickly be able to join these to form coherent good-sized paragraphs (perhaps 200 words or so). Similarly, sometimes long paragraphs include detail that can be easily trimmed or different points that can easily be split into separate points. At other times, more thought and rewriting are required to untangle the different issues being addressed.

A quick look at the presentation of your essay before submission is so much better than a long remorseful appraisal after you have received your grade. Sometimes you will identify quick fixes that improve your essay and remove obstacles between the marker and your thinking about the topic. At other times, looking at your presentation will reveal issues about content, cohesion and critique, the presentation being merely the symptom of deeper issues. If you allow time to check your essay through (see Chapter 10 for more on this), then checking your presentation can be a vital tool for identifying issues of substance which you actually have time to fix before submitting your essay. This one step – allowing time to edit – is perhaps the ultimate key to improving your work and is the focus of the next chapter.

REFLECTING ON THE CHAPTER:
Why not be professional?

If, like me, you have had the presentation of your CV held up to ridicule, you will be sensitive to the power of presentation. Presentation is not everything and it is so easy to dismiss it, seeing it as outside of the serious academic job of the essay – but, while it shouldn't be our main focus, there is a paradox – the more we treat presentation as unimportant the more prominent it will be in the minds of our reader. If we submit an untidy essay that looks like it was thrown together in haste, then poor presentation will be the first thing that the marker thinks about when they see our essay. Good presentation in an academic essay foregrounds the academic work (which certainly should be the focus), rather than distracting the reader into trying to decode what is going on with your paragraphs, your font choices, alignment or unexpected use of emojis. Good presentation also (rightly or wrongly) suggests a pride in your work and a certain degree of professionalism. Try to produce work that you would be happy to show to a future employer or a

(Continued)

postgraduate administrator – something that, if seen, would work to your advantage in getting you that great job or a place on a desirable postgraduate programme. Your essay presentation is like a window looking out onto a glorious sunrise: keep it clean and bright, so that readers can see your sparkling brilliance on the other side, rather than simply close the curtains in disgust.

TAKE AWAY POINTS FROM THIS CHAPTER

- Good presentation goes largely unnoticed, but really helps the reader to more clearly focus on your writing and thinking without being irritated and distracted.
- Presentational problems can sometimes indicate issues with the substance of our essays, acting as helpful clues for what we can improve.
- Good citation crisply conveys a sense of the sources that are relevant for your essay and enables you to discuss them effectively.
- Good referencing uses conventions to provide clear, straightforward information to your reader about the sources that you have used in your essay.
- Checking the presentation of our essay when we review and edit our work can help us identify and correct both presentational and possible underlying issues.

LINKING TO OTHER CHAPTERS

This chapter addresses how you can improve your citation, referencing and the presentation of your essay. This chapter should help you to feel empowered to clearly cite and reference relevant literature, to identify and remove presentation barriers and thereby communicate more effectively with your reader. Using a slightly different title, for example at the start of our essay, may indicate that we have not actually addressed the title in the substance of our essay. Chapter 4 provides guidance on addressing the precise essay title. Extremely long, or short, paragraphs are often associated with problems in essay structure and the smooth interconnection of ideas (Chapter 5 addresses this in more detail). This chapter discusses how your treatment of sources that you cite within your essay can facilitate or impair the way in which you describe and evaluate the ideas that you refer to. The issues of effective evaluation and description are addressed in more detail in Chapters 6 and 7 respectively. Presentation may lack a certain charisma compared with, say, 'critical evaluation', but fixing presentation tends to be one of the quickest remedies available and a small amount of work can have a big impact. So why not make citation, referencing and presentation an important focus when you edit a draft of your essay? This most crucial process of editing is covered in more detail in Chapter 10. Tackle your essay presentation, take pride in it (without becoming obsessed by it) so that nothing comes between your reader and the ideas expressed in your essay.

Chapter 10

Refine and enhance – how to effectively review and edit your essay

---

In this chapter you will learn...

- How to look at your work with a critical but constructive eye
- How you can use your 'inner critic' effectively
- How to know what to focus on when reviewing your essay
- How to tailor your reviewing and editing to the time that you have available

REVIEWING AND EDITING: WHAT THEY ARE AND WHY THEY MATTER

Touch any inanimate object within arm's reach. What have you got? A phone, a chair, a priceless Yamanka vase? That object – however simple, however complex – came into being from a dynamic tension between a creative spark on the one hand, and a process of review, reflection and refinement on the other. With artists, technicians and good academic essay writers, there is both a positive, generative process that involves producing ideas and executing them, and a critical process of appraisal and decision about what we have done (or thought of doing). We gather resources, assemble our thoughts, write our essays – but we also look and think about what we write, and this sometimes involves negating what we have written, cutting bits out or changing them.

You may think that you do not engage in the critical review aspect of your writing. I think at some level almost all students do, especially those reading these words. However, most of us struggle to get the balance right between generating words and critically reviewing them to create that optimal creative tension. That's where this chapter can help.

STOP AND THINK
The dynamism of editing and reviewing

Reviewing and editing our work brings us face to face with the key writing dynamic – between creative, generative production on the one hand and critical appraisal on the other. This creative tension is captured in the famous yin–yang image – which (among other interpretations) can be seen as acknowledging how seemingly contradictory energies can operate in a complementary and interdependent way.

Can you think of a time in your writing, or in any other creative act, when there have been moments of flowing, generative production and then a stepping back to look at and appraise what you are doing or have done? We often feel we are doing well when we experience the 'flow state', but are wasting time, hitting problems or being unproductive when we are moving to reviewing and editing, yet *both* of these and the creative tension between the two can help us to do our very best work.

WAYS OF BEING OUT OF BALANCE (AND SOME QUICK TIPS)

Have a look at these ways of being out of balance in the production and critical review of our writing. Which one(s) do you think apply most to you?

- **Critical from the start**

   When we experience being critical from the outset, we may put off getting started at all. This is one of the key factors behind procrastination (see Chapter 1 for more on this). When the inner critic is this active from the beginning, it is like being sat on by a giant – however much we may want to, we can't get up and go.

   It can help to charm our way into starting – try to make it fun and creative, not just a heavy-duty thing.

- **Critical once I start writing**

   This experience is when we manage to start writing, but each sentence drips out really, really slowly. It can be a very frustrating way to write, especially if we want that experience of being 'in the flow' and yet we can't seem to get there. This can lead to a real frustration with our writing and in turn make us procrastinate in continuing with our essay.

   Sometimes we have to write ourselves into writing. Although the right thing may be to have a break and come back later – perhaps when we are 'inspired' – there may not ever be an 'ideal' time to try again. Do try to write through – or around – some of these blocks. Many of us experience this and it doesn't mean that your writing is worse just because it is not flowing easily.

- **Critical comprehensiveness**

   Sometimes your inner critic can operate to make you feel like you have to write exhaustively on each issue you are addressing. Any one paragraph can be almost impossible to finish because you start writing about Alan Baddeley's multi-component model of memory and feel you will lose marks if you omit any important detail. Your inner critic might be prompting you to include more and more details 'just to be safe'– as a form of insurance.

It is likely that we have all had experiences – perhaps at school or college – where we suffered because we missed out something that was crucial in our work. That red pen and those teacher exclamation marks can leave their trace years down the line. With an under-graduate academic essay, it is not possible to include every detail about every reference that you draw on.

Imagine that you have a fairly short essay in which you cite 12 sources, and your sources include a book chapter, nine journal articles, a specialist book and a textbook. If you really included every detail of each of these, your word count would be similar to the total of all of these sources and we would have an essay of approximately 478,000 words ($5000 + 9 \times 7000 + 70,000 + 340,000$). Even if it was read in its entirety and the word length didn't apply, it would get a low grade because your essay would not be doing what essays are required to do, which is to draw on the details, evidence and arguments necessary to create a well-argued treatment of the specific essay title. No marker wants to see every detail of every source that you have come into contact with. Instead, markers want essays that show your scholarly thinking, one aspect of which is the distilling of the key issues that are pertinent for addressing the precise essay title.

- **Critical when I am nearing the end or about to hand in my essay**

Nearing the finish line can really awaken the critic within. Suddenly, the sense that we will be judged and our work will be found wanting looms vividly before us. This can lead to our being late with our work, never handing it in or sometimes questioning whether we should continue our studies at all.

We all want to do our best, but we are going to learn quite a bit from the process of submitting our work and seeing how it does and what feedback we get. Usually the fate of planet earth does not hinge on whatever we are trying to write, although it may feel like it does. Bear in mind the small contribution that each individual assignment typically makes towards your overall degree. By finishing this well *but imperfectly* you can complete your other assignments, learning a little more each time. Alternatively, you can wait for perfection – the only snag is you may be waiting forever.

- **Not really critical**

It may be that we don't experience the inner critic as stopping us from starting, continuing or finishing our writing. We just write and don't need to think about it – we let the marker do that instead. This may look ideal in the light of what we have considered above, but it isn't really. If we are not at all critical or evaluating of the work we submit, if we write, just generating words and putting them down with no appraisal whatsoever, we will pro-duce a stream of consciousness essay. This sort of essay is rare, although every few years I see one that comes close to this. They do not do well.

If you are likely to do this, just be aware that you are not skilfully avoiding the hard work of writing a proper academic essay by just 'going radical', 'letting it flow' and 'being creative'. If you genuinely write without any appraisal, you are unlikely to be producing what we consider to be an academic essay, and you will not be answering the question.

STOP AND THINK
Befriending your inner critic

This last issue, concerning 'not being critical' is really important. We can easily start to see our 'inner critic' as the thing that makes us procrastinate, that stops us from getting into the flow and that makes us never feel that our essay is 'ready to submit'. The inner critic becomes the enemy within – our self-defeating secret that stops us from reaching our full potential. But let's stop right there. If our inner critic is completely absent, we have stream-of-consciousness writing. The chance that this will be anything like the best we can do is probably similar to the likelihood of coming across Elvis Presley alive and well and lecturing in cognitive psychology at the University of Tasmania.

Our writing really can start to be the best we can do *when we respect our inner critic*, rather than simply going to war with it or suppressing it. When we do battle with our inner critic and see it as an entirely destructive force within us, we are missing what our inner critic can usefully contribute to our essay and we are actually making the disruptive potential that it has greater, rather than smaller. We want a non-disruptive inner critic which supports our essay writing by helping to ensure that we are answering the question, being accurate and writing well.

ACE YOUR ASSIGNMENT
Your inner critic

Let's consider how the right way of drawing on our inner critic can support our writing.

Our inner critic can raise these questions regarding our writing:

- Is it answering the question?

  The inner critic can help to make sure that you address the essay question in what you write (see Chapter 4 for more on this).

- Is it accurate?

  The inner critic can help to make sure that our relevant topic knowledge is accurate.

- Is it well written?

  The inner critic can help to make sure that we have addressed the very issues that this book has focused on concerning the features of good academic writing.

See your inner critic as a potential mentor – a wise guide, *helping us to apply* what we have learned about the essay title, the topic and good academic writing to our essays. Having this respectful relationship with our inner critic can enable it to become a helpful mentor, one that can free us from a continual struggle with an enemy partly of our own making.

Welcome your inner critic in. It is trying its best – it is keen that you do well and is worried about the ways in which you might not do your best. Give your inner critic a specific role where it can help. Planning time for critiquing, reviewing and editing your work – as you are writing and when you have finished – can free you up. Your writing can flow in the knowledge that errors, omissions and imperfections will be looked at during your review time. Acknowledging the contribution that your inner critic can make helps you to find a constructive role for it, enabling it to genuinely help you to reach your potential in your essay writing.

TRANSFORMING YOUR CRITICAL REVIEWING

Guides to writing essays will tend to note the importance of reviewing and editing essays – and that is excellent advice. Part of what makes professional writing (often) seem very well written is that it goes through a review and editing process. But these guides can sometimes assume that we all have plenty of time. While we should all aim for this ideal, if it's 12 noon and our essay is due in at 2pm, what can we do? Have no fear, here is a guide to what we can do to review our essay if we are really short of time – and what to do if we have longer.

STOP AND THINK
Before you start

Keep an eye on the time. Set an alarm before the deadline and give yourself perhaps 20 minutes more than you think you need to do all of the file uploading (or printing) and submission processes involved. There are sometimes technical issues, especially when many students are submitting work at once, so allow for these. When your alarm goes, move from editing mode to submission mode.

Save a copy of your essay as it is and save the one you are editing separately (perhaps adding 'edited' to the file name). If you suddenly find it is nearing the submission deadline and you have highlights and half-reworded paragraphs that you cannot complete in time, you will always have your original copy to fall back on. However, try to edit in a smart way here. Don't be like me when I tidy the house, creating so much upheaval that it often looks worse than when I started. Fix small, focused bits at a time, and only tackle what you have time to fix.

At the risk of oversimplifying, the three levels of editing outlined below differ in terms of their scope, and may focus, with differing emphasis, on the presentation, how the essay is written and the underlying thinking.

What is presented – what will the marker visually notice (for example, sections that are missing, paragraphs that are out of balance, typographical and other writing errors). These can be reasonably quick to spot and, depending on what is spotted, quite quick to fix.

How it is written – this gets into how well the essay is crafted. For example, does it do the sort of academic writing that this book has focused on? Is it critically evaluative? Does it have a strong introduction and conclusion and is it smoothly interconnected? This takes longer to address, but some of these concerns could be tackled without requiring a significant rethink about the ideas and content of the essay.

What is the underlying thinking – this goes deeper and requires more time. Here we might need to read more or, at the very least, think through our ideas carefully. We might need to fill in gaps to address the essay title or to re-engage with ideas we have covered to better understand, critique or conceptualise them. It's not quite 'back to the drawing board', but this level of reviewing does involve thinking through one or more sections within our essay.

The very quick review and edit

Here I am assuming that in addition to the time needed to comfortably do all of the file submission and uploading procedure (or printing and submitting by carrier pigeon), you have some time available, perhaps the time it would take to watch a typical movie, maybe 90 minutes or so. If you have more time, you've just earned a free upgrade and can choose one of the other levels of editing below. If you have less time, just be smart about what you can achieve in the time you have.

- Read through your essay with particular attention to the essay title. It may be helpful to read it aloud if time and context permits. Now, be honest – do you answer the essay title?
- If you see some obvious problems, highlight them.
- Focus on your introduction and conclusion in particular. Do you set up issues that address the essay title in your introduction? Do you capture the key issues and debates in your conclusion?
- Ensure that both your introduction and conclusion convey to the reader that you are directly addressing the essay title.
- Check for any sentences or paragraphs that go off track.
- If they are relevant, make that clear in your writing – if they are not, delete them.

Presentation of writing

Do any problems jump out at you? Perhaps some of these:

- Incomplete sentences
- Typos
- Missing citations

- Unclear sentences
- Paragraphs that are too long (check those that are over 300 words)
- Paragraphs that are too short (check those that are less than 100 words)
- Tone, words or phrases that don't seem appropriate for an academic essay.

Each of these should be reasonably quick to fix, but if you don't have long, focus on the cases that really stand out. Addressing these issues gives your essay a much better feel and enables the marker to see your thinking without these untidy distractions.

All main sections present

Most essays should have (though not necessarily under separate subheadings):

- An introduction
- A main body
- A conclusion
- A references section

It is possible that you have other guidance about required sections (perhaps concerning personal reflection or other features specific to your particular assignment). To miss these key sections is really an own goal – it will be noticed, you will lose marks – yet fixing them is reasonably quick when you consider that even a very imperfect introduction, conclusion and references section is a big improvement on having none at all. If the main body of the essay is missing, then you really have a detective mystery on your hands – where's the body gone and who is responsible?

The fairly quick review and edit

You have more time? That's great! I am assuming that these edits may typically take more than 90 minutes – but I don't know how you and your essay are working together. It is possible that you have less time and can still tackle some of these issues or that you have more time but are struggling with the edits in the previous section. See these suggestions as rough indicators and use them in any way that supports you as you review and edit your essay.

First, do the steps outlined in the very quick review and edit above. These will help to tidy up your essay, a little like polishing the car and checking that the wheels are still there before you put it up for sale. It is now time to check the engine, as we look at how ideas are handled and expressed in your essay.

Essay title (see Chapter 4 for more on this)

- Look through your essay and see if you directly answer the question throughout. Try to adopt a fair, rather than severe or lenient reader perspective.

- Move to a precise understanding of the essay title, rather than a general sense of the broad topic or key names.

- Pay particular attention to your introduction and conclusion. Both of these sections are super-important for setting up the issues of direct relevance to the essay title that are to be addressed (the introduction) and providing an intelligent conceptual reflection of the issues of relevance to the essay title (the conclusion).

- See whether you have material that does not directly address the essay question. This might be a stray paragraph or sentence, for example. If it looks suspicious, interrogate it – ask it what it's doing there. If it hasn't a good reason to be there *given the specific essay title*, then – possibly with regret – it needs to be fired/removed/deleted or sent elsewhere.

- Adopt the perspective of a mystery reader. Can you triumph with the mystery reader challenge? If your mystery reader can fairly precisely work out the title of your essay from reading your essay, then great! If they can't, this is great in another way – it means you are about to really improve your essay, making changes so that your essay more clearly conveys (without restating) the essay title.

- Most essays can be sharpened and they do not typically need a full rewrite. A relatively small amount of work can bring your essay much more sharply on track with the specific essay question, thus spreading joy to all who are lucky enough to read your essay.

Introduction (see Chapter 3 for more on this)

- Have you used a first sentence that orientates to the essay title, conveying something of how or why this is a relevant issue to address?

- This first sentence, before you outline how you will address the essay title, conveys to your reader a sense that you are aware of the important issues that the essay title raises. Orientating sentences will of course vary from essay to essay but might share something of the look and feel of this schematic sentence: 'The question of … raises important issues for our understanding of …, touching on key debates that have been central to … for …'.

- Have you a clear statement of what your essay will address (a statement of intent)? This should communicate a clear sense of what your essay will address, in what order and why it is relevant for the specific essay title.

- Your statement of intent not only conveys a sense of what's on the menu for this essay, but is also the first opportunity that you have to assure your reader that your whole essay will address the precise essay title. Your statement of intent can also convey something of your rationale, or *why* you are addressing the things you are focusing on. This schematic outline is indicative of some of the thought that can be conveyed in a statement of intent: 'In order to address these issues, this essay will first outline … and examine X's interpretation of these findings. This research will then be critiqued in terms of the potential methodological issues raised by … and …, before moving to alternative interpretations of these findings outlined by … and … In order to fully … [identify key requirement in the essay title] … the essay will then consider …. Finally, the essay will reflect on how our approach to understanding … [issue in the essay title] depends crucially on …'.

Interconnection (see Chapter 5 for more on this)

- Read through the first sentences of your paragraphs. Do they *state how they relate*? Does the first sentence tell the marker how *this* paragraph relates to the previous one? Your introduction will be different because that has to link to the essay title, and your second paragraph gets the main body going, but then we should have beautiful sentences starting each new paragraph that each *state how they relate*.

Think of the relationship between your paragraphs. Interrogate your new paragraph and think how its relationship can be captured in a sentence or two. Is your new paragraph:

  i. Providing support for the ideas in the previous paragraph (for example, 'Further evidence to support the idea of … can be found in the work of …, who argues that …')?

  ii. Offering a contrasting perspective (for example, 'In contrast to the idea that …, based on their research investigating …, X and Y argue that …')?

  iii. Arguing for some mix of the two (for example, 'The idea that … finds partial support in the work of X and Y who investigated … . <New sentence> X and Y, argue, on the one hand, that …, but on the other hand, suggest …')?

If you find a paragraph that has no relation at all to the previous one, check if it is relevant to the precise essay title. Also check that your paragraphs are all arranged in the best possible order.

EXERCISE
Practise your editing skills

We are not always editing, but we can be regularly refining our editing skills. If you have a draft essay, use the guidance in this chapter to try a quick mini edit. If you do not have any assignments due, look at a previous essay. How can you improve this work? What specific changes can you make? You may find that marker comments inform your sense of what is to be edited. Briefly note down your thoughts and save your work under a new file name. Now set a timer for 10 minutes and see how quickly you can do a mini edit. It is empowering to see how a few brief minutes can really change things.

Conclusion (see Chapter 8 for more on this)

- Does your conclusion not only indicate that your essay focuses on the essay title (see the 'very quick review and edit section' above) but also provide the reader with some sense of how they can think about the issues addressed in your essay? For example, if your essay (as most should) draws out different perspectives on an issue, does your conclusion note the different perspectives and make sense of them in terms of the different sets of assumptions or types of theoretical approaches that they represent?

Recapping on what was covered in your essay may be a good starting point but, when reviewing your conclusion, try to upgrade this to a conceptualisation of the relevant perspectives. Rather than: 'Gibson argued that it is important to consider the use of rhetoric in making sense of Milgram's results', consider something like: 'In contrast to Milgram's emphasis on the intra-psychic process of agentic shift, Gibson conceptualises Milgram's findings in terms of the rhetorical processes found in the talk of both experimenters and teacher-participants.' This draws out the broader perspectives at work (that is, 'intra-psychic' versus 'rhetorical' perspectives), demonstrating your scholarly understanding of the debates that you have covered in your essay.

Critical evaluation (see Chapter 6 for more on this)

- If there is one special ingredient you really want in your essay, it is, almost always, critical evaluation. Do you compare different perspectives to one another or merely list what each cited source says? Think of the difference between an entirely descriptive report of what witnesses say ('W says…, X says…, Y says…') and a crucial cross-examination where one claim is drawn on to make sense of another ('You say…, but X argues that…').

- Your essay is all about looking at each piece of research, each finding, each interpretation and each theory in the light of other perspectives, some of which will confirm and others of which will challenge. Looking through your essay, are you listing all of the research, findings, interpretations and theories in splendid isolation from each other – or are you giving the reader a real sense of analysing the ideas that you raise, from different perspectives?

- Check parts of your essay where there is – and is not – critical evaluation. Where critical evaluation is not present, ask whether, for all of the empirical details, findings, interpretations and theories covered, 'is there another relevant view'? If you have, or can readily find, a name associated with another (different or supporting) relevant view, then great; if not, you can still make the analytic points that come to mind (for example, 'It could be argued that…'), see Chapter 6 for more on this.

LEARN
How Jung can help with your essays

When Jung was about 80 years old, after more than a decade since starting it, he finally completed and published a book that sought to clarify much of his life's work. *Mysterium Coniunctionis* (Jung, 1970) focused on a central tension between separation, on the one hand, and synthesis, on the other. Jung's emphasis on this crucial dynamic between separate, often opposing, elements and their union or reconciliation actually captures the heart of good essay writing in psychology:

- Our essays start with identifying the different voices that are relevant (the perspectives, findings and ideas).
- In writing our essays, we develop a sense of critical thinking (and create an argumentative structure), by considering the relationship between these separable elements.
- Our conclusions offer a conceptualisation that provides a way of understanding how we can make sense of these diverging perspectives, or how we can reconcile, for ourselves (and our readers), the apparent contradictions we have investigated.

STOP AND THINK
How does this help?

When we look through our essays, we sometimes see the chaos of different ideas that don't neatly fit – but this tells us we are probably on the right track. If this is how your essay looks, then:

- Acknowledge that you have done well in identifying different perspectives.
- See how you articulate the ways in which different elements interrelate (who aligns with/disagrees with whom about what issue that is directly relevant for the title).
- In your conclusion, in particular, see if you articulate what we are to make of these clashing, difficult-to-reconcile perspectives? Are there ways of making sense of the potential chaos of these differences? What should the reader think about the issue of the essay title given these different viewpoints?

When we think like this we are involved in our own separation–synthesis conundrum. However, it is a generative one. It is from this precise tension that great essays are born. Having this in mind as we edit our essays can transform them from list-like descriptions into insightful, critical investigations.

The longer review and edit

Ensure that you have covered the points highlighted in the 'fairly quick review and edit' above. As you have more time, make sure you work through these aspects with more care and attention to detail. Finding your academic voice can take time. Reading good academic writing and thinking about what makes it good will certainly help you to develop your academic voice, but *actually writing in a reflective way*, will do most to develop this skill. Don't expect the first version of your essay to be the best that you can do. The opportunity to properly edit your work is wonderful and can really transform your writing.

Essay title (see Chapter 4 for more on this)

- It is *always* relevant when reviewing essays to check that they address the precise essay title. Follow the guidance in the preceding section with real attention to detail. You should also ask if there are gaps in terms of the literature that you have included *given the specific essay title*. Also, identify if there are gaps in your understanding or evaluation of the ideas covered. As you have longer you can start to address these issues of what you have covered and how you have engaged with the literature.

Introduction (see Chapter 3 for more on this)

- Your introduction conveys your thinking to the reader straight away, so it is worth making a good impression from the start.
- It is often worth editing your introduction once you have completed your essay in order to ensure that it really conveys the sense of a scholarly mind, engaged with the specific essay question.
- Don't just outline what is to be addressed in your essay, try to convey a sense of why these issues are important to fully address the specific essay title and how the different issues touched on relate to one another.

Interconnection (see Chapter 5 for more on this)

- Separate out the task of identifying the points you need to make from thinking about the order in which they should occur.
- Paragraphs are key to good structure. Think of each paragraph as doing a specific job in your essay – ask each one, 'What are you *doing* in my essay?' Your paragraph might be detailing empirical work, outlining a theoretical approach or identifying a contrasting approach to the essay topic – but it should be clear what it is doing and why this is important. Check that your paragraphs do a clear and important job in your essay with clarity and coherence; if you are not sure what their purpose is for this precise essay then they may need to be removed.
- Scan through your essay and consider whether there is there a better, more logical order in which this material can be placed. If so, change the order.
- Check your essay and ask, if your paragraphs were shuffled around, could someone put them back in the right order. If not, then check the order of your paragraphs and the clarity of your connecting sentences.
- As you are checking the flow of your essay be aware that non sequiturs can sometimes indicate not just a missing connecting sentence, or sub-optimal paragraph order, but also missing literature or coverage. In this longer edit see if you need to include ideas, information or perspectives that are relevant for your specific essay title.

Conclusion (see Chapter 8 for more on this)

- If you think conclusions are difficult to write – well done! This awareness is very helpful. You can transform your conclusions. It will take some effort on your part and you might actually enjoy it!

- Read through your draft conclusion and imagine yourself as the reader/marker. What would you say about your conclusion? Bring that thinking into your conclusions right now and see if you can make changes that will result in a focused, conceptual and insightful conclusion.

- With a longer edit you may have the time to articulate the overarching ideas that are relevant to your essay in your conclusion. Does your conclusion communicate a clear sense of the underlying issues (such as different perspectives on the person) that provide a way of making sense of the ideas covered in your essay (for example, the debate between different viewpoints)? If you can get at this conceptual level of thinking your conclusion really is going for gold.

ACE YOUR ASSIGNMENT
Embracing the yin and yang of conclusion writing

Embrace the yin and yang of conclusion writing. It is difficult, but your conclusions need to be *precise* (they have to focus on the specific issues identified in the essay title) and *conceptual* (they should be more focused on abstract issues rather than stuck with concrete particulars). This skill takes time to acquire, but if you read good conclusions (use this book, look at other published work and sample essays if these are made available) and practise writing them, you will make real progress.

Critical evaluation (see Chapter 6 for more on this)
Critical evaluation was touched on above, here it is assumed that you see the importance of it and have a little more time to devote to it.

- Look through your essay to see how the different ideas that you refer to relate to one another. Check whether you have brought out an emphasis on the implications that these ideas have for one another. For example, which ideas do the results that you refer to support? Who agrees and disagrees with whom in your essay? What are the points of agreement and disagreement? What does the evidence suggest? For this longer edit, you may wish to consider whether additional literature would strengthen your – directly relevant – critical evaluation.

- You should do this first with the ideas that are already present in your essay and then, if time allows, you can consider articulating different critiques. Perhaps you can spot methodological flaws or limits to an idea or argument? If time allows, you may be able to locate a source to substantiate your critique. For example, locating sources that cite a target paper can often identify subsequent sources of support and critique.

- If you have an evaluative point, but no source to substantiate it, allow a finite time to find relevant supportive literature. You could use databases to follow up citations of the target publication that you are evaluating, which may identify some subsequent relevant (and critically evaluative) publications.

- Alternatively, you might use a 'citation free' formulation such as: 'It could be argued that…' or 'one potential limitation of this experiment was that…'. It's great if the point acknowledges relevant supportive literature, but even without this it is still important to make evaluative points as long as they contribute towards addressing the essay question.

References and sources (see Chapters 2 and 9 for more on this)

- Good literature searching is like good detective work and can help you to uncover gems for your essay. If you need to do more of this when reviewing and editing your essay, be conscious of the time that this can take. A focused approach where you are seeking sources to develop specific points may work best.

- Good citation crisply conveys a sense of the sources that are relevant for your essay and enables you to discuss them effectively. Take time to look through your essay, checking that the citations follow the correct format (in many, but not all, cases this will be the American Psychological Association, APA, format).

- Good referencing uses conventions to provide clear, precise information to your readers about the sources that you have used in your essay. Taking the time to check that you have applied the appropriate conventions in your essay can give your whole assignment a more professional look.

Description and academic writing style (see Chapter 7 for more on this)

- If academic writing doesn't flow from you like torrents of water cascading over rocks, then be easy on yourself. First, it's a very specific form of writing which differs from that which most (non-academics) use in their personal and professional lives. The more you can practise and reflect on what you have written, the better you will get.

- Aim for clarity not 'cleverness'. It is so tempting to try to be clever – we've all done it. Really good academic writing is about a beautiful clarity in expressing complex ideas, not an attempt to draw attention to how clever the writer is. While some words and terms are usually less effective in academic essays for psychology (for example, 'this proves that…'), it is not really a question of 'upgrading' words but instead being really clear and precise about what you write. Your writing should be like a clear window onto your sophisticated and subtle understanding of issues directly relevant to the precise essay title.

- Write with your essay title in mind. Your essay title should inform each paragraph, from introduction to conclusion. It is well worth taking this thought to each paragraph that you write and to the totality of your essay when you review it before submission.

- Read through and check for a consistent, scholarly, on target academic tone. If you can spot passages that have slipped into a chatty style, that have too much description, or which air-drop opinions – then rejoice, you are just about to improve your essay! Look at the ideas covered in this book and *learn from those parts of your essay that are well written* to help improve and develop weaker parts.

- Feel the power of your own ability: you, yes you, really can spot these issues and improve them. Don't passively 'wait and see what the marker thinks' – see what you think first as you are writing your essay.

ACE YOUR ASSIGNMENT
Read good academic writing and write often

I once asked the children's author Jacqueline Wilson for advice that might help develop my daughter's writing talent – 'read lots and write daily' was her reply, and that is absolutely key to developing our academic writing. Reading good academic writing helps us tune in to forms of expression that work well. Writing a little bit – even for five minutes each day – will empower us to draw from what we have read and reflected on in developing our academic voice.

GETTING IT FINISHED AND LETTING GO OF YOUR ESSAY

It seems perfectly rational to complete our essay, submit it and move on to our next assignment. Delaying our current submission while we work on it (up to the deadline) seems logical, but delaying it out of worry alone less so. Worrying about our essay *after* submission seems even less sensible. But, as psychologists, we scarcely need Jung, Freud, Pascal or others to remind us that however we may present ourselves, even to ourselves, we are not entirely rational creatures. There are several reasons why we might find it difficult to complete, submit and let go of our essay.

Deadline dilemmas

While many, though not all, students can mobilise themselves to submit their essays by the deadline, others find it difficult to submit in advance of the deadline – even when this would be the most logical thing to do. Submission deadlines are often arranged so that it would be wisest to start work on the next assignment (that is, essay two) before the deadline for the current assignment (that is, essay one) has passed. In other words, if we always submit our assignment on the day of the deadline and only then move to our next assignment, we might not be distributing our time optimally. It sounds like being super-organised, but why not look – perhaps with another student or tutor – at your assignments for the term, semester or academic year and see how they fall. Planning when you will work on, *and stop working on*, your assignments may actually give you an increased sense of control and could help you to have sufficient time for completing each of them.

Not quite finished

One of the best, and worst, things about exams is that when we are instructed to stop writing, we have to do just that. There are no crises of indecision, no 'should I, shouldn't I?', and no anxiety that if I stop others may have the advantage of continuing with their exams. But with assignments that have a few weeks or more in between the release of the title and the due date there is a real dilemma. A key point to bear in mind here is that the essay that we are working on is usually not our last piece of work. We will usually have other work to do after submitting this essay – perhaps another essay or maybe exam preparation.

Although we are all often far from logical at times, let's think rationally for a moment. If you have completed your essay and had the opportunity to review and edit it and have completed the changes that you have identified as being necessary, then there are diminishing returns for the additional time and energy that you devote to 'perfecting' it. If you have the time, with no further work that you need to undertake now, then great – but if not, three hours starting a new piece of work will accrue far more marks than revisiting an essay that is, by any reasonable definition, finished.

Try to seize your agency here and think about how you can best deploy your time, especially if you tend to work consecutively on assignments (starting a new one only after you have submitted a previous one). Look at your schedule of assignments and try to work out what your 'time budget' is for each assignment. If you are like me (and most people), revise your initial estimates down, because they are far too optimistic. Having a sense of the finite time that we have can help us to think clearly and wisely about how much of it we spend on any one piece of work.

Being judged

It is easy to feel as if someone will judge the work that we submit, possibly even evaluating it on an alphanumeric scale. And we would probably be right – our assignments *are* judged in this way. We can have all sorts of baggage around being judged, particularly in an academic context. If we can start to see our academic ability as a developing, evolving capacity with individual assignments providing the opportunity to improve, we can develop a different perspective. This outlook can be harder to maintain when markers (perhaps faced with a pile of 50 or more scripts) have given minimal feedback or left us a harshly worded comment, but it is nonetheless true. The very fact that you are reading this book suggests that you have some interest in improving your essays, and completing, submitting and reflecting on your assignments is almost unsurpassable as a means of reaching your full academic potential. Don't be blown off course by incomplete or inhospitable feedback, and don't let a disappointing grade drag you down. You have a bigger project underway – something of a miracle is within your grasp. You are in the process of transformation, and what emerges is largely down to you. That capacity to grow, to change and to develop is surely the very essence of being alive and what makes life worth living.

Reaching an ending

We can have contradictory feelings about endings. Undergraduates coming out of their last exam often have this sense of poignant elation. The hooray hardly leaves the lips before a slight shadow falls across their face. Submitting essays can be like that – we can feel that it is a final end, perhaps to something that we don't entirely want to end. Some people might tell us to 'get a grip' or to 'pull yourself together' or might shake their head in disbelief if we even hinted at this thought. But, if most of therapeutic psychology is anything to go by, there is more value in acknowledging rather than judging, condemning or ridiculing such feelings.

Endings of all sorts can be difficult, for numerous reasons – we may or may not have an awareness of what (if anything) is at the root of such feelings. Acknowledging these feelings and talking them through with others, if that helps, can start to empower us to choose what we do, rather than to finding ourselves falling into a pattern of delaying or not submitting our work for no apparent reason. We can start to take back control. And honesty and kindness towards ourselves may be our first step.

REFLECTING ON THE CHAPTER:
Stopping and reviewing is always worthwhile

On 26 September 1983 Stanislav Yevgrafovich Petrov could have followed standard protocol (and orders) and reported (as his instruments suggested) that the USA had launched a nuclear missile attack on the Soviet Union. Had he done so, then this may have initiated an unimaginable nuclear war. Stanislav stopped and considered the evidence before taking action and he surmised correctly that there was no attack (just an erroneous instrument reading). His restraint prevented possible disaster on a global scale. All of us are a world away from anything like such massively consequential cold war decisions, but we might still learn that in many much more trivial and inconsequential areas of life stopping, rather than rushing ahead, can be beneficial.

It's very easy to get sucked into a world of action so that we want to rush our essay and submit it the minute it's done, rather than allowing time for anything as 'unproductive' as reviewing and editing. Surely, we should write for all the available time and then hit submit? This chapter has tried to argue that even if we have a comparatively short time – maybe a couple of hours or so – we can use that time to make a real difference to our essay. If we don't review and edit before submitting our essay we will usually lose marks, and we will get comments back *after* submission that we could have made about

(Continued)

our essay ourselves *before* submission. A short space of time reviewing and editing has a disproportionate impact on the quality of work that we submit and on our learning about the essay process. In fact, looking at what we are doing and have done is how we learn from experience or, turning it around, how experience can teach us – without it, we don't get wiser, just older.

TAKE AWAY POINTS FROM THIS CHAPTER

- Reviewing and editing is a key reason why published work looks neat and well written – enormous care is taken by skilled editors to re-read and review drafts prior to publication. Why not give your essay the review and edit treatment too?

- Writing brilliant essays involves both a productive pouring out of words and a review and appraisal process. While these often alternate throughout the writing of an essay, there should also be a dedicated time at the end of your work for reviewing and editing.

- Having a specific time when you review and edit can free you from being blocked by self-criticism – give yourself a dedicated time to consider all of your (constructive) critical ideas.

- Taking the time to read and edit your essay will transform it.

- Even with a limited amount of time, reviewing and editing your essay can have an enormous impact on the quality of what you submit.

- Reviewing and editing gives you a second chance before it is too late. All of the ideas mentioned in this book, such as writing strong introductions and conclusions and making your essays evaluative and directly relevant to the essay title, can be picked up before submission when you review and edit.

LINKING TO OTHER CHAPTERS

The ideas covered in this chapter link with almost every other chapter in the book, because reviewing and editing provides that second opportunity to ensure that your essay excels in all of the features addressed in the previous chapters. When considering what to look for in reviewing and editing your work, attention was paid to addressing the essay title (see Chapter 4), ensuring that you have an effective introduction (Chapter 3), and adopt an appropriate academic style (Chapter 7), checking for smooth interconnection (Chapter 5) and strengthening both your critical evaluation (Chapter 6) and your conclusion (Chapter 8). Consideration was also given to both chasing up additional sources if time allows (Chapter 2) and polishing the presentation and references (Chapter 9). Perhaps less obvious, though emphasised within this chapter, is the role that having a dedicated time for reviewing and editing your work can play in freeing you from the potential inhibiting effect of a strong internal critic. If you are procrastinating starting, or finishing, your work (see Chapter 1), then you may find that having a specific time to review and edit gives your inner critic a helpful and hopefully constructive role, rather than a merely destructive, inhibitory one. Reviewing and editing sounds chorish and restrictive, but try it out – it can be transformative, informative and liberating.

Chapter 11

Unseen exams

In this chapter you will learn how to:

- Identify and deal with exam stress
- Plan for your exam
- Cope with the pressure before your exam
- Remember what you need for your exam
- Perform well during your exam
- Prepare for and answer multiple-choice and essay based exams
- Tackle self-defeating thoughts

UNSEEN EXAMS: WHAT THEY ARE, WHY THEY ARE STRESSFUL AND HOW YOU CAN HELP YOURSELF

Unseen exams are the classic and most common form of exams. With these exams, we sit in examination room for a specified period of time (typically between one and three hours) and answer questions in an exam paper that we have not seen before. Other exam formats, such as 'seen' exams and 'takeaway' exams, are addressed in Chapter 12.

Exams are stressful in a similar way to any performance that is assessed, or judged, and which is consequential – when we sit an exam we are like the athlete, actor or musician about to perform when it really matters. If the exam is not being judged (for example, if you are sitting a practice paper yourself) or is not consequential (for example, it is a class-based practice or a mock exam), then any stress gently dissipates like the scent of a rose on a summer's day. This chapter focuses on exams that *are* being assessed (we will get a grade for them) and which *are* consequential (the grade counts towards our degree). With these exams, we can feel the pressure build as the exam approaches, like the increasing heat and humidity on an overcrowded train, and we may be desperate to escape from the situation or avoid the pressure by not thinking about it. If this is how you feel, fear not – this chapter is written for you!

STRESS AND EXAMS

What do you tend to do when you feel anxious? Many of us feel a compulsion to avoid thinking about what is making us anxious and instead try to distract ourselves with something less threatening – those YouTube videos of vegetables that look like human faces suddenly seem captivating. Despite the temptation, leave the vegetables and try to identify what it is that is at the heart of your worry. Try to nail down your exam fears by completing Table 11.1 in the exercise below.

EXERCISE
Identifying your exam fears

Fill in the sections that you can manage in Table 11.1. Don't turn this into a punishment; this is simply you trying to help yourself in a friendly way. Try to identify your fear and to note why – as far as you can tell – you may have this fear and what impact it has on you. What sort of friendly advice would you give to someone (like yourself) who had these concerns? Would that advice help you to make a change? If you are struggling, turn to Table 11.2 for some suggestions that may help.

TABLE 11.1
Identifying your exam fears and anxieties

It makes sense for you to construct your own table in which you outline the fears that you have about the process of sitting or preparing for exams. Try to note why – as far as you can tell – you may have this fear and what its impact is. What sort of friendly advice would you give to someone (like yourself) who had these concerns? Would that advice help you to make a change?

Exam fear	Why	Impact	To make a change

Bear in mind that your university is likely to have counsellors, well-being officers and tutors who can help you. In addition, there are online resources that can support and help you (see the online resources at https://study.sagepub.com/psychologybrilliantessays for links to these).

While it makes sense for you to create your own table of fears when preparing for or sitting examinations, in the Table 11.2, I have identified three quite common exam-related fears. How do the fears listed in Table 11.2 compare with those that you have identified as relevant for yourself?

TABLE 11.2
Exam-related fears and anxieties

Exam fear	Why	Impact	To make a change
Worry about panicking in the exam.	Had a bad experience in a previous exam.	Makes me nervous about what will happen.	Talk through with well-being/counselling/tutorial support and/or other sources of support.
			Support may enable you to sit the exam in a different location.
			Support may also help you to learn to acknowledge the fear, observing it, rather than feeling threatened or dominated by it.
			You may discover calming techniques (including mindfulness) that may assist you before and during the exam.
Feeling trapped in the room	Surrounded by so many others, I might feel exposed and self-conscious amid the sea of desks.	Finding it difficult to concentrate in the actual exam as I feel uncomfortable in the exam hall.	Talk through with well-being/counselling/tutorial support and/or other sources of support.
			Support may enable you to sit the exam in a different location.
			Support may also help you to acknowledge and work through this fear.
			You may discover calming techniques (including mindfulness) that you can use directly in the exam room.
Mind going completely blank	I might not remember anything of relevance to the exam.	The fear of this makes me panic and not want to think about the exam.	If this has already been, or you think it could be, a major issue for you, you should seek advice and support, initially using the sorts of university-based sources of support outlined above.
			Practise completing sample questions under timed conditions – you may even wish to create some formality, for example, by using a space within your university library for some of your practice. This way, you are not only learning material, you are also practising retrieving it.
			In the exam itself, you may find that recall, understanding and a capacity to interrelate ideas do not all come at once – perhaps it never does work like that anyway. Instead, even the shakiest of starts can lead to remarkably strong answers – give yourself a chance.

Is stress always bad news?

There is a danger of building exam stress into a monster to be avoided at all costs. The problem with doing this is that we then have two causes of stress – we have whatever was causing us exam stress and also the stress about feeling stressed. It's like being in some zombie film where in our attempt to slay one zombie there are now two out to get us! Don't give the zombies the upper hand. Instead, try to befriend the stress, acknowledging that, while we may benefit from help if it keeps escalating, stress can actually help us out. Think about the way in which stress often arises from our wanting the best for ourselves, reflect on the way in which great performers (whether sporting, acting or musical) seem to use the (potentially stressful) energy of the performance to excel – perhaps you can do something like that?

THINK
You're a psychologist, aren't you?

You have probably heard of the Yerkes Dodson Law, or 'inverted U' of performance under stress, which maps performance (on the y-axis) and stress or arousal (on the x-axis). The original Yerkes & Dodson (1908/1972) experiment examined how quickly participants learned a task when they were subjected to electric shocks of greater intensity. As Figure 11.1 indicates, up to a certain optimal level, even for the difficult task, the increase in stress (associated with the shocks) was understood as improving task performance.

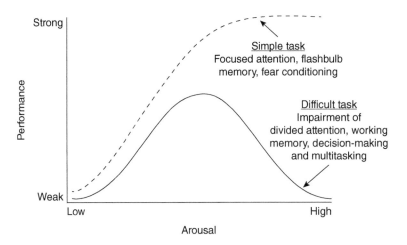

FIGURE 11.1
Yerkes-Dodson Law: The relationship between arousal and task performance

Whilst there are important issues in terms of the ethics and indeed the external validity of this research it neatly captures an idea found in much subsequent work – that stress can sometimes improve rather than impair performance. Don't exacerbate your own exam stress by believing that the very fact of feeling stress will ruin everything – it needn't be like that.

Although stress can become overwhelming – and we should seek support when it does – it need not be the villain of the piece. A certain level of stress may be just what we need in order to start – or continue – our exam preparation in advance of the exam. Similar to an athlete summoning the pressure of the situation to bring about a peak performance, we may find that the almost inevitable stress of the exam hall can be used to energise us as we seek to achieve our own personal best during the exam.

Using awareness/mindfulness techniques to tackle exam stress

A key argument made so far is that despite our impulse to run away from stress, taking time to be aware of it can really transform things for us. Noting down what makes us stressed is an example of bringing our awareness of the sources of our stress to the fore, and simply doing this can, paradoxically, reduce our stress. Another frequently used 'awareness' practice, which takes this reflection on our anxieties and sensations a little further, is 'mindfulness'.

Mindfulness is a practice which has been present in different forms for thousands of years, as being a key component of many religious, spiritual and contemplative traditions. The secular version of this practice was pioneered by Kabat-Zinn (1994) and others at the University of Massachusetts, who developed a stress reduction programme for the chronically ill. Drawing on these ideas, Shapiro, Schwartz and Bonner (1998) developed a mindfulness programme as an intervention for medical and premedical students. Shapiro et al. discovered that anxiety and other signs of psychological distress were reduced, even during exam periods, for students engaged in the programme. These findings were further confirmed in Shapiro, Oman, Thoresen, Plante and Flinders (2008), where students undertaking a secular mindfulness programme – and those following a more spiritual meditation programme – were found to experience significantly greater reduction in stress and rumination than control groups.

The various mindfulness practices used in these interventions included:

1.   A **sitting meditation**, which involved becoming aware of sensations experienced by the body as well as thoughts and emotions, with a gentle focus on the breath.
2.   In some cases, a specific **three-minute breathing space** practice, which involved, first, observing what one is experiencing (for example, 'anxiety') without trying to change it, then moving to a 'single, pointed' focus on the breath and, finally, to an awareness of sensations in the body.
3.   A **'body scan'**, where attentional focus is moved across different areas of the body.
4.   **Hatha yoga** movements and postures, or an equivalent.
5.   A **loving-kindness meditation**, which was designed to help develop greater compassion for self, others and humanity-at-large. In some cases, an additional **forgiveness meditation** was also used.

These core features of mindfulness have a strong track record of helping with anxiety and stress. You may seek to join a group (perhaps at your place of study) or read further on specific practices that could help you. Much of the empirical evidence for the effectiveness of mindfulness is based on relatively short-term but *recurrent* interventions (often lasting 7–8 weeks). This suggests that there may be a benefit in developing a regular practice of some form. However, it should also be noted that some of the specific practices (such as the three-minute breathing space practice) involve minimal time commitment and can be transported directly to stressful situations, such as waiting to enter the examination hall.

Mindfulness, in its secular or spiritual form, may be something that will help you to acknowledge the anxiety and stress that exams – and even exam preparation – can give rise to. It can help you to develop the capacity to stay with those feelings, without either desperately trying to avoid or 'fix' them, or simply becoming overwhelmed by them. Techniques that develop our awareness of what we are thinking and feeling, of what we are sensing in our bodies, and that develop our ability to come back to a focus on our breath, can offer a considerably supportive method of coping with the stress and anxiety that we all experience.

PLANNING FOR YOUR EXAM SUCCESS

If you are coming to this section with an imminent exam, you may find it helpful to flip down to the timescale that applies best to your situation. Hopefully, you are not reading this for the first time on the actual day of your exam, but sometimes this happens. So, if you are reading this on the day of your exam, there is the relevant section for you below – but please don't be late for your exam!

Set a timetable and allow for life events

As noted above, we all want to turn away from things that make us anxious. Exams are a great example of that – if they worry us, we try not to think about them, and we put off our revision. Don't let your exams creep up on you. If you have the exam dates, great! Get exam dates in your calanders as soon as you have them. If not, you are probably aware of roughly when they will take place. Write out a timetable for what you will do when – but be realistic and allow for the fact that life will not be amazingly accommodating to your exams. It is likely that there will be mishaps, illnesses and other crises that you will need to deal with, so build these into your timetable. If they start to look overwhelming, then talk to a member of staff at your university who can help you – this might be a tutor, another academic or a member of a counselling and well-being team. Members of staff will almost always prefer to hear from you sooner rather than later. They can typically advise you and outline options if circumstances do not improve for you.

If you are not a natural planner, consider software that can help you to plan or ask those you know who do have this gift for their advice, perhaps a member of your family and/or a staff member at your university. The key to the plan is realism. Without this, you won't want to look at your plan as it will just remind you of how far behind you are.

We typically tend to get more done on a 'little and often' basis, so don't underestimate what you can achieve with regular pockets of time, and don't wait for that 'day when I have nothing else to do' – it will probably never arrive. Work with what you realistically have. Often we need to start our revision just when we don't feel like it – there is always something else that 'needs' to be sorted out. But it is typically that early transition time into study that is key. If we can get a start, perhaps 30 minutes, we can usually go on and get some useful work done – but give yourself a chance by making a start.

If you are good at late bursts of frenetic activity, then you can build that into your plan – but you do need a fall-back position. What if you are ill, below par or embroiled in a crisis on the night you planned to do your marathon stint of revision? It is better to see these dramatic surges of activity as a bonus rather than the core of your exam preparation.

The days and *the night* before

The more you follow your pre-set timetable, the less that the almost mythical 'night before the exam' actually matters. Advice varies very substantially here. Some people will stress the potential effectiveness of relatively late revision, while others will focus on the need to find a relaxed state so that you can get a really good night's sleep.

The analogy of an athlete may help here. For major competitions, athletes have months – even years – of preparation and then a relatively brief performance window, when they have to run as if they were frantically trying to catch a bus, or hurl an object as if they were trying to rid their life forever of some painful memory. That combination, of long preparation and anticipation and a brief performance window, can put a lot of pressure on the days leading up to the big event and on the day itself. What is perhaps reassuring is that many athletes find that they sleep terribly the night before their big day and yet they can still perform exceptionally well. This doesn't mean that we should aim to have a disturbed night's sleep, but it does suggest that, with the exception of persistent conditions, we shouldn't make a huge deal out of it. In one of the earliest mass-circulation self-help books, Carnegie (1948), who acknowledged the struggles he had personally faced, notes: 'Worrying about insomnia will hurt you far more than insomnia' (1948: 229) (see the 'Stop and think' box below for eight tips on coping with impaired sleep).

Like an athlete, we need to find ways to facilitate our performance. The more we have a sense of (even imperfect) preparation in advance, the better placed we are to cope with a really tricky day or night before the exam. Use those days running up to the exam to practise doing what the exam will require you to do under similar (timed) conditions. Don't exhaust yourself – if the exam requires you to write three essays in three hours, you might want to write one essay in one hour, or perhaps three detailed essay plans in 45 minutes. If the exam entails 60 multiple-choice questions in two hours, then it might make sense to complete a smaller number of questions, allowing for the same average time per question (two minutes each). In this way, the size of the task is reduced (for example, taking up one hour instead of three hours), but the time allowed per answer is consistent with the actual exam conditions.

STOP AND THINK
Eight tips for coping with impaired sleep

Here are eight tips for overcoming the 'can't sleep – won't sleep' tension of the night before an exam. Try them out.

1. **Undertake some (safe and familiar) exercise**. It can be really helpful to engage in exercise on the day before the exam. It's probably not the best time to try to perform a standing backward flip for the first time, or to try and beat the world freediving record, but a walk, jog or some other low-risk and familiar exercise can help relieve stress and make you more ready for sleep that evening. Because exercise can be arousing, it is usually best to do this in the daytime rather than the evening.

2. **Reassure yourself**. You can still perform well for a brief period, even if you are short of sleep. Almost no one enters the examination hall feeling in optimal condition – and that's OK. Don't add to the tension you already have by feeling that you 'really must get to sleep now!'. Acknowledge that even lying down awake can be restful, but if it isn't, then it might make sense to get up. However, intensive work, large meals and loud choral singing are probably best avoided.

3. **Make yourself cosy**. Give yourself a good opportunity for sleep. Avoid or reduce your intake of stimulants, such as caffeine, in the evening. Try to be facilitative to yourself – like a really considerate host, make things comfortable for you.

4. **Think before you listen**. Listening to things before you sleep and as you try sleep can work – but it can also backfire. If it's music, make a sensible choice – playing 'Turn the Music Louder' or 'The 1812 Overture' at full volume might be best saved for another occasion. It makes sense to do what you have done in the past, but go easy on yourself. Nearly everyone finds sleep before an exam extra challenging. Audio books or other spoken media might work for you, but the thriller and horror genres are not really designed for this task. See what works for you, although often silence really is golden.

5. **Free yourself from your phone**. Don't post images of yourself not sleeping on the night before your exam. Put the phone down. Even in easy-on-the-eye night-setting mode, your phone is likely to keep you awake, so why not put it down, and then you and your phone can both enjoy a good rest.

6. **Use relaxation methods**. You may find it helpful to listen to a guided relaxation – ideally one that you are familiar with. You can use what is sometimes referred to as a 'body scan', 'progressive relaxation' or Savasana to help you to relax. This involves lying on your back and bringing your awareness to different parts of your body in turn. So you might bring your attention to your toes, then your foot, your ankle, your lower leg and so on, moving usually from extremities to your core and ending with your head. Some techniques involve tensing and then relaxing each area that you focus on; others use mere awareness without tension.

7. **Don't panic if it all goes wrong**. This might be the night when a car alarm goes off at 1am, when an estranged relative calls you at 3.30am to talk through your relationship, and when someone you live with practises their yodelling in the bathroom at 5am. Try not to get into the 'must' mentality – 'I must sleep' – or catastrophic thinking that 'this is a disaster'. Even with these issues, it is usually the case that you will actually get more rest than you think. And remember, even when sleep deprived you can still perform well. The anxiety, tension and frustration you may feel as you get up can be just the energy you need to help you through that exam – although you may want a word with your yodelling flatmate at a later stage.

8. **Try it out in advance**. It makes sense to try out all of these ideas in advance, so that you have a range of options to help you when you need them.

The day of the exam

Make sure you get to the examination room early. At best, arriving late will make you more stressed and short of time, and at worst, it can mean that you are not admitted to the exam. You may want time for a quiet look through your notes or think through before the exam. The idea that 'if you don't know it now, you never will' was probably developed by someone who was keen to convince themselves – and others – that it was OK to stop revising and do something else, perhaps checking out unusual vegetables on YouTube. It can be helpful to look over some key ideas or some essay plans, but don't go all heavy and stressful, 'cramming' facts into your head like bulky clothes into a small suitcase. Have a relaxed look through, perhaps with a favourite beverage, or in a quiet spot that you find calming – but not if this is in a different city, country or continent to where your exam is taking place.

The moment of the exam

Waiting outside and then entering the examination hall is enough to make anyone feel stressed. Finding your seat and waiting to see the exam paper (in some cases, you are allowed to see this, without writing anything, before the exam officially starts) can build the stress further, but do bear in mind that you don't need to fight off the stress – you can use this energy. Also remind yourself that you can raise your hand and let an invigilator know if you need any help.

When you have the opportunity to see the paper, read it through carefully. This is especially true for essay-based exams; with multiple-choice exams (which tend to involve too many questions to be scanned in five minutes or less), check how many questions you need to answer and where and how you should note your answers – and only then allow yourself a brief look at some of the questions.

For essay-based exams, it may help to use essay plans before starting your answer. You may have formed tentative plans beforehand, and that is great, but don't forget that the crucial point for any exam question is *to read the question carefully*. This message should be in neon lights in every examination hall in the world. Once you have read the question carefully, *read it again*.

Try to work out what the question is asking you to do, and thus what aspects of the broad topic are directly relevant. Your preparation (the practice essay plans, timed attempts and notes) should inform your answer, but you will almost certainly need to shape and adapt your knowledge to the specific question in front of you. *Your answer should convince the examiner that you are directly answering the precise question.*

In the exam, it is very likely that you will feel that you can only remember a small amount of the relevant material. Don't panic – we can't hold all that we know in conscious awareness at any one time. You know more than is in your mind right now or at any moment in the exam. Once you start writing your essay plan and then writing your actual essay, further relevant information will come to mind. Try to use your essay plan to keep your essay well-structured and to ensure that you build evaluation throughout your essay.

The aftermath of the exam

After the exam can be difficult because we rarely give a perfect performance at any time. It is very likely that some ideas, some references and other information that could have been included were omitted. Allow yourself to be exhausted after the exam – unless you have another one immediately, in which case you may need to defer feeling exhausted. Eating and resting and being kind towards yourself can help your recovery. Think of an athlete taking care of themselves after a huge performance.

When your results come through, you may find that you have done well – fantastic. Try to learn from and be energised by your experience. If your results are disappointing, then do not despair – we have all been there. It can really help to discuss disappointing results with well-meaning friends and family, but bear in mind that in terms of procedural advice they may not be fully aware of the options that your university has in place. It is well worth overcoming any awkwardness and talking with a relevant tutor if your results are disappointing. In many cases, your lowest grades do not count towards your overall degree classification, so if this is the case for you, then the low grade you are worried about may not have any impact on your overall degree. If you have failed an exam, then normally you will have an opportunity to resit the exam, although it may be the case that the subsequent grade is capped at a bare pass. If there were circumstances in your life that affected your performance, then it is worth discussing these with a relevant tutor, as in some cases even retrospective mitigation might be considered. Whatever the case, try to learn what you can from your exam. While feedback on exams is rarely given, try to make sense of your performance, reflect on your preparation and use this to inspire yourself for your next exam.

THE MEMORY FACTOR

How will I remember it all?

This is, I think, one of the biggest fears that many of us have experienced going into exams. If you search for advice on exams online, you can find lots of people talking enthusiastically about key techniques, many of which tackle the issue of memory head on. But first a little warning – much of what we need to remember for academic exams involves meaningful units of information. Meaningful ideas and arguments are different from isolated items (for example, lists of names, dates, etc.) or strings of items whose sequence has no intrinsic meaning or structure (for example, the order of a series of playing cards).

Some of the methods for memory are really great at getting a handle on essentially meaningless items – by imbuing them with associations that have a familiarity and/or meaning to us. These can be useful for remembering aspects of academic ideas as well – perhaps helping us to recall trigger names, models and theories – but do remember that:

- Most academic content is centred around an idea, perspective, finding, interpretation or critique – that is, it has an intrinsic meaning at some level.
- Much of what we need to do in an exam is different from mere recall. It may be identifying a correct answer (in a multiple-choice exam) or drawing on our knowledge to produce a written response to a question (in an essay-based exam), and both are really different from mere recall.

STOP AND THINK
Memory for meaningful information

You may well be under the impression that you will quickly forget information that you learn. Sometimes psychological research can reinforce this idea. We might recall Ebbinghaus's (1913/2013) 'forgetting curve' which suggests that we can very quickly forget much of what we have learnt. If we combine this thought with our everyday experience of forgetting we can become quite anxious about how long the memory trace of our revision will last.

But memory research in the century since Ebbinhaus's famous experiment has provided a more reassuring picture. First, the deeper, more elaborated and more extensive our thinking about the items to be remembered, the more accurate and comprehensive our recall appears to be. This concept that extensive, deep and elaborated thinking can improve our recall is drawn on below in discussing the benefits of active revision.

A second strand notes that building associations can assist our recall. The use of imagery to link faces and names is an example of this, as is the 'method of loci' and memory palaces, where things to be remembered are located in visualised familiar places. Memory palaces and the method of loci are discussed below as a tool for enhancing our recall in examinations.

But perhaps the most reassuring point is that research which suggests how quickly lists of words might be forgotten (like Ebbinghaus's) and our own everyday experiences of forgetting (such as an item we meant to purchase) are quite different from the potentially more meaningful and interconnected ideas that our exams require us to remember. What we need to learn for undergraduate and postgraduate examinations typically does have meaning to us and forms intrinsically coherent structures. These features of intrinsic meaning and structure give us a great starting point and can be used to effectively support our revision.

Link to location

When I was 11 years old I had a booked called '*How to develop a superpowered memory*' (Lorayne, 1977). I had the particular humiliation of having forgotten where I'd left it one day and it was subsequently returned to me in front of a large audience. I can assure you that the irony of 'forgetting' a book about developing a 'superpower memory' was not lost on the person present-ing my misplaced book to me. This book dealt with one of the most famous and long-established methods of memory call, the 'method of loci' – put your hand up if you have heard of it. OK, now put your hand up if you have heard of 'memory palaces' – I know it sounds weird, but I sense more hands up in the air right now.

Memory palaces

The 'method of loci' has informed a popular approach to memory, known as 'memory palaces'. This technique involves choosing a place that is familiar to you (this could be outdoors, within a building or a combination of the two) and thinking of a route through it which takes you past several identifiable features (a step, a window, a door, a plant, a table, a lamp-post, etc.). Items that are to be remembered are then linked to these locations. The following steps are typical:

1. Choose a place with which you are familiar, so that you can picture it clearly in your head.
2. Think of a clear route through that place, one that is quite obvious or memorable, so that you are likely to be able to repeat that route the next time you think of it.
3. Note identifiable elements that you visualise as you think of yourself travelling along your route through your familiar place.
4. Now identify the items that you want to remember.
5. Think of links between the items that you want to remember and the elements that you have identified on your route through your familiar place.
6. Where possible, try to have the items to be remembered interacting with the identifiable elements, using exaggeration and humour to make a more vivid image.
7. Repeat your mental 'walk through' your familiar place, taking the same route through and noting the identifiable elements and the items to be remembered that are linked to each one.

People who use this technique do seem able to remember lots of isolated bits of information. Some people report that across their numerous 'memory palaces' they are able to contain, and thus remember, a vast array of items. Users of memory palaces often note that this method enables one to remember isolated facts with little or no intrinsic meaning (for example, names) and that the memory is effective even when the items to be remembered are not understood.

Let's pick out some features here: 'isolated facts', 'little or no intrinsic meaning' and 'not understood'. In one sense, this is remarkably helpful – lists (e.g. a shopping list) tend to be comprised of isolated items, sometimes things do not have an intrinsic meaning (e.g. names and phone numbers) and we may want to remember things that we do not fully understand (e.g. an important procedure that is new to us). But these features have led some who use memory palaces to see them as not ideally suited to all test situations. If knowledge has to be understood, interconnected and/or applied, then this framework – and the revision time spent thinking of isolated bits of knowledge linked to separate locations – may be less useful than other sorts of exam preparation.

Perhaps more troubling is that thinking about relevant ideas and debates in terms of isolatable, separate units might take you away from the meaningful and complex connections that you could and should make. The 'method of loci', including memory palaces, can help us to recollect items to be remembered and perhaps even form rudimentary links: placing Russell after Milgram might help me to remember that there is *some* sort of link between the two. Perhaps I can even think of a linking image to indicate that the two agree or disagree. But the understanding that is key to most undergraduate exam questions has to already be in place for this to be useful. If I have not spent time *understanding* what Russell argued in relation to Milgram's work, then it would be difficult to answer this exam essay title:

'Critically evaluate Milgram's interpretation of his experiments that investigated obedience to authority.'

And even this multiple-choice question:

Which of the following was one of the Strain Reducing Mechanisms that Russell noted was significant in facilitating participants' obedience in Milgram's series of experiments?

a.   Proximity to the learner.
b.   Distance from the learner.
c.   Ideology of advancing scientific knowledge.
d.   The rhetorical persuasion of the experimenter.
e.   The ethical beliefs of the participant.

Rather than give a generic thumbs up – or thumbs down – to this method, the best advice is perhaps to use it wisely. It is probably best not to see this technique as the central focus of your revision, especially for an exam that is mainly concerned with assessing your understanding and evaluation of psychological phenomena and how they interrelate. However, it may be that the method of loci in general, or memory palaces specifically, can have a supplementary role if you need the prompt of a name or idea to release the understanding that you already have in place.

There is often a danger of defaulting to thinking of exams as essentially about memory, when it is more accurate to see that as a component of exams, rather than the principal focus. Awareness of different research findings and their interpretations, along with knowledge of relevant ideas and perspectives *and how they interrelate*, is so central to psychology that it is *these* aspects that most undergraduate exams seek to assess. Whatever techniques you use to support your recall, it makes sense to ensure that your exam preparation is fundamentally focused on *meaning*. In other words, it pays to use your exam preparation to think about what the research, ideas and perspectives actually mean and how they relate to one another.

Focusing on *meaningful* understanding – and practising the sorts of answers that the exam requires (timed essays, multiple-choice, short-answer, etc.) – helps to ensure that our exam preparation is aligned with what the exam is seeking to assess. With this at the core of our revision, we are doing all that we can to help ensure that we fulfil our potential in the exams that we have to sit.

UNDERSTANDING THE MULTIPLE-CHOICE EXAM INSIDE OUT

Multiple-choice examinations differ from the essay, which has been the focus of this book. On the face of it, they may seem easier – our answer is just the stroke of a pen (or actually a pencil) or the press of a key. There is no need for structure, carefully worded critical evaluation and conceptual conclusions – just pick 'a', 'b', 'c', 'd' or 'e'. But reaching your full potential in a multiple-choice examination (MCE) does involve avoiding a few traps and snares. An essay assignment, or an essay-based exam, doesn't have wrong answers luring you into their lair – MCEs do. The right answer is there, but it is in among three, or more usually four, other wrong answers. How can you avoid getting tricked and find the correct answer? One really useful way is to switch perspective and to see how things look from the point of view of the person (or people) writing your MCE.

THINK
Taking the position of the examiner

Imagine for a moment that you have to write a multiple choice exam paper – it would actually be quite a hassle. Marking multiple-choice exams is easy as answer sheets are often scanned into a machine that (pretty much) does it for you, or the whole exam is online and is marked automatically. However, if you were writing a multiple choice exam, you may find that you are quickly overwhelmed with having to:

- Write quite a lot of questions
- Cover most, or much, of the course content
- Write questions that have clearly correct answers
- Write wrong answers (distractors) for each question that are plausible yet unequivocally incorrect

ACE YOUR ASSIGNMENT
What can I do in preparation?

Given the distinctive features of an MCE, it is really important to practise the very specific skills needed for identifying the correct answer.

Warning: Only read on if you want to do really well!

To do really well try to write a small number of multiple-choice questions (MCQs). Be informed by past and sample papers if they are available. Go through the key topics, choose perhaps four or five of these and try to write one MCQ for each of them. Doing this will help you because:

- You will be thinking deeply about the sorts of examinable issues that you have covered
- You will remember the issues, having processed them quite deeply
- You will better understand the role that the incorrect options (distractors) play and how to avoid them

Doing this – and reading the guidance below – will help you to enter the mind of the examiner. As long as you can find a way back out of there, this is extremely helpful as you will get a clearer sense of how to locate the correct response for each question.

Let's think about these issues for a moment. Multiple-choice exams are typically multi-question exams. While an essay-based exam might have a relatively small number of questions – perhaps requiring students to choose two questions from a list of six or seven options – an MCE will often comprise somewhere between 20 and 60 questions.

The questions for your MCE will normally be drawn from a selection of the entire material covered in a course, representing a more comprehensive selection of issues than most essay-based exams involve.

If you think that's tricky, look at how hard it is to write *good* multiple-choice questions. You need to word your questions so that they have a right answer. Think how debate-rich psychology is – there is nearly always another perspective on most of the issues covered in psychology. Your MCE questions (MCQs) need to have one (and only one) correct answer; the three, four or five other options should be incorrect, or not fully and completely correct, *distractors*.

Enough to make you stop? I know how you feel. You now need to write several wrong but credible alternatives. This type of question, with blatantly incorrect options, just won't do:

Who argued that obedience to authority could be thought of in terms of agentic shift?

a.   Stanley Milgram
b.   Carl Jung
c.   Richard Gregory
d.   Boris Johnson
e.   Donald Trump

The options need to be credible and test some refinement of knowledge, so the false options should usually be (at least partly) connected to the issue being asked about (for example, associated with the same broad area of psychology).

It is harder still to write an MCE when you consider that, while 'Who was it?' type questions are easy to write, most academics wouldn't want to have a whole paper with a 'guess the name' type format. Instead, MCQs often seek to assess students' understanding of ideas rather than simple recognition of names and dates. As soon as we move away from framing the concrete, quiz-show type of question we have a challenge. How do we have one, and only one, fully correct response, amid a range of credible but not fully correct options?

This would be a poor MCQ because it is possible to see more than one answer as correct:

Which of the following is a key factor for understanding aggression from a Social Identity Theory perspective?

a. Deindividuation
b. Shared, or group, identity issues
c. Intergroup differentiation
d. Bias against 'out-groups'
e. Evolutionary factors

The above question has three correct responses – b, c and d – and so the question is flawed. Hopefully the rigorous processes of putting an exam paper together will mean that you do not encounter such a problematic question. But this example demonstrates that it can be a challenge to write an MCQ that only provides one clearly correct response, yet includes distractors that are credible but incorrect (or not *fully and completely* correct). Sometimes, partly because of this challenge, MCQs have 'grouped' response options. The two most frequently used are 'all of the above' and 'none of the above', and these and other more complex grouped responses are considered below.

ACE YOUR ASSIGNMENT
Read, write and answer MCQs

- Practise *reading* multiple-choice questions (MCQs) from practice papers and past papers. Look at the sorts of topics they focus on and what they ask about them. See how wrong answers (distractors) are used and how the correct answer fits the question.
- Practise *writing* MCQs on the topics that you will be examined on. This helps to demystify them, and shows you how they work, while deepening your knowledge and understanding of the topic.
- Practise *answering* MCQs. There really is a skill in discarding distractors and identifying the correct response to questions. Getting used to doing this – on the topic you are preparing – in advance of the exam is an excellent idea.

Dealing with 'grouped' response options in MCQs

Often MCEs contain options that *refer to other options in some way*. The two grouped response options that I use in writing MCEs are 'all of the above' and 'none of the above'.

'All of the above'

One way to deal with the problem of writing plausible, but not fully correct, distractors is to have several correct options and then include a grouped response – see how easy that makes it to fix the problems in the MCQ we have just considered? We simply add another feature of a Social Identity Theory understanding of aggression and then finish with an 'all of the above' option.

> Which of the following are key factors for understanding aggression from a Social Identity Theory perspective?
>
> a.   Perceptions of others as belonging to an 'out-group'
> b.   Shared, or group, identity issues
> c.   Intergroup differentiation
> d.   Bias against 'out-groups'
> e.   All of the above

But, *yikes*, there could be a problem for us in the context of a time-pressured examination. 'All of the above' does run the risk of leading to a very understandable error. The danger here is that if you are rushing through, anxious about the time ticking by, you might immediately spot that, say, option 'a' or 'b' is correct and select the first 'correct' answer that you see. You would, paradoxically, be correct in selecting option 'a', but would be graded as being 'incorrect' if options 'b', 'c' and 'd' were also correct. Then (as in the above example), clearly, option 'e', 'all of the above', would be the *fully and completely correct* answer. Whenever you see 'all of the above' as a response, please take action to save your marks – *double-check that other options are not also correct*.

'None of the above'

'None of the above' is quite straightforward, none of the preceding answers correctly answer the question. Don't assume when you see 'none of the above' that it can't ever (or always will) be correct – take it on its merits. There is the potential to be tricked into reading through the options, trying to imagine how one of them might be true if stretched or interpreted in a certain way, but if you are doing too much stretching and far-fetched interpretation, try to stop! Carefully check through that you haven't missed a correct option sneaking past you. If not, then 'none of the above' is the logical response.

More complex question groupings: 'a and b only' or 'b, c and d'

With both 'all of the above' and 'none of the above', the last option is simply referring to all of the others – in a five-option MCE, option 'e' is referring to 'a', 'b', 'c' and 'd'. However, sometimes you will find more complex groupings where only some of the other responses are grouped together to form another option. It can look like this:

a.   xx
b.   xx

     c.   xx

     d.   a and b only

     e.   a, b and c

Note here that both options 'd' and 'e' refer to groupings of the preceding options. Many people who write MCQs avoid multiple groupings of this nature as they can cause students to trip up, not through a lack of knowledge or understanding, but from the potential confusion caused by the question format in exam conditions. However, they are sometimes used – partly in an effort to more precisely test students' knowledge and also perhaps to help with the difficult job of writing four credible distractors in a five-option MCQ.

When you are faced with a question like this, don't panic – you need to take your time. I would first look at the non-grouped options 'a', 'b' and 'c' and, taking each in turn, ask if it is a correct response to the question. You may then want to make notes, if permitted, on the question paper (perhaps ticking the correct responses) or on scrap paper, noting which of 'a', 'b' and 'c' are correct. If more than one of the single item options (a, b and c) is correct, which grouping captures the configuration of correct responses that you have identified once you have solved this you can record your response on the answer sheet.

Managing your timing

Well in advance of the exam, get really clear about how many questions you have to answer in what period of time. This is so important, but frequently overlooked and that fuzzy uncertainty about how long you have, or how many questions you need to answer is just what you don't need as you enter the exam room. Prior to the exam, work from sample and past papers if available and try to do about 10 multiple-choice questions (MCQs) and time yourself. Do check how the actual exam that you will sit relates to any practice papers or quizzes that you use, and try to allow the same number of minutes per question. In practising MCQs your timing will vary and you may find yourself taking longer with questions that have more text, involve interpreting a complex table, ask a complex question or require you to choose between two or more plausible answers. To get a more accurate sense of timing, you should make sure that you include some of the more time-consuming sample questions in your practice, that you have not previously seen the questions and that you do this, if possible, on more than one occasion (many people find they get quicker with practice). This practice gives you a sense of approximately how long you spend per question.

Once you are in your exam, double check your exam paper, confirming the duration and numbers of questions (which you have checked in advance). Knowing this will help you with managing your time in the examination. A long line of MCQs can be quite scary in an exam, but if you know that you take about 1 minute 15 seconds per question and the exam allows 1 minute and 45 seconds per question, it gives you a bit of reassurance. This means that you can afford to spend a little longer on some of the trickier items (although you won't want to spend too long on them, especially if the difficult questions carry the same marks as the easier ones).

ACE YOUR ASSIGNMENT
What can I do in the examination?

It's all very well understanding how MCQs work and preparing for the examination by practising and writing MCQs, but what about managing the examination itself?

Managing your answering process

When you are staring a real MCQ in the face, what should you do? Plump for the first option that looks right and then speed on? I would advise against that. Imagine that it was a convincing distractor and the correct answer is one of the other options, or perhaps all of the responses 'a', 'b', 'c' and 'd' are correct and the fully and completely correct answer is 'e', 'all of the above'. It is easy to lose marks that really are yours by a simple, hasty rush through the question like this. Instead, try this:

- Read the question through twice.
- Think about what topic, issue or ideas this links to – just your immediate responses, nothing heavy.
- Look through each response option.
- If you spot the correct answer, great. If you have time, scan those options again – to be safe.
- If you are torn between two or more options, are there any that you can eliminate? If it is possible, perhaps clearly note this (but not on the answer sheet or booklet). Now read the question again.

TACKLING SELF-DEFEATING THOUGHTS

With exams, more than with other forms of assessment, we can carry a lot of baggage. Our own assessment history – and, crucially, *the stories we tell ourselves and others about our past experiences* – are vividly with us when we have exams to sit. But our thoughts might work against our best interests, leading us to avoid working on our exams, to underperform or to turn a challenging time into an impossible one. Below, some common self-defeating thoughts are outlined, but it is also worth identifying *your own* self-defeating thoughts. Don't give yourself a hard time over your self-defeating thoughts. Instead, congratulate yourself for identifying them – that is the first step to freedom.

'If I don't know it now, I never will'

This thought can be used to call a halt to revision. Sometimes we do this to provide a sense of psychological relief by creating an arbitrary end point to the stress of revision. This is the thought we tell ourselves when we close our laptop, close the books and leave our notes. It can feel reassuring to have a stop point, but it might work better to have stop *points* along the way. These are times when we allow ourselves some down-time, away from revision, rather than a full and final *finito*. If you have this thought, then, yes, you may want to schedule in breaks, but is there really a point of no return, as this thought suggests? It can be helpful to allow ourselves to put away our work and stop revising. That may be part of being calm and grounded as we are about to sit an exam, or it may facilitate sleep the night before an exam. However, we can do this as an active choice: 'It is wise for me to stop or take a break now', not out of some fear that 'it's all too late now'.

'I'm too stressed to revise'

It can be stressful to revise, but sometimes it is even more stressful to think about the fact that you *should* be revising. See if you can make your revision a more positive experience. You really can learn without punishing or overly stressing yourself. Finding a creative or playful way into your work can be great, so make it a nice experience for yourself – it can be more holiday camp than boot camp.

'I should have… I shouldn't have…'

Do you get the feeling of having an angry tyrant/sergeant major/authority figure oppressing you with a sense of what you *should* have done? Even if these '*should* haves' make good sense – and often they are quite misguided – they are not helpful unless we have a working and reliable time machine. So, if you are Dr Who, you could step into your Tardis and set about doing and undoing some long list of 'shoulds' and 'shouldn'ts', but if you are not Dr Who, let's find another way.

It is probably best to avoid this sort of internal dialogue:

Inner tyrant: 'You should have started revising three months ago.'

You: 'Go away you, err, nasty inner tyrant you!'

Inner tyrant: 'Not so fast oh lazy one; I haven't even got going yet.'

You: 'Stop oppressing me, you fiend!'

Inner tyrant: 'This is so typical of you. You had your chance to revise properly and you blew it.'

An alternative is to avoid battling with your 'inner tyrant' – if you battle, you are caught in this inner dynamic that is taking you further away from exam preparation. Why not befriend your inner tyrant? Connect with the essence of a concern about your well-being. In amongst these thoughts there is some wisdom about preparing that can help you next time, when you click into exam preparation sooner rather than later. For now, channel these thoughts into finding ways of making your revision focused and targeted. Get smart about how you will revise, given that you don't have much time. These prods needn't be argued down – they can help you next time and help you to devise a cunning plan to optimise your revision with the time you have right now.

'Exams are so unfair'

In a sense this is true, exams share this with all forms of assessment – they are an imperfect and often unfair means of assessment. We probably all have a tale of the unfairness of exams, but they keep being used because the alternatives are also unfair, just in different ways. It is possible to acknowledge the unfairness of exams without letting it erode our sense of agency and control in our exam preparation. It is worth bearing in mind that the more we conceptualise exams as essentially a memory test, the more vividly we are likely to feel depowered by the perceived unfairness of exams. While undergraduate exams have a memory element to them, they are – or should normally be – an imperfect means of assessing the clarity and depth of our understanding of a topic. Don't get depowered by worries about the fundamental unfairness and the sense that you are helpless in the face of this. Rather, focus on the fundamentals of really understanding the material and, if possible, falling in love with (or developing an inquiring respect for) the material that you are revising. Practise *active revision*, where your preparation involves doing some of the sorts of things the exam will require you to do (e.g. completing multiple-choice questions, writing time-limited essays, etc.).

'I'm rubbish at exams'

The more accurate thought here is likely to be that you have experienced some disappointment with exams that you have sat in the past. If these were the same exams that you need to sit now (that is, you are preparing for resits), then you are in a different place now, because you have the benefit of all that you have been through. If your disappointment with your exam performance related to different exams, then not only have you developed over time, but the exam itself is so different that previous performance (on different exams) might well be a very poor predictor this time around.

Why not acknowledge that you have faced disappointment in the past, but don't generalise. While we are alive, we are never entirely static: the you now, with the exams you have ahead of you, is different from the you that sat an exam less successfully in the past. Instead, why not learn from your previous experience? If it worked out badly in the past, what can you learn from that and do differently this time? Be kind and supportive towards yourself. You needn't be deluded that 'things can only get better', but you can acquire wisdom from previous disappointment that can help you to support yourself in reaching your potential.

LESSONS FROM THE EXAMINATION ROOM

You can contrast some of your demotivating and discouraging thoughts with what you might notice in an exam room. If you have ever been in an exam room with the exam underway, which you yourself are observing rather than actually sitting, you will probably be struck by the productive energy in the room. There is usually a maximal productivity period, starting a few minutes after the beginning of the exam. When this happens, the room is filled with a pulsing energy – as if it were electrically charged. Many students who, in other circumstances, typically delay starting their essay, abandon it soon after starting or find that they can't really 'get going' in their writing, are transformed. Here in the exam room they are on it and engaged in it, busy writing and intensely focused. I often wish for the students (and myself) that we could bottle up this energy and dip into it so that we could all reach this peak productivity, whenever we need it.

We can sometimes be free of procrastination

These observations of the exam room teach us something about how we can switch out of procrastination when the chips are down, when we have to do it. It suggests something about the atmosphere in which we are writing, and how a quiet, concentrated atmosphere can – for many – be incredibly productive. This productivity might be expressed in our writing outside of the exam room – it can also be expressed in our engaged, concentrated attention during revision. It shows what we can do when we are not distracted by social media, videos of talking dogs and being outbid for a 3D printer.

We know more than we think we know

These observations also suggest something about the amount of knowledge that is latent within us. Many students do not realise how much they know until they are in the process of writing it down. While we can have a sense of what we know about an area of psychology, it can seem worryingly sketchy. In the midst of revising, perhaps even as we enter the examination room, we can't hold all of our topic knowledge in consciousness at once and that can make our knowledge feel a bit lightweight. It is when we start writing that we show ourselves, and others, what we know.

We can get 'in the flow' in exams

I think this also teaches us something that is directly relevant for the next exams we may have to sit. There is potential in us – both in terms of knowledge and the capacity to express that in our writing. We can actually amaze ourselves with what we can do, accessing ideas and understandings that we were not sure we had and being able to convey them effectively in our writing in an exam situation. Those students sitting and being in the flow of ideas and writing are at their peak productivity. Most do not ordinarily manage to write so many hundreds of words in so short a period of time. Yes, there are moments when they stop and think and then they restart. So often we, or circumstances, put up walls that block us from reaching this state of what is possible – it's beautiful to watch work without walls, and I think we can all experience something of this.

REFLECTING ON THE CHAPTER:
Use psychology to help yourself

There is a potency of the unknown at the heart of many of our deepest fears. With unseen exams, we have both the unknown of how we will perform and the additional unknown of not knowing *exactly* what we have to do. 'Don't worry', 'You'll be fine', 'It's just an exam' are words that might help, but probably not very much. Psychology gives us a better toolkit than well-meaning, but clichéd words of encouragement.

Therapeutic and counselling psychology has long emphasised that acknowledging our feelings, in particular our fears and anxieties, provides the key for relating to them constructively. Honest acknowledgement of what we feel, perhaps using mindfulness or related approaches, perhaps through talking things through with counsellors, can create a subtle transformation where stress no longer inhibits our ability and may (as early psychological experiments suggested) actually enhance our preparation and performance.

The psychology of memory and task performance offers further wisdom that we – because we are so lucky to be psychologists – can apply to our situation. We can note that building associations for what we need to recall (possibly supported by various mnemonics, such as 'memory palaces') can play a supportive role for some of our exam preparation. We can further learn from psychology that processing meaningful information deeply helps to really encode information in a way we are much more likely to recall. Finally, using the format of the performance to inform our (pre-performance) practice is a key tool that sports psychologists and coaches use to get the best performance out of elite athletes. We can shape our exam preparation to make sure it includes practising writing essays and completing multiple-choice or short-answer questions, that is, practising just the sort of things that we need to do in the exam itself. You may want to 'enact' aspects of the exam at certain points, such as having a specific time that you start and end your practice exam (although perhaps for a shorter duration than the actual exam) or perhaps sitting at a desk and completing the sort of ID details that you will have to use in the real exam. In other words, you are closing the gap between performance and preparation. If we close this gap, especially as the exam approaches, we will be making the most of what performance psychology has to offer us.

Use your psychology to help yourself. Reach out to others when anxieties and concerns keep escalating, but also see the potential that you have in acknowledging stress, processing relevant ideas and information deeply, and practising in advance the very things that you will need to do in the exam itself.

TAKE AWAY POINTS FROM THIS CHAPTER

- Acknowledge stress and recognise that sometimes a bit of stress can help us.
- Make use of appropriate support when anxiety and stress start to become overwhelming.
- Consider awareness/mindfulness practices.
- See exam preparation as an active process where you use past papers and practice papers to practise answering questions, at least occasionally in timed conditions.
- When practising answering essay questions, pay attention to developing some level of interconnection between ideas and ensure that critical evaluation is a key feature of your exam essays.
- Support your memory, but don't transform your exam into a memory test (unless it really is one).
- Demystify multiple-choice questions by reading them, writing them and answering them.
- Don't do battle with destructive thoughts, but quietly and kindly observe them and let them fade away.

- Note the potential that exam conditions hold as a potent source of productive energy, and think how you can use this energy in – and out – of exams yourself.

LINKING TO OTHER CHAPTERS

The ideas covered in this chapter link most directly to Chapter 12, which addresses the counterpart of *unseen* exams, namely *seen* exams. The anxiety, which is so much a part of exams, can lead us to procrastinate – so as to avoid and escape from the discomfort they pose. Chapter 1 addresses procrastination issues. Use these ideas to charm your way into exam preparation gently. While the material on multiple-choice exams differs from the focus of the rest of this book, essay-based exam preparation and performance link to everything that has been considered about writing an effective essay in Chapters 3–8. Chapter 10's focus on reviewing and editing provides a useful overview of many of the key ideas across Chapters 3–8, and this can be a useful, quick-reference support for writing effective essays as you prepare for essay-based exams. Use the ideas from previous chapters to strengthen your exam preparation, informing your practice essays and essay plans. Doing a lot of relevant thinking prior to the exam (for example, about what sorts of different perspectives you might draw on and how you could organise your arguments) will massively help your performance on the day itself. Practising *what you will actually do in the exam* in advance is like reaching out a hand of support to yourself right there, sitting at that exam desk, reducing the multiple complex tasks in that high-pressure situation. These chapters can help you in developing structure, evaluation and tentative conclusions for potential essays in advance – and even if the actual exam essays are very different, the mere fact of practising in advance will help enormously.

Chapter 12

Seen and takeaway exams

In this chapter you will learn...

- How to avoid common mistakes with these exam formats
- How to develop the best strategy for seen and takeaway exams, including: using your exam preparation time effectively, coping with the pressures associated with both types of exam and performing on the day effectively
- How to apply these ideas to seen exams
- How to apply these ideas to essays that need to be completed urgently

SEEN AND TAKEAWAY EXAMS: WHAT THEY ARE AND WHY THEY MATTER?

In Chapter 11 the focus was on a conventional exam, where the questions are not seen in advance and which is sat in an examination hall (or other examination room) for a period of (usually) between one and three hours. However, some exams have a different format. In some cases, the questions on the exam paper are released in advance of the exam. These are called 'seen' exams. In these exams, there is no mystery about what the questions will be and preparation for the exam will be targeted at the precise questions on that 'seen' exam paper. Another, less common, format is the 'takeaway' exam. This exam typically involves an unseen paper, which is released at the moment that the exam starts. Students sitting the exam then take this exam paper away (from the examination room or wherever it was issued) and complete it at a place that they choose within a specified time period, usually between 24 and 72 hours.

Do these exam formats sound almost too good to be true? Thinking about the problems and possibilities that these exam formats offer, when compared to a conventional unseen exam, can help us – *even if we are not sitting these exam formats.*

EXERCISE
The advantages and disadvantages of seen and takeaway exams

Try to think of one or two advantages and disadvantages of sitting a 'seen' exam.

Advantages:

Disadvantages:

Now do the same for the 'takeaway' exam.

Advantages:

Disadvantages:

Thinking about the pros and cons of the 'seen' exam can highlight issues about how we draw on *information* in our essays (exam and coursework assignments). Similarly, thinking about the 'takeaway' exam raises issues concerning how we manage time and resources in completing the complex task of writing an essay.

If you were told that your forthcoming exam won't be an 'unseen' paper as you had expected, but it will be 'seen' one, or that you won't have two hours in an examination hall but 48 hours in your home and library to complete it, what would you really feel? You might grin like a maniac when you are told you have a 'seen' exam because you needn't worry about what's on the paper. Perhaps you'd do the same when it's a 'takeaway' exam as there is no need to frantically write everything you know in 120 minutes. But you could soon feel a different pressure when you start to consider what the marker's expectations might be for a 'seen' and a 'takeaway' exam. It could also occur to you that if the exam is 'seen' by you, it is seen by everyone else sitting it. Similarly, if you have 48 hours to complete the paper, so does everyone else.

DESPERATE LAST-MINUTE ESSAY WRITING

If you do not actually have a 'seen' or 'takeaway' exam, there are elements in this chapter that can still support you. If you find yourself, like some central character in an action movie, having just 24 hours to save the, er, essay, then the tips for a takeaway exam will also apply to your (perhaps self-imposed) time-pressured essay.

STOP AND THINK
These don't apply to me, so what's the point?

The strategies for a formally 'seen' exam are actually useful even when the exam paper is not strictly 'seen'. Preparing for a seen exam can encourage you to think of whole-essay responses rather than simply 'what do I know about X?'. That is, you can start to think about how you should structure your exam answers in advance of the exam rather than leave this as yet another thing to do from scratch in the pressure of the examination hall. Bringing this thinking into unseen exams can really help your answers too. Practising answering sample questions, or possible questions (that you or others might create), can really help you in the difficult job of drawing your information into a well-structured, evaluative essay – it is so much better to have practised doing this before the actual exam itself.

Learning how to tackle the takeaway exam can be amazingly helpful too – not least because sometimes we find ourselves in (or put ourselves into) exactly this situation. Have you ever found that you have 48 hours to complete the assignment? In this situation, you don't have the time to read and apply all of the advice in the first ten chapters of this book, you need to act fast. This chapter will help you whether you are sitting a takeaway exam, a severely time-limited essay assignment or, in all honesty, have kind of wound up in that situation, with just a short time to complete your assignment. It feels like being in a movie plot – never mind '*48 Hours*', '*24 Hours*' or '*24 Hours to Live*', you are in your own thriller, *48 (or perhaps less) hours to hand in*. If you are in that predicament, or sitting this exam format – don't panic. Let's focus on this together and find an effective way through – your essay drama can have a positive ending.

This chapter tackles the specific pressures that these less common exam formats bring and how you can cope with the stress, avoid the common pitfalls and fulfil your potential whatever the exam format. We will also note how some of these ideas can help you to achieve a strong essay answer for conventional unseen exams and – just in case – for other times when you only have 24 or 48 hours to complete your essay.

SUCCEEDING WITH THE SEEN AND TAKEAWAY EXAM

At first when we realise our exam paper is 'seen' (questions released in advance) or 'takeaway' (to be completed outside an examination hall in 24 hours or more) we probably punch the air with joy, relief and other feelings of well-being. However, even mid-punch, we might be aware that the expectations for these exam formats will probably be higher than for non-seen and non-takeaway exam papers.

On the plus side, with the seen exam, all of that guessing about 'what's coming up on the exam paper?' has gone; we know the questions and can focus our exam preparation on those questions and those alone. With the takeaway exam you may hope for a favourable question (or questions), but at least you know you have access to books, papers and other resources to help you find the answer (however hazy your memory is) and you have some time to understand the relevant issues and perfect your answer.

But here is our conundrum – how are we to use the advantages of seeing the exam paper in advance or having an exam that we can take away and complete over a period of between 24 and 72 hours? What are the expectations of those who will mark these papers? What are they looking for and how can we succeed with these exam formats?

The seen exam

This exam format may be unfamiliar to you, but it is sometimes used to get away from some of the problems with conventional 'unseen' exams that are completed in a specified time (perhaps two hours) in the examination hall. Releasing the exam questions several weeks or months in advance of the exam may help to reduce the stress for students of not knowing what the questions are, enabling them to focus their efforts on the questions they know will be on the exam paper. It also means that luck – some students get questions that they have thoroughly revised and understood, while others do not – has less of an impact on exam performance. Finally, it enables students (in these more favourable conditions) to show the markers what they are capable of in a controlled exam environment. With a 'seen' exam, the examiners can mark the students' understanding, conceptualisation and critical thinking around the issues identified in the exam paper, rather than what the students managed under the more adverse (and typical) conditions of the 'mystery' (unseen) exam. At least, that is the intention.

With the seen exam we are relieved that the game of guessing the questions can be put to one side. However, we are also aware that everyone else sitting the exam is in the same position as we are – and we may feel that the examiner(s) are likely to expect a substantially stronger performance than for an equivalent unseen exam. In this situation, we are often tempted to act on factors that seem most easily within our control and which give us a measurable sense of progress. Memorising more detail feels within our control – it is not as flaky or capricious as *deepening* our understanding, which we might, or might not, achieve after an hour of effort. Similarly, attention to getting factual details under our belt gives a wonderfully reassuring sense of progress. In 45 minutes we might be struggling to critically evaluate a theory or an interpretation of empirical evidence with nothing much to show for it, but in that same time look at how many PowerPoint slides or paragraphs of notes you can memorise!

Given our anxiety to make real, identifiable progress in our exam preparation, it is not surprising that we are tempted to focus on those things that reassure us that we *are* doing well. In Chapter 11 we looked at some of the issues and techniques concerned with memory. As noted, this has a place, but we are probably mistaken if we treat memory as the principal issue being assessed in our undergraduate psychology exams. It is this mistake that perhaps explains why often, but not always, seen exam answers can be weaker (in particular, more descriptive and less evaluative) than their unseen counterparts, and why some examiners, having switched from a seen to an unseen exam format in the hope of reading critically and conceptually rich answers, are tempted to switch back!

The takeaway exam

With the takeaway exam, we may think, great – we can use resources to help us. But this sense of expectation can be even worse. Everyone else also has 24, 48 or 72 hours. They are – we tell ourselves – going to be completing brilliant essays in that time period and those totally efficient robots can probably even do so without sleeping!

These anxieties sometimes lead to a performance that is not only sub-optimal, but can actually be below that which is obtained in more standard, unseen, examination-hall exam formats. One of the dangers is that we feel that we need to 'cram it all in' – like neurotic travellers going on a long vacation. If we would normally cite 10 sources in our essay, let's cite 50 – that'll be impressive! If we normally give a little bit of detail, let's knock the marker's socks off with our intricate knowledge of the papers that we refer to. These considerations are not always and for all times 'wrong', but they run a risk, and that risk can be thought of as the 'information avalanche'.

Potential pitfalls – avoiding the information avalanche

Often seen and takeaway exams can tempt us into information overload – where we lose sight of answering the actual question as we attempt to squeeze more and more information into our essays. Nervous that others might be putting in information that we are leaving out, the impulse to add more information can be so strong for these essays that they become packed with detail, leaving no room for critical evaluation or conceptualisation. The essay that we have worked so hard on – struggling to put in every last reference and every detail we can fit in – may be rich in detail but poor in thinking. The marker may see no sign of critical evaluation or conceptualisation because the avalanche of information has overwhelmed the entire essay.

In seen exams in particular, things can get still worse when we have 'too much' information to handle or when we have not practised drawing our information into a clear, concise and critical essay in advance of the exam. We may find that we have so much rich detail that we not only fail to develop critique and conceptualisation of the material, but we also miss important ideas and perspectives out all together because we run out of time.

Try to become an expert on what your module tutors are looking for in your examinations – what are the criteria they will be applying in marking your exams? Finding these criteria, locating relevant guidance and talking to tutors about what is and is not being sought may seem a hassle, but it can be amazingly helpful. You will typically find that knowledge of the relevant material is an important component of excellent exam answers, but that something else is also being examined. This 'something else' is sometimes referred to (a little vaguely) as 'a mind at work' or 'a scholarly approach', but think of it as showing that you not only know the relevant ideas, findings and interpretations, but can also write intelligently about how they relate with each other.

Potential possibilities – what to aim for

To avoid the dangers of the information avalanche, bear in mind what the markers want to see in an excellent essay. They want to see a scholarly mind at work. The ideal essay shows the following:

- An understanding of the essay question.
- An awareness and understanding of the relevant literature.
- A capacity to structure relevant material into a coherent essay.
- A capacity to think critically about relevant ideas, findings, interpretations and perspectives.
- An ability to conceptualise the issues of direct relevance to the essay title.

We must draw on relevant literature and the details within to service these essay priorities (noting, of course, the particular guidance that we have received concerning what is expected of a strong answer for this particular exam). The point is that the information should not be seen simply as an end in itself – don't think 'I've mentioned X that will get me another 4%'. Instead think:

- How can I use X to intelligently answer this specific essay question?
- How does the work of X relate to other relevant material?
- How can I critique X's work or use it to critique that of others?
- How can X's work best be conceptualised in ways that are relevant to the specific essay title?

The following sections will address ways in which you can stay calm and succeed in both your exam preparation and on the exam day (or days)!

STRATEGIES FOR THE SEEN EXAM

Acknowledging the stress

It is great that you don't have the guessing game, there is no need to wake at 3am in a cold sweat asking yourself, or anyone else, 'What's coming up in the exam?'. But exam stress is still there – it just takes a different form. Instead of the worries about 'what's on the exam paper?' you have these (dis)comforting thoughts:

- Will I remember all of the things I have prepared?
- Will I be able to write everything down in time?
- Have I understood the question correctly?
- Have I included all of the right material?

- Have I understood the relevant ideas?
- Have I drawn on enough sources?
- Is my essay long enough?
- Is my essay critical enough?
- Is my essay structured correctly?
- Does my essay have a good conclusion?
- Are others better prepared than me?

EXERCISE
Take five

Take five minutes to acknowledge the particular stresses that you feel about your seen or takeaway exam. If you are using this chapter to help you quickly finish an assignment that is due imminently, you can still do this exercise. It may seem that you are wasting valuable time, but the five minutes that you use here can help you clear your mind and focus on the tasks ahead.

Put a timer on and just acknowledge your feelings in this stressful situation. You may find that it helps to do so, sitting upright and sipping a pleasant (non-alcoholic) beverage. See this as time that you are giving to yourself – it is not a punishment. You are giving yourself space to experience your feelings just as you might give that opportunity to someone else whom you care about.

When the five-minute timer goes off, breathe with awareness as you gracefully move into your various tasks. You know that you really can do this.

Many of these issues identified above are addressed in the preparation section below. Remember that these anxieties can actually be good friends to us, they can spur us to prepare in an intelligent and helpful way, to plan our answers and to practise answering the question(s) in timed conditions. It is usually best not to go into battle with your anxiety, but to use the helpful part of that energy to your own advantage and to find ways of taking care of yourself during these highly stressful times.

Chapter 11 provides further guidance for thinking about exam anxiety, but for now it is worth thinking that it is sensible to let others (such as relevant tutors and counselling/well-being support at your university) know if your anxieties are starting to impede your work, keeping you awake or having other adverse effects on you. It is also worth considering practices that can support you in stressful times. These might include versions of mindfulness and breathing exercises (discussed in Chapter 11). Sometimes stress encourages our flight response – we want to run away from any-thing to do with the thing that is creating anxiety for us (in this case, the exam) – but some exam preparation can actually be an effective way of not only 'dealing with stress', but also channelling that stress to our advantage.

Preparation

STOP AND THINK
Past papers for perspective

You might think that past papers have no value if the actual exam paper is released in advance of the exam, but you could be missing out if you take this perspective. If the current paper has not been released yet, past papers can inform your preparation; if they have been released, past papers might help you unlock what the current paper is trying to get at and what a brilliant answer might look like.

Past exam papers can help with your preparation before the release of the paper that you will be sitting. If the actual paper is not released until relatively close to the exam, then rather than waiting anxiously, as if waiting to unwrap an exciting present, Amazon delivery or official-looking envelope, there is an advantage in having your revision informed by past papers. Have a look through the past questions to get a feel for the sort of topical focus that questions have and what the questions ask you to do.

When you have the actual exam paper, the past papers can enable you to see the paper that you will be sitting, in the context of the different ways in which questions on various topics can be phrased. Past papers can help not to predict what the wording of the questions will be (that's not especially helpful when you have the current paper), but to more clearly identify what the wording of the actual paper is trying to get at. By seeing the wording of the actual paper and the target question(s) that you will answer in the context of past papers, you will better appreciate what each question means and what answers would be best fitted to it.

However, a slight word of warning is necessary here. Don't be too semantically sensitive – often there are 'exam crib sheets' that try to decode the meaning of each question framing. This sometimes involves assumptions that super-fine distinctions between, for example, 'compare and contrast different approaches' and 'critically discuss different perspectives' are key, and that each requires a radically different sort of essay answer. This approach can work well with some exams that you might encounter before (perhaps even after) your undergraduate degree. However, it has the danger of taking you away from the fact that at undergraduate level, essay-based exam questions nearly always require a scholarly, critically evaluative treatment of the question topic, in which different, directly relevant approaches are knowledgeably drawn on and evaluated with a sense of how they interrelate.

It really makes sense to use past papers to get a sense of what is being examined this time, particularly in regard to the precise topical focus in the way the question is framed. Used wisely, this can help you to answer the precise essay question(s) rather than trigger an information dump of 'everything I know about X'. Where possible, it is wise to approach relevant tutors to discuss either the actual paper (if they are happy to do so) or past papers, for example: 'With this question from last year, what would be expected from a strong answer?'; 'Would it be appropriate to answer a question like this by…'; 'Was this question focusing on X?'; 'Would it be relevant to refer to Y in a question like this?'. But – obvious warning time – although past papers, used intelligently, can be very helpful, do remember the actual paper that you are going to sit.

Preparing in this way means that you really are giving yourself every possible advantage to succeed in the seen exam that you are about to sit.

Creating a strong answer

One of your key bits of preparation is creating a strong answer. It might be that there is a word limit and a time limit, but it is more often the case that you have just the two hours or so of the exam with no actual word limit.

Essay length and citation density

One of your challenges is to discover what you can write, in terms of length and citation density, within the time that the exam allows. In addition to asking the relevant tutors about what is expected, it makes sense to see for yourself what you can do. This is something you can practice. Two important components of this are the essay length and the number of sources that you cite. With a seen exam, it is quite possible and relatively straightforward to work out roughly what you can write in a specific timeframe.

Assemble the relevant sources, with a focus on how you will use them in your essay. In particular, sources can help you add depth to that all-important critical evaluation that you need to develop in your essays. Don't be tempted, because it is a seen exam, into learning lots of names and ideas and dumping them like a huge pile of snow at the examiner's door. Yes, it's great to see citation of relevant sources, including *directly relevant* material that evidences wider reading, but your exam isn't a memory test. Don't allow 'social loafers' amongst your cited sources, who are there for the sake of it. Make your citations do some work for you. They should support ideas that are being developed and critiqued in your essay. Using citations in this way is one of the hallmarks of excellent, scholarly writing.

Earlier on in your preparation, as you are likely to have less information to draw on, it is a good idea to try timed writing for a shorter duration than will be the case in the actual exam. For example, if your exam will involve answering three essay questions in three hours, then you may want to see the length of your answers (and extent of your citation) within a 20- or 30-minute time limit. As your knowledge and thinking about the topics increase, you can extend this – but don't go crazy, finishing your own three-hour practice paper minutes before your actual three-hour exam is not well thought out. Think of an athlete trying to prepare for a big championship race so that they peak (rather than fall asleep) when it really matters!

Addressing the precise question

In many respects, it is easier to go off track in a seen exam than in an unseen exam. Having time to think about the title can result in our expanding what we think we should include – our sense of what's potentially relevant can get wider and wider, and soon we feel almost all of psychology might be relevant in some way. Look at your essay title, consult relevant tutors and exam guidance and, together with lecture notes and resources, carefully consider *what are the key issues and debates that are directly relevant for this specific essay title.*

Being different

In some ways, most of us want to fit in and yet stand out at the same time. When it comes to essays, our desire to stand out can lead us to do unexpected things – perhaps we will include completely unexpected material, fill the essay with rich personal anecdotes, or switch to another style of writing (poetry, journalism, detective fiction). Why not instead go for great scholarship – that will be distinctive, rather than just different for the sake of it.

Being critical

Develop a sense of how you can critique throughout your essays. Most essays will include just one or two critical observations and often these will be quite generalised and predictable. The evaluative comments which simply assert that 'further', 'more up-to-date', 'larger scale', 'longitudinal' and 'real-world' research is needed are airdropped everywhere. They are like the pop up adds I get when I am online (which increasingly advertise hair loss treatments and funerals as I have got older); they pop up anytime, anyplace, anywhere.

It is not that these 'evaluative comments' are not relevant, but rather that the argument has not been made, the author has not made it specific enough. What sort of 'further' research is needed? What, specifically, would larger or longitudinal research enable us to consider? What sort of 'real-world' research does the author have in mind and what would that tell us? Furthermore, these arguments are more convincing if there is an awareness of similar work that has been done, or other sources that have made these arguments are cited. In other words, if you are going for these sorts of evaluations, demonstrate real specificity and relevant sources.

See the development of genuinely thoughtful, well-informed and specific critique as an absolutely key component of your preparation. Having a seen exam gives you the opportunity to develop intelligent, specific and appropriately referenced critical evaluation – where you think about the questions and issues that one perspective has raised for others. Look at Chapter 6 for more detail on developing critical evaluation in your writing and apply those principles to your exam preparation. Use this to plan relevant critical evaluation for each of the key issues you raise in your essay.

The conclusion itself is so often the trickiest part of any essay and what you may want to say in your conclusion is likely to change as your understanding deepens. In essence, a brilliant conclusion does not simply restate what you have said in your essay, nor flip to vague generalisations (e.g. 'There are lots of different ideas and further research is needed.'). Instead, it *conceptualises* what is at the heart of the issue(s) raised by the essay title and addressed in your essay (e.g. 'Fundamental to the question of … is the debate between perspectives which emphasise … and those which focus on …'). The conclusion generously gives your reader a way of making sense of the debates and perspectives that you have drawn on in your essay – it's like that bit of a detective story (the *denouement*) where the Poirot, Holmes or Miss Marple makes sense of it all. A detective story without the *denouement* is often less satisfying, so why not spread the joy and treat your examiners to a lovely conclusion that makes sense of what you have covered in your essay? This conceptual thinking can take a while to develop, and even after you have written thousands of words of psychology conclusions it can remain the most challenging part of any essay to write. Use the ideas addressed in Chapter 8 to develop this crucial skill – and enjoy it!

Planning your answer

Planning out your answer is the best way to ensure that you address the question, include relevant content and critique, and that the essay reads as a smooth interconnected response to the question. The very act of planning enables you to experiment with different information and different evaluative ideas, to explore different ways of positioning the ideas that you will cover, and how you can cope with the agreements and disagreements between the perspectives that you draw on. It's great fun. If you like Lego – and even if you don't – you will enjoy (if you try) planning out your answer and it really does help you to remember the material.

To plan effectively, it is best to think in terms of the different paragraphs within your essay. You can do this in lots of different ways:

- Digitally
- On large sheets of paper
- In colour
- In monochrome
- With arrows linking points and ideas
- Using numbers or letters to indicate the order of your arguments

It can help to have a couple of lines/sentences or a few key words to indicate the content of each tentative paragraph. This makes it easy to quickly represent them and the order in which you might write them. It can be frustratingly fun to scribble out your paragraphs, redraw the arrows between them and renumber the order of them as you think more deeply about the essay. Please try to enjoy it – it's quite creative and you're not 'locked in' to one 'correct format' so see what works, and then see how it can be improved, so that the order is even more logical and the evaluation is even more powerfully present.

The special free bonus with essay structure is that it helps you to remember the material because you have processed it more deeply and you have focused on the link from one component of your relevant knowledge to another. These links facilitate moving from the material you plan to address in one paragraph to the material for the next paragraph. Some students may wish to supplement this with mnemonics (see Chapter 11), but focusing on how the ideas relate (e.g. 'Z critiqued Y's ideas about the issue being considered, arguing that…') is so key to the actual requirements of most essay-based exams that emphasising the *meaningful relationship between ideas* in your exam preparation is the best thing you can do.

Performance

When you enter the exam room, try to use all of that stress-inducing energy to pull off a really good performance. All of that adrenalin can keep you awake and focused and help you to write more in that two- or three-hour period than you usually do in a whole day. Seizing the energy of the occasion is what many athletes, actors and musicians do to achieve a great performance. It is not that the stress has gone, but rather they have harnessed it, and used it to energise what they are about to do, or are doing. If you can do even a little of this – or even acknowledge that stress can sometimes be our friend in pressured situations – it can really help.

You may find it helpful to write down your essay plan(s). If you have more than one essay to complete, you may wish to write them one at a time before answering each question or, alternatively, you may want to note down all of your plans in one go before you tackle each essay in turn. Don't spend so long on the plan that your essay itself suffers, but try to include details or prompts that you find helpful. If you do not remember all of the plan, jot down what you can and leave a space for what you can't quite remember.

As you start to follow your plan and write your essay, you might struggle to remember ideas, arguments or perhaps words and phrases that you planned to use in your essay. Don't panic – first, it is not surprising and, second, it probably matters less than you think it does. If you come up with different words and phrases now, that is absolutely fine and may well be a good thing. It is worth checking with specific tutors associated with the exam subject what they suggest in circumstances where you can't remember passages of relevance in the exam. One approach might be to leave some additional lines of space *between* paragraphs – this means information can be inserted without any paragraph looking conspicuously incomplete. However, tutors do vary in their preferences in terms of how this is dealt with, so talk to them and find out in advance.

You may be aware that your essay as it develops does not seem quite the same as the essay(s) that you prepared. Keep the focus on the fact that your exam is not assessing 'how well does the student remember their exam preparation essay(s)', but something a little bit different, specifically, 'how well does the student address the precise essay title?'. During the exam do not add extra pressure to yourself by trying to replicate the exam preparation essay that you may have produced; rather, draw on that and your essay plan to guide you to write the best answer that you can to the essay title in the actual exam right now. All of those things that you did in preparation are there to help you – they are your helpful friends and supports, not some tough point of comparison against which your exam performance will be judged.

STRATEGIES FOR THE TAKEAWAY EXAM

Preparation

Here is a bit of writing wisdom which you should test out against your own experience. Writing can be fluent and self-evidently productive at times, and at other times it can be extremely slow and painful. Nothing surprising so far. But bear in mind these three things:

1. Both the fluent and the struggling phases of writing can be productive (even though we often only treat fluent phases as being so).
2. The sorts of things that we are doing in the less fluent phases often involve trying to understand ideas, findings and interpretations and how these interrelate.
3. When we are taking an exam, it is sensible to do the less fluent struggling with the ideas, findings and interpretations (and how these interrelate) *in advance* of the exam.

You should try to do the difficult leg-work *before* your 'takeaway' exam paper is released. That is, you should try to locate the core ideas that are likely to inform the exam and grapple with them early on. Try to think critically and conceptually about the sorts of issues, ideas and interpretations that are likely to come up.

You may well find that there is a voice inside you saying something like this: 'Yes, but I don't know what's coming up – it will be a waste of time. I'm too busy to spend time on issues that might not even be relevant for the exam. I'll have 48 hours anyway, so it's probably better if I wait until then.' The answer to this is 'No, it's not "better"; it is much, much worse to "wait until then"'. If you really leave to one side thinking about issues that might be relevant for a takeaway exam, you are piling pressure upon pressure. Don't do this to yourself. Instead, ask, enquire and find out (from module convenors, lecturers and tutors) what sorts of things you can usefully look at as part of your exam preparation.

Making effective notes

Unusually for this exam format, you are (typically) allowed as much access to your own notes as you want. This makes it incredibly important and valuable to create supportive notes. With this format you really can give yourself a helping hand with relevant notes (unless you are told otherwise), so your notes should be a key component of your exam preparation.

You should develop notes that help *you* to sharply understand the relevant theoretical ideas, empirical investigations and interpretations of data. Your notes should also identify ways in which you can critique and interrelate relevant work. It can be a challenge to write for different audiences, who have different experiences and are looking for different things from your writing, but in this exam preparation you simply have to write notes that work brilliantly well for you!

When you are writing, do you notice that some bits flow and others take absolutely ages to form. Work out your own recurrent slow points in essay writing. What features of good essays (e.g. critical evaluation), parts of an essay (e.g. conclusion) or types of content (e.g. unfamiliar ideas) are often most difficult for you to write? It is these exact issues – as long as they are directly relevant to the forthcoming takeaway exam – that you need to front-load and try (as far as you realistically can) to practise and prepare in advance.

ACE YOUR ASSIGNMENT
Getting the information (and search tools) lined up in advance

Use the advice in Chapter 9 to locate relevant information (including the publications that you will use in your essay) and to gain familiarity with all of the search tools and search techniques you can use (e.g. how to combine and isolate search terms, how to locate publications that subsequently cite the key references that you locate, etc.). This will help you to avoid adding a further element of panic when the clock starts ticking on your assignment. If you have relevant material to hand and have practised searching for further publications, you are empowered and ready to go!

Managing pressure

Time management

Doing a takeaway exam almost invariably means having an amount of time that can be, or at least feel, difficult to structure. When you have 24, 48 or 72 hours to complete the exam, what should you do about eating, sleeping or taking down time? Whatever you do, you may find yourself worrying whether others have hit on a more effective formula than you have. Are they snacking or eating high (or low) carb meals? Are they sleeping – or not? Do they give themselves any down time? Or have they achieved some optimal arrangement that puts you at a relative disadvantage? We can be torn with anxiety, not knowing what we should do for the best and/or suffering from sleep or food deprivation, perhaps feeling our efficiency and focus slowly drain away, or anxiously trying to sleep, feeling that we are neither resting nor working.

There is another time management issue which arises from having an 'in-between' amount of time – longer than a typical exam, but shorter than a typical essay. In a standard two- or three-hour examination we often do not have the time to do our essay differently – to consider starting again from scratch in an effort to perfect it. Instead, in those environments we usually feel up against the clock, desperately struggling to complete our essays in the time allocated. In a standard unseen exam we may have the opportunity to briefly revisit our work, but seldom do we have the chance for a major rethink. With the takeaway exam we have the blessing – and the curse – of more time. This tension of the clock is real even in the extended exam time of 24, 48 or 72 hours. We can be caught between a sense of 'having' and 'not having' time. For example, we may be uncertain as to whether it is best to restart or carry on with our essay. We have some time to stop, think and restart, but it is still finite, we do not have the luxury of being able to take a really long break or engage in a very substantial rethink. Coming back after a two-day break can make sense for conventional assignments, but would be a truly terrible idea for a 48-hour exam.

STOP AND THINK
Acknowledging the stress

It is helpful to acknowledge the particular stress of the takeaway exam. If you ever sit in a library where students sitting a takeaway exam have located themselves, you will pick up on a tense, tetchy atmosphere. The room will be charged with energy, conveying the vivid sense that if anyone even coughs unexpectedly, they could be struck down by the electrical charge of the group – or at the very least wilt away under their withering stares. Often, when I think of stress even today, I think of seeing students sitting a takeaway examination when I was an undergraduate. I could feel the prolonged tension, and could understand the dilemmas about when to sleep – or even *if* to sleep – and the crushing sense that these students had of worrying about what *other* students would be doing during each hour of the exam that they had remaining.

It is important to acknowledge that while this exam format *may* have a little less *anticipatory* stress, it has an enhanced and considerably extended *performance* stress. You may worry less about what is coming up on the paper and if you will remember all that you need to, but the anxiety of actually performing well in the exam is likely to be increased.

Controlling the setting

One of the chief sources of tension is the struggle to create an advantageous environment for ourselves or, at the very least, to ensure that we do not find ourselves at a disadvantage. The examination hall is to some extent a great equaliser as students are in the same working location and will (largely) have the same resources available. But in the takeaway examination, the location and resources might not be the same for everyone. As a student sitting a takeaway exam, we may be concerned that others have found a more suitable location, have a more supportive and facilitative living environment and have managed to get access to helpful resources that we haven't thought about or been able to locate.

Performance on the day itself

As soon as you have your takeaway exam, you should stop, look and think – you may of course want a calming beverage (preferably a non-alcoholic one). It really is wise to bring a little mindfulness into this very tense situation. Something like the three-minute meditation practice (see Chapter 11) can be helpful. However, if there is a rush to retrieve key, non-digitised, reference materials from the library – then that may take priority. As soon as you can after receiving your exam paper, you could sit quietly and be aware of what you are sensing in your body and what emotions you are experiencing. Observing what you are feeling, *without any sense of judging or even trying to change it*, can be very liberating in itself. You might follow this by focusing on your breath (the out-breath in particular) and becoming aware of sensations in your body. At its heart, any relaxation technique provide a non-burdensome way of being mindful right in the middle of exam stress. That patient, non-judgemental awareness of whatever you are feeling doesn't necessarily zap your anxiety, vaporising it like some sci-fi ray gun, but it can give you a different way of relating to it. You can start to feel more empowered and less like you have been taken over and are being driven by whatever difficult circumstances and emotions you are dealing with.

STOP
Take a moment

However many hours we are told we have for a takeaway exam, there is an understandable impulse to rush ahead, because we are anxious not to lose a second. Just stop for a moment to make sure that you are on the right track.

LOOK
Check what you are required to do

Look carefully at the exam paper and make sure that you very clearly understand what is required of you.

First, check what is called the exam rubric. How many questions do you need to answer? Is there a specified format for your answer? Is a required, or recommended, word length specified.

Second, check the form that the answer must take. You should, of course, be aware of this already. Is it an essay that addresses a specific title, or does it require some other form of answer, such as a review of a journal article? Are there some other specific forms of writing required, for example, personal reflection?

Third, read the question through carefully. It may help to imagine that you need to explain the question to someone else.

THINK
Think like a marker

As you look at the question that you have to answer (or the task that you have to complete) imagine you are the marker. What would you give marks for? It can help to take the perspective of the marker as you think about the following issues:

- What is the relevant information and where can it be located?
- What is there to be discussed and debated?
- What are the different perspectives that should be drawn on?
- Are any overarching concepts at work?

As you think about the question (or task to be completed), look for the diamonds – or gold, if you prefer. Look for the controversies, critiques and concepts. Don't be worried by complexities, but delight in them – that's where the marks are.

From panic to poise: Actively engaging with your (time-constrained) essay

When we have 24, 48 or even 72 hours to complete an assignment it is easy to get frantic. Often this means desperately grabbing at information. When we do this, we are worried that we are going to miss things out, important things, things that others will include. Take a deep breath – and do please, continue to keep breathing hereafter. It can make sense to waste no time in accessing relevant information – particularly, as noted above, if there is limited access (for example, if there are insufficient hard copies of a crucial, non-digitised, text). But, going for an information-grab approach can lead us down the path of passive writing.

Let's consider two approaches that might help you to tackle your time-constrained essay in a productive manner.

Approach one: Developing and executing a rational plan for your essay

The first approach provides a sensible plan for writing your essay, particularly when you have limited time as with a takeaway exam, or for times when you have wound up with 48 hours to complete your essay. Some people will be drawn to the fact that the different tasks here are segmented, so that they can be ticked off in order. You could quite easily subdivide these further. For example, you could think of the different components of your essay that you need to write, and note when you have completed each of these.

1. Read the title very carefully several times.
2. Think about what you already know and what you need to know.
3. Start to plan the structure that your essay will take.
4. Search for relevant publications that will inform your essay.
5. Revise your essay plan in the light of what you have found.
6. Write your essay.
7. Review and edit your essay.

This plan makes absolute sense, but you may find the slightly more fluid approach detailed below (or a combination/modification of the two) more helpful. These are tools to help you commence, continue and complete your work – use whatever is most facilitative and supportive for you.

Approach two: Acknowledging the dynamic interplay in the different phases of writing

Orientating phase

When you see the essay title, you have to spend time reading and understanding it and start to bring yourself to this title (for example, thinking about what you do and don't know). You have to be with the essay title – not triggering off all that you know (then you are not with the title) and not drastically grabbing at information that will tell you the answer (then you are not with yourself). You need a genuine meeting between the exact title – and all that is very directly relevant to that – and yourself. In this encounter, you should become really aware of what the essay title wants: what an excellent answer to this essay might include, what you can currently bring, and what thoughts, ideas and understandings you have and what you will further investigate.

Exploring and structuring phase

This phase is where the fun begins. If you are creatively minded, you can draw diagrams or use colours, images, anything that helps you to think about the ideas and information that might be relevant and how these ideas might relate. This process involves a dynamic interplay between an expansive reflection on what ideas and arguments may be relevant for the essay and thoughts about how they may interrelate in an essay. On the one hand, you need to be able to accumulate a sense of what is directly relevant – the names and ideas, the critique and argument. On the other hand, you can start to play with structuring these elements – what sorts of essays can you build, what goes where and what flow or order would be the most clear and compelling?

Writing and thinking

We often think that we need to straighten out our ideas before we start the serious business of academic writing. This image depicts writing as a sort of divine inspiration or outpouring of genius, when for most of us it's not really like that. We write not just to express our understanding but to feel our way towards our answer(s). There is a mixture of understanding and knowledge and wondering and uncertainty, and this makes writing creative – once we have written about something, we arrive at a different understanding to that which we had previously.

Some knowledge and understanding relevant to your essay title will get you going with your writing, and this then acts like a torchlight, highlighting aspects you can think about further. Your thinking then, in turn, progresses your writing. This is not a depiction of writing gone wrong, but of writing gone right – where your writing expresses your understanding and highlights the limits of that understanding by raising questions. You may have to read specific information and/ or reflect on your ideas – but this is brilliant, it is on-target thinking, identified by the fact that you have started to write. Using this tension between writing and thinking creatively – embracing both as being intertwined with the other – is a feature of really excellent academic work: develop this and enjoy it.

Reviewing and editing

It's easy to yawn at the idea of reviewing and editing. It can feel like cleaning the fridge, backing up your important files or reducing the time you spend on social media – you know you should do it, but you don't quite get around to it. But try to see the reviewing and editing as something that you really can do, that needn't be a burden, that can almost be fun to do and can make an absolutely massive difference. It often helps to print out the essay and to read it through, although always bear in mind how long you have got to do this.

Focus on what is straightforward to address in the time that you have available (see Chapter 10 for guidance on this precise issue). A simple 'rule of thumb' is that the more intellectually involved the task is, the longer the editing will take. Thus, typos are quick to fix, but rethinking your understanding of key theories will take longer to fix. Even if you only have a short amount of time, you would be surprised how you can start to address not only typos, citations and references, but also structural issues, such as including a statement of intent in your introduction (see Chapter 3) and developing sentences at the beginning of each new paragraph to help to link it to the preceding one (see Chapter 5). Don't miss out on something that can have such a high impact on the quality of your work for a very modest investment of time and energy. Even a brief time of reviewing and editing will make a difference. And, as a bonus, once you've done this – you can sort the fridge out.

STOP AND THINK
From information grab to intelligent searching

Look at the two scenarios below. The takeaway essay title is:

'Outline and evaluate the Elaboration Likelihood Model of persuasion.'

Scenario one

Larissa feels that there's not a moment to lose. Diving straight into Google Scholar and using the search term 'Elaboration Likelihood Model of persuasion', Larisa finds approximately 87,500 results. She then puts in the whole essay title, which helps a little, and she now has only 25,700 results to wade through. Limiting her results to the last four years gives Larissa a mere 18,000 results. Larissa calculates that if she spends just an hour reading and understanding each of these, she should be ready to start writing her essay in two years and 20 days. Larissa stares into the middle distance, wondering why no one has invented a reliable time machine.

Poor Larissa. I think we have all experienced turning to a search engine and being overwhelmed by the results. Our sense of, 'Isn't it great that I can get 18,000 results in 0.12 seconds' is soon replaced with, 'How do I find the few results that are really relevant'. What is needed is a more proactive approach. This is illustrated by Laxman in scenario two.

Scenario two

Laxman reads the question through several times with care. From this he starts to plan what a strong, directly relevant and evaluative essay might look like. For three quarters of an hour or so he develops a few different essay plans. These are not at all detailed, but they do highlight how the different elements relevant to the essay title (the ideas, findings, interpretations and perspectives) relate to each other. Someone picking up these plans would note that they convey a sense of which theories or theorists agree with each other and which disagree. They would also note that every idea included is directly relevant to the essay title.

Laxman is familiar with using relevant search engines. This means that he has several tools at his disposal straight away, and he does not have the added stress of needing to learn how to use them. Having practised using the search tools previously, Laxman knows how to use them intelligently. He has learnt how to use different search terms to find specific, relevant publications or ideas. For example, his notes indicate that discursive approaches form an important critique of the Elaboration Likelihood Model, so he includes this in his search. He is better able to use the abbreviated descriptors that are returned in search results to sift through them. Doing this identifies relevant journal titles, which he then uses, along with other search parameters for subsequent searches (for example, authors, publication dates and specific terms occurring in the title). When Laxman has found (or already knows) a specific relevant publication, he uses

(Continued)

the cited by/cited in function to locate publications that refer to the target paper. This is an excellent way to investigate how the target paper has been endorsed, critiqued and developed. When this in turn yields too many results, the skills of sifting, changing and re-specifying search parameters and specifying exact search terms helps to narrow the results to a manageable number. Be like Laxman, not Larissa – actively use sources as vital resources for ideas and arguments to be developed in your essay. Chapter 2 deals with these issues in some detail.

Making the most of existing understanding

Even if we search intelligently and arrive at a manageable number of references, it can be very stressful to try to quickly understand lots of unfamiliar, or not-previously-understood, ideas when we feel that the final countdown has begun. There is a key lesson here and – if your deadline is imminent, I apologise for this – learning takes time. During our course, in preparing our notes, we should focus on the clarity of our understanding. If that is in place, fantastic; often we may find that it is *partly* in place. The more we have a foundation of relevant understanding the easier it is to build our essay.

Hitting the wall

Often when we are well underway with our writing – perhaps more than half-way through –we can have the academic writing equivalent of what distance runners refer to as 'hitting the wall'. We have got a long way through the process but, with a sizeable chunk still to go, we feel stuck. If we are just returning to our writing (having stopped at 'the wall' previously) it may resolve itself, but often it feels just as bad, or even worse. The temptation for distraction is massive at these points in your academic writing – cleaning a kitchen cupboard, watching a YouTube video of painting a toilet wall, reading a message from a remote acquaintance announcing that they had muesli for breakfast – all of this, however bland and uninspiring, can pull you away at this point. Here are some pointers that can get you back on track:

Stay with your writing even if you move to a different section. Just being around the essay (or other academic writing) can help. This is especially true if you are writing about the main focus of the essay, but – to some extent – applies even if you are doing other essay work, such as completing the reference section, this can be a means to get back to completing your essay.

Avoid the negative narratives nightmare. It is so easy to tell yourself how impossible it is and to have this sort of internal dialogue:

'I can't do it!'

'I have to do it!'

'It's impossible!'

'I've got 10 hours, five minutes and seven seconds to complete this!'

'Mmm. Zara had sugar free muesli for breakfast today – let me just check...'

Heavy negative thinking is like taking a direct flight to Distraction Central in the heart of Avoidance Land. Keep going at yourself like this and you are likely to avoid work. Instead, reassure yourself and be gentle with yourself. If you've got stuck midway through your writing, you are almost certainly doing something right – well done!

It is not impossible, there are just different choices available. Being stuck often means you are aware of options, perhaps different interpretations, different ways of linking, or different ways of developing your ideas in your writing. All the words you have written can sometimes get in the way of clearly seeing the argument(s) that you are developing and the best way forward. Don't lose sight of the wood or forest as a whole because you are staring at a couple of large trees. Get in your metaphorical helicopter, pilot it to 2000 feet and see the topography of your essay. Print your essay out and make notes on it, sketch a flowchart briefly noting what you cover in each paragraph, make an extremely simple essay plan of what your essay has covered and may cover – do any or all of these to get the picture of your essay and where it might go. Seeing the whole of your essay helps enormously, try it out – you and your essay are worth it!

Having nothing to say is not the same as not knowing. The sense of not knowing what to write can spring from knowledge, rather than ignorance. Don't spiral into self-criticism; instead go free form, write down, maybe on a scrap of paper or in a separate file or in a different colour font, any ideas that come to mind. Even things that look banal or barmy can lead to other thoughts and ideas that might work out.

Needing to know doesn't mean starting from scratch. Sometimes being stuck highlights a thing we need to find out. It is not a 'red alert – all-hands-on-deck' situation, but rather, a regular feature of academic writing. We often write and then get to a point where we need to check our knowledge. This will typically be an aspect, feature or detail of an idea that we are in the process of referring to. Please don't panic. Look to find the aspect of knowledge that you need, clarify what it is that you need to know and check if you have notes that you have already created that may hold the answer. Look at your notes (as these probably encapsulate your understanding of the broad topic and should be quick to grasp) before checking further.

Don't get derailed. When we need to check things or even think things through it is so easy to get off track. If this is happening to you, don't chastise yourself, but charm yourself back onto task. You have done well, you can do this. Writing your essay is a challenge, but that means it can also be rewarding, satisfying and something you will feel really good about having done.

Be kind to yourself. Without a doubt, takeaway exams involve consistent high pressure. You will need food and rest and you will go through times that are more and less productive. Don't always stop when it gets tricky. Although that is sometimes the right thing to do, it can make the essay hard to come back to (who wants to pick up a task at a really tricky point in the process?). You might find that working to blocks of time and being appropriately disciplined about that is helpful and supportive and enables you to have breaks. The 'Pomodoro Technique' (and some other 'chunking' strategies), suggest just this idea of working for an interval (of perhaps 25 minutes) separated by short breaks (Cirillo, 2018). Chunking your work like this may suite you, and reduce the risk of giving up in a state of confusion and exhaustion. The more you know your own strengths, weaknesses and general quirkiness, the better you can support yourself to achieve your full potential.

REFLECTING ON THE CHAPTER:
Prepare for peak performance

Knowing that our exam is one that we will see in advance, or that we can take away and spend two or three days completing, can lead us to think that preparation is perhaps less important. We can suddenly swing from this complacency to near panic when we think how others are taking advantage of the seen exam, and how they are 'on task' 24 hours a day for the takeaway exam. Preparing in advance can be amazingly helpful – it really makes all the difference.

It can be useful to think that preparing for seen and takeaway exams has a lot in common with an athlete preparing for a major championship. Unlike the 'unseen' exam, you know what the task is that you need to accomplish (or, with the takeaway exam, you will have perhaps two or three days in which to complete the task), but you still have the pressured duration of the examination in which to pull off your peak performance.

In a seen exam, your preparation will involve searching for relevant sources, checking your understanding, working out the best way of structuring information, developing an effective introduction and conclusion, and ensuring that you critically evaluate throughout. In your seen exam preparation, you might write one or more essays, or very extensive essay plans, in advance. Even if you don't remember the essays that you have prepared in advance word for word, the very fact of having done this work will enable you to remember the key ideas, arguments and critiques which will help your exam essay to really sparkle. In the exam itself, you are drawing on that deep thinking within the time constraints of the examination.

In the takeaway exam, the preparation will be to locate and engage with materials that are potentially relevant and to plan relevant essay structures and develop relevant critique and tentative conclusions for the potential essay questions that you might be confronted with. You may be surprised how even preparing for an essay title that does not come up provides invaluable practice and a fund of deep thinking that will help with the actual essay title that you are faced with in the exam. The takeaway exam has a major, extended performance dimension, and managing yourself across that period of perhaps two or three days is a real challenge. Like an athlete competing in the heptathlon or decathlon, there is a consistent, unrelenting demand to perform that does place you under considerable stress. This chapter has provided advice for managing that stress – it won't zap the stress away like magic, but it can stop it from becoming overwhelming and destructive.

To achieve your full potential, keep these two aspects in mind: preparation and performance. Preparation should involve the hard, slow, difficult thinking work; and performance the maximum effective use of the time you have available to draw on all of the difficult thinking and preparatory work that you have already done. Don't become overwhelmed whether you have a seen exam, a takeaway exam or an essay that you have left to the last minute – use the tips in this chapter to support you. You will be surprised at what you are actually capable of.

TAKE AWAY POINTS FROM THIS CHAPTER

- Beware of the information avalanche – do not see your task as piling lots of information into your mind for it to be offloaded into your essay.

- In your exam preparation and in writing your exam essays, try to convey a sense of a scholarly mind at work (not just of someone who would do well in a quiz show focused on this topic).

- Acknowledge the specific stress that seen and takeaway exams entail.

- See the relevance of the advice for takeaway exams for times when we have left ourselves with just 24 hours to complete our essay.

- Make good use of essay plans so that you can build in structure, critique and an intelligent conclusion.

- When searching for material, be targeted and intelligent – this is a great skill to practise in advance, but very stressful to learn during a time-constrained takeaway exam.

- For takeaway exams, do the slow work (locating sources, reading, understanding and making good notes) in advance, as much as possible.

- Allow for the different phases of writing and don't let understandable anxiety or uncertainty over how to proceed derail you – you may be really close to a great breakthrough, go for it!

LINKING TO OTHER CHAPTERS

This chapter covering seen and takeaway exams links directly to its counterpart addressing unseen exams (Chapter 11). Much of the advice found there concerning coping with exam stress and using exam preparation effectively also applies for many seen exam situations. As with unseen exams, the inevitable anxiety involved in all exams can mean that preparation is sometimes shelved as part of a general avoidance of anything to do with the 'far too worrying exam'. Chapter 1's advice concerning procrastination can be drawn on to support you in handling your anxieties by finding a positive, non-threatening way to get started with your exam preparation. For essay-based seen exams and takeaway exams, all of the preceding chapters can help to inform relevant preparation, with Chapters 3–8 providing the basis for an excellent essay and Chapters 2 and 9 helping with the appropriate use of sources and referencing and presentation issues respectively. For the takeaway exams in particular, the guidance on reviewing and editing (Chapter 10) and ensuring that your essay is professional (Chapter 9) is especially helpful, both for preparation in advance of the exam and for enhancing and refining your essay during the extended examination period itself. Similarly, the advice given in this chapter about completing an extended exam essay within perhaps 48 or 72 hours can be applicable for completing other essay assignments where the deadline is looming. All exam formats are stressful, even if they are seen or takeaway exams. This chapter and the preceding ones in this book will support you in bringing your preparation forward, so that the strain of the exam itself is reduced and the standard of your exam performance is increased. These ideas are relevant for every time we want to write a brilliant essay.

REFERENCES

Anderson, C. A., Shibuya, A., Ihori, N., Swing, E. L., Bushman, B. J., Sakamoto, A., … & Saleem, M. (2010). Violent video game effects on aggression, empathy, and prosocial behavior in Eastern and Western countries: A meta-analytic review. *Psychological Bulletin, 136*(2), 151. http://dx.doi.org/10.1037/a0018251

American Psychological Association. (2020). *Publication Manual of the American Psychological Association* (7th ed.). https://doi.org/10.1037/0000165–000

Arendt, H. (1963). *Eichmann in Jerusalem: The banality of evil*. Viking Press.

Bartlett, D., Ora, J. P., Brown, E., & Butler, J. (1971). The effects of reinforcement on psychotic speech in a case of early infantile autism, age 12. *Journal of Behavior Therapy and Experimental Psychiatry, 2*(2), 145–149.

Billig, M. (1987). *Arguing and thinking: A rhetorical approach to social psychology*. Cambridge University Press.

Billig, M. (1991). *Ideology and opinions: Studies in rhetorical psychology*. Sage.

Billig, M. (1996). *Arguing and thinking: A rhetorical approach to social psychology* (2nd ed.). Cambridge University Press.

Block, J. (2002). *Personality as an affect-processing system: Toward an integrative theory*. Lawrence Erlbaum. http://dx.doi.org/10.4324/9781410602466

Boag, S. (2006). Can repression become a conscious process? *Behavioral and Brain Sciences, 29*, 513–514. http://dx.doi.org/10.1017/S0140525X06239116

Brehm, J. W. (1966). *A theory of psychological reactance*. Academic Press.

Buzan, T. (1993). *The mind map book*. BBC Books.

Carnegie, D. (1948). *How to stop worrying and start living*. The World's Work.

Case, R. (1998). The development of conceptual structures. In R. S. Siegler & D. Khun (Eds.), *Handbook of child psychology: Vol. 2 Cognition, perception, and language* (5th ed., pp. 745–800). Wiley.

Cirillo, F. (2018). *The Pomodoro Technique: The life changing time management system*. Random House.

Charcot, J. M., & Bernard, D. (1883). Un cas de suppression brusque et isolée e de la vision mentale des signes et des objets (formes et couleurs). *Le Progres Medical, 11*, 568e571.

Chomsky, N. (1959). A review of BF Skinner's Verbal behavior. *Language, 35*(1), 26–58.

Cotter, R. B., Burke, J. D., Loeber, R., & Navratil, J. L. (2002). Innovative retention methods in longitudinal research: A case study of the developmental trends study. *Journal of Child and Family Studies, 11*, 485–498.

Decety, J., Bartal, I. B., Uzefovsky, F., & Knafo-Noam, A. (2016). Empathy as a driver of prosocial behaviour: Highly conserved neurobehavioural mechanisms across species. *Philosophical Transactions of the Royal Society of London. Series B, Biological Sciences, 371*, 20150077. http://dx.doi.org/10.1098/rstb.2015.0077

DeYoung, C. G. (2010). Toward a theory of the Big Five. *Psychological Inquiry, 21*, 26–33. https://doi.org/10.1080/10478401003648674

Dickerson, P. (2012). *Social psychology: Traditional and critical perspectives*. Pearson.

Donaldson, M., & McGarrigle, J. (1974). Some clues to the nature of semantic development. *Journal of Child Language, 1*, 185–194. http://dx.doi.org/10.1017/S0305000900000635

Downing, P., Liu, J., & Kanwisher, N. (2001). Testing cognitive models of visual attention with fMRI and MEG. *Neuropsychologia, 39*, 1329–1342. http://dx.doi.org/10.1016/S0028-3932(01)00121-X

Drury, J., & Reicher, S. (2000). Collective action and psychological change: The emergence of new social identities. *British Journal of Social Psychology, 39*(4), 579–604. http://dx.doi.org/10.1348/014466600164642

Ebbinghaus, H. (1913/2013). Memory: A contribution to experimental psychology. *Annals of Neurosciences, 20*, 155–156. http://dx.doi.org/10.5214/ans.0972.7531.200408

Edwards, D., & Potter, J. (1992). *Discursive psychology*. Sage.

Elliott, M. A., Armitage, C. J., & Baughan, C. J. (2007). Using the theory of planned behaviour to predict observed driving behaviour. *British Journal of Social Psychology, 46*, 69–90. http://dx.doi.org/10.1348/014466605X90801

Enoksen, A. E., & Dickerson, P. (2018). 'That proves my point': How mediums reconstrue disconfirmation in medium–sitter interactions. *British Journal of Social Psychology, 57*, 386–403. http://dx.doi.org/10.1111/bjso.12241

Erdelyi, M. (2006). The unified theory of repression. *Behavioral & Brain Sciences, 29*, 499–511. http://dx.doi.org/10.1017/S0140525X06009113

Fischer, P., Krueger, J. I., Greitemeyer, T., Vogrincic, C., Kastenmüller, A., Frey, D., Heene, M., Wicher, M., & Kainbacher, M (2011). The bystander-effect: A meta-analytic review on bystander intervention in dangerous and non-dangerous emergencies. *Psychological Bulletin, 137*, 517–537. http://dx.doi.org/10.1037/a0023304

Fiske, S. T. (2010). Interpersonal stratification: Status, power, and subordination. In S. T. Fiske, D. T. Gilbert, & G. Lindzey (eds.), *Handbook of social psychology* (5th ed., Vol. 2, pp. 941–982). Wiley.

Freud, S. (1913). *The interpretation of dreams*. (A. A. Brill, Trans). MacMillan. (Original work published 1900). https://doi.org/10.1037/10561-000

Gaertner, L., Sedikides, C., & Graetz, K. (1999). In search of self-definition: Motivational primacy of the individual self, motivational primacy of the collective self, or contextual primacy? *Journal of Personality and Social Psychology, 76*, 5. http://dx.doi.org/10.1037/0022-3514.76.1.5

Gibson, S. (2013). Milgram's obedience experiments: A rhetorical analysis. *British Journal of Social Psychology, 52*, 290–309. http://dx.doi.org/10.1111/j.2044-8309.2011.02070.x

Gibson, S. (2019). *Arguing, obeying and defying: A rhetorical perspective on Stanley Milgram's obedience experiments*. Cambridge University Press.

Gladwell, M. (2008). *Outliers: The story of success*. Little, Brown and Company.

Greenwald, A. G., McGhee, D. E., & Schwartz, J. L. K. (1998). Measuring individual differences in implicit cognition: The Implicit Association Test. *Journal of Personality and Social Psychology, 74*, 1464–1480. http://dx.doi.org/10.1037/0022-3514.74.6.1464

Haslam, S. A., & Reicher, S. D. (2006). Stressing the group: Social identity and the unfolding dynamics of responses to stress. *Journal of Applied Psychology, 91*, 1037–1052. http://dx.doi.org/10.1037/0021-9010.91.5.1037

Haslam, S. A., Reicher, S. D., & Van Bavel, J. J. (2019). Rethinking the nature of cruelty: The role of identity leadership in the Stanford Prison experiment. *American Psychologist*, *74*, 809–822. http://dx.doi.org/10.1037/amp0000443

Hayne, H., Garry, M., & Loftus, E. F. (2006). On the continuing lack of scientific evidence for repression. *Behavioral and Brain Sciences*, *29*, 521–522. http://dx.doi.org/10.1017/S0140525X06319115

Holyoke, T. T., & Brown, H. (2019). After the punctuation: Competition, uncertainty, and convergent state policy change. *State Politics & Policy Quarterly*, *19*, 3–28. http://dx.doi.org/10.1177/1532440018788564

Hovland, C. I., Janis, I. L., & Kelley, H. H. (1953). *Communication and persuasion: Psychological studies in opinion change*. Yale University Press.

Jayawickreme, E., Meindl, P., Helzer, E. G., Furr, R. M., & Fleeson, W. (2014). Virtuous states and virtuous traits: How the empirical evidence regarding the existence of broad traits saves virtue ethics from the situationist critique. *Theory and Research in Education*, *12*, 283–308. http://dx.doi.org/10.1177/1477878514545206

Jung, C. G. (1959). *The collected works of C. G. Jung. Vol. 9(2): Aion: Researches into the phenomenology of the self*. Edited by H. Read, M. Fordham, & G. Adler. Trans. R. F. C. Hull. Routledge. (Original work published in 1955 & 1956.) http://dx.doi.org/10.1515/9781400851058

Jung, C. G. (1970). *The collected works of C. G. Jung. Vol. 14: Mysterium coniunctionis: An inquiry into the separation and synthesis of psychic opposites in alchemy* (2nd ed.). Edited by H. Read, M. Fordham, & G. Adler. Trans. R. F. C. Hull. Routledge. (Original work published in 1955 & 1956.) http://dx.doi.org/10.1515/9781400850853

Kabat-Zinn, J. (1994). *Wherever You Go, There You Are: Mindfulness Meditation in Everyday Life*. Hyperion Books.

Kail, R. (2000). Speed of information processing: Developmental change and links to intelligence. *Journal of School Psychology*, *38*, 51–56.

Kelley, H. H. (1967). Attribution theory in social psychology. In D. Levin (Ed.), *Nebraska symposium of motivation* (Vol. *15*, pp. 192–238). University of Nebraska Press.

Kihlstrom, J. F. (2006). Does neuroscience constrain social-psychological theory. *Dialogue [Society for Personality & Social Psychology]*, *21*, 16–17.

Latané, B., & Darley, J. M. (1970). *The unresponsive bystander: Why doesn't he help?* Appleton–Century–Crofts.

Lorayne, H. (1977). *How to develop a super-power memory*. Pan Books.

Macnamara, B. N., Hambrick, D. Z., & Oswald, F. L. (2014). Deliberate practice and performance in music, games, sports, education, and professions: A meta-analysis. *Psychological Science*, *25*, 1608–1618. http://dx.doi.org/10.1177/0956797614535810

Malle, B. F., Knobe, J. M., & Nelson, S. E. (2007). Actor–observer asymmetries in explanations of behavior: New answers to an old question. *Journal of Personality and Social Psychology*, *93*, 491. http://dx.doi.org/10.1037/0022-3514.93.4.491

Maze, J. R., & Henry, R. M. (1996). Psychoanalysis, epistemology and intersubjectivity: Theories of Wilfred Bion. *Theory & Psychology*, *6*, 401–421. http://dx.doi.org/10.1177/0959354396063004

McArthur, L. A. (1972). The how and what of why: Some determinants and consequences of causal attribution. *Journal of Personality and Social Psychology*, *22*, 171. http://dx.doi.org/10.1037/h0032602

Mewburn, I., Firth, K., & Lehmann, S. (2019). *How to fix your academic writing trouble: A practical guide*. Open University Press.

Milgram, S. (1963). Behavioral study of obedience. *Journal of Abnormal and Social Psychology*, *67*, 371–378. http://dx.doi.org/10.1037/h0040525

National Robotics Network. (2020). *Heritage*. www.nationalroboticsnetwork.org/?page_id=217

Neill, C. (2016). *Midnight marked: A Chicagoland vampires novel*. Gollancz.

Nesse, R. M. (1990). The evolutionary functions of repression and the ego defenses. *Journal of the American Academy of Psychoanalysis*, *18*, 260–285. http://dx.doi.org/10.1521/jaap.1.1990.18.2.260

Onorato, R. S., & Turner, J. C. (2004). Fluidity in the self-concept: The shift from personal to social identity. *European Journal of Social Psychology*, *34*, 257–278. http://dx.doi.org/10.1002/ejsp.195

Osborn, A. F. (1953). *Applied imagination: Principles and procedures of creative thinking*. Scribner.

Petty, R. E., & Cacioppo, J. T. (1986). The elaboration likelihood model of persuasion. In L. Berkowitz (ed.), *Advances in experimental social psychology*, (Vol. *19*, pp. 123–205). Elsevier. http://dx.doi.org/10.1016/S0065-2601(08)60214-2

Piaget, J. (1928). *The child's conception of the world*. Routledge and Kegan Paul.

Piaget, J., & Inhelder, B. (1956). *The child's conception of space*. Routledge and Kegan Paul.

Potter, J., Stringer, P., & Wetherell, M. S. (1984). *Social texts and context: Literature and social psychology*. Routledge and Kegan Paul.

Reicher, S., & Haslam, S. A. (2011). After shock? Towards a social identity explanation of the Milgram 'obedience' studies. *British Journal of Social Psychology*, *50*, 163–169. http://dx.doi.org/10.1111/j.2044-8309.2010.02015.x

Rofé, Y. (2008). Does repression exist? Memory, pathogenic, unconscious and clinical evidence. *Review of General Psychology*, *12*, 63–85. http://dx.doi.org/10.1037/1089-2680.12.1.63

Ross, L. (1977). The intuitive psychologist and his shortcomings: Distortions in the attribution process. In *Advances in experimental social psychology* (Vol. *10*, pp. 173–220). Academic Press. http://dx.doi.org/10.1016/S0065-2601(08)60357-3

Russell, N. J. C. (2011). Milgram's obedience to authority experiments: Origins and early evolution. *British Journal of Social Psychology*, *50*(1), 140–162. http://dx.doi.org/10.1348/014466610X492205

Shallice, T., & Warrington, E. K. (1975). Word recognition in a phonemic dyslexic patient. *The Quarterly Journal of Experimental Psychology*, *27*, 187–199. http://dx.doi.org/10.1080/14640747508400479

Shapiro, S. L., Oman, D., Thoresen, C. E., Plante, T. G., & Flinders, T. (2008). Cultivating mindfulness: Effects on well-being. *Journal of Clinical Psychology*, *64*, 840–862. http://dx.doi.org/10.1002/jclp.20491

Shapiro, S. L., Schwartz, G. E., & Bonner, G. (1998). Effects of mindfulness-based stress reduction on medical and premedical students. *Journal of Behavioral Medicine*, *21*, 581–599.

Silvia, P. J. (2005). Deflecting reactance: The role of similarity in increasing compliance and reducing resistance. *Basic and Applied Social Psychology*, *27*, 277–284. http://dx.doi.org/10.1207/s15324834basp2703_9

Skinner, B. F. (1957). *Verbal behaviour*. Appleton-Century-Crofts.

Sroufe, L. A., Egeland, B., & Kreutzer, T. (1990). The fate of early experience following developmental change: Longitudinal approaches to individual adaptation in childhood. *Child Development*, *61*, 1363–1373. http://dx.doi.org/10.2307/1130748

Stein, S. (1995). *Stein on writing*. St Martin's Griffin.

Stott, C., Ball, R., Drury, J., Neville, F., Reicher, S., Boardman, A., & Choudhury, S. (2018). The evolving normative dimensions of 'riot': Towards an elaborated social identity explanation. *European Journal of Social Psychology*, *48*(6), 834–849. http://dx.doi.org/10.1002/ejsp.2376

Tajfel, H. (1979). Individuals and groups in social psychology. *British Journal of Social and Clinical Psychology*, *18*, 183–190. http://dx.doi.org/10.1111/j.2044-8260.1979.tb00324.x

Tajfel, H., Flament, C., Billig, M., & Bundy, R. (1971). Social categorization and intergroup behavior. *European Journal of Social Psychology*, *1*, 149–178.

Wicker, A. W. (1969). Attitudes versus actions: The relationship of verbal and overt behavioral responses to attitude objects. *Journal of Social Issues*, *25*, 41–78. http://dx.doi.org/10.1111/j.1540-4560.1969.tb00619.x

Wiggins, S., & Potter, J. (2003). Attitudes and evaluative practices: Category vs. item and subjective vs. objective constructions in everyday food assessments. *British Journal of Social Psychology*, *42*, 513–531. http://dx.doi.org/10.1348/014466603322595257

Wilbrand, H. (1892). Ein Fall von Seelenblindheit und Hemianopsie mit Sectionsbefund. *Deutsche Zeitschriftfir Nervenheilkunde*, *2*, 361–387. http://dx.doi.org/10.1007/BF01667704

Wong, S., & Goodwin, R. (2009). Experiencing marital satisfaction across three cultures: A qualitative study. *Journal of Social and Personal Relationships*, *26*, 1011–1028. http://dx.doi.org/10.1177/0265407509347938

Yerkes, R. M., & Dodson, J. D. (1908). The relation of strength of stimulus to rapidity of habit-formation. *Journal of Comparative Neurology and Psychology*, *18*, 459–482. http://dx.doi.org/10.1002/cne.920180503

Zimbardo, P. G. (2006). On rethinking the psychology of tyranny: The BBC prison study. *British Journal of Social Psychology*, *45*, 47–53. http://dx.doi.org/10.1348/014466605X81720

INDEX